12th International Conference on Computational Semantics (IWCS 2017)

Long Papers

Montpellier, France
19 – 22 September 2017

Editors:

Claire Gardent
Christian Retore

ISBN: 978-1-5108-5282-2

Proceedings of **IWCS 2017 long papers volume, ACL anthology W17-68xx.**

12th International Conference on Computational Semantics, Montpellier 19-22 September 2017

Edited by Claire Gardent (CNRS, LORIA Nancy) & Christian Retoré (Université de Montpellier & LIRMM)

Out of the 37 long submissions that we received, 17 were accepted and presented in Montpellier. We thank the authors for their submissions, as well as the program committee listed below for their help with the reviews and the selection process.

Claire Gardent & Christian Retoré

IWCS PROGRAM COMMITTEE		
First Name	**Last Name**	**Affiliation**
Claire	**GARDENT (co-chair)**	**CNRS LORIA Nancy**
Christian	**RETORÉ (co-chair)**	**Université de Montpellier et LIRMM**
Rodrigo	AGERRI	IXA NLP Group, UPV/EHU
Nicholas	ASHER	IRIT-CNRS Toulouse
Timothy	BALDWIN	The University of Melbourne
Daisuke	BEKKI	Ochanomizu University
Emily M.	BENDER	University of Washington
Raffaella	BERNARDI	University of Trento
Gemma	BOLEDA	Universitat Pompeu Fabra
António	BRANCO	University of Lisbon
Chris	BREW	Digital Operatives
Paul	BUITELAAR	Insight - National University of Ireland, Galway
Harry	BUNT	Tilburg University
Aljoscha	BURCHARDT	DFKI
Stergios	CHATZIKYRIAKIDIS	CLASP University of Gothenbourg
Ivano	CIARDELLI	ILLC - Universiteit van Amsterdam
Philipp	CIMIANO	Bielefeld University
Vincent	CLAVEAU	IRISA - CNRS
Dick	CROUCH	A9
Montse	CUADROS	Vicomtech-IK4
Philippe	DE GROOTE	INRIA Nancy
Valeria	DE PAIVA	Nuance Comms
Rodolfo	DELMONTE	Universita' Ca' Foscari
Pascal	DENIS	INRIA
Marc	DYMETMAN	Xerox Research Centre Europe
Markus	EGG	Humboldt-Universität Berlin
Katrin	ERK	Univ Texas
Arash	ESHGHI	Heriot-Watt University
Raquel	FERNANDEZ	University of Amsterdam
Tim	FERNANDO	Trinity College Dublin
Claire	GARDENT	CNRS/LORIA Nancy
Jonathan	GINZBURG	Université Paris-Diderot (Paris 7)
Iryna	GUREVYCH	Technische Universität Darmstadt
Aurelie	HERBELOT	University of Trento
Agata	JACKIEWICZ	Université Paul Valéry Montpellier
Makoto	KANAZAWA	National Institute of Informatics
Dimitri	KARTSAKLIS	University of Cambridge
Ralf	KLABUNDE	Ruhr-Universitt Bochum
Shalom	LAPPIN	CLASP, University of Gothenburg
Zhaohui	LUO	Royal Holloway College, University of London
Louise	MCNALLY	Universitat Pompeu Fabra
Marie-Francine	MOENS	KU Leuven
Richard	MOOT	CNRS (LaBRI) & Bordeaux University
Erwan	MOREAU	Trinity College Dublin
Alessandro	MOSCHITTI	Qatar Computing Research Institute
Larry	MOSS	Indiana University Mathematics Department
Shashi	NARAYAN	University of Edinburgh
Vincent	NG	University of Texas at Dallas
Malvina	NISSIM	University of Groningen
Ekaterina	OVCHINNIKOVA	KIT, Karlsruhe & ICT, Uni Heidelberg
Alexis	PALMER	University of North Texas
Denis	PAPERNO	CNRS LORIA Nancy
Laura	PEREZ-BELTRACHINI	Free University of Bozen-Bolzano / LORIA
Paul	PIWEK	The Open University
Thierry	POIBEAU	LaTTiCe-CNRS
Christopher	POTTS	Department of Linguistics, Stanford University
Violaine	PRINCE	Université de Montpellier & LIRMM-CNRS
Matthew	PURVER	Queen Mary University of London
James	PUSTEJOVSKY	Brandeis University
Livy	REAL	IBM Research
Christian	RETORE	Université de Montpellier & LIRMM-CNRS
German	RIGAU	IXA Group, UPV/EHU
Laura	RIMELL	University of Cambridge
Stephen	ROLLER	The University of Texas at Austin
Michael	ROTH	Saarland University
Mehrnoosh	SADRZADEH	Queen Mary University of London
David	SCHLANGEN	Bielefeld University
Sabine	SCHULTE IM WALDE	Universität Stuttgart
Rolf	SCHWITTER	Macquarie University
Joanna Ut-Seong	SIO	Nanyang Technological University
Mark	STEEDMAN	University of Edinburgh
Matthew	STONE	Rutgers
Mary	SWIFT	IBM Watson
Stefan	THATER	Saarland University
Tim	VAN DE CRUYS	IRIT & CNRS
Benjamin	VAN DURME	HLTCOE, Johns Hopkins University
Eva Maria	VECCHI	University of Cambridge
Shan	WANG	The Education University of Hong Kong
Roberto	ZAMPARELLI	Università di Trento

Contents of IWCS 2017 long papers (available on ACL Anthology)

A Type-Theoretical system for the FraCaS test suite: Grammatical Framework meets Coq

Jean-Philippe Bernardy
University of Gothenburg
`jean-philippe.bernardy@gu.se`

Stergios Chatzikyriakidis
University of Gothenburg
`stergios.chatzikyriakidis@gu.se`

Abstract

We present a type-theoretical framework for formal semantics, which leverages two existing well established tools: Grammatical Framework (GF) and Coq. The framework is the semantic equivalent of GF's resource grammars: every syntactic construction is mapped to a (compositional) semantics. Our tool thus extends the standard GF grammar with a formal semantic backbone. We evaluated our framework on 5 sections of the FraCaS test-suite (174 examples) and significantly improved on the state of the art by 14 percentage points, obtaining 83% accuracy. Our semantics is free software and available at this url: `http://github.com/GU-CLASP/FraCoq`

1 Intro

Roughly put, Natural Language Inference (NLI) is the task of determining whether a Natural Language (NL) hypothesis can be inferred from an NL premise. NLI is central within a theory of formal semantics for Natural Language (NL), given that humans do not only have the ability to understand infinitely many NL sentences, but can further reason about them. In effect, understanding a NL sentence amounts (among others) to knowing what can be inferred or not from such a sentence.

Natural Language Inference has been also central in the field of computational semantics. As Cooper et al. aptly put it 'inferential ability is not only a central manifestation of semantic competence but is in fact centrally constitutive of it' (Cooper et al., 1996). A number of test suites have been proposed throughout the years and different computational approaches have been put forth in order to deal with NLI. The most well-known platforms are the FraCaS test suite (Cooper et al., 1996), the Pascal Recognizing Textual Entailment tasks (RTE) (Dagan et al., 2006), and recently the Stanford Natural Language Inference platform (SNLI) (Bowman et al., 2015). At least until a few years ago, a bipartite classification of NLI accounts depending on whether a translation to an intermediate logical language was performed or not existed. On the one hand, one got logical approaches where such a translation, usually to first-order or even weaker logics like Natural Logic, is performed (Blackburn et al., 2006; Bos and Markert, 2005; Pulman, 2013; Mineshima et al., 2015) and on the other, approaches where this is not the case (e.g. bag of words approaches or other approaches using various machine learning techniques) (Romano et al., 2006; Glickmann et al., 2005; Hickl et al., 2005; MacCartney et al., 2008). Recently, Mineshima et al. (2015) have argued that using higher order logic can significantly increase accuracy of systems using logic, compared to those where weaker logics are used.

In this paper, we show how to construct a formal system for NLI that bridges the gap between two well-studied systems, the Grammatical Framework (GF) (Ranta, 2011) on the one hand, and the proof assistant Coq on the other. Concretely, we map the GF parse trees for NLI problems to Coq propositions. The NLI solutions then become Coq proofs. We thus obtain a complete system which leverages GF for parsing and Coq for reasoning. We evaluate against 5 sections of the FraCaS (almost half of it, 174 examples in total) and show that our approach can outperform the state of the art in logical approaches by 14 percentage points. The structure of the paper is as follows: in Section 2, we present the background to our approach, GF, Type Theoretical (TT) semantics and the proof assistant Coq. In Section 3, we describe the FraCoq system concentrating on the most important and linguistically relevant aspects of the system. In Section 4, we first briefly present the FraCaS test suite. Then, we evaluate our system against it and present the results. We further discuss the issue of proof automation. In Section 5 we conclude and further point to future research directions.

2   Background: GF, TT semantics and Coq

2.1   GF

In GF, abstract syntax is comprised of: a) a number of syntactic categories, and b) a number of syntactic construction functions, which provide the means to compose basic syntactic categories into more complex ones. For example, the constructor $AdjCN : AP \to CN \to CN$ expresses that one can append an adjectival phrase to a common noun and obtain a new common noun. Additionally GF comes with a library of mappings from abstract syntax to concrete natural language syntaxes. These mappings can be inverted by GF, thus offering parsers from natural text into abstract syntax. Yet in this project we skip the parsing phase and use the parse trees constructed by Ljunglöf and Siverbo (2011), thereby avoiding any syntactic ambiguity.

2.2   TT semantics

In the tradition of formal semantics, we interpret abstract syntax into logic. The type of logics that we are employing here have been dubbed as modern or rich type theories (MTTs) by researchers like Luo (2012); Chatzikyriakidis and Luo (2014); Cooper et al. (2015) and are constructive TTs within the tradition of Martin-Löf (1971); Martin-Löf (1984). There is a considerable body of work on doing semantics using MTTs going back at least to Sundholm (1989) and Ranta (1994). Recent approaches of this kind can be found in Luo (2012); Retoré (2013); Chatzikyriakidis and Luo (2014); Tanaka et al. (2015); Cooper et al. (2015); Bekki and Mineshima (2017); Chatzikyriakidis and Luo (2017); Cooper (2017); Grudzińska and Zawadowski (2017) among many others. Compared to simple type theories (e.g. Church's TT), MTTs have been claimed to offer a number of advantages. The most important of these are summarized below:

1. Type many-sortedness. This usually refers to the possibility of using a more structured domain for the monolithic domain of individuals (e) one finds in systems based on simple type-theory, e.g. Montague Semantics (Montague, 1973). Even though we do not make use of this feature here, it remains an attractive feature that brings fine-grainedness to semantic interpretations.

2. Dependent Typing. Here we mention two instances of dependent typing:

   (a) Dependent sum types, or Σ-types, often written $\sum_{x:A} B[x]$ and which have product types $A \times B$ as a special case when B does not depend on x.

   (b) Dependent product, Π-types, often written ($\prod_{x:A} B[x]$), and which have arrow-types $A \to B$ as a special case. Dependent Π are very useful because they generalise function types and universal quantification. Additionally they offer type polymorphism, a very useful feature for semantic interpretation (see for example our treatment of VP based on Π).

3. Proof-theoretical specification and support for effective reasoning. The latter is evident from the fact that the most powerful interactive theorem provers (proof assistants) are based on type-theory. That is, the machinery *par excellence* for reasoning with formal structures implement MTTs (for example, the proof assistants Coq and Agda).

We will not delve here into further details: a complete discussion of MTTs for formal semantics is out of the scope of this paper. We will instead introduce any relevant features in discussing the transition from GF trees to semantic representations in Coq in the next section.

2.3 Coq

Coq is a proof assistant based on the calculus of inductive constructions (CiC), which is itself a lambda calculus with dependent types. Coq is arguably one of the leading proof assistants. Indeed, it has famously been instrumental in formalising a proof of the four-color theorem (Gonthier, 2008), a proof of the odd order theorem (Gonthier et al., 2013), as well as developing CompCert, a formally verified compiler for C (Leroy, 2013). Faithful to our actual development, our semantics will be presented in Coq syntax. While the reader should turn to a proper textbook Bertot and Castéran (2013) for reference, the main two features that we use are Π types (in Coq syntax $\prod_{x:A} B[x]$ is written `forall (x:A), B` or (simply `A` $\rightarrow$ `B` when `B` does not depend on x) and record types, which generalise Σ-typed and are encoded as (trivial) inductive types with a single constructor. In particular the type $\sum_{x:A} B[x]$ is encoded as follows:

```
Inductive Sigma : Type := mkPair : forall (x:A)(y:B) → Sigma.
```

3 The FraCoq system

As already mentioned, we do not perform parsing, but use the existing treebank of Ljunglöf and Siverbo (2011). The bulk of the work is thus to take these trees to their type-theoretical counterparts.[1]

3.1 From GF trees to semantic representations in Coq

The structure of our semantic representation is the following:

1. Every GF syntactic category C is mapped to a Coq Set, noted $[\![C]\!]$.

2. GF Functional types are mapped compositionally : $[\![A \rightarrow B]\!] = [\![A]\!] \rightarrow [\![B]\!]$

3. Every GF syntactic construction function $f : X$ is mapped to a function $[\![f]\!]$ such that $[\![f]\!] : [\![X]\!]$.

4. GF function applications are mapped compositionally: $[\![t(u)]\!] = [\![t]\!]([\![u]\!])$.

Theorem 1 (Semantic interpretations are type sound). *For every applicative expression e in GF, if $e : X$ then $[\![e]\!] : [\![X]\!]$.*

Proof. By induction over the GF typing relation, resting on the fact that the GF type-system is a subset of that of Coq. □

We proceed and describe the details of the interpretation $[\![\cdot]\!]$ for several key syntactic constructions.

Sentences As customary, we interpret sentences as propositions: $[\![S]\!] = Prop$, or in Coq syntax:

```
Definition S := Prop.
```

Consequently, checking entailment can be done by checking logical entailment of the interpretations. Namely, to verify that P entails H, we prove the proposition $[\![P]\!] \rightarrow [\![H]\!]$.

Common nouns We represent common nouns as customary in typed formal semantics, namely as predicates over an abstract object type:

---

[1]One could use other systems to perform parsing, e.g. a CCG parser would be also suitable. Indeed, this is the parser used by Mineshima et al. (2015) in their system. Perhaps the most important reason for choosing GF over another well-suited parser was the existence of a GF treebank for FraCaS Ljunglöf and Siverbo (2011).

```
Parameter object : Set.
Definition CN := object → Prop.
```

Another option would be to follow the common nouns as Types paradigm, an approach found in Ranta (1994); Luo (2012); Chatzikyriakidis and Luo (2017) among others. This would allow common nouns to be basic types and every common noun to be associated with a base type in a type theoretic CN universe. A subtyping relation could then be used to encode semantic relations between the types. Indeed, this is the approach taken in Chatzikyriakidis and Luo (2014) in dealing with inference in Coq. However, for the current task, the need for subtyping is not crucial. In contrast it is needed to test whether an object belongs to a CN as a proposition, which is tricky to encode compositionally we we simply have $[\![CN]\!] = Type$, so a fully-fledged universe would be required.[2]

Verb phrases Like common nouns, verb phrases are traditionally represented as predicates over the subject. Here, we additionally parameterize over the *noun* of the subject (using Π types). This allows in particular for comparative copulas to know which class they refer to, which is often needed in FraCas.

```
Definition VP := forall (subjectClass : CN) (subject : object), Prop.
```

Adjectival phrases and adjectives Adjectives and adjectival phrases are represented as modifiers of common nouns.

```
Definition A := CN → CN.
```

The test suite further requires to refine adjectives as intersective, subsective, extensional subsective, privative and non-commital, as it is standard in the formal semantics literature (Kamp, 1975; Partee, 2007, 2010). For a full discussion of adjectives and in general modification within a constructive setting, see Chatzikyriakidis and Luo (2017). For concision we show how to deal with intersective and extensional subsective only.

An intersective adjective (`IntersectiveA`) is fully defined by a predicate over objects. The adjectival meaning is the conjunction of such predicate and the bare noun (`wkIntersectiveA`). Additionally, to relieve the user from calling this semantic function in in many places, we declare it as an implicit coercion.

```
Definition IntersectiveA := object → Prop.
Definition wkIntersectiveA : IntersectiveA → A
        := fun a cn (x:object) ⇒ a x ∧ cn x.
Coercion wkIntersectiveA : IntersectiveA ↣ A.
```

Extensional subsective adjectives are characterised by a noun-modifier a, and the property that if two noun classes p and q are extensionally equivalent, then $a(q)$ implies $a(p)$ (again, note the use of a dependent type):

```
Inductive ExtensionalSubsectiveA : Type :=
   mkExtensionalSubsective :
     forall (a : (object → Prop) → (object → Prop)),
     forall (ext : forall (p q:object → Prop),
               (forall x, p x → q x) → (forall x, q x → p x) → forall x, a p x → a q x),
     ExtensionalSubsectiveA.
```

---

[2]For example, a sentence like "John is a man" would be interpreted as a typing judgment in the common nouns as Types paradigm, $John : [\![Man]\!]$. Then, one would want some extra mechanism to turn this into a proposition in order to reason about it in Coq. Indeed, this is feasible as shown in Chatzikyriakidis and Luo (2017) but this is something that we have not pursued in this paper. Working on the common nouns as Types approach is left for future work, and we hope that results will shed light on the theoretical advantages of the two approaches.

The adjectival semantics is that of a subsective adjective: the bare noun holds in conjunction with the modified noun:

```
Definition apExtensionalSubsectiveA
        : ExtensionalSubsectiveA → A
        := fun a cn (x:object) ⇒ let (aa,_) := a in
             aa cn x ∧ cn x .
Coercion apExtensionalSubsectiveA : ExtensionalSubsectiveA ↣ A.
```

In the same way we treated intersective adjectives, we add the semantics as a coercion for subsectives as well. It should be stressed that it suffices to declare an adjective as extensional subsective for Coq to remember the extensional property, even though it does not appear in the interpretation as a coerced general adjective.

Adverbs Adverbs are similar to adjectives, except that they modify verbal predicates or propositions instead of nouns. In the FraCaS test suite we only find VP adverbs (verbal predicates). Furthermore, the test suite does not require the noun class to be passed to the adverb semantics, and thus we omit it. *A contrario*, the test suite requires many adverbs to be veridical and covariant. Thus, as for adjectives, we define a refined subclass to capture these properties.

```
Definition ADV := (object → Prop) → (object → Prop).
Definition Adv := ADV.
Definition VeridicalAdv :=
  { adv : (object → Prop) → (object → Prop)
    & (forall (x : object) (v : object → Prop), (adv v) x → v x) *
      (forall (v w : object → Prop),
        (forall x, v x → w x) → forall (x : object), adv v x → adv w x)
  }.
```

The plain adverbial semantics are recovered by extracting the *adv* component. Similarly to extensional adjectives, veridical adverbs the additional properties are made available solely by declaring lexical entries as belonging to the correct class. A coercion between *VeridicalAdv* and *Adv* is further defined (in effect we define veridical adverbs to be subtypes of adverbs). To give an example, consider the veridical adverb *on_time*. This will have the entry:

```
Parameter on_time_Adv : VeridicalAdv .
```

Noun phrases and predeterminers The literature usually defines the semantics of noun-phrases as a predicate over verb phrases:

```
Definition NP0 := VP → Prop.
```

Unfortunately, such a clean definition cannot work with GF's abstract syntax. The main issue is that predeterminers, which include "most", "at least", "all", etc. are parsed as modifiers of noun phrases: $PredetNP : Predet \to NP \to NP$. A moment of thought suffices to be convinced that predicates over verb-phrases are too rigid to be "pre-determined" in this way. Therefore the semantics that we use is a tuple of the components of noun-phrases: number, quantifier, and common noun:

```
Inductive NP : Type := mkNP : Num → Quant → CN → NP.
```

Predeterminers can then update the quantifier part of the NP. For example, the "all" and "most" predeterminers replace the quantifier part by the corresponding quantifier:

```
Definition Predet := NP → NP.
Definition all_Predet : Predet := fun np ⇒ let (num,qIGNORED,cn) := np
                                  in mkNP num all_Quant cn.
Definition most_Predet : Predet := fun np ⇒ let (num,qIGNORED,cn) := np
                                   in mkNP num MOST_Quant cn.
```

One may wonder if it is justified to simply ignore the quantifier in such a way. We answer positively, because in practice, a noun-phrase with a useful quantifier is never equipped with the "all" predeterminer — in fact, in this case GF introduces a dummy indefinite article which *must* be overwritten in the semantics.

Numerals, cardinals   An important part of the NP is the number. Here we record as precisely as possible the information given by the syntax; which can be a singular, a plural, a precise cardinality or even the "more than" modifier.

```
Inductive Num : Type   :=
  singular : Num        |
  plural :  Num         |
  unknownNum : Num      |
  moreThan : Num → Num  |
  cardinal : nat → Num .
```

Generalised quantifiers and articles   Generalised quantifiers turn a number and a common noun into a (usual) noun-phrase (which we call $NP0$).

```
Definition Quant := Num → CN → NP0.
```

Certain quantifiers ignore the number, and are thus given usual definitions:

```
Definition all_Quant : Quant :=fun (num:Num) (cn : CN) (vp : VP) ⇒ forall x, cn x→ vp cn x.
```

Some others, such as "at most" make essential use of the number:

```
Definition atMost_quant : Quant
  := fun num cn vp ⇒ interpAtMost num (CARD (fun x ⇒ cn x ∧ vp cn x))
```

In the above, `interpAtMost` checks that the given number is less than the given cardinality. The function `CARD` is a context-dependent abstract function which turns a predicate into a natural number. We equip `CARD` with common-sense axioms of set cardinality, such as monotonicity:

```
Parameter CARD : (object → Prop) → nat.
Variable CARD_monotonous : forall a b:CN, (forall x, a x → b x) → CARD a <= CARD b.
```

The `CARD` variable is used to interpret several other quantifiers, including "most":

```
Definition MOST_Quant : Quant :=
    fun num (cn : CN) (vp : VP) ⇒ CARD (fun x ⇒ cn x ∧ vp cn x) >= MOSTPART (CARD cn).
```

where `MOSTPART` is another context-dependent abstract function from natural to natural. To support FraCas examples, it is sufficient to equip it with a monotonicity axiom:

```
Parameter MOSTPART: nat → nat.
Variable MOST_mono : forall x, MOSTPART x <= x.
```

As usual, articles are special cases of quantifiers. When a useful number is provided by the NP, the indefinite article enforces it. Otherwise it generates an existential quantification.

```
Definition IndefArt:Quant:= fun (num : Num) (P:CN)⇒  fun Q:VP⇒  match num with
  cardinal n ⇒ CARD (fun x ⇒ P x ∧ Q P x) = n                  |
  moreThan n ⇒ interpAtLeast n (CARD (fun x ⇒ P x ∧ Q P x))    |
  _          ⇒ exists x, P x∧ Q P x end                        .
```

The definite article checks for plural noun phrases, in which case it implements definite plurals (universal quantification). Otherwise, it looks up the object of discourse in an abstract *environment*, which is a function which turns a common noun into an object: $environment : CN \to object$.

```
Definition DefArt:Quant:= fun (num : Num) (P:CN)⇒ fun Q:VP⇒ match num with
plural ⇒ (forall x, P x → Q P x) ∧ Q P (environment P) ∧ P (environment P) |
_ ⇒ Q P (environment P) ∧ P (environment P) end.
```

Prepositions Prepositions are interpreted as values transforming simplified noun phrases (1) to predicates. This transformation is veridical (2) and covariant (3). These three aspects are captured in three fields of a record, as follows.

```
Definition NP1 := (object → Prop) → Prop.
Inductive Prep : Type :=
  mkPrep : forall
  (prep : NP1 → (object → Prop) → (object → Prop)),              (* 1 *)
  (forall (prepArg : NP1) (v : object → Prop) (subject : object),    (* 2 *)
    prep prepArg v subject → v subject) →
  (forall (prepArg : NP1) (v w : object → Prop),
  (forall x, v x → w x) → forall x, prep prepArg v x → prep prepArg w x) (* 3 *)
    → Prep.
```

Comparatives We interpret comparatives as functions from adjective and NP into an adjectival phrase. We use the common noun (class) provided by the NP as a common reference class for the quality (or adjective, denoted a below) under comparison. Note that we additionally obtain the class of the object, but we ignore it. (Future work may want to unify those two classes).

```
Definition ComparA : A → NP → AP
 := fun a np cn x ⇒ apNP np (fun yCN y ⇒ (a cn y → a cn x)
                                ∧ (not (a cn x) → not (a cn y))).
Definition ComparAsAs : A → NP → AP
 := fun a np cn x ⇒ apNP np (fun _class y ⇒ a cn x ↔ a cn y).
```

We define 'as ... as' as an equivalence of the quality a between the subject and the object. We define 'more ... than' as an implication of the quality a in the appropriate direction, and the converse implication in the opposite direction. Note that the treatment of comparatives does not involve any reference to scales or degrees: this was not needed at least for the examples at hand, even though many fine-grained treatments of comparatives take these into consideration.[3]

Relative clauses Relative clauses are interpreted as verb phrases and used intersectively when building noun phrases:

```
Definition RS := VP.
Definition RelNPa : NP → RS → NP
  := fun np rs ⇒ let (num,q,cn) := np
  in mkNP num q (fun x ⇒ cn x ∧ rs cn x).
```

4 Evaluation

4.1 The FraCaS test suite

The FraCaS test suite is a test suite for natural language inference (NLI) (Cooper et al., 1996). It arose out of the FraCas Consortium, a huge effort with the aim to develop a range of resources related to computational semantics. The goal of the suite is to reflect what an adequate theory of NL inference should be capable of capturing. It contains 346 NLI examples in the form of one or more premises followed by a question along with an answer to that question. There are three potential answers to the question: a) YES, indicating that the declarative sentence formed out of the question follows from the premise(s), b) NO, indicating that the negation of the declarative sentence follows from the premise(s),

---

[3]For a first treatment in MTTs, the interested reader is directed to Chatzikyriakidis and Luo (2014, 2017).

and c) UNK, indicating that neither the declarative sentence nor its negation follow from the premise(s). The suite is structured according to the semantic phenomena involved in the inference process for each example, and contains 9 sections. As such, there are sections on quantifiers, adjectives, comparatives, plurals etc. Some representative examples from the suite are shown below:[4]

(1)   An Irishman won the Nobel prize for literature.
      An Irishman won a Nobel prize.
      Did an Irishman win a Nobel prize? [Yes, FraCaS 017]

(2)   No delegate finished the report.
      No delegate finished the report on time.
      Did any delegate finished the report on time? [No, FraCaS 038]

(3)   Smith, Jones or Anderson signed the contract.
      Jones signed the contract.
      Did Jones sign the contract? [UNK, FraCaS 083]

The FraCaS test suite has considerable weaknesses, for example its small size as well as the artificial nature of the examples.[5] However, FraCaS covers a wide range of phenomena associated with NLI and it remains possibly the best suite to test logical approaches as regards NLI.

4.2   Evaluating FraCoq against the FraCaS

We evaluated FraCoq against 5 sections of the FraCaS test suite, a total of 174 examples. We excluded the sections where a whole lot of context-dependency has to be taken into consideration (sections on anaphora, ellipsis and temporal reference), plus the very short section dubbed as 'verbs', including aspectual class and collective predication test cases.[6] We classify as YES if a proof can be constructed from the premises to the hypothesis, NO if a proof of the negated hypothesis can be constructed and UNK otherwise.[7]

	Section	# examples	Ours	MINE	Nut	Langpro
1	Quantifiers	75	.96	.77	.53	.93 (44)
2	Plurals	33	.76	.67	.52	.73 (24)
3	Adjectives	22	.95	.68	.32	.73 (12)
4	Comparatives	31	.56	.48	.45	-
5	Attitudes	13	.85	.77	.46	.92 (9)
6	Total	174 (181)	0.83	0.69	0.50	0.85

The above result reveals a considerable improvement over earlier approaches in terms of accuracy. Still there are some cases that present difficulties. For example, the section on comparatives was quite challenging. Mostly, this was due to examples like the following, where one needs not only to provide adequate semantics for *more* but also to make sure that the elliptical fragment is also correctly reconstructed:

(4)   ITEL won more orders than APCOM.
      ITEL won some orders.
      Did ITEL win some orders? [Yes, FraCaS 233]

---

[4]The examples are taken from Bill Maccartney's xml conversion of the suite. Note that in the xml conversion, the declarative hypothesis formed out of the question is also included.

[5]These weaknesses have given rise to the creation of other NLI platforms, like RTE and SNLI. For more information on these platforms the interested reader should consult Dagan et al. (2006) and Bowman et al. (2015) respectively. The discussion on what type of NLI platform is better suited for computational semantics is out of the scope of this paper.

[6]However see the discussion in section 5 for relevant ideas for future research.

[7]"Ours" refers to the approach presented in this paper, "MINE" refers to the approach in Mineshima et al. (2015), "NUT" to the CCG system that utilizes the first-order automated theorem prover *nutcracker* described in Bos (2008), and "Langpro" to the system presented in Abzianidze (2015).

Another example case concerns the semantics of definite plurals. The problem there is that definite plurals sometimes give rise to a universal interpretation, and sometimes to an existential one. We have used the universal interpretation for definite plurals, so the examples involving the existential interpretation were not predicted correctly. The example below is a case where our system will find the proof, contrary to what we would want:

(5)   The inhabitants of Cambridge voted for a Labour MP.
        very inhabitant of Cambridge voted for a Labour MP.
        Did every inhabitant of Cambridge vote for a Labour MP? [UNK, FraCaS 094]

As can be seen from the table, our system outperforms both Mineshima et al. (2015) and the Nutcracker system. We evaluate on 7 fewer examples than Mineshima et al. (2015), 174 instead of 181 (we have not evaluated against the "verbs" section), and get an overall accuracy of 0.83 compared to 0.69 by Mineshima et al. (2015), an overall improvement of 14 percentage points. Note that the Langpro system as described in Abzianidze (2015) shows an accuracy of 0.85. However the system is only evaluated against 92 examples and the comparatives section, which was the most difficult part to cope with for all systems, was not taken into consideration. If the comparatives section is taken out, our system shows an accuracy of 0.88 for 143 examples.

4.3 Automation

One issue to be discussed is automation. So far, our proofs are not automated, which means that there are a number of steps (usually very few), that are needed in order to produce a proof. In the earlier approaches using the proof-assistant Coq, i.e. Chatzikyriakidis and Luo (2014); Mineshima et al. (2015), the authors use Coq's tactical language LTAC to create macros of proof tactics that automate the proofs. However, we believe that such automation says little of the system's ability to provide a general automated procedure for examples outside the ones tested. Indeed, one can trivially automate all the examples at hand by just going through all the proof tactics or observe the tactics that are used in the proofs to create a macro that will automate the proofs. Yet, can that macro of tactics generalize outside the suite? Unfortunately, only to a limited extent: when exactly the same set of tactics yields a proof. For this reason, we have not automated proof search to obtain the results presented in this paper. Yet if someone were to automate the proof search for the examples looked at, in the same sense as Mineshima et al. (2015), this is not difficult to do.

Another issue with automating the work is that this would make an unprincipled use of higher-order logic (HOL): indeed, in HOL, there is no algorithm which can decide if a proposition has a proof or not. This means that we must use heuristics both to search for proofs and to decide when to give up searching. Fortunately, in FraCas, most problems have either obvious proofs or obviously lack a proof. From a logical perspective, the most difficult inferences involve veridicality and covariance, yet the premises involving those are sufficiently clear to guide the search in a clear direction. Still, due to its heuristic nature the proof search necessarily contains a human component, which is problematic to make a statement about the suitability of FraCoq outside FraCas from the percentages observed in the above table. This issue compounds with the small size of FraCas and the lack of separation between a development and a testing subset. (At the limit, one can construct a tool with 100% success rate by simply using a lookup table.)

A related shortcoming is that we sometimes use specialised semantics for specific entries in the lexicon — which may themselves trigger the need for more heuristics in proof search.

5   Conclusions and Future work

A first improvement to this work would be to address the issue of automation. We could take the unprincipled approach outlined above. A more principled approach would be to define a decidable fragment of the logic and only work within such fragment. Then, we would be able to concisely characterize how our approach generalises. In the meantime, users of our framework must understand the semantics defined above in order to grasp their scope.

Another area of improvement is at the GF level. An obvious advance would be to improve the syntax of predeterminers, to make it more suitable for compositional semantics, as we have hinted at above.

Similarly, the GF syntax for "more than" makes it very hard to recover the elliptical component of the phrase (see example (4) above). Indeed, in phrases such as "more orders than APCOM", "more" is often in a different syntactic subtree than "than APCOM", which renders a compositional semantics infeasible. (When "than APCOM" is attached to the verb phrase the connection to "more" is not naturally recoverable.) In cases where "than APCOM" is in the correct subtree, it is construed as an adjectival phrase built from a prepositional phrase. Again, unsuitable for compositional semantics.

Lastly, a mid-term improvement to our work would be to support anaphora. A straightforward, if tedious, way to do so would be to thread an environment of mentioned objects throughout phrases.

In summary, we have connected two well-defined systems based on type-theory by providing a resource semantics for GF. We have underlined how approaches based on higher-order (and to a lesser extent even first-order) logic are inherently limited in how they generalize. Despite this limitation, we have shown that it is possible to achieve very precise semantics for specific domains. This translates into high accuracy for NLI, as exemplified by our results on the FraCas test suite. We hope that in the future such approaches will be used in performing inference tasks on controlled natural language domains and/or applications having such a component.

References

Abzianidze, L. (2015). A tableau prover for natural logic and language. In *Proceedings of EMNLP2015*, pp. 2492–2502.

Bekki, D. and K. Mineshima (2017). Context-passing and underspecification in dependent type semantics. In S. Chatzikyriakidis and Z. Luo (Eds.), *Modern Perspectives in Type-Theoretical Semantics*, pp. 11–41. Springer.

Bertot, Y. and P. Castéran (2013). *Interactive theorem proving and program development: Coq?Art: the calculus of inductive constructions*. Springer Science & Business Media.

Blackburn, P., J. Bos, M. Kohlhase, and H. d. Nivelle (2006). separate performative account of the german right dislocation,. In *Proc. of Sinn und Bedeutung 10*.

Bos, J. (2008). Wide-coverage semantic analysis with boxer. In *Proceedings of the 2008 Conference on Semantics in Text Processing*, pp. 277–286. Association for Computational Linguistics.

Bos, J. and K. Markert (2005). Recognising textual entailment with logical inference. In *Proc. of the 2005 Conference on Empirical Methods in Natural Language Processing (EMNLP),*, pp. 98–103.

Bowman, S. R., G. Angeli, C. Potts, and C. D. Manning (2015). A large annotated corpus for learning natural language inference. In *Proceedings of EMNLP*, pp. 632–642.

Chatzikyriakidis, S. and Z. Luo (2014). Natural language inference in coq. *Journal of Logic, Language and Information 23*(4), 441–480.

Chatzikyriakidis, S. and Z. Luo (2017). Adjectival and adverbial modification: The view from modern type theories. *Journal of Logic, Language and Information 26*(1), 45–88.

Cooper, R. (2017). Adapting type theory with records for natural language semantics. In S. Chatzikyriakidis and Z. Luo (Eds.), *Modern Perspectives in Type-Theoretical Semantics*, pp. 71–94. Springer International Publishing.

Cooper, R., D. Crouch, J. van Eijck, C. Fox, J. van Genabith, J. Jaspars, H. Kamp, D. Milward, M. Pinkal, M. Poesio, and S. Pulman (1996). Using the framework. Technical report lre 62-051r, The FraCaS consortium. http://www.cogsci.ed.ac.uk/ fracas/.

Cooper, R., S. Dobnik, S. Larsson, and S. Lappin (2015). Probabilistic type theory and natural language semantics. *LiLT (Linguistic Issues in Language Technology) 10*, 1–43.

Dagan, I., O. Glickman, and B. Magnini (2006). The pascal recognising textual entailment challenge. In *Machine learning challenges. evaluating predictive uncertainty, visual object classification, and recognising tectual entailment*, pp. 177–190. Springer.

Glickmann, O., I. Dagan, and M. Koppel (2005). Web based probabilistic textual entailment. In *Proceedings of the PASCAL Challenges Workshop on Recognizing Textual Entailment.*

Gonthier, G. (2008). Formal proof–the four-color theorem. *Notices of the AMS 55*(11), 1382–1393.

Gonthier, G., A. Asperti, J. Avigad, Y. Bertot, C. Cohen, F. Garillot, S. Le Roux, A. Mahboubi, R. OConnor, S. O. Biha, et al. (2013). A machine-checked proof of the odd order theorem. In *Interactive Theorem Proving*, pp. 163–179. Springer.

Grudzińska, J. and M. Zawadowski (2017). Generalized quantifiers on dependent types: A system for anaphora. In S. Chatzikyriakidis and Z. Luo (Eds.), *Modern Perspectives in Type-Theoretical Semantics*, pp. 95–131. Cham: Springer International Publishing.

Hickl, A., J. Williams, J. Bensley, K. Roberts, B. Rink, and Y. Shi (2005). Recognizing textual entailment with lCC's groundhog system. In *Proc. of Second PASCAL Challenges Workshop on Recognizing Textual Entailment*, pp. 80–85.

Kamp, H. (1975). Two theories about adjectives. In E. Keenan (Ed.), *Formal Semantics of Natural Language*. Cambridge Univ Press.

Leroy, X. (2013). The compcert c verified compiler: Documentation and users manual. http://compcert.inria.fr/man/manual.pdf.

Ljunglöf, P. and M. Siverbo (2011). A bilingual treebank for the FraCas test suite. Clt project report, University of Gothenburg.

Luo, Z. (2012). Formal semantics in modern type theories with coercive subtyping. *Linguistics and Philosophy 35*(6), 491–513.

MacCartney, B., M. Galley, and i. C.D. Manning (2008). A phrase-based alignment model for natural language inference. In *Proceedings of EMNLP-08*, pp. 802–811.

Martin-Löf, P. (1971). An intuitionistic theory of types. manuscript.

Martin-Löf, P. (1984). *Intuitionistic Type Theory*. Bibliopolis.

Mineshima, K., Y. Miyao, and D. Bekki (2015). Higher-order logical inference with compositional semantics. In *Proceedings of EMNLP*.

Montague, R. (1973). The proper treatment of quantification in ordinary english. In *Approaches to natural language*, pp. 221–242. Springer.

Partee, B. (2007). Compositionality and Coercion in Semantics: The Dynamics of Adjective Meaning. In *Cognitive Foundations of Interpretation*. Royal Netherlands Academy of Arts and Sciences.

Partee, B. (2010). Privative Adjectives: Subsective plus Coercion. In R. Bauerle, U. Reyle, and T. Zimmermann (Eds.), *Presuppositions and Discourse: Essays Offered to Hans Kamp*, Volume 21 of *Current Research in Semantics/Pragmatics Interface*. Emerald Group Publishing Ltd.

Pulman, S. (2013). Second order inference in NL semantics. Talk given at the KCL Language and Cognition seminar, London.

Ranta, A. (1994). *Type-Theoretical Grammar*. Oxford University Press.

Ranta, A. (2011). *Grammatical framework: Programming with multilingual grammars*. CSLI Publications.

Retoré, C. (2013). The montagovian generative lexicon Tyn: a type theoretical framework for natural language semantics. In R. Matthes and A. Schubert (Eds.), *Proc of TYPES2013*.

Romano, L., M. Kuylekov, I. Szpektor, I. Dagan, and A. Lavelli (2006). Investigating a generic paraphrase-based approach for relation extraction. In *Proceedings of EACL 2006.*, pp. 409–416.

Sundholm, G. (1989). Constructive generalized quantifiers. *Synthese 79*(1), 1–12.

Tanaka, R., K. Mineshima, and D. Bekki (2015). Factivity and presupposition in dependent type semantics. In *Proceedings of TyTLeS, ESSLLI2015*.

Extracting word lists for domain-specific implicit opinions from corpora

Núria Bertomeu Castelló
UFS Cognitive Sciences
Universität Potsdam, Germany
parlamind GmbH, Berlin
nuria@parlamind.com

Manfred Stede
UFS Cognitive Sciences
Universität Potsdam, Germany
stede@uni-potsdam.de

Abstract

Sentiment analysis relies to a large extent on lexical resources. While lists of words bearing a context-independent evaluative polarity ('great', 'bad') are available for many languages now, the automatic extraction of domain-specific evaluative vocabulary still needs attention. This holds especially for implicit opinions or so-called polar facts. In our work, we focus on German and on a genre that has not received much attention yet: customer emails. As the prime downstream application is identifying customers' complaints, we concentrate here on finding negative words, but our method applies to positive ones as well. Using a seed list approach, we provide a comparative analysis along three dimensions: effect of different seed lists, different linguistic analysis units, and different statistical correlation tests.

1 Introduction

One interesting and difficult subtask of sentiment analysis is the automatic recognition of so-called *implicit opinions* or *polar facts*: Statements that express a valuation yet do not include context-independent polar words that belong in standard sentiment (polarity) dictionaries. With a polar fact, an author gives a description of some state of affairs, which prima facie appears to be an objective statement, but for the particular target at hand (or more precisely, all targets of its class) entails a polar opinion. They have been studied for product reviews (Toprak et al., 2010) and minutes of meetings (Wilson, 2008), but are also relevant in many other genres such as political or legal discourse.

By their nature, polar fact expressions are domain-specific (see, e.g., Blitzer et al. (2007)). Therefore, it is important to be able to acquire the vocabulary for a domain when high-quality sentiment analysis is to be applied. In this paper, we provide a comparison of several variants of a seed-list approach to generating lists of such lexical items. The starting point is a list of standard opinion words, which we use as seeds to extract collocating polar fact words and phrases from their contexts. The genre we tackle is customer emails, and our data comes from four different content domains, which we illustrate with examples:

- Fashion: "The seam's coming undone."

- Food: "Those cookies were really hard."

- Beauty: "The perfume does not smell!"

- Eyewear: "With these lenses my sight is blurry."

Not surprisingly, most of such customer emails are negative rather than positive: People usually write to the vendor when there is something to complain about. Being able to automatically identify such messages in a company's email stream is an important downstream application for the task we study here. For that reason, in this paper we will focus on extracting negative polar lexical items; the method, however, would apply to positive items as well.

Our target language is German, but the method is language-neutral, and furthermore it should be applicable to other genres and domains, too. So far there is only little related work on polar fact identification in general, and we are not aware of any that has addressed German. The central aims of our study are to investigate the effects of two different seed sets (varying in origin and size), and of different notions of "minimal unit" for defining the collocation context, and to compare the utility of different measures for lexical association.

The following section summarizes the relevant previous work, and Section 3 introduces our data set. Then, Section 4 presents our experiments and results on word list generation, and Section 5 provides conclusions and an outlook on the next steps of this project.

2   Related Work

Our goal is related on the one hand to the SemEval shared task 2a of 2013 (re-run in 2014 and 2015), where Twitter messages with marked words were given, and the words had to be classified for their polarity. It also resembles SemEval shared task 9 of 2015 on detecting the implicit polarity of events. In contrast to both, however, we are aiming at extracting domain-specific lists of lexical and phrasal items, which can then be applied to the task of finding polar facts. In the following, we thus review previous research on these two aspects: the automatic recognition of polar facts and the generation of word lists for purposes of sentiment analysis.

2.1   Recognizing polar facts

The importance of polar facts has been acknowledged in schemes for manual sentiment annotation by Wilson (2008), Toprak et al. (2010) and de Kauter et al. (2015). There is, however, very little work so far on identifying polar facts automatically. Chen and Chen (2016) extract them from Chinese hotel reviews, but their emphasis is on the additional problem of implicit aspects. Their basic idea is similar to ours in this paper: They collect two adjacent segments, where one contains an explicit opinion word (and an aspect term), and the second one does not, and then project the explicit opinion from one to the other segment (making the assumption that it has the same polarity). New words are learned via the chi-squared test and PMI methods, and candidates are manually inspected for the construction of an opinion word list; the accuracy observed was 70.46%.

2.2   Generating word lists

On the side of *explicit* sentiment, the idea of generating word lists based on a seed set has been employed quite often, and we mention here the successful system of Mohammad et al. (2013); Kiritchenko et al. (2014) for Twitter sentiment classification. Working on two domains, the authors gathered large amounts of unlabelled web data (reviews) and extracted word lists from them. Following Turney and Littman (2003), each term received a sentiment score:

$$score(w) = PMI(w, pos) - PMI(w.neg) \tag{1}$$

with *pos* and *neg* denoting positive and negative reviews, respectively. PMI is calculated as:

$$PMI(w, neg) = log_2 \frac{freq(w, neg) * N}{freq(w) * freq(neg)} \tag{2}$$

with $freq(w, neg)$ the number of times a word appears in negative reviews, $freq(w)$ its total frequency in the corpus, $freq(neg)$ the total number of tokens in negative reviews, and N the total number of tokens in the corpus. Terms that occurred less than five times in the positive or negative reviews were ignored. When $PMI(w, pos)$ is calculated in the analogous way, a positive $score(w)$ indicates that w is more associated with positive sentiment, and a negative one indicates negative sentiment. A simple heuristic negation score recognizer was used to make sure that negated words were treated as different items. The resulting word lists were used in conjunction with other lexicons and contributed significantly to the performance in the overall task of computing aspect-based sentiment (lexicons as a whole increased the F-score by 8 points).

Participating in the same SemEval tasks on Twitter sentiment, Severyn and Moschitti (2015) use a distant supervision method: A large Twitter corpus with noisy polarity labels (inferred from hashtags and emoticons) is mapped to a lexicon of labeled unigrams and bigrams from those Tweets. Then an SVM classifier is trained on these lexical features. The authors show that their method outperforms the PMI-induced lexicon method of Kiritchenko et al. (2014) on the same datasets. Similarly, Vo and Zhang (2016) show that a prediction-based neural network implementation yields a better accuracy than the counting-based method of Mohammad et al. (2013) when comparing to an existing (manually-annotated) "gold" lexicon.

For German, Sidarenka and Stede (2016) compare two families of methods for generating sentiment lexicons and evaluate them on Twitter data: dictionary-based methods starting from WordNet, and corpus-based methods, including the two mentioned above. They found that dictionary-based methods generally outperform corpus-based ones, and that – more importantly for our purposes here – the results of corpus methods depend heavily on the specific seed sets employed in the various approaches. One of the German lexicons available today, SentiWS (Remus et al., 2010), used a method similar to ours – counting co-occurrences, applying log likelihood as association measure, and involving human judgements – and achieved an accuracy of 49.5% for negative polarity words.

3   Our data: Email corpus

Customer care emails are a genre that has not been studied much in the literature, but is highly relevant for several practical applications, including topic identification, sentiment or emotion detection, and automatic mail response systems. Polar facts play an interesting role in these texts, because customers often point out that a product did not meet their expectations, without using explicitly-polar words (see the examples in Section 1). In order not to tie our work too closely to a particular domain, we selected different clients of parlamind GmbH (a company providing customer service solutions) as sources for our email corpus. In a first step we filtered for those emails that actually mention a product, using the Google product taxonomy[1]. The main reason for only selecting e-mails about products is that products are domain-specific (there are e.g. fashion products, eyewear products, beauty products, etc.), while other contact reasons in customer-care e-mails are general accross all the domains (e.g. payment, shipping, withdrawal). Since this work is concerned with finding domain-specific polar words or expressions, we select e-mails with product-related contact reasons. Below we give the number of mails selected by this filter, the sizes of the original sets, and the proportion of the selection.[2] An example email, together with its English translation, is given in Figure 1.

- Fashion (2 clients): 18.358/203.085 emails (9%)

- Food (2 clients): 5.519/35.712 emails (15%)

- Beauty (1 client): 12.819/131.980 emails (10%)

- Eyewear (1 client): 2.087/5.406 emails (39%)

- TOTAL: 38.783/376.183 (10%)

---

[1]https://support.google.com/merchants/answer/6324436?hl=de

[2]Mails that do no mention a product contain general feedback to the company or its service, ask questions not related to a product, or can be qualified as spam.

Sehr geehrte Damen und Herren,
ich habe am Freitag die Sonnenbrille, die ich bestellt hatte, erhalten. Jedoch fand ich, dass diese Brille nicht gut genug für den Versand verpackt war. Beim Aufsetzen der Brille hat sich mein Gedanke dann bestätigt. Sie ist schief und ist wirklich sehr locker beim Aufsetzen. Sie sitzt so, als wäre sie total ausgeleiert.
Deshalb will ich sie gerne zurück schicken und eine neue, richtig eingepackte Brille zugeschickt bekommen.
Mit freundlichen Grüßen, NAME

Dear Sir or Madam,
on Friday I received the sunglasses that I had ordered, but I noticed that the glasses were not packed up well enough for shipping. When wearing the glasses, this impression was confirmed. They are bended and really very loose when putting on. It feels like they are completely worn out.
Therefore I would like to return them and have new, adequately-packaged sunglasses being shipped to me.
Yours sincerely, NAME

Figure 1: Sample email from 'Eyewear' domain

4 Experiments on word list generation

The system described below was implemented for both positive and negative words, but as explained earlier, we will focus here on the negative set and provide evaluations only for that. The basis for our approach is a seed list of negative words, and we experiment with two variants here: The first is a list of 170 domain-independent negative German words (lemmas) that we compiled manually from various sources, targeting specifically the customer-care email genre. Some translated examples from this list are: *unsatisfactory, unpleasant, dirty, pointless, weak, fault, unfortunately, unreliable, sad.*

The second was obtained from automatically computing the intersection of negative entries in three existing German sentiment lexicons, see (Sidarenka and Stede, 2016). It consists of 9004 words. Henceforth, we abbreviate these lists as NEG-170 and NEG-INTER, respectively.

For computing the polarity of segments, we also use a list of manually-compiled of positive words, POS-100.

The central goal of the experiments is to assess the influence of

- two different ways of obtaining a seed list for negative words,

- different notions of "minimal unit" for the polarity analysis (in the related work above, these were always complete Tweets; we need a more elaborate definition), and

- different measures for computing lexical association.

4.1 Preprocessing

Our pipeline starts with segmenting the emails into minimal units that define the context for computing lexical association between candidate words/phrases and polarity. As there is no generally established definition of that unit, we experimented with four different variants:

- paragraphs (as determined by the newline character)

- sentences (as determined by punctuation, i.e., via sentence splitting)

- discourse units comprising a single or multiple clauses which exhibit discourse continuity among each other. We use discourse markers expressing contrast, such as "aber", "obwohl", "sondern" ("but", "although", "but rather") etc. in order to split mails into discourse units. We perform the splitting in three ways, depending on the type of discourse connective:

- In the presence of a coordinating discourse marker expressing contrast, such as "aber", "sondern", "doch", "andererseits" ("but, "but rather", "however", "on the other hand") etc., the text is split and a new discourse unit is created, starting with the marker.

  - In the presence of a subordinating discourse marker, such as "obgleich", "ausser", "abgesehen von" ("despite, "besides", "disregarding") etc., the text is split and a new unit is created that starts with the marker and ends with the next punctuation sign encountered. After that a new discourse unit starts.

  - Finally, if an utterance contains the adverb "leider", we create a new discourse unit starting at the beginning of the utterance.[3]

- clauses: main clauses and subordinate clauses are split according to coordinating and subordinating conjunctions and punctuation (final punctuation or comma occurring after a finite verb). Infinitive clauses, complement clauses, irrealis conditional clauses[4] and indirect questions are not split because the main clause has incomplete meaning without the subordinated clause.

The example in Figure 1 consists of four paragraphs, most of them very short; the second gets segmented into five sentences. In turn, two of these sentences get split into two clauses. The e-mail contains two discourse units.

Generally, sentences that are questions get removed from the corpus, as we do not expect to find opinions in there. For POS tagging, we use the Apache OpenNLP[5] tagger with its German model, but performed additional training on a manually-annotated email corpus, in order to improve the performance on our genre. Based on the POS tags, we then mark the candidate items that will be considered for our lexicon: nouns, adjectives, and verbs. In addition, we extract predicate/argument tuples: For each verb, we build a set of tuples containing all combinations of the verb with the respective heads of the subject, object and indirect object. I.e., for a transitive verb, as in *We process the order*, three such tuples are being built: *(process,we)*, *(process,order)* and *(process,we,order)*. The tuples are extracted from predicate-argument structures. Those are obtained using chunking heuristics and morphological information to identify the syntactic roles in the sentence. When it is unambiguous, morphological case informs the selection of syntactic roles, otherwise constituent-order is used. This can be considered a "light" version of dependency analysis (full parsing has generally turned out to be too noisy on the email data).

As part of the predicate/argument analysis, we check for the presence of negation operators, i.e., words such as "nicht", "kein", "keins", "niemand", "nie", "nirgendwo" ("not", "no", "none", "noone", "never", "nowhere") etc. and heuristically determine their scope: negated verbs and negated arguments are stored as such. If a clause contains some negated argument, it is stored as negated, too. Therefore if a tuple contains any negation, it is stored as negated.

We then mark all instances of negative and positive words (from our seed lists) in all the segments and add their polarity as a feature. Again, we check for negation scope and reverse the polarity if necessary. Based on these assignments, the final step is to label each segment with its estimated polarity:

- positive: If there is a majority of positive instances (having factored in the negation scope);

- negative: (likewise);

- neutral: if the number of positive and negative words is equal.

---

[3]This decision is based on the observation that customer-care e-mails expressing complaints very often start with a small narrative introduction and then signal the start of the complaint with an adverb such as "unfortunately". For example: "On Friday the shirt that I had ordered arrived. Unfortunately, the shirt is too small for me." Here, the adverb "unfortunately" behaves similarly to a discourse marker like "but".

[4]For example: "Es wäre schön, wenn Sie mir das noch mal zuschicken könnten." ("It would be nice if you could send it to me again.")

[5]https://opennlp.apache.org

Polarity	Item	Not Item	Total
-1	6 (c12)	19172	19178 (c1)
0,1	0	146699	146699
Total	6 (c2)	165871	165877 (n)

Table 1: Sample contingency table, as built for each candidate item (word, pred/arg tuple)

At the end of this preprocessing phase, we have for each of the four domains a set of segments (coming in four variants, as described above) with a polarity label and all potential candidate items (word, pred/arg tuples) included therein.

4.2 Scoring and ranking the candidates

For building our different variants of domain-specific lexicons, we now consider each candidate item and count how often it occurs in a positive, negative, and neutral segment. For building a list of negative items (which is the goal scenario for the rest of the paper), we compute a score for each item, following six different methods. Similar to the related work, we remove items that occur less than three times in all the negative segments. Then, for each of the scoring methods, a ranked lists of the items is produced. (Recall that this complete process is also run for each of the above-mentioned notions of elementary unit.) In the following, we describe the scoring methods, based on the sample contingency table shown in Table 1. (Such a table is constructed for each word/item under consideration.) It uses the following variables:

- $c12$: co-occurrence of the item and the currently-considered polarity

- $c1$: total counts of the considered polarity

- $c2$: total counts of the considered item

- n: total number of units (segments)

Bayesian test We use two binary variables: pol = polarity (1 = negative; 0 = not negative) and i = item (1 = present; 0 = not present). Then we estimate the probability that the polarity is negative, given that we have observed the item:

$$P(pol = 1|i = 1) = k * (P(pol = 1) * P(i = 1|pol = 1)) = (c1/n) * (c12/c1) \tag{3}$$

where k is a normalizing constant, so that $P(pol = 1|i = 1) + P(pol = 0|i = 1) = 1$.

Frequency classes difference test Here we consider that we have two (sub-)corpora: one with segments of the negative polarity under consideration and one with other segments. The approach is for a given item to find out whether it belongs to a different frequency class in each of the corpora, and if so, how distant those frequency classes are. The lower the frequency class, the more frequent is the word in the given corpus.

- Polarity-Frequency-Class: $log_2(c1/c12)$

- Reference-Frequency-Class: $log_2((n - c1)/(c2 - c12))$

- Difference: $log_2(c1/c12) - log_2((n - c1)/(c2 - c12))$

Relative likelihood ratio test   The relative likelihood ratio test assumes the same two sub-corpora. It is the ratio of the probability of seeing an item given the negative polarity over the probability of seeing the same item given the non-negative polarity. It is calculated as follows:

$$\frac{c12/c1}{(c2 - c12)/(n - c1)} \tag{4}$$

Likelihood ratio test   We use the same binary variables *pol* and *i* as in the Bayesian test. Then we calculate the ratio of the null hypothesis (a given item and a given polarity are independent) over the alternative hypothesis (the given item and polarity are dependent):

- H1 (null hypothesis) $= P(pol = 1|i = 1) = p = P(pol = 1|i = 0)$

- H2 (alternative hypothesis) $= P(pol = 1|i = 1) = p1 \neq p2 = P(pol = 1|i = 0)$

- $log(L(H1)/L(H2)) = logL(c12, c2, p) + logL(c1 - c12, N - c2, p) - logL(c12, c2, p1) - logL(c1 - c12, N - c2, p2)$, where

  - $L(k, n, x) = x^k(1 - x)^{(n-k)}$
  - $p = c1/n$
  - $p1 = c12/c2$
  - $p2 = (c1 - c12)/(N - c2)$

Chi-squared test   The Chi-squared test sums the differences between observed and expected values in all squares of the table, scaled by the magnitues of the expected values.

$$\frac{n * ((o11 * o22) - (o12 * o21))^2}{(o11 + o12) * (o11 + o21) * (o12 + o22) * (o21 + o22)} \tag{5}$$

where

- $o11 = c12$

- $o12 = c1 - c12$

- $o21 = c2 - c12$

- $o22 = n - c12 - o21$

PMI test

$$log_2 \frac{c12/n}{(c1/n) * (c2/n)} \tag{6}$$

From each of the domain-specific ranked lists of items (as they result from the different combinations of segmentation units and statistical tests), we take the top 350 items. The 350 top words cut-off is motivated both by the amount of items our annotators could manage and by the perceived lower (negative) quality of the words appearing after the 350 cut-off. This perceived lower quality is later confirmed by the probability of 0.57 of being negative in the Bayesian test of the words occurring after the threshold and the precision of 0.528 on the cut-off. See section 4.3 for evaluation scores on different thresholds.

In the following, we present the procedure and evaluation for the Fashion domain, as it has the largest amount of data. Here, the union of the sets of 350 words amounts to 2146 unique items. For these, we obtained human judgements as to whether they are indeed negative, given the domain in question. (For example, in the Fashion domain, the tuple (have,hole) would be judged as a proper negative item.) Our annotators confirmed that 559 of the 2146 items are negative (in their respective domain).[6]

These 559 "gold" items are the basis for the evaluation of the various settings we are interested in: choice of seed list, type of minimal unit, and association measure.

---

[6]At this point we did not compute inter-annotator agreement for the polarity assignments; this is left for future work.

Bayesian	Chi-squared
(reklamiren,Mangel) *(complain,fault)*	klein *small*
(unterlaufen,Box) *(occur,box)*	feststellen *notice*
(haben,Mangel) *(have,fault)*	eng *tight*
(zeigen,Mangel) *(show,fault)*	muss *must*
(feststellen,Rücksendung) *(notice,return shipping)*	musste *had to*
(setzen,Defekt) *(sit,defect)*	groß *large*
(erwarten,Monat) *(expect,month)*	(haben,Problem) *(have,problem)*
(scheinen,Fehler) *(appear,mistake)*	unterlaufen *occur*
leiert *worn out*	weit *wide*
(haben,Defekt) *(have,defect)*	Qualität *quality*
(verändern,Farbe) *(change,color)*	(unterlaufen,Fehler) *(occur,mistake)*
(entstehen,Problem) *(originate,problem)*	technisch *technical*

Table 2: Top items of the generated "Fashion" term list (negative) for two methods

4.3 Evaluation and results

For each ranked list of negative items as produced by one of the settings, we again consider the top 350 items and measure how many of them are indeed negative (i.e., they are among the 559 confirmed ones). We determined these accuracy scores for the Fashion domain. For illustration, Table 2 shows the top 12 entries in the lists of the extracted negative items for two association measures. Evidently they differ in favouring single words versus tuples, which we comment on below. The verb 'unterlaufen' *happen* in German collocates predominantly with negative event nouns ('Fehler', *mistake*) but is not by itself negative. Thus, the items in the Bayesian list indeed all indicate negative sentiment; two thirds of them contain a generally-negative word such as *problem*, while one third represent domain-specific polar facts (e.g., *(change,color)*). The Chi-squared list, on the other hand, has several items that cannot be identified as negative without knowing further context (e.g., *small, large*). We surmise that they are often used with the intensifier 'zu' *too*, which then yiels a negative judgement. The modal verb 'müssen' *must* in a customer email has a negative ring, similar to 'unterlaufen' *occur*, which is present in this list as well.

Table 3 contains twenty top negative words for the domains Fashion and Eyewear obtained with the Bayesian method, all of them with probability 1.0 of being negative. Tuples containing generally-negative words, such as *problem*, have been filtered out for presentation. As you can see, both lists contain genre-specific domain-independent words and tuples (such as "(notice, return shipping)"or "(transfer, bill)"), but also domain-specific or at least domain-relevant words and tuples (such as "worn out" and "loosened", for the Fashion domain, and "exact-FALSE"[7] and "(have, assembly, glasses)-FALSE", for the Eyewear domain). Many tuples and words are not negative per se, but they appear as negative because in the customer-care-genre and the specific domains they are only mentioned in relation to some trouble or issue; otherwise they are seldom the topic of some mail (e.g. "loose money pocket"or "water-repellent")[8]. So, even if this kind of words are not polar, it may be helpful to consider them for the purpose of identifying complaints.

Seed set. We consistently obtained much better results for NEG-170 than for NEG-INTER. For example, the overall best result (any unit, any association measure) for NEG-INTER is 0.35, while for NEG-170 we often get results over 0.5, as can be seen in Table 4. We assume that the long, automatically-generated NEG-INTER list has too much noise and produces many irrelevant results for our type of task. Another possibility is that NEG-INTER does not contain some genre-specific sentiment words that occur particularly often in customer-care e-mails (e.g. "Schrott" *(scrap)*, "unerklärlich" *(unexplicable)*). This

---

[7]The suffix "-FALSE" is to be understood as negation, e.g. "not exact".

[8]Please take into account that orders are always taken automatically in the online-shop and only very seldom per e-mail. So those domain-relevant words are usually only mentioned in the context of complaints.

Fashion	Eyewear
(feststellen,Rücksendung) *(notice,return shipping)*	Paketversand *packet shipping*
(unterlaufen,Box) *(occur,box)*	(unterlaufen, Bestellung) *(occur, order)*
leiert *worn out*	erfolglos *unsuccessful*
(haben, Etikett) *(have, label)*	(erhalten, Rückmeldung)-FALSE *(receive, response)-FALSE*
(zeigen,Herstellerlabel) *(show, producer label)*	abhanden *lost*
Frontseite *front side*	(haben, Fertigung)-FALSE *(have, assembly)-FALSE*
(vermeiden, Rücklastschriftgebühren, Mahnkosten) *(avoid, return debit note fee, dunning costs)*	Rücksendung-FALSE *return-FALSE*
DHL-Lieferantin *DHL-delivery woman*	(durchführen, Messung) *(take, measurements)*
(angeben, Hosengrösse) *(provide, trousers size)*	genau-FALSE *exact-FALSE*
erwischen *to catch*	angerechnet *charged*
(zusenden, bitte, Beutel) *(send, please, bag)*	Ring *ring*
loesten *loosened*	herausgestellt *turned out*
erst-FALSE *first-FALSE*	(haben, Fertigung, Brille)-FALSE *(have, assembly, glasses)-FALSE*
reklamiren *to complain*	wasserabweisend *water-repellent*
Retoureschein-FALSE *return voucher-FALSE*	Zustand *state*
(gutgeschrieben, Herr, Betrag, Rechnung)-FALSE *(booked, Mister, amount, bill)-FALSE*	(verlegen, Rechnung) *(transfer, bill)*
begangen *commited (e.g. error)*	(gelten, Rücksendung)-FALSE *(be valid, return)-FALSE*
Paketanfrage *packet inquiry*	schicht *coating*
Kleingeldfach *loose money pocket*	laufen-FALSE *work-FALSE*
(verwundern, Situation) *(wonder, situation)*	spät *late*

Table 3: Top items of the generated "Fashion" and "Eyewear" term lists (negative) without tuples containing seeds

Segmentation	rel. likel. ratio	freq. class	log likel.	chi-squared	Bayesian	PMI
clauses	0.53	0.53	0.36	0.41	0.53	0.53
sentences	0.52	0.52	0.31	0.31	0.52	0.52
disc. units	0.46	0.46	0.25	0.23	0.46	0.46
paragraphs	0.40	0.41	0.21	0.19	0.41	0.41

Table 4: Results (accuracy) for the NEG-170 seed set, Fashion domain

suggests that having genre-specific seed words (in this case, customer-care sentiment words) may be more useful to obtain domain-specific lists of words (e.g. for Fashion, Eyewear, Beauty, ...) than using general sentiment seeds.

Unit. In Table 4, and in our other experiments, we find that clauses are generally the most successful unit of analysis for our task. This can be related to the genre of the customer emails, which very often are a mix of neutral reporting ("I received the ordered box last week", etc.) and a single specific complaint. Sometimes, this complaint is actually part of a contrastive sentence ("I like the color of the blouse, but it really doesn't fit", etc.). This is in contrast to text-level sentiment analysis, as needed for product or movie reviews, where the general tone of the overall text is to be determined.

Association measure. Overall, the relative likelihood ratio test, the frequency classes difference test, the Bayesian test and the PMI test achieve the best results. The fact that the log likelihood and Chi-square tests turn out considerably worse might be a result of our setting where tuples play an important role and have generally a better chance to get a positive vote from the human annotators; in particular, a verb-object combination is often more easily judged as negative in the domain than just the single verb. The two last-mentioned tests, however, yield more individual words than the others do, because the words occur more frequently than the tuples, and the two tests are more sensitive to this than the others are (which are based on probabilities independent of the absolute frequency in the corpus). In general, the other tests rank higher items occurring only in one polarity, independently of their frequency.

Overall best results. Besides accuracy, we also measured precision, recall, and F1 for the various combinations of settings that we investigated, and with various thresholds. The maximum F1 score we obtained is 0.55 (for a threshold of 0.742, using the Bayesian measure), with precision at 0.65 and recall at 0.48. The optimal precision is (also using the Bayesian measure, with a threshold of 0.957) 0.73, accompanied by a recall of 0.4.

4.4 Comparison to a baseline

In order to substantiate the findings on unit size and on the influence of our preprocessing, we also implemented a baseline that follows the approach of Turney and Littman (2003): There is no segmentation; instead, for each seed word found, we look for collocation candidates within a fixed window of ten words to the left and to the right of the seed word. We do not identify negation operators and compute any associated polarity reversals. Only single words are being considered, no predicate/argument tuples. The correlation measure is PMI, but with counts replacing probabilities (as also done by Turney and Littman).

For the setting with NEG-170, as reported in Table 4, this methods yields an accuracy of only 0.09, which is substantially worse than the PMI results for the other units, which include the preprocessing measures.

5   Conclusion

Customer emails are a genre that invites many practical applications involving sorting the mails according to the presumed intention of the sender. Negative sentiment in a mail tends to indicate a complaint, and is thus an important feature for a processing pipeline. Recognizing the sentiment, however, is to a large extent dependent on the ability to recognize implicit opinions (or 'polar facts'), which is in turn a domain-dependent task. In the experiments reported here, we worked with German mails from four different domains and selected 'Fashion' as the one to run the evaluations for.

The basic idea we employ here, using domain-neutral seed words to identify further domain-specific negative items, is not new. But we constructed a number of variants of the task, in order to determine some crucial features for a working solution. In our experiments, we thus combined one of two seed lists, one of four notions of minimal unit for allocating candidate items, and one of six different lexical association measures, in order to find the overall most promising combination. In the absence of a large amount of test data, we used human judgements of interim results (the union of the top 350 items suggested by the best-performing combinations) in order to produce the confirmed lexical items (many of them domain-specific) that were then used to evaluate the approach. Although not directly comparable, because different corpora are used, our method, with accuracies of 0.53, seems to be competitive to the earlier work on generating German negative words by Remus et al. (2010) (see Section 2), which achieved an accuracy of 0.495.

A further difference to earlier work is our use of tuples of verb and dependents in addition to individual lexical tokens (or bigrams). These tuples represent a step toward syntactically-motivated analysis while avoiding the full parsing problem (which we found to be quite hard for the email genre). The lists generated by our best-performing settings contain many such tuples, which indicates the potential of this approach. Further improving this minimal syntactic analysis (e.g., by handling verb suffixes) is one of our goals for the future work.

To our knowledge, the influence of using a specific notion of minimal unit for the computation of lexical associations with seed words has not beed studied before. For one thing, much of the earlier work used token windows of a fixed size; in addition, much work has been done on Tweets, which were taken as a complete unit of analysis. For emails, experimenting with units of different size is an important step, and we found that (heuristically-determined) clauses are the best choice, outperforming discourse units (also computed heuristically, drawing on the presence of connectives) and larger units (sentences, paragraphs).

Furthermore, we found that a carefully-selected genre-specific seed list of 170 negative words significantly outperforms a list that is derived from the intersection of three widely-used German sentiment lexicons; these have been built with semi-automatic methods, and apparently contain too much noise for the task at hand here and lack relevant sentiment words in the customer-care e-mail genre.

While the association measures have some diverging properties and are therefore not straightforwardly comparable, we found that generally, the chi-squared and log likelihood tests performed worse than the four others we had implemented.

In order to develop our findings further toward a practical procedure for determining domain-specific negative items, one important task is to empirically motivate a threshold for the ranked list of generated items, which is taken to separate the items regarded as "trustworthy" from those that are not. So far, we used a fixed 350-item cutoff for our experiments, motivated in part by the volume that could be handled by our human judges in dis/confirming the suggestions by the algorithm and by our initial intuitions regarding the quality of the items according to their rank. Our ongoing experiments with precision/recall measurements (some of which we mention in Section 4) are a step into this direction, which constitutes a major aim of our future work.

Acknowledgments

The work reported here was financially supported by the German Federal Ministry for Education and Research (BMBF) through grant 03EFFBB037 in the 'EXIST Forschungstransfer' programme. The authors thank Uladzimir Sidarenka for helpful comments on earlier versions of the paper, and the anonymous reviewers for their constructive suggestions.

References

Blitzer, J., M. Dredze, and F. Pereira (2007). Biographies, Bollywood, boom-boxes and blenders: Domain adaptation for sentiment classification. In *Proceedings of the 45th Annual Meeting of the Association of Computational Linguistics*, Prague, Czech Republic, pp. 440–447. Association for Computational Linguistics.

Chen, H.-Y. and H.-H. Chen (2016). Implicit polarity and implicit aspect recognition in opinion mining. In *Proceedings of the 54th Annual Meeting of the Association for Computational Linguistics (Volume 2: Short Papers)*, Berlin, Germany, pp. 20–25. Association for Computational Linguistics.

de Kauter, M. V., B. Desmet, and V. Hoste (2015). Guidelines for the fine-grained analysis of polar expressions. Technical Report LT3 14-02, Ghent University.

Kiritchenko, S., X. Zhu, C. Cherry, and S. Mohammad (2014). NRC-Canada-2014: detecting aspects and sentiment in customer reviews. In *Proceedings of the 8th International Workshop on Semantic Evaluation (SemEval 2014)*, Dublin, Ireland, pp. 437–442. Association for Computational Linguistics and Dublin City University.

Mohammad, S., S. Kiritchenko, and X. Zhu (2013). NRC-Canada: building the state-of-the-art in sentiment analysis of tweets. In *Second Joint Conference on Lexical and Computational Semantics (*SEM), Volume 2: Proceedings of the Seventh International Workshop on Semantic Evaluation (SemEval 2013)*, Atlanta, Georgia, USA, pp. 321–327. Association for Computational Linguistics.

Remus, R., U. Quasthoff, and G. Heyer (2010). SentiWS - a publicly available German-language resource for sentiment analysis. In *Proceedings of the Seventh International Conference on Language Resources and Evaluation (LREC'10)*, Valletta, Malta.

Severyn, A. and A. Moschitti (2015). On the automatic learning of sentiment lexicons. In *Proceedings of the 2015 Conference of the North American Chapter of the Association for Computational Linguistics: Human Language Technologies*, Denver, Colorado, pp. 1397–1402. Association for Computational Linguistics.

Sidarenka, U. and M. Stede (2016). Generating sentiment lexicons for German Twitter. In *Proceedings of the Workshop on Computational Modeling of People's Opinions, Personality, and Emotions in Social Media (PEOPLES) at COLING*, Osaka, Japan, pp. 80–90.

Toprak, C., N. Jakob, and I. Gurevych (2010). Sentence and expression level annotation of opinions in user-generated discourse. In *Proceedings of the 48th Annual Meeting of the Association for Computational Linguistics*, Uppsala, Sweden, pp. 575–584. Association for Computational Linguistics.

Turney, P. and M. L. Littman (2003). Measuring praise and criticism: Inference of semantic orientation from association. *ACM Transactions on Information Systems 21*(4).

Vo, D. T. and Y. Zhang (2016). Don't count, predict! an automatic approach to learning sentiment lexicons for short text. In *Proceedings of the 54th Annual Meeting of the Association for Computational Linguistics (Volume 2: Short Papers)*, Berlin, Germany, pp. 219–224. Association for Computational Linguistics.

Wilson, T. (2008). Annotating subjective content in meetings. In *Proceedings of the 6th conference on language resources and evaluation (LREC)*, pp. 2738–2745.

Is Structure Necessary for Modeling Argument Expectations in Distributional Semantics?

Emmanuele Chersoni
Aix-Marseille University
emmanuelechersoni@gmail.com

Enrico Santus
Singapore University of Technology and Design
esantus@mit.edu

Philippe Blache
Aix-Marseille University
philippe.blache@univ-amu.fr

Alessandro Lenci
University of Pisa
alessandro.lenci@unipi.it

Abstract

Despite the number of NLP studies dedicated to thematic fit estimation, little attention has been paid to the related task of composing and updating verb argument expectations. The few exceptions have mostly modeled this phenomenon with *structured* distributional models, implicitly assuming a similarly *structured* representation of events. Recent experimental evidence, however, suggests that human processing system could also exploit an unstructured "bag-of-arguments" type of event representation to predict upcoming input. In this paper, we re-implement a traditional structured model and adapt it to compare the different hypotheses concerning the degree of structure in our event knowledge, evaluating their relative performance in the task of the argument expectations update.

1 Introduction

An important trend of current research in linguistics and cognitive science aims at investigating the mechanisms behind anticipatory processing in natural language (Kamide et al., 2003; DeLong et al., 2005; Federmeier, 2007; Van Petten and Luka, 2012; Willems et al., 2015). It is, indeed, uncontroversial that our cognitive system tries to predict incoming input on the basis of prior information, and this strategy is probably crucial for dealing with the rapidity of linguistic interactions (Christiansen and Chater, 2016). By means of different experimental paradigms, several studies have focused on the role of event knowledge in the activation of expectations on verb arguments (McRae et al., 1998, 2005; Hare et al., 2009; Bicknell et al., 2010). During sentence processing, verbs (*arrest*) activate expectations on their typical argument nouns (*crook*), and nouns do the same for other arguments frequently co-occurring in the same events (*cop-crook*). The explanation proposed by these studies is that the human ability to anticipate the incoming input depends on general knowledge about events and their typical participants. This knowledge, stored in the semantic memory, 'reacts' to the linguistic stimulus: the more the processed information is coherent with a prototypical event scenario, the easier for the comprehension system is to constrain the range of the events potentially described by the sentence and to predict the upcoming sentence arguments.

According to one of the most influential accounts of event-based prediction, the event representation includes both the thematic roles and the lexical meanings of the arguments, as well as the relations between different roles. Therefore, there is the assumption of a *structural distinction* between the participants filling the roles (Kim et al., 2016) (i.e. some arguments are good *agents*, other are good *patients* etc.). Such an account has been challenged by the experimental evidence for a 'bag-of-arguments' mechanism of verb predictions, discussed by Chow et al. (2015). Their experiments with Event-Related Potentials (ERPs) focused on the N400 component,[1] whose amplitude is generally interpreted as reflecting the predictability of a word in context (Kutas and Hillyard, 1984). One of their findings was that there is no significant difference in the N400 amplitude at the target verb in sentences like (1a) and (1b) (normal vs. *role-reversed* argument configuration):

(1)   a.   The restaurant owner forgot which **customer** the **waitress** had *served* during dinner yesterday.

         b.   The restaurant owner forgot which **waitress** the **customer** had *served* during dinner yesterday.

That is to say, even if different roles are assigned to *customer* and *waitress* in (1a) and (1b), this difference seems to have no impact on the N400 amplitude.

Given the lack of influence of the structural roles, in order to circumscribe their hypothesis (which we will henceforth refer to as the *bag-of-arguments hypothesis*), the authors set up another experiment, in which they tested whether the predictions could be influenced also by other co-occurring words (i.e., not necessarily arguments; we will refer to this possibility as the *bag-of-words hypothesis*). In order to carry out this test, they compared the amplitudes for sentences like (2a) and (2b) (argument substitution), finding a significantly smaller N400 component for the first sentence type.

(2)   a.   The <u>exterminator</u> inquired which **neighbor** the **landlord** had *evicted* from the apartment complex.

         b.   The <u>neighbor</u> inquired which **exterminator** the **landlord** had *evicted* from the apartment complex.

Chow et al. (2015) concluded that only the event *arguments* can influence predictions about a verb, and that arguments are represented in a sort of unstructured collection (i.e., *bag-of-arguments*). Therefore, according to them, predictions would be sensitive to the meaning of the arguments, but not to their structural roles, which are computed later. For example, the difference between typical agents and typical patients, according to this account, would not be included in the representation of an event.

In the last few years, a related issue has been debated in the field of distributional semantics, i.e. whether there is any added value in using structured representations of linguistic contexts over bag-of-words ones (e.g., contexts represented as co-occurrence windows). While structured models have been shown to outperform the latter in a number of semantic tasks (Padó and Lapata, 2007; Baroni and Lenci, 2010; Levy and Goldberg, 2014), some bag-of-word models proved to be extremely competitive, at least under certain parameter settings (Baroni et al., 2014). A recent paper by Lapesa and Evert (2017) explicitly addressed the question of whether using structured distributional semantic models is worth the effort, by comparing the performance of syntax-based and window-based distributional models on four different tasks. The authors showed that, even after extensive parameter tuning, the former have a significant advantage only in one task out of four (i.e., noun clustering). Interestingly, in the discussion they leave open the question of whether their results can generalize to linguistically challenging task such as the prediction of thematic fit ratings.

In this paper, we specifically investigate this point. The main questions we want to address are: what are the implications of the *bag-of-arguments hypothesis* for current models of thematic fit? More precisely, is it really necessary to have *structured* representations to carry out a thematic fit-related task, such as the argument expectation update?

In order to answer our questions, we implemented three models of argument expectations, adapting them to the above-mentioned hypotheses (i.e., *structured* and *unstructured*, the latter including both the *bag-of-arguments* and the *bag-of-words* hypothesis), and we compared their performance in a binary selection task.

---

[1]The N400, one of the most well-studied ERP components, is a negative-going deflection that peaks around 400 ms after the presentation of a stimulus word.

2 Related Work

One of the most influential distributional model of thematic fit was introduced by Baroni and Lenci (2010), who represented verb semantic roles with a *prototype vector* obtained by averaging the dependency-based vectors of the words typically filling those roles (i.e. the *typical fillers*). Within the Distributional Memory (DM) framework, which was based on syntactic dependencies, Baroni and Lenci used grammatical functions such as subject and object to approximate the thematic roles of agent and patient, and they measured role typicality by means of a Local Mutual Information score (Evert, 2004) computed between verb, arguments and syntactic relations. The basic assumption is that the higher the distributional similarity of a candidate argument with a role prototype, the higher its predictability as a filler for that role will be. As a gold standard, the authors used the human-elicited thematic fit ratings collected by McRae et al. (1998) and Padó (2007), and they evaluated the performance by measuring the correlation between these ratings and the scores generated by the model (as already proposed by Erk et al. (2010)).

Lenci (2011) later extended this 'structured-approach' to account for the dynamic update of the expectations on an argument, which depends on how other roles in the sentences are filled. For instance, given the agent *butcher* the expected patient of the verb *cut* is likely to be *meat*, while given the agent *coiffeur* the expected patient of the same verb is likely to be *hair*. By means of the same DM tensor, this study tested an additive and a multiplicative model (Mitchell and Lapata, 2010) to compose the distributional information coming from the agent and from the predicate of an agent-verb-patient triple (e.g., *butcher–cut–meat*), generating a prototype vector which represents the expectations on the patient filler, given the agent filler. The triples of the Bicknell dataset (Bicknell et al., 2010), which were used for the first time to evaluate such a model, are still today, at the best of our knowledge, the only existing gold standard for this type of task.

Although the 'structured-approach' to thematic fit was influential for a number of other works (Sayeed and Demberg, 2014; Sayeed et al., 2015; Greenberg et al., 2015; Sayeed et al., 2016; Santus et al., 2017), the task of modeling the update of the argument expectations has received relatively little attention. An exception is the work by Tilk et al. (2016), who trained a neural network on a role-labeled corpus in order to optimize the distributional representation for thematic fit estimation. Their model was also tested on the task of the composition and update of argument expectations, where it was able to achieve a performance comparable to Lenci (2011) on the triples of the Bicknell dataset.[2] Notice that both the models of Lenci (2011) and Tilk et al. (2016) necessarily rely on the hypothesis that the arguments are structurally distinct, since they are trained either on argument tuples containing fine-grained dependency information, or on sentences labeled with semantic roles.

Outside the specific area of study of thematic fit modeling, Ettinger et al. (2016) successfully used a type of unstructured representation for another sentence processing-related task, i.e. modeling N400 amplitudes with distributional spaces. The authors proposed a method based on word2vec (Mikolov et al., 2013) to build vector representations of sentence context, and to quantify the relation of an upcoming target word to the context. After training their word vectors on the Ukwac corpus (Baroni et al., 2009) with the Skip-Gram architecture, they modeled the mental state of a comprehender at a certain point of a sentence as the average of the vectors of the words in the sentence up to that point. The predictability of a target word in a sentence was measured as the cosine similarity between its vector, and the context-vector obtained by averaging the vectors of the preceding words. Ettinger and colleagues tested their method on the sentences used in the ERP study by Federmeier and Kutas (1999), in which three different conditions were defined, and they observed that the context-target similarity scores across conditions were following the same pattern of the N400 amplitudes of the original experiment. Thus, this work shows how data on N400 variations can be modeled even by means of vectors with minimal or no syntactic information.

---

[2]Chersoni et al. (2016) presented a research work testing a similar method on the Bicknell dataset. However, their model does not really update argument expectations on the basis of other arguments, computing instead a global score of semantic coherence for the entire event representation, on the basis of the mutual typicality between all the participants.

3 Experiments

Rationale. Baroni and Lenci (2010) computed the thematic fit for a candidate *filler* (e.g., *policeman*) in an argument *slot* (e.g., agent) of an *input* lexical item (e.g., *arrest*) as the similarity score between the vector of the candidate *filler* and a prototype of the typical *slot* filler, built by summing the vectors for the top-k most typical fillers of *input* for *slot* (e.g., the typical agents for the *arrest*-event, such as *cop*, *officer*, *policewoman*, etc.). In this model, syntactic relations were used to approximate verb-specific semantic roles and to identify the most typical fillers. For example, the agent role is approximated by the subject relation, so that the typical *fillers* for the agent *slot* are the typical subjects of the *input* verb. Similarly, the patient role is approximated by the object relation, so that the typical *fillers* for the patient *slot* are the typical objects of the *input* verb.

We propose an extension of the model by Lenci (2011) and we interpret thematic fit as *the expectation of an argument* (i.e., what the prototype vector is meant to represent: $EX_{slot}(input)$), claiming that the update on expectations for a filler caused by new input (e.g. a verb combining with an agent) could be modeled by means of a function $f(x)$ that combines the prototypes built for every input:

$$EX_{slot}(\langle input_1, input_2 \rangle) = f(EX_{slot_1}(input_1), EX_{slot_2}(input_2)) \qquad (1)$$

where the function $f(x)$ is the sum or the pointwise multiplication between the prototype vectors. Once the expectations are calculated, the *filler* fit for the *slot* of $\langle input1, input2 \rangle$ can be computed by measuring the similarity (e.g., by vector cosine) between the *filler* and the expectations. As an example, if we want to estimate how likely is *burglar* as a patient of *the policeman arrested the...*, we build a prototype out of the vectors of typical objects co-occurring with the subject *policeman-n*, then we do the same for the vectors of typical objects of the verb *arrest-v*, and finally we combine the prototype vectors through $f(x)$, by either sum or multiplication. At this point, we can estimate the *filler* fit by calculating the following similarity:

$$EX_{patient}(burglar|\langle police, arrest \rangle) =$$
$$sim(burglar, f(EX_{cooc\_patient}(policeman), EX_{patient}(arrest))) \qquad (2)$$

Since distributional similarity is used as a measure of the predictability of a filler for a certain role, we expect that the thematic fit score of *burglar* for the patient *slot* of $\langle policeman, arrested \rangle$ will be much higher than for *singer-n*. Indeed, *burglars* are more typical patients in this type of situation than *singers* are. Notice that while in Lenci (2011) the update function modified the association scores between the predicate and the fillers, in the present case $f(x)$ directly composes the prototype vectors associated with $\langle input1, input2 \rangle$.

Models. In our experiments, we compared three different distributional semantic models (henceforth DSMs), all inspired by Lenci (2011): i) a structured model, which is similar to the one presented in Lenci (2011) (**DEPS**); ii) a variation of this system, modeling the *bag-of-arguments hypothesis* (**BOA**); iii) a baseline relying on the *bag-of-words hypothesis* (**BOW**). The key difference between our models is to be found in the selection of the fillers (see Table 1):

- **DEPS**: Similarly to Lenci's system, DEPS makes use of information on specific syntactic relations to select role fillers: the agent-role prototypes will be built out of the most typical subjects, the patient-role prototypes out of the most typical objects, and so on (see the last two rows of Table 1).[3] This means that not only the semantic information is taken in consideration (e.g. *policeman*), but also the thematic role of the filler (e.g. *sbj:policeman, obj:policeman*, etc.). Since dependencies

---

[3]Since the roles are approximated by syntactic relations identified by the parser (i.e. Malt-parser (Nivre and Hall, 2005)), their accuracy is subordinate to the accuracy of the parser. Ideally, we would expect clean lists of fillers for the typical subjects (agents) and objects (patients) of a verb, but – as it can be seen in Table 1 – this is not the case.

	Target	Fillers
BOW	steal-v	car-n, money-n, show-n, base-n, thief-n, good-n, item-n, property-n, someone-n, horse-n, limelight-n, vehicle-n, attempt-n, cattle-n, food-n, wallet-n, bike-n, identity-n, thunder-n, key-n
BOA	steal-v	show-n, money-n, car-n, base-n, food-n, thunder-n, march-n, limelight-n, horse-n, idea-n, key-n, wallet-n, heart-n, property-n, jewel-n, identity-n, cattle-n, body-n, purse-n, treasure-n
DEPS	steal-v (agent)	thief-n, someone-n, man-n, burglar-n, gang-n, money-n, robber-n, handbag-n, criminal-n, wallet-n, computer-n, thou-n, horse-n, equipment-n, boy-n, crook-n, disciple-n, cash-n, somebody-n, dog-n
DEPS	steal-v (patient)	show-n, money-n, car-n, base-n, food-n, thunder-n, march-n, limelight-n, horse-n, idea-n, key-n, wallet-n, heart-n, property-n, identity-n, cattle-n, jewel-n, body-n, purse-n, treasure-n

Table 1: Top-20 filler nouns for the word *steal-v* in our three models (for DEPS, we provide the fillers for the agent and the patient slot, while in the other models there is no distinction).

are used to filter fillers entering in the role representation, this model is the closest one to theories assuming *structured* event knowledge.

- **BOA**: Almost identical to the DEPS model, except for the fact that the most typical arguments are not bound to a specific syntactic slot. Indeed, according to Chow et al. (2015), the arguments of a verb like *to serve* (*customer*, *waitress*, *tray*, etc.) are represented like an *unstructured* collection. In this type of model, thus, the top-*k* typical fillers will include *all the strongly associated arguments*, abstracting away from the specific syntactic relation.

- **BOW**: In this baseline, the typical fillers are not arguments, but words typically co-occurring with the targets in a window of fixed width (possibly having no syntactic relation to the targets).

Going back to the previous example, the core idea of the DEPS model is that processing a sentence fragment like *the policeman arrested the...* leads to the activation only of the typical *patients* of such events, since the event knowledge is assumed to be structured. Therefore, the predictability of an argument is measured in terms of its similarity with the prototype built out of the activated patients.

On the other side, the BOA model assumes no distinction between the arguments (i.e., whether they are agents, patients, locations or others), and consequently the sentence fragment above would activate all the typical arguments of the verb *arrest*. This means that the predictability of an argument will be equivalent to its similarity with the prototype of a generic argument of the verb.

Finally, the BOW baseline has no notion of structure at all, not even the underspecified argument relation of the BOA model, and thus the prototypes of this model are just representations of the typical neighbors of the target words. It should be recalled at this point that a *bag-of-words* account of prediction was ruled out by the experimental results by Chow et al. (2015), since only arguments turned out to have an impact. Nonetheless, since we have chosen a *bag-of-words* model with a very narrow window (i.e., two words on the left and right of the target), BOW could also capture indirectly syntactic information (i.e., words frequently co-occurring with the targets within a narrow window are very likely to be also syntactically related to them). Therefore, we expect it to be a reasonably strong baseline.

Corpus and DSMs. Distributional information is derived from the concatenation of the British National Corpus (Leech, 1992) and of the Wacky (Baroni et al., 2009) corpus. Both were parsed with the Malt-parser (Nivre and Hall, 2005). From this concatenation, we built a dependency-based DSMs, where the tuples are weighted by means of Positive Local Mutual Information (PLMI, Evert (2004)). Given the co-occurrence count O_{trf} of the target t, the syntactic relation r and the filler f, we computed the expected count E_{trf} (i.e., the simple joint probability of indipendent variables, corresponding to the product of the probabilities of the single events).[4]

---

[4]The DSM were built by means of the scripts of the DISSECT framework (Dinu et al., 2013)

The PLMI for each target-relation-filler tuple is computed as follows:

$$LMI(t, r, f) = log\left(\frac{O_{trf}}{E_{trf}}\right) * O_{trf} \tag{3}$$

$$PLMI(t, r, f) = max(LMI(t, r, f), 0) \tag{4}$$

Our DSM contains 28,817 targets (i.e., all nouns and verbs with frequency above 1000 in the training corpora), and all syntactic relations were included.[5] We also built a window-based DSM to extract co-occurrence information for the BOW model, counting only the co-occurrences between the nouns and the verbs of the list above within a word window of width 2.

Prototypes The prototypes of all models were built out of the vectors of the k most typical fillers for each model type, and we tested 10, 20, 30, 40, and 50 as values of k.[6]

As in previous studies, PLMI values were used as typicality scores: in the DEPS model, the typicality ranking of the fillers for a given role takes into account *only the fillers occurring in the corresponding syntactic slot* (e.g. the subject for the agent, the object for the patient etc.), whereas in the BOA model the typicality of a filler only depends on the PLMI score with the target, thus ignoring the type of syntactic relation.[7] As for the BOW baseline, the words used for building the prototype are simply co-occurring with the targets within a word window of width 2, and such co-occurrences have been PLMI-weighted as well.

Compositional Functions. The compositional functions that we used to combine the prototypes are the vector sum and the pointwise vector multiplication (Mitchell and Lapata, 2010). An important difference between the compositional functions lies in the fact that, while the sum retains the dimensions that are not shared by both prototype vectors, the multiplication sets them to zero those dimensions. This has an obvious impact on the computation of the cosine, as it could drastically reduce the number of dimensions on which the similarity score is computed.

Datasets and Evaluation. The models were tested on the datasets from the ERP experiments by Bicknell et al. (2010) and Chow et al. (2015).

The Bicknell dataset was introduced to test the hypothesis that the typicality of a verb direct object depends on the subject argument. With this purpose in mind, the authors selected 50 verbs, each paired with two agent nouns that significantly changed the scenario evoked by the subject-verb combination. They obtained typical patients for each agent-verb pair by means of production norms, and they used such data to generate triples where the patient was congruent with the agent and with the verb. For each congruent triple, an incongruent triple was generated as well, by combining each verb-congruent patient pair with the other agent noun, in order to have items describing atypical situations.

The final dataset is composed by 100 plausible-implausibile triples, which were used to build the sentences for a self-paced reading and for an ERP experiment. The subjects were presented with sentence pairs such as:

- *The journalist checked the spelling of the last report.* (plausible)

- *The mechanic checked the spelling of the last report.* (implausible).

Bicknell et al. (2010) reported shorter reading times and smaller N400 amplitudes for the plausible condition. The goal, for a thematic fit model of the argument expectations update, is to assign a higher

---

[5] We added the extra relation VERB, accounting for the link between typically co-occurring subjects and objects. An analogous relation was already in Baroni and Lenci (2010).

[6] The choice of the parameter range is in line with previous NLP studies on thematic fit (Sayeed et al., 2015; Greenberg et al., 2015).

[7] It goes without saying that using syntactic functions to identify the fillers of semantic roles is just an approximation. Nonetheless, the good performances reported by syntax-based thematic fit estimation systems suggest that, at least for agents and patients, such an approach is empirically justified.

cosine similarity score to the plausible triple, as in Lenci (2011). Moreover, Tilk et al. (2016) evaluated their systems on two different versions of this task, since the triple pairs can be created by combining either triples differing only for the agent, or triples differing only for the patient. Following the terminology from this latter study, we will refer to **Accuracy 1** meaning the accuracy of the models in scoring differing-by-patient triples, and to **Accuracy 2** meaning the accuracy in the classification of the differing-by-agent ones.

We also turned into similar triples the 50 verb-arguments combinations of the role reversal experiment by Chow et al. (2015), by creating triple pairs corresponding to the normal and to the role-reversed condition. For example, the sentences in Example (1) were turned into the form: *customer-n waitress-n serve-v* (normal) and *waitress-n customer-n serve-v* (role-reversed). Notice that we preserved the order in which the experimental subjects saw the arguments and the verb, with the latter at the end. Consequently, instead of composing the prototype vectors of the typical fillers of the patient role given an agent and a predicate, as we did for the Bicknell dataset, we derive the expectation vector for the verb from the composition of the prototypes of the typical predicates of the agent and of the patient.

The binary selection task is the same used with the Bicknell dataset, the only difference being that the goal for our models is to assign higher scores to the triples in the standard argument configuration (i.e., the expectation vector should be closer to the verb vector in the normal condition). Only the DEPS results are reported for the Chow dataset, because unstructured models assign exactly the same score to normal and role-reversed triples (independently of the order in which the prototypes of the head verb for each argument are created, the combined prototype will be the same). This is, of course, consistent with the report of the ERP experiment by Chow and colleagues, who found no differences in the N400 amplitudes elicited by the two sentence types.

The performance of the DEPS model on the Chow dataset is of particular interest, as the model has the structural information that is lacking in the other two. If DEPS has to reproduce the N400 pattern found by Chow and colleagues, the scores for the normal and for the role-reversed conditions should not differ significantly.

4   Results

In Table 2 and 3, we report the results for the three model types on the Bicknell dataset for the two kinds of prototype composition and $k = 20$. This latter value is the most common in the literature (Baroni and Lenci, 2010; Greenberg et al., 2015), and the one that gave us the highest accuracy scores.

The DEPS model is almost always the best performing one on the Bicknell dataset, with the exception of a single drop for the multiplicative model in the Accuracy 1 evaluation. The sum turned out to be the most efficient combination function in the majority of the models, and a possible explanation is that the application of multiplication to dependency-based prototype vectors led to sparsity problems. The results obtained by the DEPS Sum model are the highest ones, and the Accuracy 2 score for $k = 20$ is extremely close to the best performance reported in Lenci (2011) (73%).[8] The task of classifying differing-by-patient triples turns out to be harder, as the accuracies are lower and none of the models is significantly better than a random baseline (p-values were computed with the χ^2 statistical test)[9], whereas the Accuracy 2 scores of both the Deps Sum Model and the Deps Multiplication Model have a significant advantage (for both of them, $p < 0.05$).

We also carried out the Wilcoxon rank sum test on the scores generated by all models, and we found that the DEPS-sum model is the only one that manages to assign significantly different scores to the sentences in the two conditions ($W = 5660, p < 0.05$; for all the other models, $p > 0.1$) (see Figure 1). The BOA model was found instead to be worst performing one, even lower than the BOW baseline, and often the recorded accuracy scores are very close to a random baseline. Also, the differences between conditions were far from significance in any of the versions of the model.

---

[8] The only result available for comparison in the literature is the one obtained by Lenci (2011) on the Accuracy 2 task, since the evaluation of Tilk et al. (2016) was carried out on a way smaller subset of the Bicknell dataset (64 triples).

[9] Also the Accuracy 1 scores reported by Tilk et al. (2016) confirm the higher difficulty of this version of the task.

Model	Sum	Multiplication
BOW	59%	57%
BOA	53%	59%
DEPS	**62%**	56%

Table 2: Accuracy 1 on Bicknell (100% coverage) for $k = 20$

Model	Sum	Multiplication
BOW	60%	56%
BOA	58%	57%
DEPS	**72%**	68%

Table 3: Accuracy 2 on Bicknell (100% coverage) for $k = 20$

Figure 2 shows the performance variation of the Sum models on Bicknell dataset, while varying the number of fillers used to build the prototype. At a glance, we can observe that DEPS models achieve higher accuracies with fewer fillers. This is kind of expected, since the good performances of such models are likely to be due to a more restrictive selection of the fillers. With higher values of k, the selection of more weakly-related fillers is probably introducing noise in the prototype. On the other hand, BOA models slightly improve when more fillers are used, but in general their performance is almost always equivalent to BOW models. This indicates, in our view, that the underspecified dependency relation of the BOA model is insufficient to build a precise representation of the expectations on an upcoming argument, unless a larger number of fillers is taken into account. Moreover, even if typical arguments are selected by virtue of a dependency relation, the absence of information on the dependency type makes these models essentially equivalent to window-based ones. Finally, as for the difference between the scores in the two conditions, the Wilcoxon rank sum test returns a significant difference only for the DEPS Sum model with $k = 10, 20$ (in both cases, $p < 0.05$).

Concerning the performance of DEPS on the Chow dataset, it can be seen in Table 4 that the system identifies the triple in the normal condition with a level of accuracy between 62% and 68%. The scores are quite steady, independently from k, and again, the Sum models are generally performing better (but never significantly better than a random baseline: for all parameter settings, $p > 0.05$).

Interestingly, after applying the Wilcoxon rank sum test, it turns out that the differences between the assigned scores never differ significantly between the normal and the argument reversal condition (for all values of k, $p > 0.05$; see also Figure 1). This result is coherent with the outcome of the role-reversal experiment by Chow and colleagues, who found no difference between the N400 elicited by the two sentence types. In other words, structural information does not help in predicting the upcoming verb.

k	Sum	Multiplication
10	68%	66%
20	62%	64%
30	64%	62%
40	64%	62%
50	66%	62%

Table 4: Accuracy on Chow (100% coverage) for the DEPS model for different values of k

In the same way as the unstructured representations used by Ettinger et al. (2016), our models show that the distributional similarity between a target and its context (a structured one, in our case) can accurately reflect the N400 amplitude patterns found in the experimental studies. Notice however that only a model based on the notion of a structured event knowledge was able to mirror the patterns of both the studies of Bicknell et al. (2010). Together with the better performance reported on the Bicknell dataset for the binary classification task, these results suggest that the presence of structural information is an advantage for distributional models of thematic fit.

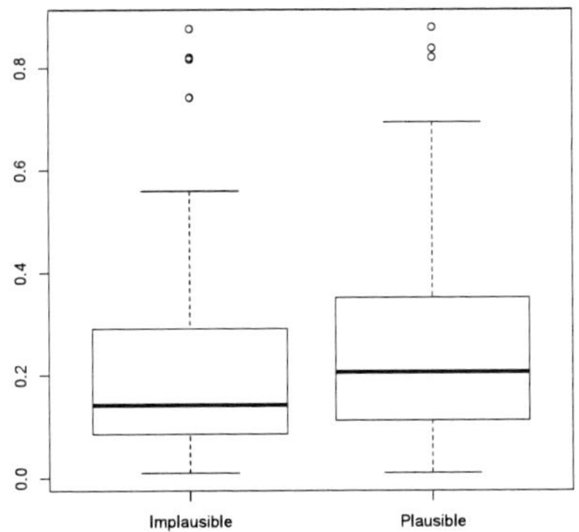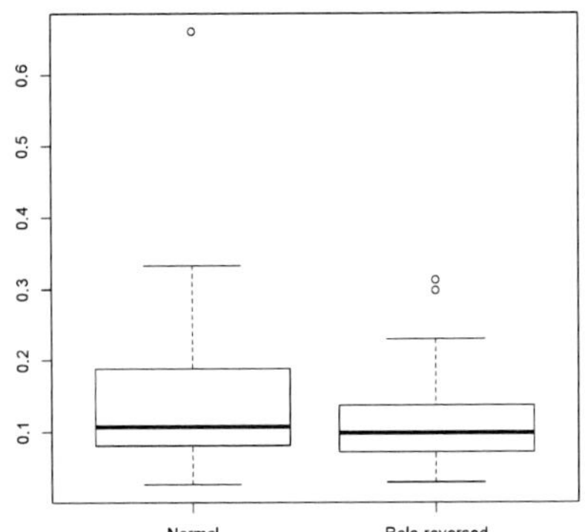

Figure 1: Cosine scores assigned by DEPS-sum model ($k = 20$) for the Bicknell dataset (left) and for the Chow dataset (right).

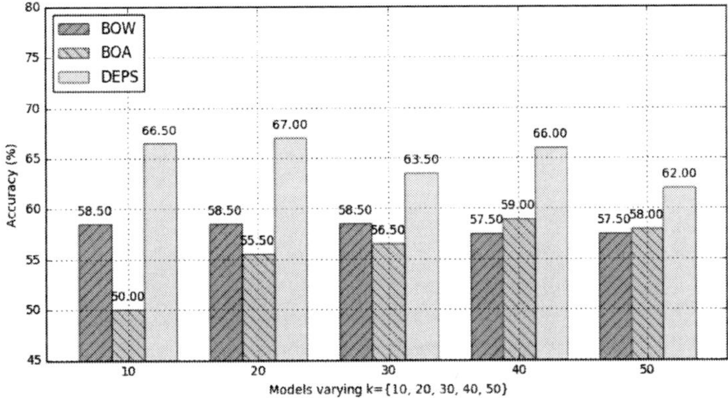

Figure 2: Average of Accuracy 1 and Accuracy 2 on Bicknell dataset, for all the Sum models for different values of k

5 Conclusions

In this paper, we addressed the question of whether structured information is necessary to model the argument expectation update. With this purpose in mind, we have implemented a traditional system for composing and updating thematic fit estimations (Lenci, 2011) and we adapted it to model both structured and unstructured representations (the latter including both the *bag-of-arguments* and the *bag-of-words* hypotheses). We compared the performance of these models on the binary selection task of the argument expectation update and on their ability to replicate the experimental results from the studies by Bicknell et al. (2010) and Chow et al. (2015).

Our results show that structured models perform better in a task of composing and updating argument expectations, and can reproduce the ERP results reported for both datasets. On the other hand, the *bag-of-arguments* model had lower scores in the classification task on the Bicknell dataset, and it was not able to discriminate between the plausible and the implausible condition.

It should be recalled that the *bag-of-arguments* hypothesis was proposed to account for the results of an experiment on initial verb predictions, where the participants could see the verb only at the end (see Examples 1 and 2). In absence of any cue facilitating the mapping between arguments and syntactic positions (consider also that the arguments in the dataset do not differ by animacy), it is reasonable to hypothesize a delay in the assignment of the thematic roles. Moreover, as already pointed out by Kim et al. (2016), the N400 component is generally not sensitive to the implausibility derived by thematic role reassignments, but the presence of event knowledge violation in such cases can be signaled by other ERP components.[10] In sum, the idea of a structure in the event knowledge does not seem to be incompatible with the findings of Chow and colleagues, since our structured DSMs replicated the lack of significant differences between normal and role-reversed sentences. On the other side, models with no structural information struggle in modeling the results of datasets where the items differ for their context-sensitive argument typicality, like the one from Bicknell et al. (2010).[11]

The performance of the DEPS model also complies with the conclusions of Ettinger et al. (2016), which showed how DSMs could be used to reproduce the N400 variations. Such a component is known to be tied to the general semantic relatedness of a target word to its sentential context, and not to syntactic anomalies.[12] From this point of view, it is interesting that our structured models, despite their coherence with the ERP results by Chow et al. (2015), are still able to distinguish the sentence in the normal condition from the role-reversed one with an accuracy always above 60%. Future research could explore in which measure thematic fit models can be sensitive to differences between syntactically-composed representation. Finally, with reference to Lapesa and Evert (2017), our results make the expectation update task a good candidate for being among those that clearly benefit from using fine-grained syntactic information, as it seems to require knowledge about the relation types and about the interdependencies between participants.

Future works might aim at comparing these model types on other NLP tasks, to check how many of them effectively take advantage from structured representations. For the moment, we can conclude that structure is an important added value for thematic fit models.

Acknowledgments

This work has been carried out thanks to the support of the A*MIDEX grant (nANR-11-IDEX-0001-02) funded by the French Government "Investissements d'Avenir" program.
We would like to thank the anonymous reviewers for their comments and for their helpful suggestions.

References

Baroni, M., S. Bernardini, A. Ferraresi, and E. Zanchetta (2009). The WaCky Wide Web: A Collection of Very Large Linguistically Processed Web-crawled Corpora. *Language Resources and Evaluation 43*(3), 209–226.

Baroni, M., G. Dinu, and G. Kruszewski (2014). Dont Count, Predict! A Systematic Comparison of Context-counting vs. Context-predicting Semantic Vectors. In *Proceedings of ACL*.

Baroni, M. and A. Lenci (2010). Distributional Memory: A General Framework for Corpus-based Semantics. *Computational Linguistics 36*(4), 673–721.

Bicknell, K., J. L. Elman, M. Hare, K. McRae, and M. Kutas (2010). Effects of Event Knowledge in Processing Verbal Arguments. *Journal of Memory and Language 63*(4), 489–505.

---

[10]Kim et al. (2016) point out that role-reversed sentences typically elicit en enhanced P600 components compared to their plausible counterparts (see also the experiments in Kim and Osterhout (2005) and Kim and Sikos (2011)).

[11]The 'bag-of-arguments' mechanism described by Chow et al. (2015) actually concerns a very early stage of the comprehension process. Moreover, in a later response article, Chow et al. (2016) brought evidence that verb predictions become sensitive to structural roles of the arguments if more time is available for prediction.
We thank one of our reviewers for pointing this out.

[12]The study of Chow et al. (2015) is an example of experimental evidence for this claim, but see also the results from Fischler et al. (1985) on the N400 insensitivity to the introduction of negations.

Chersoni, E., P. Blache, and A. Lenci (2016). Towards a Distributional Model of Semantic Complexity. *Proceedings of the COLING Workshop on Computational Linguistics for Linguistic Complexity*.

Chow, W.-Y., S. Momma, C. Smith, E. Lau, and C. Phillips (2016). Prediction as memory retrieval: timing and mechanisms. *Language, Cognition and Neuroscience 31*(5), 617–627.

Chow, W.-Y., C. Smith, E. Lau, and C. Phillips (2015). A 'Bag-of-arguments' Mechanism for Initial Verb Predictions. *Language, Cognition and Neuroscience (Advance online publication) 31*(5), 577–596.

Christiansen, M. H. and N. Chater (2016). The Now-or-Never Bottleneck: A Fundamental Constraint on Language. *Behavioral and Brain Sciences 39*.

DeLong, K. A., T. P. Urbach, and M. Kutas (2005). Probabilistic Word Pre-activation During Language Comprehension Inferred from Electrical Brain Activity. *Nature Neuroscience 8*(8), 1117–1721.

Dinu, G., N. T. Pham, and M. Baroni (2013). DISSECT-DIStributional SEmantics Composition Toolkit. In *Proceedings of the ACL System Demonstrations*.

Erk, K., S. Padó, and U. Padó (2010). A Flexible, Corpus-Driven Model of Regular and Inverse Selectional Preferences. *Computational Linguistics 36*(4), 723–763.

Ettinger, A., N. H. Feldman, P. Resnik, and C. Phillips (2016). Modeling N400 Amplitude Using Vector Space Models of Word Representation. In *Proceedings of the 38th Annual Conference of the Cognitive Science Society*, pp. 1445–1450.

Evert, S. (2004). *The Statistics of Word Cooccurrences: Word Pairs and Collocations*. Ph. D. thesis.

Federmeier, K. D. (2007). Thinking Ahead: The Role and Roots of Prediction in Language Comprehension. *Psychophysiology 44*(4), 491–505.

Federmeier, K. D. and M. Kutas (1999). A Rose by any Other Name: Long-term Memory Structure and Sentence Processing. *Journal of Memory and Language 41*(4), 469–495.

Fischler, I., D. G. Childers, T. Achariyapaopan, and N. W. Perry (1985). Brain Potentials During Sentence Verification: Automatic Aspects of Comprehension. *Biological Psychology 21*(2), 83–105.

Greenberg, C., A. B. Sayeed, and V. Demberg (2015). Improving Unsupervised Vector-space Thematic Fit Evaluation via Role-filler Prototype Clustering. In *Proceedings of HLT-NAACL*.

Hare, M., M. Jones, C. Thomson, S. Kelly, and K. McRae (2009). Activating Event Knowledge. *Cognition 111 2*, 151–67.

Kamide, Y., G. T. Altmann, and S. L. Haywood (2003). The Time-course of Prediction in Incremental Sentence Processing: Evidence from Anticipatory Eye Movements . *Journal of Memory and Language 49*(1), 133 – 156.

Kim, A. E., L. D. Oines, and L. Sikos (2016). Prediction During Sentence Comprehension is More than a Sum of Lexical Associations: the Role of Event Knowledge. *Language, Cognition and Neuroscience 31*(5), 597–601.

Kim, A. E. and L. Osterhout (2005). The Independence of Combinatory Semantic Processing: Evidence from Event-related Potentials. *Journal of Memory and Language 52*(2), 205–225.

Kim, A. E. and L. Sikos (2011). Conflict and Surrender During Sentence Processing: An ERP Study of Syntax-semantics Interaction. *Brain and Language 118*(1), 15–22.

Kutas, M. and S. A. Hillyard (1984). Brain Potentials During Reading Reflect Word Expectancy and Semantic Association. *Nature 307*, 161–163.

Lapesa, G. and S. Evert (2017). Large-scale Evaluation of Dependency-based DSMs: Are They Worth the Effort? In *Proceedings of EACL*.

Leech, G. (1992). 100 Million Words of English: the British National Corpus (BNC). *Language Research 28*(1), 1–13.

Lenci, A. (2011). Composing and Updating Verb Argument Expectations: A Distributional Semantic Model. In *Proceedings of the ACL Workshop on Cognitive Modeling and Computational Linguistics*.

Levy, O. and Y. Goldberg (2014). Dependency-Based Word Embeddings. *In Proceedings of ACL*.

McRae, K., M. Hare, J. L. Elman, and T. Ferretti (2005). A Basis for Generating Expectancies for Verbs from Nouns. *Memory & Cognition 33*(7), 1174–1184.

McRae, K., M. J. Spivey-Knowlton, and M. K. Tanenhaus (1998). Modeling the Influence of Thematic Fit (and Other Constraints) in On-line Sentence Comprehension. *Journal of Memory and Language 38*, 283–312.

Mikolov, T., K. Chen, G. Corrado, and J. Dean (2013). Efficient Estimation of Word Representations in Vector Space. *arXiv preprint arXiv:1301.3781*.

Mitchell, J. and M. Lapata (2010). Composition in Distributional Models of Semantics. *Cognitive Science 34*(8), 1388–1429.

Nivre, J. and J. Hall (2005). Maltparser: A Language-independent System for Data-driven Dependency Parsing. In *Proceedings of the Workshop on Treebanks and Linguistic Theories*, pp. 13–95.

Padó, S. and M. Lapata (2007). Dependency-Based Construction of Semantic Space Models. *Computational Linguistics 33*(2), 161–199.

Padó, U. (2007). *The Integration of Syntax and Semantic Plausibility in a Wide-coverage Model of Human Sentence Processing*. Ph. D. thesis.

Santus, E., E. Chersoni, A. Lenci, and P. Blache (2017). Measuring thematic fit with distributional feature overlap. In *Proceedings of EMNLP*.

Sayeed, A. and V. Demberg (2014). Combining Unsupervised Syntactic and Semantic Models of Thematic Fit. In *Proceedings of CLIC-IT*.

Sayeed, A., V. Demberg, and P. Shkadzko (2015). An Exploration of Semantic Features in an Unsupervised Thematic Fit Evaluation Framework. *Italian Journal of Linguistics*.

Sayeed, A., C. Greenberg, and V. Demberg (2016). Thematic Fit Evaluation: an Aspect of Selectional Preferences. In *Proceedings of the ACL Workshop on Evaluating Vector-Space Representations for NLP*.

Tilk, O., V. Demberg, A. B. Sayeed, D. Klakow, and S. Thater (2016). Event Participant Modelling with Neural Networks. In *Proceedings of EMNLP*.

Van Petten, C. and B. J. Luka (2012). Prediction During Language Comprehension: Benefits, Costs, and ERP Components. *International Journal of Psychophysiology 83*(2), 176–190.

Willems, R. M., S. L. Frank, A. D. Nijhof, P. Hagoort, and A. Van den Bosch (2015). Prediction During Natural Language Comprehension. *Cerebral Cortex*, bhv075.

Semantic Variation in Online Communities of Practice

Marco Del Tredici and Raquel Fernández
Institute for Logic, Language and Computation
University of Amsterdam
{m.deltredici|raquel.fernandez}@uva.nl

Abstract

We introduce a framework for quantifying semantic variation of common words in Communities of Practice and in sets of topic-related communities. We show that while some meaning shifts are shared across related communities, others are community-specific, and therefore independent from the discussed topic. We propose such findings as evidence in favour of sociolinguistic theories of socially-driven semantic variation. Results are evaluated using an independent language modelling task. Furthermore, we investigate extralinguistic features and show that factors such as prominence and dissemination of words are related to semantic variation.

1 Introduction

In computational linguistics and NLP, variation in word meaning has mostly been studied in the abstract, as lists of possible word senses (Navigli, 2009; Yarowsky, 2010). In contrast, other neighbouring fields such as sociolinguistics and psycholinguistics have emphasised the link between semantic variation and the activities and interactions of speakers. For example, the psychologist Herbert Clark appeals to the notion of 'common ground' to characterise patterns of word usage: *"Word knowledge, properly viewed, divides into what I will call* communal lexicons, *by which I mean sets of word conventions in individual communities [...] When I meet Ann, she and I must establish as common ground which communities we both belong to simply in order to know what English words we can use with what meaning"* (Clark, 1996); while the sociolinguist Hasan Ruqaiya argues that *"there is evidence of sociosemantic variation"* which must be taken into account *"unless the concept of meaning is arbitrarily constrained"* (Hasan, 1989). The distinction between the two approaches is relevant: while the former is based on the idea that, for a given word, a finite list of discrete senses is available, the latter builds on a more dynamic concept, namely that a new meaning can emerge in any interaction among speakers, who use it in order to make communication more effective.

Understanding the intricate ways in which patterns of word use and communities of individuals are related is essential for characterising the interests and the expressive means of sub-cultures, as well as to develop NLP tools that are effective in the face of variation (Hovy, 2015; Yang and Eisenstein, 2017). In this paper, we study how word meaning (as captured by distributed vector representations) varies across and within different online communities. We take online communities, such as online discussion forums, to be excellent examples of *communities of practice* (Wenger, 2000; Eckert and McConnell-Ginet, 1992), that is, aggregates of individuals not defined by a location or a population, but rather by social engagement in some common endeavour. Using computational modelling techniques and statistical analyses, we show that community-specific conventional meanings of common word forms (as opposed to jargon) do arise and can be reliably detected, which is consistent with the theoretical standpoint of Clark (1996), among others.

The paper makes the following contributions: We adapt a model for geographically located language introduced by Bamman et al. (2014) to learn word representations for different online communities of practice. We introduce a framework for quantifying semantic variation and apply it to several Reddit sub-communities engaged in discussing two broad domains, Football and Programming. We evaluate our framework extrinsically against a language modelling task, showing that the semantic shifts we detect on common words are strong enough to affect performance.

Our results show that distinct meaning conventions arise within communities engaged in discussing a shared domain, but also that the domain itself is not the only determinant of semantic variation: sub-communities concerned with discussing the same general topic may also develop their own conventional meanings for common words, which supports the view that the main factors driving semantic variation are local accommodation effects presumably arising during interaction.

In addition, our findings indicate that, besides frequency-related factors, the level of dissemination of a word among community members plays a key role in understanding the dynamics of meaning variants.

2   Related Work

The present investigation is related to several strands of research in computational sociolinguistics and historical linguistics. Within the former, a substantial amount of work has used NLP techniques to study correlations between linguistic variables and macro-sociological categories such as age (Nguyen et al., 2013), gender (Nguyen et al., 2014; Burger et al., 2011; Ciot et al., 2013), and other demographic factors (Eisenstein et al., 2014). A related line of research has explored the interplay between language use and social relations among community members. For example, Cassell and Tversky (2005) and Huffaker et al. (2006) investigate the correlation between linguistic features and the strength of the relations among users in newborn communities; Danescu-Niculescu-Mizil et al. (2012) and Noble and Fernández (2015) show how variations in linguistic style can provide information about power differences in social groups. Yet other related work has focused on how acceptance into existing communities is mediated by the adoption of community norms (Nguyen and Rosé, 2011; Tran and Ostendorf, 2016) and on how the process whereby linguistic innovations become norms can be leveraged to predict the permanence of a user in a community (Danescu-Niculescu-Mizil et al., 2013).

Common to all approaches mentioned above is the exploitation of language features to implement predictive models for *non-linguistic* features (such as gender, power differences, or community permanence). Less attention has been payed to investigating linguistic variation in its own right. Those approaches that do address this aspect have concentrated almost exclusively on community-specific jargon and slang, i.e., neologisms, unique acronyms and abbreviations — e.g., *'dx'* for 'diagnosis' in breast cancer discussion forums (Nguyen and Rosé, 2011) or *'scrim'* for 'practice match' in online gaming (Kershaw et al., 2016). They have therefore ignored the fact that social interaction among speakers often leads to semantic variation of common word forms: that is, word that *"belong to many communal lexicons, though with very different conventional meanings"* (Clark, 1996). In the present study we concentrate on precisely this type of semantic variation.

Our approach takes a synchronic perspective, i.e., we do not look into the temporal dynamics of meaning variation. Nevertheless, in terms of methodology, our work is related to computational historical linguistics. Diachronic meaning change has been studied at different time scales, from a few decades to several centuries. A variety of techniques have been explored: Latent Semantic Analysis (Sagi et al., 2011; Jatowt and Duh, 2014), topic clustering (Wijaya and Yeniterzi, 2011) and dynamic topic modelling (Frermann and Lapata, 2016). More recently, word embeddings (Mikolov et al., 2013) have proved useful for investigating meaning change over time. The most common approach consists in creating independent vector representations for consecutive time spans and then using a transformation matrix to map vectors from one space to another one (Kulkarni et al., 2015; Zhang et al., 2015; Hamilton et al., 2016). Similarly to this strand of research, our work leverages the power of word embeddings, but exploits a different approach originally introduced by Bamman et al. (2014) to account for geographical variation. As we will explain in detail in Section 4, this approach is an extension of the skip-gram vector model (Mikolov et al., 2013) that allows us to learn meaning representations per community that build upon shared representations.

Meaning variation determined by geographical location — including that of Bamman et al. (2014) — has often focused on dialectal varieties in the USA using data from Twitter (Eisenstein et al., 2010;

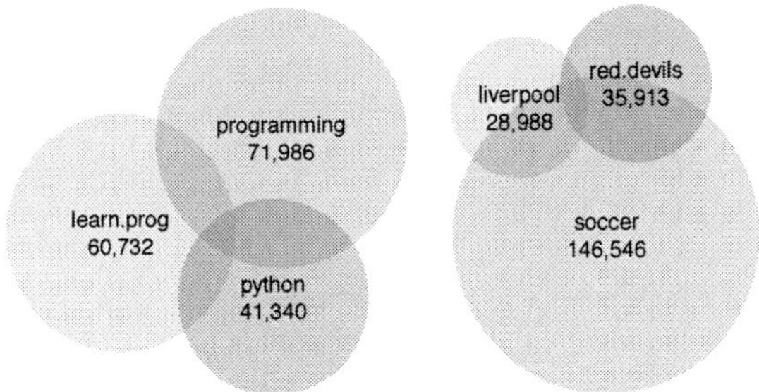

community	years	million tokens
programming	10	21
python	8	18
learn.prog	7	21
soccer	8	65
liverpool	8	55
red.devils	6	66
global	–	50

Figure 1: Left: total number of members and their overlap in the Programming and Football supra-communities. Right: main statistics (time span and number of word token) in each community dataset.

Doyle, 2014; Eisenstein et al., 2014). In contrast to this line of work, as pointed out in the introduction, we are interested in investigating semantic variation in *communities of practice* (Wenger, 2000; Eckert and McConnell-Ginet, 1992): communities defined by social engagement rather than geo-location or other demographic variables.

3 Experimental Setup

Online communities offer an unprecedented opportunity to study linguistic variation and its dynamics. For our investigation of semantic variation, we collected data from Reddit, a large on-line community which includes approximately 1 million sub-communities called 'subreddits'.[1] A subreddit is essentially a discussion forum where individuals with a shared interest on a topic or activity interact: once a user has subscribed to a subreddit, she can post any kind of content (text, links, pictures), reply to existing posts as well as 'upvote' or 'downvote' them. Subreddits can therefore be considered *communities of practice* in the sense of (Eckert and McConnell-Ginet, 1992).

We collected data from 6 different subreddits: half of them (programming, learn.programming and python)[2] are concerned with the domain of computer programming, while the other half (soccer, liverpool, and red.devils) are related to the domain of sports, in particular football.[3] We refer to the subreddits as *communities* and to the two groups of subreddits related by a common theme, Programming and Football (with a capital), as *supra-communities* or domains. It is important to note that Reddit does not have a hierarchical structure whereby subreddits are classified into groups. We base this grouping on the common theme and on shared membership. The communities programming and soccer have a somewhat special status as they are more general in terms of topic and larger in terms of number of members. Figure 1 shows the total number of members in each community and the pattern of shared membership within a supra-community. Over 12% and 15% of members within Programming and Football, respectively, belong to at least two communities in the respective domain. The communities within a domain are thus substantially interconnected. In contrast, the Programming and Football supra-communities share less than 2% of users.

For each community, we crawled the contents created by all members during its whole lifespan (between 6 and 10 years). In the present study, we do not make use of the longitudinal character of the corpus, i.e., we abstract away from the temporal aspect and consider each of the community datasets synchronically as a whole.[4] Since the resulting datasets had different sizes in terms of number of tokens, we randomly subsampled some of them (those crawled from soccer, programming, and

---

[1] https://www.reddit.com

[2] The actual names of the latter two subreddits are learnprogramming and Python; we have slightly modified the names for clarity and simplicity.

[3] The subreddit liverpool (actual name LiverpoolFC) consists of fans of Liverpool Football Club, while red.devils (actual name reddevils) groups fans of the Manchester United Football Club.

[4] The temporal information is a valuable feature of the corpus, which we plan to exploit in future work – see Section 7.

`learn.programming`) in order to make them comparable in size to the other communities within the same domain. The table in Figure 1 summarises the main statistics for each community.

Finally, in order to obtain a sample of community-independent linguistic practices, we created an additional dataset by randomly crawling posts and comments exchanged within any of the existing subreddits during January 2017. We refer to this dataset as the *global* community. The global community includes 50 million tokens from hundreds of thousands of different subreddits, contributed by more than 445k different users. Less than 1% of these users are members of the Programming and Football supra-communities. We consider the linguistic practices present in this dataset as a proxy for general language use.

This experimental setup allows us to investigate different types of semantic variation taking place at different levels: (1) meaning variants deviating from the general language and shared by communities concerned with a common domain, and (2) meaning variants specific to a community and differing both from general language and from other communities within the same domain. In the next section, we define a framework for capturing these two types of semantic shift in a precise, quantitative manner.

4 Framework

We describe the vector-space model we use to learn word representations for online communities of practice and then introduce two indices to measure semantic variation.

4.1 Vector space model

Let C be a set of *communities of practice* and let g denote the *global community*, reflecting general (community-independent) language use. We use subsets such as $D \subset C$ to denote sets of communities related by a certain *domain* (Programming and Football in the experimental setup we use here).

We adapt the model introduced by Bamman et al. (2014) for geo-located language, which in turn is an extension of the skip-gram model by Mikolov et al. (2013). The model relies on a set of contextual variables—geographical locations in the case of Bamman et al. (2014) and Kulkarni et al. (2016), and online communities of practice in our setup. Instead of using a single embedding matrix containing a single real-valued vector for every word in the vocabulary, several matrices are defined: a main matrix W, which is learned by considering all occurrences of each target word in the entire corpus, and one matrix W_c per community (including one matrix W_g for the global community). During training, given an input word w used in a message exchanged within community c, the hidden layer is calculated as the sum $h = w^{\top} W + w^{\top} W_c$. Back-propagation via stochastic gradient descent then updates both embedding matrices.

This joint parametrisation has several desirable properties: the model learns different embeddings for the same word (one per community: $w_{c1}, w_{c2}, \ldots, w_g$) that are part of the same vector space and therefore can be compared to each other. Furthermore, the word representations share information across communities (via the main matrix W), which, intuitively, operates as a regularizer, thus capturing the intuition that the use of a word in a given community is not radically different from its use in other settings but rather a modulation of conventions built upon general shared common knowledge (Clark, 1996).

We tokenise the datasets described in Section 3 (no further preprocessing is applied), and create two independent vector space models for the Programming and Football supra-communities, respectively. We consider only those words that appear at least 100 times in each community dataset and learn word embeddings with 200 dimensions using L2 regularisation. The global community dataset is used in both models.

4.2 Measures of semantic variation

The model described above allows us to derive word embeddings w_c, w_g for each word w and community c in a domain D, encoding how w is used within that community and in the global community g, respectively.

For any two vectors $v, v' \in \mathbb{R}^k$, let $\text{sim}(v, v')$ denote their *cosine similarity*. Given two sets of communities $A, B \subseteq C \cup \{g\}$, we use $\text{Sim}^w_{A,B}$ to refer to the following multiset of similarity values for word w:[5]

$$\text{Sim}^w_{A,B} = \{\text{sim}(w_a, w_b) \mid (a, b) \in A \times B \text{ with } a \neq b\}$$

Let S and S' be two such multisets of similarity values. To measure the extent to which these values are higher in S than in S', we use the following index, where μ and σ are the mean and the standard deviation, respectively:

$$\mathbb{I}(S, S') \quad = \quad [\mu(S) - \sigma(S)] - [\mu(S') + \sigma(S')]$$

We can now use this generic index to construct several specific indices to quantify different types of semantic variation.

Variation at domain level: We consider that a word w exhibits a domain-specific semantic shift if its meaning is relatively constant across communities with a common domain, while being distinct from its use in the global community. The *domain shift index* $\textbf{dsi}^w(D)$ captures exactly this, for a given domain $D \subset C$ and word w:

$$\textbf{dsi}^w(D) \quad = \quad \mathbb{I}(\text{Sim}^w_{D,D}, \text{Sim}^w_{D,\{g\}})$$

For words with positive **dsi** values, the higher the index, the more pronounced their semantic shift across a domain with respect to the language use of the global community.

Variation at community level: We now want to quantify the degree to which a given word exhibits a semantic shift specific to a community, i.e., not shared by other communities concerned with the same domain D. This type of semantic variation is particularly interesting because, when present, it arguably shows that meaning variants can arise in a community independently from the topic discussed.

In particular, we focus on capturing scenarios where the meaning of a word w in a community $c \in D$ has drifted away from its general use in g, while in other domain-related communities the meaning remains closer to that observed in the global community. This is what the *community shift index* below captures, where $D \setminus \{c\}$ denotes the set of communities in domain D except for c:

$$\textbf{csi}^w_c(D) \quad = \quad \mathbb{I}(\text{Sim}^w_{D \setminus \{c\}, \{g\}}, \text{Sim}^w_{\{c\}, \{g\}})$$

Again, for words with positive $\textbf{csi}^w_c(D)$ values, the higher the index, the stronger the shift in c relative to other domain-related communities.

Using the community-specific word embeddings learned with our vector space model, we compute $\textbf{dsi}^w(D)$ and $\textbf{csi}^w_c(D)$ values for all words per domain and community, respectively.

Figure 2 shows the distribution of **dsi** values for the Football domain and the **csi** values of the communities belonging to the domain.[6] All the distributions present a common pattern: few words undergo a strong semantic shift in the domain / community (left tail of the graph), while the majority of the words present a small or null shift, corresponding to **dsi** / **csi** values included in the range between 0 and 0.2. Note that on average **dsi** values are larger than **csi** ones because, intuitively, the **dsi** captures the shift in the domain vocabulary compared directly to the global community, while **csi** represents the more subtle shifts within communities belonging to the same domain. The right tail of negative values has different interpretations for the domain and the communities. Negative values of **dsi** are assigned to the same words that have high **csi** values, i.e. words that show a strong shift in just one of the communities part of the general domain. Finally, for each community, negative **csi** values are assigned to words that undergo strong semantic shift in *another* community of the same domain.

---

[5] In practice, in case $A = B$, we only compute one cosine similarity value for every unordered pair rather than for every ordered pair. Observe that this does not affect either the mean or the standard deviation of the multiset.

[6] Similar results are found for the Programming domain and its communities.

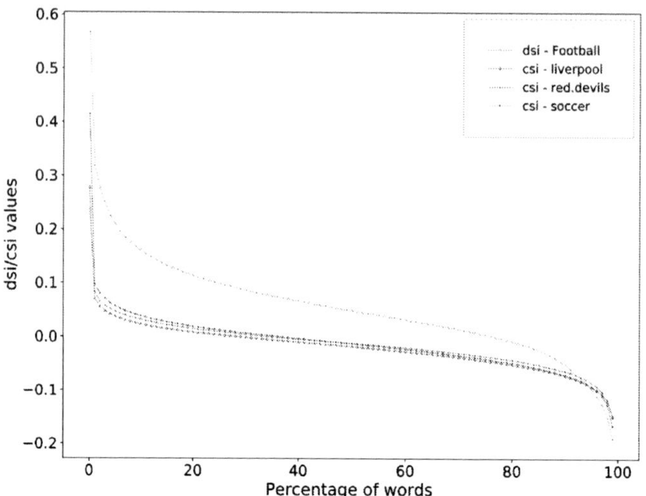

Figure 2: The **dsi** and **csi** values (on the y-axis) for the Football domain and the communities which belong to it. On the x-axis the number of words (in percentage): since we consider only words in the shared vocabulary (see Section 3) the total amount of words is the same for all the communities and for the domain.

5   Evaluation

In order to verify whether the measures proposed in the previous section capture semantic variation that is noticeable beyond cosine distances in semantic space, we evaluate them using an independent language modelling task.

5.1   Method

We implement a neural language model (NLM) using an existing encoder-decoder LSTM[7] with 2 layers of size 200. We randomly split the dataset of each community into training (70%), validation (15%), and test (15%) sets and train one NLM per community using the word embeddings previously learned for that community with the vector space model described in Section 4.1. We train the models for 40 epochs, using Adam estimation (Kingma and Ba, 2014) for parameter update and dropout for regularisation. The same procedure is also carried out for the global community. All the community language models reached an average test perplexity between 45 and 67 on the task of predicting the upcoming word given the preceding word (window size = 1) — a performance in line with the state of the art, (e.g., Zaremba et al. (2014)).

For each domain D, we define two sets of target words: a `shift` set containing the top 10 words with the highest $\mathbf{dsi}^w(D)$ values, and a `no.shift` set containing the 10 bottom words with the lowest positive $\mathbf{dsi}^w(D)$ values. We do the same per community c: the `shift` set includes the ten words with the highest $\mathbf{csi}_c^w(D)$, while the `no.shift` set includes the ten words with the lowest $\mathbf{csi}_c^w(D)$ per communtiy.

At test time, given a set of target words, we compute the average perplexity for each target word w on predicting $w + 1$ with the original w embeddings used for training (ppl_{train}^w) and with *alternative* embeddings for w learned from another community (ppl_{alt}^w). We then measure change in performance as relative perplexity increase:

$$\mathrm{ppl}_{change}^w \;=\; \frac{\mathrm{ppl}_{alt}^w - \mathrm{ppl}_{train}^w}{\mathrm{ppl}_{train}^w}$$

---

	shift		no.shift	
domain	$c \rightarrow D\backslash\{c\}$	$c \rightarrow g$	$c \rightarrow D\backslash\{c\}$	$c \rightarrow g$
Programming	6.04	64.9 (*)	5.77	9.02
Football	2.40	40.47 **	-0.78	-1.04
community	$g \rightarrow D\backslash\{c\}$	$g \rightarrow c$	$g \rightarrow D\backslash\{c\}$	$g \rightarrow c$
programming	0.24	3.87	4.92	10.05
python	6.73	26.83 **	0.68	8.83
learn.prog	11.85	56.77 *	9.57	13.28
soccer	11.32	8.92	13.33	11.93
liverpool	2.45	17.70 **	3.84	5.31
red.devils	4.98	55.84 **	2.98	5.60

Table 1: Perplexity increase medians in each setting with significance level of Wilcoxon signed-rank test ($***p < .001$, $**p < .01$, $*p < .05$).

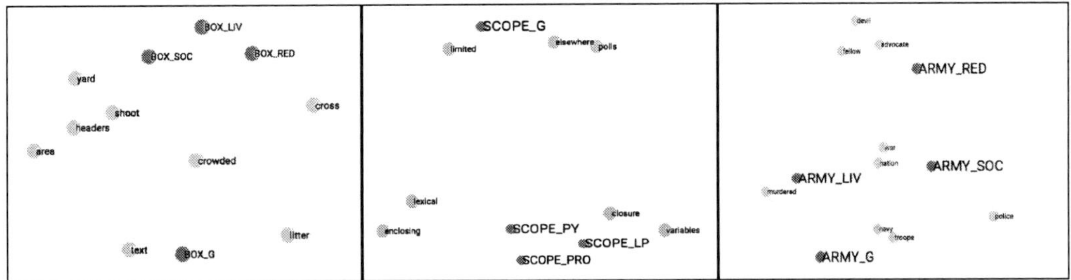

Figure 3: Two-dimensional representation in semantic space of meaning variants for words 'box' (high **dsi**(Football)), 'scope' (high **dsi**(Programming)), and 'army' (high $\mathbf{csi}_{\texttt{red.devils}}$(Football)).

The rationale behind this method is the following: Regarding domain variation, we hypothesise that for shift words the increase in perplexity of the NLM of a given community will be significantly higher when testing on alternative embeddings belonging to the general community than on alternative embeddings belonging to another domain-related community. Regarding community-specific variation, we hypothesise that, when leveraging the NML of the global community, using embeddings of shift words in community c as alternative embeddings will yield significantly higher perplexity than using alternative embeddings from other communities within the same domain.[8] In all cases, we expect that for no.shift words (i.e., words for which there is no semantic variation according to our indices) the change in perplexity with different embeddings will be negligible.

We evaluate these hypotheses by calculating ppl^w_{change} values for shift and no.shift words and checking for significance with Wilcoxon signed-rank test.

5.2 Results

Table 1 shows an overview of the results. For conciseness, we only show the median ppl^w_{change} values. Regarding domain variation, as predicted, for words with low $\mathbf{dsi}^w(D)$ values (no.shift), we never observe a significant difference in perplexity when different embeddings are used. In contrast, for words with high $\mathbf{dsi}^w(D)$ values (shift) the increase in perplexity is always significantly higher when the original embeddings of a community are substituted with those of the general language ($c \rightarrow g$), while perplexity remains reasonably stable when the alternative embeddings come from another domain-related community ($c \rightarrow D\backslash\{c\}$). This holds for both domains, Football and Programming, with the exception of the programming community, for which there is no significant difference in perplexity when

---

[8] Recall that $\mathbf{csi}^w_c(D)$ is meant to capture a meaning variant of w in c that has drifted away from w's use in the global community more than in other domain-related communities.

`learn.programming` and general language embeddings are used — indicated by (*) in Table 1.

As for community-specific variation, again we never observe a significant difference in perplexity for words with low $\mathbf{csi}_c^w(D)$ values (`no.shift`). For words with high $\mathbf{csi}_c^w(D)$ values (`shift`), our hypothesis is confirmed for the more specific communities `liverpool`, `red.devils`, `python` and `learn.programming`: there is a significant increase in perplexity when the embeddings from these communities are used with the global NLM ($g \rightarrow c$), which is in line with the presence of a community specific semantic variant within the domain. This is not confirmed for the more general communities `programming` and `soccer`. This latter negative result is in fact intuitive: it is unlikely that these more general and larger communities will exhibit meaning variants that are further away from general language use than the more specific, smaller communities.

Figure 2 shows some examples of meaning shift captured by our indexes. The words 'box' and 'scope' are among the ten words with the highest **dsi** for Football and Programming, respectively. As a consequence, the domain-related variants are closely located, while the variant of the general community is farther away in semantic space. Difference in meaning is also evident from the nearest neighbours.[9] The word 'army' has high **csi** in the `red.devils` community. In the other domain-related communities, the word has meaning variants that are closer to its use in the general community. In the `red.devils` community, however, 'army' is conventionally used to denote the Manchester United fans (e.g., 'we need all types of supporters to make the red army'), as evidenced by its closest neighbours.

6 Factors Influencing Semantic Variation

Having confirmed that the semantic shift indices proposed in Section 4.2 capture variation that is noticeable in an external language modelling task, we now turn to analysing the factors that may be related to the presence of such variation.

6.1 Features

We consider four features capturing different properties of word *forms* and investigate their effect on meaning variation:

Frequency. It is known that more frequent words have a tendency to be more polysemous (Zipf, 1949), are more semantically stable over time (Hamilton et al., 2016), and evolve at slower rates across languages (Pagel et al., 2007). Word frequency may therefore play a role in semantic variation across communities of practice. We compute word frequency as the log-scaled relative frequency of a word in a given community:

$$\text{Freq}(w, c) = \log_{10}(N_c^w / N_c)$$

where N_c is the total number of words in the sample dataset of community c and N_c^w the number of occurrences of word w in that sample. Frequency in a domain $\text{Freq}(w, D)$ is calculated equivalently.

Prominence. Many measures have been proposed to weight the prominence of a word in a language sample, including TF-IDF. Our choice here is inspired by literature on terminology extraction (Velardi and Sclano, 2007). We compute the prominence of w as its frequency in a community (N_c^w) relative to its frequency in a domain, or as its frequency in a domain (N_D^w) relative to its frequency in general language use (N_g^w):

$$\text{Pro}(w, c) = N_c^w / (N_c^w + N_{D \setminus \{c\}}^w)$$
$$\text{Pro}(w, D) = N_D^w / (N_D^w + N_g^w)$$

---

[9]In the domain of Football, 'box' has come to mean the penalty area, which is associated with game actions such as 'cross', 'shoot' and 'headers'.

	Freq	Pro	Spe	Dis
Programming	0.96 ***	0.72 ***	0.46 ***	0.37 ***
Football	1.32 ***	0.81 ***	0.52 ***	0.63 ***
python	0.12	1.0 ***	0.09	0.21 ***
learn.prog	0.02	0.63 ***	0.32 *	0.23 **
liverpool	0.26 **	0.47 **	0.18	0.38 ***
red.devils	0.16	0.42 **	0.16	0.20 *

Table 2: Effect size (Cohen's d) and unpaired two-sample t-test significance level (***$p < .001$, **$p < .01$, *$p < .05$) for each feature.

Community-specific jargon or slang words will typically have very high prominence. In contrast, we hypothesise that common words exhibiting semantic variation as a result of community conventions — which are our focus here — are likely to *not* be singled out by very high prominence values. Nevertheless, their level of prominence may still be a determiner of variation.

Specificity. Besides frequency-related aspects, we also want to capture the extent to which a given word w appears in a restricted set of contexts. We approximate this by computing the collocational score of every bigram containing w and then scoring them using log-likelihood ratio as association measure (Dunning, 1993; Manning and Schütze, 1999).[10] We take the value of the highest ranked bigram as a proxy for the contextual specificity of w in community c ($\mathrm{Spe}(w, c)$) or domain D ($\mathrm{Spe}(w, D)$). The feature values are normalised to obtain scores in the range $[0, 1]$.

Dissemination. Finally, we consider the range of individuals using a given word. A priori, words with the same frequency, prominence, or contextual specificity may differ in their level of social dissemination, i.e., in the proportion of community members using them. We compute a word's dissemination within a community c as follows:

$$\mathrm{Dis}(w, c) \;=\; (U_c^w / U_c) \times (1 - \mathrm{RelFreq}(w, c))$$

where U_c^w is the number of community members who use word w and U_c the total number of members in community c. Since words with very high frequencies (such as function words) will be used across the board, we weight the ratio U_c^w / U_c by the inverse of w's relative frequency. Dissemination in a domain $\mathrm{Dis}(w, D)$ is calculated equivalently.

Word dissemination has been shown to be predictive of changes in word frequency over time (Altmann et al., 2011). Here we investigate whether it is a determiner of semantic variation.

6.2 Results

To investigate the role of the features introduced above, we test whether their values are significantly different in words that exhibit a strong semantic shift (words with **dsi / csi** values equal or larger than 2 standard deviations above the mean within a domain or community) and words with no semantic variation (with index values lower than one standard deviation above the mean).

At the domain level, we find very robust patterns for all features: the words that have undergone a strong domain shift have significantly higher frequency, prominence, contextual specificity, and social dissemination in each respective domain, Programming and Football. Table 2 shows the significance level of a unpaired two-sample t-test and the effect size for each feature.

At the community level, since the shifts for the `programming` and `soccer` communities were not validated in our extrinsic evaluation (Table 1), we do not consider these communities here. For the other 4 communities, we find a systematic pattern: words that exhibit a semantic shift particular to a community

---

[10]We used the NLTK implementation described at `http://www.nltk.org/howto/collocations.html`

are significantly *more* prominent in that community than in other domain-related communities, and *less* disseminated within that community than words that do not exhibit a shift. The significance of frequency and specificity vary per community. A summary is given in Table 2.

6.3   Qualitative analysis

As hypothesised, words with high **dsi** / **csi** values have significantly higher levels of prominence in the respective domain or community, but lower levels than jargon. For example, 'box' and 'believers', which have high **dsi** in Football and high **csi** in `liverpool`, respectively, have prominence values of 0.7, in contrast to jargon terms such as 'hat-trick' (Pro=1 in Football) and 'bitwise' (Pro=1 in Programming), which are not singled out by our semantic shift indices. This confirms that our measures of semantic variation identify meaning variants of *common* words (such as 'box' and 'believers') that arise in communities of practice.

From qualitative analysis, we observe that contextual specificity, which is significantly higher in words that exhibit a variant at the domain level, can give rise to different semantic phenomena. For instance, in the case of 'box' (see footnote 9), we observe semantic *broadening*, a generalisation of meaning possibly as a consequence of metaphorical use. While in other cases, specificity is related to semantic *narrowing*. This holds, for instance, for 'yellow', which has come to mean 'yellow card' in the Football domain. The strength of the collocation 'yellow card' seems to have made possible a narrower interpretation of 'yellow', as in 'Terry got a very stupid *yellow*'.

In contrast to domain-level variation, specificity and frequency do not play an important role across the board for semantic shift at the community level (see Table 2). Meaning variants that are specific to a particular community are not highly frequent and thus it is less likely that they take part in collocations (see e.g., Shin and Nation (2008)). As mentioned, we find that words with high **csi** values are less disseminated within the community. We see this as potentially related to the general process of linguistic innovation and diffusion descibed in Chambers and Trudgill (1998) and usually represented by a sigmoid function (see, for example, Fagyal et al. (2010)). Linguistic variants originate among and are initially adopted by a circumscribed number of members. At this stage (corresponding to the left tail of the function) few users use the innovation, which is therefore not highly disseminated in the community. Our intuition is that the **csi** index captures innovations which are in this phase. Some variants may then rapidly spread within the community (central part of the function) and possibly to other domain-related communities, until they reach a plateau, in terms of frequency of use (right tail of the function). This is the stage which is captured by our **dsi** index: the innovation, at this point, has been largely adopted, and, consequently, has a high dissemination value.

It is also possible that some community-specific semantic variants are used as identity markers (e.g., 'army' in `red.devils` or 'believers' in `liverpool`), which are then presumably not likely to spread to other communities. Such uses may be limited to members who are particularly invested in the community and thus not part of other domain-related communities, which may lead to lower dissemination (since different communities within a domain share a substantial number of members, as shown in Figure 1). These speculations, however, need to be verified with further analysis, which we leave to future work.

7   Conclusions

We have investigated meaning variation from the perspective of social engagement in online communities of practice, exploring the hypothesis that meaning conventions are not only topic dependent, but that different meanings can emerge in communities discussing the same topic. We verified our research hypothesis using a large dataset from Reddit discussion forums, and showed that our quantitative measures allow us to identify semantic variation in the use of common (non-slang) words at both domain and community levels. We evaluated our findings using an extrinsic language modelling task.

Our analysis of the factors that influence socially-driven semantic variation should be seen as a preliminary investigation, which we believe opens the door to more in-depth studies we plan to conduct in the future. The most natural extension of the current work is an investigation of the social dynamics that lead to meaning variation: while in the present work we have shown the outcome of such dynamics, i.e. the observable meaning shift in different communities of practice, in our future work we plan to focus on the interactions among speakers, which are at the base of observable variation. Directly related to this is the consideration of the diachronic dimension, linking the presence of semantic variation to the more general dynamics of meaning change. Our aim in this direction is to consider the evolution of meaning conventions in time while taking into account the network structure of communities of practice.

In parallel, we plan to explore other aspects within the synchronic perspective, such as the relationship between semantic variation and demographic factors, e.g., geo-location, age, or gender — in particular, in light of the fact that the datasets we are using here are likely to be biased towards the language use of male speakers. Finally, we want to extend our investigation to a larger set of communities, in order to make our findings and claims more robust.

References

Altmann, E. G., J. B. Pierrehumbert, and A. E. Motter (2011). Niche as a determinant of word fate in online groups. *PLoS ONE 6*(5), e19009.

Bamman, D., C. Dyer, and N. A. Smith (2014, June). Distributed representations of geographically situated language. In *Proceedings of the 52nd Annual Meeting of the Association for Computational Linguistics (Volume 2: Short Papers)*, pp. 828–834.

Burger, J. D., J. Henderson, G. Kim, and G. Zarrella (2011). Discriminating gender on twitter. In *Proceedings of the Conference on Empirical Methods in Natural Language Processing*, pp. 1301–1309. Association for Computational Linguistics.

Cassell, J. and D. Tversky (2005). The language of online intercultural community formation. *Journal of Computer-Mediated Communication 10*(2), 00–00.

Chambers, J. K. and P. Trudgill (1998). *Dialectology*. Cambridge University Press.

Ciot, M., M. Sonderegger, and D. Ruths (2013). Gender inference of twitter users in non-english contexts. In *EMNLP*, pp. 1136–1145.

Clark, H. H. (1996). *Using language*. Cambridge University Press.

Danescu-Niculescu-Mizil, C., L. Lee, B. Pang, and J. Kleinberg (2012). Echoes of power: Language effects and power differences in social interaction. In *Proceedings of the 21st international conference on World Wide Web*, pp. 699–708. ACM.

Danescu-Niculescu-Mizil, C., R. West, D. Jurafsky, J. Leskovec, and C. Potts (2013). No country for old members: User lifecycle and linguistic change in online communities. In *Proceedings of the 22nd international conference on World Wide Web*, pp. 307–318. ACM.

Doyle, G. (2014). Mapping dialectal variation by querying social media. In *EACL*, pp. 98–106.

Dunning, T. (1993). Accurate methods for the statistics of surprise and coincidence. *Computational Linguistics 19*(1), 61–74.

Eckert, P. and S. McConnell-Ginet (1992). Communities of practice: Where language, gender, and power all live. In K. Hall, M. Bucholtz, and B. Moonwomon (Eds.), *Locating Power, Proceedings of the 1992 Berkeley Women and Language Conference*, pp. 89–99.

Eisenstein, J., B. O'Connor, N. A. Smith, and E. P. Xing (2010). A latent variable model for geographic lexical variation. In *Proceedings of the 2010 Conference on Empirical Methods in Natural Language Processing*, pp. 1277–1287. Association for Computational Linguistics.

Eisenstein, J., B. O'Connor, N. A. Smith, and E. P. Xing (2014). Diffusion of lexical change in social media. *PloS one 9*(11), e113114.

Fagyal, Z., S. Swarup, A. M. Escobar, L. Gasser, and K. Lakkaraju (2010). Centers and peripheries: Network roles in language change. *Lingua 120*(8), 2061–2079.

Frermann, L. and M. Lapata (2016). A bayesian model of diachronic meaning change. *TACL 4*, 31–45.

Hamilton, W. L., J. Leskovec, and D. Jurafsky (2016). Diachronic word embeddings reveal statistical laws of semantic change. In *Proceedings of ACL 2016*.

Hasan, R. (1989). Semantic variation and sociolinguistics. *Australian Journal of Linguistics 9*(2), 221–275.

Hovy, D. (2015). Demographic factors improve classification performance. In *Proceedings of the 53rd Annual Meeting of the Association for Computational Linguistics and the 7th International Joint Conference on Natural Language Processing (Volume 1: Long Papers)*, pp. 752–762.

Huffaker, D., J. Jorgensen, F. Iacobelli, P. Tepper, and J. Cassell (2006). Computational measures for language similarity across time in online communities. In *Proceedings of the HLT-NAACL 2006 workshop on analyzing conversations in text and speech*, pp. 15–22. Association for Computational Linguistics.

Jatowt, A. and K. Duh (2014). A framework for analyzing semantic change of words across time. In *Proceedings of the 14th ACM/IEEE-CS Joint Conference on Digital Libraries*, pp. 229–238. IEEE Press.

Kershaw, D., M. Rowe, and P. Stacey (2016). Towards modelling language innovation acceptance in online social networks. In *Proceedings of the Ninth ACM International Conference on Web Search and Data Mining*, pp. 553–562. ACM.

Kingma, D. and J. Ba (2014). Adam: A method for stochastic optimization. *arXiv preprint arXiv:1412.6980*.

Kulkarni, V., R. Al-Rfou, B. Perozzi, and S. Skiena (2015). Statistically significant detection of linguistic change. In *Proceedings of the 24th International Conference on World Wide Web*, pp. 625–635. ACM.

Kulkarni, V., B. Perozzi, and S. Skiena (2016). Freshman or fresher? quantifying the geographic variation of language in online social media. In *ICWSM*, pp. 615–618.

Manning, C. D. and H. Schütze (1999). *Foundations of statistical natural language processing*. MIT Press.

Mikolov, T., K. Chen, G. Corrado, and J. Dean (2013). Efficient estimation of word representations in vector space. *arXiv preprint arXiv:1301.3781*.

Navigli, R. (2009). Word sense disambiguation: A survey. *ACM Computing Surveys 41*(2), 10.

Nguyen, D. and C. P. Rosé (2011). Language use as a reflection of socialization in online communities. In *Proceedings of the Workshop on Languages in Social Media*, pp. 76–85. Association for Computational Linguistics.

Nguyen, D., D. Trieschnigg, A. S. Doğruöz, R. Gravel, M. Theune, T. Meder, and F. De Jong (2014). Why gender and age prediction from tweets is hard: Lessons from a crowdsourcing experiment. In *Proceedings of COLING 2014, the 25th International Conference on Computational Linguistics: Technical Papers*, pp. 1950–1961.

Nguyen, D.-P., R. Gravel, D. Trieschnigg, and T. Meder (2013). "How old do you think I am?" A study of language and age in Twitter. In *Proceedings of the Seventh International AAAI Conference on Weblogs and Social Media*. AAAI Press.

Noble, B. and R. Fernández (2015, June). Centre stage: How social network position shapes linguistic coordination. In *Proceedings of the 6th Workshop on Cognitive Modeling and Computational Linguistics*, Denver, Colorado, pp. 29–38. Association for Computational Linguistics.

Pagel, M., Q. D. Atkinson, and A. Meade (2007). Frequency of word-use predicts rates of lexical evolution throughout indo-european history. *Nature 449*(7163), 717–720.

Sagi, E., S. Kaufmann, and B. Clark (2011). Tracing semantic change with latent semantic analysis. *Current methods in historical semantics*, 161–183.

Shin, D. and P. Nation (2008). Beyond single words: The most frequent collocations in spoken english. *ELT journal 62*(4), 339–348.

Tran, T. and M. Ostendorf (2016). Characterizing the language of online communities and its relation to community reception. *arXiv preprint arXiv:1609.04779*.

Velardi, P. and F. Sclano (2007). "termextractor: a web application to learn the common terminology of interest groups and research communities". In *"7th Conference on Terminology and Artificial Intelligence"*, pp. 85–94.

Wenger, E. (2000). *Communities of practice: Learning, meaning, and identity*. Cambridge University Press.

Wijaya, D. T. and R. Yeniterzi (2011). Understanding semantic change of words over centuries. In *Proceedings of the 2011 international workshop on DETecting and Exploiting Cultural diversiTy on the social web*, pp. 35–40. ACM.

Yang, Y. and J. Eisenstein (2017). Overcoming language variation in sentiment analysis with social attention. *Transactions of the Association for Computational Linguistics*.

Yarowsky, D. (2010). Word sense disambiguation. In *Handbook of Natural Language Processing, Second Edition*, pp. 315–338. Chapman and Hall/CRC.

Zaremba, W., I. Sutskever, and O. Vinyals (2014). Recurrent neural network regularization. *arXiv preprint arXiv:1409.2329*.

Zhang, Y., A. Jatowt, S. S. Bhowmick, and K. Tanaka (2015). Omnia mutantur, nihil interit: Connecting past with present by find-ing corresponding terms across time. In *Proc. of ACL*, pp. 645–655.

Zipf, G. (1949). *Human Behavior and the Principle of Least Effort: an Introduction To Human Ecology*. Addison-Wesley.

Defeasible AceRules: A Prototype[*]

Martin Diller
Faculty of Informatics
Technical University of Vienna, Austria
mdiller@kr.tuwien.ac.at

Adam Wyner
Department of Computing Science
University of Aberdeen, Scotland, UK
azwyner@abdn.ac.uk

Hannes Strass
Computer Science Institute
Leipzig University, Germany
strass@informatik.uni-leipzig.de

Abstract

The paper adapts the syntax of the AceRules system, an existing controlled natural language (CNL), and pipes the resulting output rules to a defeasible inference engine. With this, we can represent and reason with knowledge bases (KB) with strict and defeasible rules. For strict rules, the consequent of a strict rule must hold if the premises hold; for a defeasible rule, the consequent of a defeasible rule ought to hold if the premises hold. Strict rules are always applied whenever applicable, while defeasible rules are maximally applied (in terms of rule subsets), subject to consistency. In the CNL, defeasible rules are expressed in terms of what is "usual". The CNL expressions of rules are parsed and semantically represented so as to be used by an inference engine to accurately generate possible states of affairs. A verbaliser expresses the results in natural language, which facilitates understanding. The approach to defeasible rules is contrasted with available approaches, e.g. negation-as-failure, exceptions, and the use of abnormality predicates. The work is broadly set in the context of *argumentation*. The paper overviews the underlying formalism and the CNL; it provides an extended example.

1 Introduction

We set this work in the context of argumentation, where a central aim is to reason from premises to a conclusion using a rule, e.g. the reasoning pattern *Modus Ponens* is an argument in classic Propositional Logic. Recent efforts to formalise and instantiate "abstract" argumentation have focused on reasoning with defeasible knowledge bases (KBs) (Dung, 1995; Prakken, 2010 among others). Another development is argument mining, which attempts to extract arguments, e.g. rules as well as the premises and conclusions of the rules, from large textual corpora and structure them (Lippi and Torroni, 2016). Between abstract argumentation and argument mining, there is a substantial gap: while abstract argumentation can reason with defeasible KBs, its abstraction from linguistic information limits its applicability; argument mining can extract information from text, yet it does not extract fine-grained, highly structured semantic representations that can be used for inference. Motivated by this gap, the paper begins to address it using a controlled natural language (CNL) interface to a formal, implemented theory of reasoning from defeasible KBs. A CNL takes an *engineering approach* to natural language. On the one hand, a CNL can be used as a "target" for homogenisation and structuring of mined information, and on the other hand, it can be used as an input tool to provide well-structured KBs for a defeasible inference engine.

In this context, the paper, which develops from the works of Strass and Wyner (2017) and Wyner and Strass (2017), contributes a CNL that is augmented with a defeasible sentential operator *it is usual that* and integrated with an implemented defeasible inference engine: the system enables the input of

---

[*]This research has been supported by the Austrian Science Fund (FWF) through projects I2854 and W1255-N23.

defeasible KBs in natural language, reasoning with the knowledge base, then output of consistent answer sets in natural language. The presentation is grounded with an extended example. Schematically, the flow of analysis from source text, to inference, to natural language output consists of steps 1–9 as illustrated below. For the purposes of this paper, we focus on steps 3–7 and 9, presuming steps 1 and 2.

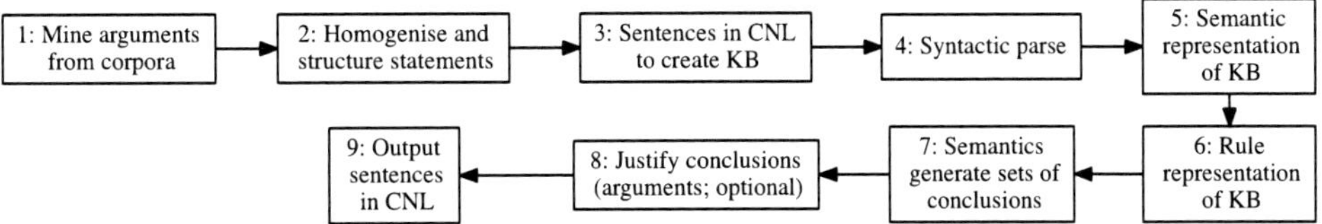

In Section 2, we briefly sketch some of the main component approaches to argumentation analysis, mining, and CNLs. We outline the defeasible semantics in Section 3. The main body of the paper is in Sections 4 and 5, where we first discuss how we have adapted a CNL to work with defeasible rules, and then we present examples and the inferences we draw. Finally, Section 6 closes with some general observations and future work.

2 Background

In this section, we briefly outline some of the context of our contribution, leaving as out of scope aspects of argumentation such as typologies of arguments or dialogue.

Abstract argumentation A central problem in formal reasoning is the treatment of inconsistency and non-monotonicity. Abstract argumentation (Dung, 1995) has emerged as an integrated approach. In abstract argumentation, arguments are "nodes" in a graph, where "attacks" are directed arcs that represent inconsistency. The semantics are used, essentially, to derive consistent subsets of arguments. Thus, from a globally inconsistent knowledge base, we can derive consistent information and reason further. *Instantiated argumentation* (e.g. ASPIC+; Prakken, 2010) realises the arguments as structures of strict and defeasible rules from a knowledge base. Once constructed as a graph, reasoning proceeds as in abstract argumentation. However, the construction of arguments in instantiated argumentation (e.g. in ASPIC+) itself leads to issues of overgeneration and opacity (Strass and Wyner, 2017).

Argument mining To use formal argumentation, significant KBs need to be created. Automatically mining arguments from large corpora of natural language texts has developed as a way to create corpora, primarily using machine learning approaches (Lippi and Torroni, 2016). While there have been advances, such approaches often treat the annotated passages as atomic propositions (Toni and Torroni, 2011) or without regard to linguistic structure (Cabrio and Villata, 2012), thus missing semantically meaningful, structured information that is relevant for fine-grained inference in formal logic. Rule-based approaches (Wyner et al., 2015), which can extract arguments and some of the information within sentences, are not yet sufficiently well-developed to extract highly structured information for a KB.

CNLs Controlled natural languages (CNLs) are engineered languages with finite lexicons and fixed grammatical constructions (Kuhn, 2014). Among the variety of purposes and applications, we focus on CNLs which provide unambiguous translations to machine readable semantic representations of First-order Logic such as Attempto Controlled English (ACE) with associated Prolog inference engine RACE (Fuchs et al., 2008; Fuchs, 2016) or Processable English (PENG[ASP]; Guy and Schwitter, 2017) with associated inference engine in answer set programming (ASP). Both ACE and PENG[ASP] provide some facility for non-monotonic reasoning using negation-as-failure, which we discuss further later. The constraints of CNLs are useful, particularly to control ambiguity and help to focus attention on particular phenomena. CNLs often have useful auxiliary functionalities such as input editors and verbalisers from semantic representations. As neither RACE nor PENG^{ASP} are open source, we work with the ACE related open source tool AceRules (Kuhn, 2007). While there are powerful, wide-coverage tools for parsing and semantic representation, e.g. C&C/Boxer (Bos, 2008), which could be used as CNLs, they require restraint in application and lack the useful auxiliary functionalities. In other related work, Gervasi and Zowghi (2005) use logical reasoning on (controlled) natural language for inconsistency management in software requirement analysis; the approach is based on Poole's THEORIST (1988), which is much like our direct-stable semantics, but for formulas instead of rules (Strass and Wyner, 2017).

3   Defeasible theories and reasoning

In this section, we give a brief formal overview of our approach to defeasible theories and defeasible reasoning, which underpins our implementation of defeasible reasoning.[1] The rationale for our approach to defeasiblity is discussed in Sections 4 and 5.

Defeasible theories   For a set $\mathcal{P}$ of atomic propositions, the set of its literals is $\mathcal{L}_\mathcal{P} = \mathcal{P} \cup \{\neg p \mid p \in \mathcal{P}\}$. A *rule* over $\mathcal{L}_\mathcal{P}$ is a pair (B, h) where the finite set $B \subseteq \mathcal{L}_\mathcal{P}$ is called the *body* (premises) and the literal $h \in \mathcal{L}_\mathcal{P}$ is called the *head* (conclusion). For $B = \{b_1, \ldots, b_k\}$ with $k \in \mathbb{N}$, we can write rules thus: a *strict* rule is of the form "$b_1, \ldots, b_k \to h$"; a *defeasible* rule is of the form "$b_1, \ldots, b_k \Rightarrow h$". In case $k = 0$ we call "$\to h$" a *fact* and "$\Rightarrow h$" an *assumption*. The intuitive meaning of a rule (B, h) is that whenever we are in a state of affairs where all literals in B hold, then also literal h (always/usually, depending on the type of rule) holds. A *defeasible theory* is a tuple $\mathcal{T} = (\mathcal{P}, \mathcal{S}, \mathcal{D})$ where $\mathcal{P}$ is a set of atomic propositions, $\mathcal{S}$ is a set of strict rules over $\mathcal{L}_\mathcal{P}$, and $\mathcal{D}$ is a set of defeasible rules over $\mathcal{L}_\mathcal{P}$. Note that there is no *negation-as-failure* in this approach; we contrast our approach with one that uses *negation-as-failure* in Section 5.1. In this paper, we will consider defeasible theories with first-order predicates, variables, and constants, treating predicates on variables or constants as short-hand versions of their ground instantiations. More details can be found in the work of Strass and Wyner (2017).

The semantics of defeasible theories are a topic of ongoing work in argumentation theory (Caminada and Amgoud, 2007; Amgoud and Besnard, 2013; Strass, 2013; Wyner et al., 2015). For the purposes of this paper, we express no preference, abstracting away from any concrete manifestations of existing approaches. For our purposes here, we make a few (mild) assumptions about the approach to assigning semantics to defeasible theories that is used to draw inferences (the "back-end"). More specifically, we assume that the reasoning back-end:

1. accepts a defeasible theory $\mathcal{T} = (\mathcal{P}, \mathcal{S}, \mathcal{D})$ as input. An additional step might be needed to transform $\mathcal{T}$ into the reasoner's native input format, a point we raise again later.

2. can produce "interpretations" (consistent viewpoints, e.g. extensions) and/or (sets of) credulous/sceptical conclusions of the defeasible theory with respect to one or more semantics, e.g. stable, complete, preferred, grounded (Dung, 1995). We comment further on this below.

3. can produce graph-based justifications for its conclusions as a derivation of that literal as obtained from an argument extension.

It may be more or less straightforward to lift these restrictions, depending on the concrete approaches. Our assumptions cover considerable common ground of the various approaches in the literature; they are a meaningful and non-trivial starting point for our own work.

As mentioned above, defeasible theories can be interpreted with respect to the direct-stable semantics as defined by Strass and Wyner (2017). The direct-stable semantics is defined for the grounded instances of defeasible theories with variables, i.e. the result of replacing each rule in the defeasible theories with all possible rules that can be obtained by substituting the variables occurring in the rules with all possible

---

[1]This section is adapted from (Wyner and Strass, 2017).

constants. The result of evaluating a grounded defeasible theory with respect to the direct-stable semantics consists in sets of grounded literals, the stable sets of the theory. Informally, stable sets are consistent sets of literals where *all strict rules hold*, a *subset-maximal set of defeasible rules* hold subject to consistency, and every literal can be derived from the facts and assumptions, which are strict or defeasible rules without bodies respectively, using the remaining rules of the theory in a non-circular manner.

More concretely, for a stable set to be consistent means that no two dual literals (i.e. an atom and its negation) can be in the set. That a rule "holds" in a set means that whenever the literals in the body of the rule are in the set, so is its head. All strict rules must hold and a $\subseteq$-maximal subset of the defeasible rules should hold without making the set inconsistent. Finally, there being a derivation of each literal from the facts and assumptions means that each literal is either a fact or an assumption or in the head of some rule in the theory having the property that each literal in the body of the rule can itself be derived from the facts and assumptions. A derivation of a literal should use the minimal set of rules needed to derive the literal. The requirement that the derivation be non-circular is cashed out by imposing a partial order on the rules used in the derivation.

4   Adding defeasibility to AceRules

In this section, we discuss the main advance reported in the paper, which is to adapt a CNL to accept natural language expressions of defeasible rules which are then provided to a defeasible reasoning engine. We adopt the Attempto Controlled English (ACE) framework (Fuchs et al., 2008), which has a parser (APE). In particular, we have adapted the AceRules tool (Kuhn, 2007), which is open source and processes ACE compatible parsed text into representations suitable for rule-based reasoners. We outline the implementation. The specific adaptation is to add defeasibility to the ACE language, then pipe the semantic representation to an implementation of the direct-stable semantics for defeasible theories of Strass and Wyner (2017). In what follows we sketch out what this means. However, due to space limitations, we do not rehearse the complex specifics or ideosyncracies of ACE other than to say it provides a fixed lexicon and grammar which provides unambiguous semantic representations. Some specific, relevant issues are detailed.

AceRules builds on APE, which parses ACE input sentences into discourse representation structures (DRSs) (Blackburn and Bos, 2005), a syntactical variant of first-order logic that supports the representation of aspects of discourse. AceRules disallows DRSs from APE which cannot be represented in the given rule language. An important component of AceRules is thus the process of "intelligent grouping" (Kuhn, 2007), the transformation of DRSs generated by APE which are not directly compliant with a rule language into DRSs that are compliant with the rule language. Grouping works by "aggregating" predicates, replacing complex expressions with equivalent simpler expressions, e.g. expressions inside of negation or in the head of a conditional. Moreover, grouping often also involves removing implicitly quantified variables (see the work of Kuhn, 2007, for examples).

Target rule languages supported by AceRules are, on the one hand, logic programs with strong as well as default negation (negation-as-failure) and, on the other hand, acyclic logic programs with both forms of negation as well as priorities over rules ("override" statements). The first are intended to be interpreted with respect to stable semantics of Gelfond and Lifschitz (1990), while the second with respect to the courteous semantics of Grosof (1997). AceRules relies on external tools (e.g. SModels and LParse) for interpreting programs with respect to stable semantics, while the courteous semantics is implemented natively. Crucially, AceRules also includes a verbalisation component, whereby the outputs of the interpreter-component are recast in DRSs which can then be verbalised by (the paraphrasing mechanism of) APE.

In contrast to the AceRules supported rule languages, in our rule language we disallow default negation and priorities over rules, while extending the input language accepted by AceRules with the constructs *"It is usual that . . . "* and *"If . . . then it is usual that . . . "*, which are respectively interpreted as assumptions and defeasible rules. For a discussion of the linguistic semantics see the discussions of Lewis (1975) and Kratzer (2012); however, while loosely related, we do not explicitly tie our analysis to that discussion. From the point of view of the interpretation of the CNL in a formal language, i.e. at the level of the DRSs, we treat defeasible rules analogously to strict rules and hence are able to make use of the techniques for translating from the output of APE (the DRSs) to the rule languages accepted by AceRules. The crucial difference is that we distinguish between the types of rules for the purposes of reasoning with the resulting defeasible theory, which amounts to having two forms of conditionals also at the level of the DRSs.

To exercise our approach we have implemented a script[2] that makes use of AceRules (and APE) as well as the answer set encodings for interpreting defeasible theories and the answer set solver (clingo) as described by Strass and Wyner (2017). More concretely, we make separate use of the AceRule parser and the verbaliser components, thus enabling our approach to be implemented by a simple interleaving of calls to the AceRules (and APE) parser, transformation to rules, solver for the direct-stable semantics (via encodings and a solver for answer set programming), and finally the AceRules (and APE) verbaliser.

Crucially, we pre-process the input text removing all constructs indicating defeasibility and make use of the AceRules parser "as if" all rules in the input were strict, but at the same time externally tracking which rules are defeasible and which are not. By differentiating the rules in this way, we are able to use the encodings for the direct-stable semantics later on in the pipeline. At the level of the stable sets, the distinction between strict and defeasible rules is irrelevant; and we are, hence, also able to make direct use of the AceRules (and APE) verbaliser component with the caveats that we mention later on in Section 5.2. We have followed this rather quick strategy for the implementation because our objective to this point was to have a prototype testing-ground for our approach as well as to develop an in depth understanding of the issues before us. Clearly, this work demonstrates that we can adapt AceRules to work with defeasible rules and to tie it in to the encodings for the direct-stable semantics.

5 Natural language interface

In this section, we discuss an extended working example, then address some of the subtleties. Our main aim in this section is to demonstrate by example the added value of defeasible rules and reasoning using a CNL. We only discuss the examples, results, and issues; the DRSs (without "usual") can all be viewed using ACE's online APE webclient.[3]

5.1 Working example: extending AceWiki with defeasible rules

We now exemplify and further motivate our approach by showing its use in the context of AceWiki (Kuhn, 2009),[4] a prototype of an encyclopedia in the style of the popular Wikipedia,[5] but where articles are written using ACE rather than unrestricted natural language. The advantage to using ACE in a wiki is that non-expert users can edit AceWiki entries, while at the same time users can use complex question answering and draw inferences. As it currently stands, AceWiki can represent a consistent KB about some domain and uses only strict rules.

Although the use of full ACE in the context of AceWiki is desirable, the undecidability of ACE (see Fuchs et al., 2008) also means that it is not feasible in practice. Restricting ACE to efficiently decidable fragments, e.g. via translation to a form of rule language, provides a more promising way forward. We base our example on current entries in the AceWiki about geographical information,[6] which have been restricted to a variant of ACE that can be translated into the rule language OWL 2 RL, and thus also, in principle, into the fragment of ACE admitted by AceRules. However, AceWiki could similarly be deployed in other fields such as Biology, Medicine, or more generally in any context where a structured KB would be useful.

---

[2]The script together with other necessary files as well as the examples in this paper is available at `https://www.dbai.tuwien.ac.at/proj/adf/dAceRules`.

[3]APE webclient: `http://attempto.ifi.uzh.ch/site/resources/`

[4]AceWiki can be accessed at `http://attempto.ifi.uzh.ch/acewiki/`.

[5]`https://www.wikipedia.org/`

[6]`http://attempto.ifi.uzh.ch/webapps/acewikigeo/`

As a motivating example, consider the entry for *island* in the geographical AceWiki. Some straightforward statements pertaining to the strict definition of *island* appear, e.g. *Every island is a land-mass* and *Every island is surrounded by a body of water*. Using ACE, such statements can be written in a straightforward manner and are automatically translated to a rule language:[7]

```
(1)  Every island is a land-mass.
(2)  If X is an island then a body-of-water surrounds X.
```

Statement (1) leads to a rule like *island*$(x) \rightarrow$ *land-mass*(x) with a first-order variable x (cf. Section 3). Due to a lack of space, we will not explicitly present further rules in the paper; in any case, they can be obtained from the presented text via AceRules.

ACE enables the addition of lexical entries, such as proper names *Mainland-Shetland* or *St-Ninians-Isle*. Moreover, ACE is often able to deduce the word class for words that are not in its lexicon from the context. There are some interactions in ACE/AceRules in relation to the verb form, quantifier scope, and the verbaliser (among other subtleties) such that, for example, we have represented (2) as a rule; we suppress further such incidental comments. We do however further note that rule (2) illustrates the situation where the input text introduces an implicitly quantified variable in the head of a rule (here, referring to a body-of-water), which needs to be treated by the grouping-mechanism of AceRules we alluded to in Section 4.

The problem, which we develop, is to add a new entry for *tied-island* to this AceWiki. However, as we show, this would lead to inconsistency were we to only have strict rules. According to Wikipedia, tied islands "are landforms consisting of an island that is connected to land only by a tombolo: a spit of beach materials connected to land at both ends."[8] With slight simplification, this definition can be written into AceWiki as follows:

```
(3)  Every tied-island is an island.
(4)  Every tied-island attaches-to a land-mass.
```

A prominent example of a *tied-island* according to the Wikipedia entry is *St. Ninian's Isle*, which is attached to *Mainland Shetland*, the largest of the Shetland Islands off the coast of Scotland. Thus, entries for St. Ninian's Isle and Mainland Shetland in AceWiki would be:

```
(5)  Mainland-Shetland is an island.
(6)  St-Ninians-Isle is a tied-island.
(7)  St-Ninians-Isle is a part of the Shetland-Islands.
```

According to the Wikipedia entry for St. Ninian's Isle, during the winter strong wave action removes sand from the tombolo that connects St. Ninian to Mainland Shetland such that the tombolo is usually covered at high tide and occasionally throughout the tidal cycle. Hence, simply stating that *St. Ninian's Isle attaches to Mainland Shetland* would be incorrect. Spelling out the exact conditions under which St. Ninian's Isle is connected to Mainland-Shetland, which corresponds to using exceptions in strict rules, seems quite difficult if even possible (or desirable) and would be rather uncommon for an application like AceWiki. Rather, an easy solution is provided by the use of the predicate *it is usual that* applied to a statement:

```
(8)  It is usual that St-Ninians-Isle attaches-to Mainland-Shetland.
```

Let us now turn to a more fundamental reason for being able to distinguish between defeasible and strict statements in a CNL. Consider now the result of having all of the above statements in the AceWiki together with the following fairly uncontroversial statements referring to the meanings of *being attached to a land mass*, *being surrounded by water*, and *being a part of*. We initially highlight the issue using

---

[7]We extended the lexicon of ACE with some further terms, e.g. *land-mass* and *body-of-water*, but suppress further discussion.

[8]`https://en.wikipedia.org/wiki/Tied_island` (accessed on 4/4/2017)

further strict rules. In particular, statements (12) and (13) are needed too, because we need to define in the wiki's KB that St. Ninian's Isle is attached to exactly one land mass, namely Mainland Shetland.

```
(9)  If X attaches-to a land-mass then it is false that a body-of-water
     surrounds X.
(10) If a body-of-water surrounds X then it is false that X
     attaches-to a land-mass.
(11) If St-Ninians-Isle attaches-to Mainland-Shetland then St-Ninians-Isle
     is a part of Mainland-Shetland.
(12) If St-Ninians-Isle attaches-to Mainland-Shetland then St-Ninians-Isle
     attaches-to a land-mass.
(13) If St-Ninians-Isle attaches-to a land-mass then St-Ninians-Isle
     attaches-to Mainland-Shetland.
```

Since according to (6) St. Ninian's Isle is a tied island, and according to (3) every tied island is an island, and both (3) as well as (6) are strict rules, the direct stable semantics forces one to conclude that St. Ninian's Isle is an island. Now, because St. Ninian's Isle is an island and following (2), we conclude that a body of water surrounds St. Ninian's Isle. But from the fact that St. Ninian's is also a tied island and (4), St. Ninian's Isle attaches to a land mass. This leads to a contradiction according to statements (9) and (10). Hence, the entire AceWiki is deemed inconsistent and further reasoning is invalidated.

Note that the AceWiki remains inconsistent even after removing statement (8); the reason for the apparent contradiction in the Wiki is the fact, as is stated in the Wikipedia entry referring to St. Ninian's Isle,[9] that "[d]epending on the definition used, St. Ninian's is [...] either an island, or a peninsula." This reveals that the definition for *tied-island* in (3) should also be *defeasible*. However, in contrast to the reasons for the defeasiblity of (8), this is now due to the fact that there is no consensus on the meaning of *tied island*. Thus, we replace (3) with the more accurate statement:

```
(3') If X is a tied-island then it is usual that X is an island.
```

The consequence is that there is now one stable set:

```
ANSWER-TEXT #1:

There is a body-of-water X1.
St-Ninians-Isle is a tied-island.
Mainland-Shetland is a land-mass.
Mainland-Shetland is an island.
St-Ninians-Isle is a part of Shetland-Islands.
St-Ninians-Isle is a part of Mainland-Shetland.
St-Ninians-Isle attaches-to a land-mass.
The body-of-water X1 surrounds Mainland-Shetland.
St-Ninians-Isle attaches-to Mainland-Shetland.
It is false that Mainland-Shetland attaches-to a land-mass.
It is false that a body-of-water surrounds St-Ninians-Isle.
```

Here the conclusion is that St. Ninian's Isle is a tied island that is attached to Mainland Shetland, while nothing can be said regarding whether St. Ninian's is also an island or not. The reason is that since statement (4) is strict, (8) is also effectively interpreted as a strict rule; that is, (8) strictly holds. To make (4) consistent with the *intended reading* of (8), (4) should be replaced with:

```
(4') If X is a tied-island then it is usual that X attaches-to a
     land-mass.
```

The result is that there are now two stable sets (answer-texts), which have in common the statements:

---

[9]`https://en.wikipedia.org/wiki/St_Ninian's_Isle` (accessed on 4.4.2017)

```
There is a body-of-water X1.
St-Ninians-Isle is a tied-island.
Mainland-Shetland is a land-mass.
Mainland-Shetland is an island.
St-Ninians-Isle is a part of Shetland-Islands.
The body-of-water X1 surrounds Mainland-Shetland.
It is false that Mainland-Shetland attaches-to a land-mass.
```

One stable set contains the following statements in addition to the common statements:

```
St-Ninians-Isle is a part of Mainland-Shetland.
St-Ninians-Isle attaches-to a land-mass.
St-Ninians-Isle attaches-to Mainland-Shetland.
It is false that a body-of-water surrounds St-Ninians-Isle.
```

The other stable set contains the following statements in addition to the common statements:

```
There is a body-of-water X2.
St-Ninians-Isle is a land-mass.
St-Ninians-Isle is an island.
The body-of-water X2 surrounds St-Ninians-Isle.
It is false that St-Ninians-Isle attaches-to a land-mass.
```

The interpretation of the latter set of statements is that St. Ninian's Isle is a tied island, but can only be called an island when it is not attached to Mainland-Shetland. Also relaxing the definition of *island* by changing (2) to

```
(2') If X is an island then it is usual that a body-of-water
     surrounds X.
```

has the consequence that St. Ninian's Isle can also (always) be considered an island, despite the fact that the isle is not always surrounded by water.

Summarizing, we have shown that by distinguishing between defeasible and strict statements, we can resolve apparent inconsistencies such as might arise, in our example, because of the use of generic statements that allow for exceptions or because different meanings can be attached to certain words.

However, our approach does not require explicit statement of exceptions or alternatives. Using non-artificial, specific exceptions together with negation-as-failure in strict rules is often not feasible nor desirable. More fundamentally, using artificial exceptions, e.g. *abnormality* predicates specific to each rule, will usually not lead to a satisfactory result. Consider, for instance the effect of having the statement (8") below rather than the statement (8) mentioned previously, while replacing (3) with (3") rather than (3'), (4) with (4") rather than (4'), as well as (2) with (2") rather than (2').

```
(8'')If it is not provable that it is false that St-Ninians-Isle attaches-to
     Mainland-Shetland then St-Ninians-Isle attaches-to Mainland-Shetland.
(3'') If X is a tied-island and it is not provable that X is not an
      island then X is an island.
(4'') If X is a tied-island and it is not provable that it is false that
      X attaches-to a land-mass then X attaches-to a land-mass.
(2'') If X is an island and it is not provable that it is false that a
      body-of-water surrounds X then a body-of-water surrounds X.
```

The resulting text does not have any answer set under the standard stable semantics for logic programs.[10] Interpreting the text under the courteous semantics does produce a unique answer set, but this approach

---

[10]This is not to say that it is not possible to simulate the evaluation of ACE texts under the direct-stable semantics by using logic programs without the defeasible conditional; in fact the encodings by Strass and Wyner (2017) provide such a simulation (via disjunctive logic programs). On the other hand, the complexity results by Strass and Wyner (2017) also suggest that any such simulation via normal or extended logic programs will involve a worst-case exponential blow-up in general (unless the polynomial hierarchy collapses to its first level), at least for ACE texts which can be parsed as *grounded* defeasible theories.

is unsatisfactory in general. First, because the rules must be acyclic and second because the resulting answer is often uninformative or somewhat arbitrary. In the current case, the rules are in fact cyclic and hence no answer is produced.

An auxiliary point is that the discussion above shows the utility of the tool, for it allows us to experiment using natural language with alternative inputs to determine alternative outputs (and compare semantics between them). From such alternatives, we can identify our preferred inputs, semantics, and outputs, which are intuitively plausible and computationally feasible.

5.2   Subtleties of defeasibility

In the previous section, we have seen what follows from different statements about what is defeasible. Which statements are strict or defeasible is not always explicit in natural language statements, but might be implicit or contextual. There appears to be no lexical distinction between strict and defeasible conditionals. Yet such a distinction seems essential in a CNL, which requires some explicit representations of the input. This is similar to the issue of whether negation in natural language out to be represented as strict or as negation-as-failure. Making an explicit distinction between strict and defeasible rules is especially pressing in the context of an application like AceWiki, where the claim can be made that, given the possibility of error, (virtually) all statements be considered defeasible.

We now consider another more fundamental issue that arises when introducing defeasibility in a controlled natural language. This is an issue that arises with similar constructs such as "it is false that ..." and "it is possible that ..." and is the question of the *semantic scope* of the operator *usual*. Consider the following two sentences in ACE extended with *usual*:

```
It is usual that Mainland-Shetland is damp and eerie and desolate.
Mainland-Shetland is not eerie.
```

In our current approach using AceWiki, the first sentence in the text above gets parsed as the conjunction of "it is usual that Mainland-Shetland is damp", "it is usual that Mainland-Shetland is eerie", and "it is usual that Mainland-Shetland is desolate", the only stable set hence being one where Mainland Shetland is damp and desolate, but not eerie.

Although this approach of having *usual* "distribute" over complex expressions within its scope seems satisfactory in the above example, further study is needed to determine whether this distribution always respects the intended meaning. As one possible counter-example, consider the following fragment of text, where the scope of *usual* in the second sentence includes an indefinite pronoun.

```
It is usual that Mainland-Shetland is inaccessible from Aberdeen.
It is usual that a ferry that starts in Aberdeen services Mainland-Shetland.
If a ferry that starts in Aberdeen services Mainland-Shetland then
Mainland-Shetland is not inaccessible from Aberdeen.
```

The result of evaluating this fragment of text is that there are four stable-sets, one in which Mainland Shetland is accessible via a ferry that starts in Aberdeen, while in the context of the remaining three stable sets Mainland Shetland is not accessible from Aberdeen. In each of these latter stable sets Mainland Shetland is inaccessible because: there is a ferry that starts in Aberdeen, but it does not service Mainland-Shetland; there is a ferry that services Mainland-Shetland, but it does not start in Aberdeen; and finally and anomalously, there simply is no ferry (while, at the same time, it being the case that were there a ferry, it would start in Aberdeen and service Mainland-Shetland).

The issue here is the particularities of AceRules parsing and semantic representation. The sentence "It is usual that a ferry that starts in Aberdeen services Mainland-Shetland" gets parsed as the conjunction of "It is usual that there is a ferry X1", "It is usual that the ferry X1 services Mainland-Shetland", and "It is usual that the ferry X1 starts in Aberdeen". However, one could argue that the result of the parse should be "it is usual that there is a ferry X1 that starts in Aberdeen" and "it is usual that the ferry X1 services Mainland-Shetland".

Indeed, this issue can be taken as support for our approach in that we can, first of all, enforce our intended reading by input of:

```
There is a ferry that starts in Aberdeen.
It is usual that the ferry services Mainland-Shetland.
```

Secondly, one can envision instances in which it is not desirable that "there being a ferry X1" grammatically associates with "starting in Aberdeen". For example in the following structurally very similar text:

```
It is usual that a ferry that starts early services Mainland-Shetland.
It is usual that a ferry that starts late services Mainland-Shetland.
If a ferry that starts early services Mainland-Shetland then it is
false that a ferry that starts late services Mainland-Shetland.
If a ferry that starts late services Mainland-Shetland then it is
false that a ferry that starts early services Mainland-Shetland.
```

one would expect it be possible to derive, concordantly with the direct stable semantics, that there is a ferry that services Mainland-Shetland, independently of whether the ferry in question starts late or early.

In our current implementation, we issue a warning whenever a statement corresponding to a defeasible rule is "split" or "distributed" into several defeasible rules. This is particularly important as such a distribution can lead to errors when verbalising the resulting answer sets. In particular, the mentioned fourth anomalous stable-set mentioned previously cannot be verbalised (in the current implementation) because of the fact that the stable set contains facts referring to something starting in Aberdeen and servicing Mainland-Shetland while at the same time there being no concrete object to which this "something" can be associated with (i.e. the ferry). The impact of these observations are that one must take care to integrate the syntax, semantic representation, and inference engine in order to obtain accurate and plausible (if not intended) output.

6 Conclusion

The paper has motivated the development of a CNL with defeasible reasoning, adapting the AceRules system with defeasible rules. We have provided background on defeasibility and reasoning, along with a discussion about how defeasible rules are introduced to AceRules. We have an extended example to exercise the tool, showing the utility and advantages of representing and reasoning with defeasible rules.

There are numerous opportunities for further development. ACE's APE parser can be augmented with capacities to represent tense, additional verb constructions, and subordinate clauses for justifications such as *because*. The example can be incrementally extended, testing the output results to ensure they comply with intuitions. There are a range of issues to address about the verbalisation, most importantly to provide some means to reconstruct claims and justifications in the output results, e.g. "X because Y", rather than producing a list of statements. A possible starting point is the direct-stable semantics implementation's ability to produce derivations of concluded literals.

More fundamentally, the interactions between the rule expressions output by AceRules, the rule language of the inference engine, and the verbaliser need greater study and development. As it is, AceRules uses grouping to adjust DRSs to the rule language, which raises several complexities; whether this can be relaxed to taken advantage of recent advances in rules languages remains to be seen. Relatedly, further work needs to be carried out on the complexity of grounding of variables and optimisations to limit blow-up, which has not been discussed in this paper. Other avenues of investigation might be rule decomposition, which could help to optimise grounding. More generally, we expect to incorporate other natural language expressions of defeasibility or genericity into a CNL with defeasible rules. Clearly, the approach we have developed opens a range of avenues for future research.

References

Amgoud, L. and P. Besnard (2013). A formal characterization of the outcomes of rule-based argumentation systems. In *SUM*, Volume 8078 of *LNCS*, pp. 78–91. Springer.

Blackburn, P. and J. Bos (2005). *Representation and Inference for Natural Language: A First Course in Computational Semantics*. CSLI Publications.

Bos, J. (2008). Wide-coverage semantic analysis with Boxer. In J. Bos and R. Delmonte (Eds.), *Semantics in Text Processing. STEP 2008 Conference Proceedings*, Research in Computational Semantics, pp. 277–286. College Publications.

Cabrio, E. and S. Villata (2012). Natural language arguments: A combined approach. In *ECAI 2012 - 20th European Conference on Artificial Intelligence. Including Prestigious Applications of Artificial Intelligence (PAIS-2012) System Demonstrations Track, Montpellier, France, August 27-31 , 2012*, pp. 205–210.

Caminada, M. and L. Amgoud (2007). On the evaluation of argumentation formalisms. *Artificial Intelligence 171*(5–6), 286–310.

Dung, P. M. (1995). On the acceptability of arguments and its fundamental role in nonmonotonic reasoning, logic programming and n-person games. *Artificial Intelligence 77*(2), 321–358.

Fuchs, N. E. (2016). Reasoning in Attempto Controlled English: Non-monotonicity. In B. Davis, G. J. Pace, and A. Wyner (Eds.), *Controlled Natural Language – 5th International Workshop, CNL 2016, Aberdeen, UK, July 25-27, 2016, Proceedings*, Volume 9767 of *Lecture Notes in Computer Science*, pp. 13–24. Springer.

Fuchs, N. E., K. Kaljurand, and T. Kuhn (2008). Attempto Controlled English for knowledge representation. In *Reasoning Web*, pp. 104–124.

Gelfond, M. and V. Lifschitz (1990). Logic programs with classical negation. In D. H. D. Warren and P. Szeredi (Eds.), *Logic Programming, Proceedings of the Seventh International Conference, Jerusalem, Israel, June 18-20, 1990*, pp. 579–597. MIT Press.

Gervasi, V. and D. Zowghi (2005). Reasoning about inconsistencies in natural language requirements. *ACM Trans. Softw. Eng. Methodol. 14*(3), 277–330.

Grosof, B. N. (1997). Prioritized conflict handling for logic programs. In J. Maluszynski (Ed.), *Logic Programming, Proceedings of the 1997 International Symposium, Port Jefferson, Long Island, NY, USA, October 13-16, 1997*, pp. 197–211. MIT Press.

Guy, S. and R. Schwitter (2017). The PENG^{ASP} system: Architecture, language and authoring tool. *Language Resources and Evaluation 51*(1), 67–92.

Kratzer, A. (2012). Modals and conditionals.

Kuhn, T. (2007). AceRules: Executing rules in controlled natural language. In *Web Reasoning and Rule Systems, First International Conference, RR 2007, Innsbruck , Austria, June 7-8, 2007, Proceedings*, Volume 4524 of *Lecture Notes in Computer Science*, pp. 299–308. Springer.

Kuhn, T. (2009). AceWiki: A semantic wiki using controlled English. In *Proceedings of the Poster Session at the 6th European Semantic Web Conference (ESWC09)*.

Kuhn, T. (2014). A survey and classification of controlled natural languages. *Computational Linguistics 40*(1), 121–170.

Lewis, D. (1975). Adverbs of quantification. In *Formal Semantics of Natural Language*, pp. 178–188. Cambridge University Press.

Lippi, M. and P. Torroni (2016). Argumentation mining: State of the art and emerging trends. *ACM Transactions on Internet Technology 16*(2), 10:1–10:25.

Poole, D. (1988). A logical framework for default reasoning. *Artificial Intelligence 36*(1), 27–47.

Prakken, H. (2010). An abstract framework for argumentation with structured arguments. *Argument & Computation 1*(2), 93–124.

Strass, H. (2013, September). Instantiating knowledge bases in Abstract Dialectical Frameworks. In *Proceedings of the Fourteenth International Workshop on Computational Logic in Multi-Agent Systems (CLIMA XIV)*, Volume 8143 of *LNCS*, pp. 86–101. Springer.

Strass, H. and A. Wyner (2017, February). On automated defeasible reasoning with controlled natural language and argumentation. In R. Barták, T. L. McCluskey, and E. Pontelli (Eds.), *Proceedings of the Second International Workshop on Knowledge-based Techniques for Problem Solving and Reasoning (KnowProS)*.

Toni, F. and P. Torroni (2011). Bottom-up argumentation. In *Theorie and Applications of Formal Argumentation - First International Workshop, TAFA 2011. Barcelona, Spain, July 16-17, 2011, Revised Selected Papers*, pp. 249–262.

Wyner, A., T. Bench-Capon, P. Dunne, and F. Cerutti (2015). Senses of 'argument' in instantiated argumentation frameworks. *Argument & Computation 6*(1), 50–72.

Wyner, A. Z., W. Peters, and D. Price (2015). Argument discovery and extraction with the argument workbench. In *Proceedings of the 2nd Workshop on Argumentation Mining, ArgMining@HLT-NAACL 2015, June 4, 2015, Denver, Colorado, USA*, pp. 78–83.

Wyner, A. Z. and H. Strass (2017). dARe – Using argumentation to explain conclusions from a controlled natural language knowledge base. In S. Benferhat, K. Tabia, and M. Ali (Eds.), *Proceedings of the Thirtieth International Conference on Industrial Engineering and Other Applications of Applied Intelligent Systems, IEA/AIE 2017*, Volume 10351 of *Lecture Notes in Computer Science*, pp. 328–338. Springer.

Semantic Composition via Probabilistic Model Theory

Guy Emerson and Ann Copestake
Computer Laboratory
University of Cambridge
{gete2,aac10}@cam.ac.uk

Abstract

Semantic composition remains an open problem for vector space models of semantics. In this paper, we explain how the probabilistic graphical model used in the framework of Functional Distributional Semantics can be interpreted as a probabilistic version of model theory. Building on this, we explain how various semantic phenomena can be recast in terms of conditional probabilities in the graphical model. This connection between formal semantics and machine learning is helpful in both directions: it gives us an explicit mechanism for modelling context-dependent meanings (a challenge for formal semantics), and also gives us well-motivated techniques for composing distributed representations (a challenge for distributional semantics). We present results on two datasets that go beyond word similarity, showing how these semantically-motivated techniques improve on the performance of vector models.

1   Introduction

Vector space models of semantics are popular in NLP, as they are easy to work with, can be trained on unannotated corpora, and are useful in many tasks. They can be trained in multiple ways, including count methods (Turney and Pantel, 2010) and neural embedding methods (Mikolov et al., 2013). Furthermore, they allow a natural and computationally efficient measure of similarity, in the form of cosine similarity.

However, even if we can train models that produce good similarity scores, a vector space does not provide natural operations for other aspects of meaning. How can vectors be composed to form semantic representations for larger phrases? Can we say that one vector implies another? How do we capture how meanings vary according to context? An overview of existing approaches to these questions is given in §2, but these issues do not have clear solutions.

In contrast, the framework of Functional Distributional Semantics (Emerson and Copestake, 2016) (henceforth E&C) aims to overcome such issues, not by extending a vector space model, but by learning a different kind of representation. Each predicate is represented not by a vector, but by a *function*, which forms part of a probabilistic graphical model. In §3, we build on the description given by E&C, and explain how this graphical model can in fact be viewed as encapsulating a probabilistic version of model theory. With this connection, we can naturally transfer concepts in formal semantics to this probabilistic framework, and we culminate in §3.5 by showing how generalised quantifiers can be interpreted in our probabilistic model. In §4, we look at how to naturally derive context-dependent representations, and further, how these representations can be used for certain kinds of inference and semantic composition.

In §5, we turn to using the model in practice, and evaluate on three tasks. Firstly, we look at lexical similarity, to show it is competitive with vector-based models. Secondly, we consider the dataset produced by Grefenstette and Sadrzadeh (2011), which measures the similarity of verbs in the context of a specific subject and object. Finally, we consider the RELPRON dataset produced by Rimell et al. (2016), which requires matching individual nouns to short phrases including relative clauses. Our aim is to show that, not only does the connection with formal semantics give us well-motivated techniques to tackle these disparate datasets, but this also leads to improvements in performance.

2   Related Work

One approach to compositionality in a vector space model is to find a composition function that maps a pair of vectors to a new vector in the same space. Mitchell and Lapata (2010) compare a variety of such functions, but they find that componentwise addition and multiplication are in fact competitive with the best functions they consider, despite being symmetric and hence insensitive to syntax.

Another approach is to use a recurrent neural network, which processes text one token at a time, updating a hidden state vector at each token. The final hidden state can be seen as a representation of the whole sequence. However, the state cannot be directly compared to the word vectors – indeed, they may have different numbers of dimensions. Other architectures have been proposed, aiming to use syntactic structure, such as recursive neural networks (Socher et al., 2010). However, this still does not use semantic structure – for example, there is no connection between active and passive voice sentences.

Coecke et al. (2010) and Baroni et al. (2014) introduce a tensor-based approach, where words are represented not just by vectors, but also by higher-order tensors, which combine according to argument structure: nouns are vectors, intransitive verbs are matrices (mapping noun vectors to sentence vectors), transitive verbs are third-order tensors (mapping pairs of noun vectors to sentence vectors), and so on. However, Grefenstette (2013) showed that quantifiers cannot be expressed in this framework.

Furthermore, in all the above methods, it is unclear how to perform inference, While we can use the representations as input features for another system, they do not have an inherent logical interpretation. Balkir et al. (2016) extend the tensor-based framework to allow inference, but rely on existing vectors, and must assume the dimensions have logical interpretations. Lewis and Steedman (2013) use distributional information to cluster predicates, but this leaves no graded notion of similarity. Garrette et al. (2011) and Beltagy et al. (2016) incorporate a vector space model into a Markov Logic Network, in the form of weighted inference rules (the truth of one predicate implying the truth of another). However, this assumes we can interpret similarity in terms of inference (a position defended by Erk (2016)), and requires existing vectors, rather than directly learning logical representations from distributional data.

Many proposals exist for contextualising vectors. Erk and Padó (2008) and Thater et al. (2011) modify a vector according to syntactic dependencies. However, by proposing new operations, they make assumptions about the properties of the space, which may not apply to all models. Erk and Padó (2010) build a context-specific vector, by combining the most similar contexts in a corpus. However, this reduces the amount of training data. Lui et al. (2012)'s "per-lemma" model uses Latent Dirichlet Allocation to model contextual meaning as a mixture of senses, but this requires training a separate LDA model for each word. Furthermore, all of these methods focus on a specific kind of context, making it nontrivial to generalise them to arbitrary contexts.

Our notion of probabilistic truth values is similar to the Austinian truth values in the framework of probabilistic Type Theory with Records (TTR) (Cooper, 2005; Cooper et al., 2015). Sutton (2015, 2017) takes a similar probabilistic approach to truth values to deal with philosophical problems concerning gradable predicates. Our stochastic generation of situations is also similar to the approach taken by Goodman and Lassiter (2015), who represent semantics with the stochastic lambda calculus, using handwritten probabilistic models to show how semantics and world knowledge can interact. While these approaches are in principle compatible with our work, they do not provide an approach to distributional semantics. We use Minimal Recursion Semantics (Copestake et al., 2005), as it can be represented using dependency graphs – this allows a more natural connection with probabilistic graphical models, as explained in §3.4.

Others have also proposed representing the meaning of a predicate as a classifier. Larsson (2013) represents the meaning of a perceptual concept as a classifier of perceptual input, in the TTR framework. Schlangen et al. (2016) train image classifiers using captioned images, and Zarrieß and Schlangen (2017a,b) build on this, using distributional similarity to help train such classifiers. However, they do not learn an interpretable representation directly from text; rather, they use similarity scores to generalise from one label of an image to other similar labels. McMahan and Stone (2015) represent the meaning of a colour term as a probabilistic region of colour space, which could also be interpreted as a probabilistic classifier. However, this model was not intended to be a general-purpose distributional model.

3 From Model Theory to Probability Theory

In this section, we show how model theory can be recast in a probabilistic setting. The aim is not to detail a full probabilistic logic, but rather to show how we can define a family of probability distributions that capture traditional model structures as a special case, while also allowing structured representations of the kind used in machine learning. In this way, we will be able to view Functional Distributional Semantics as a generalisation of model theory.

3.1 Background: Model Theory, Neo-Davidsonian Events, and Situations

A standard approach to formal semantics is to use an extensional model structure (Cann, 1993; Allan, 2001; Kamp and Reyle, 2013). We first define a set of 'individuals' (or 'entities') in the model. We then define the meaning of a predicate to be its extension – the subset of individuals for which the predicate is true. The extension can also be characterised in terms of a truth-conditional function – a function mapping from individuals to truth-values. Individuals in the extension of the predicate are mapped to true, and all other individuals to false.

We take a neo-Davidsonian approach to event semantics (Davidson, 1967; Parsons, 1990). This treats events as also being individuals, and verbal predicates are one-place relations, which can be true of event individuals. Other participants in an an event are indicated by two-place relations, linking the event to the argument individual. For example, a sentence like *pictures tell stories* would be represented with three individuals and five relations: $picture(x)$, $tell(y)$, $story(z)$, $\text{ARG}1(y, x)$, $\text{ARG}2(y, z)$. Here, the ARG1 and ARG2 relations express the argument structure of the telling event.

Finally, we take an approach in the spirit of situation semantics (Barwise and Perry, 1983), and assume that the model contains a set of *situations*. Each situation consists of a small number of individuals (unlike a possible world, which would consist of many individuals), and the relations that stand between them. As we are taking a neo-Davidsonian approach, this means that we take a situation to be set of individuals, where each predicate assigns a truth value to each individual, and where there are two-place relations between individuals, to express argument structure.

3.2 Model Structures as Probability Distributions

In this section, we generalise this notion of a model structure in two ways. Firstly, rather than a set of situations, we will consider a probability distribution over a set of situations. Secondly, rather than deterministic truth-conditional functions, we will consider probabilistic truth-conditional functions.

A probability distribution over a set of situations is naturally more general than the set itself, since it provides more information – as well as knowing that a situation is in the set, we additionally know its probability. From the formal linguistic point of view, this might seem irrelevant to the notion of truth. However, from the machine learning point of view (and perhaps also from the acquisition point of view), it is very helpful – if our aim is not just to *represent* what is true, but also to *learn* what is true, we do not know in advance what situations should be part of the model structure. By using probability distributions, we can smoothly change between different models. This lets us use continuous optimisation algorithms, such as methods based on gradient descent, which are generally more efficient than discrete optimisation algorithms. Intuitively, as we learn about what kinds of situations exist, we can update the model appropriately.

A truth-conditional function can be defined as a function mapping from a set of individuals to the set $\{0, 1\}$, where 0 denotes falsehood, and 1 truth. We can generalise this to a function mapping from a set of individuals to the range $[0, 1]$. This allows us to naturally model the fuzzy boundaries of concepts, by using intermediate values between 0 and 1. This idea was used by Labov (1973) to model the fuzzy boundaries between concepts like *cup*, *mug*, and *bowl*. For an unusual object that is intermediate between a typical cup and a typical bowl, we can say that the predicates for *cup* and *mug* both have an intermediate probability of being true of the object. As with our previous generalisation step, allowing a continuous range of values is also helpful during learning, since we can smoothly change a function between assigning truth or falsehood to a particular individual.

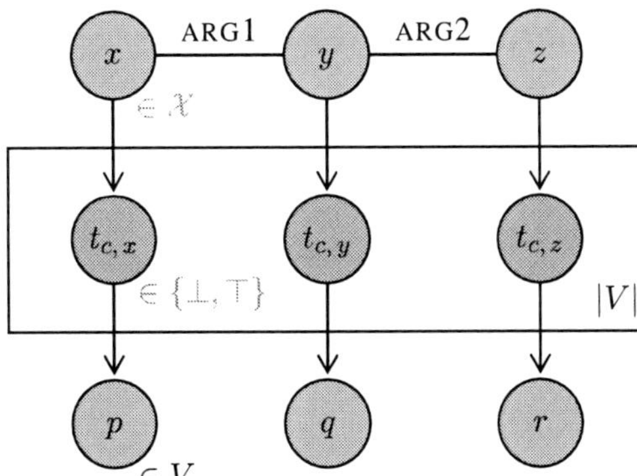

Figure 1: A simplified DMRS graph, which could be generated by Fig. 2 below. Such graphs are observed during training.

Figure 2: Probabilistic graphical model for Functional Distributional Semantics (E&C, Fig. 3). Each node denotes a random variable. The plate (box in middle row) denotes repetition of random variables. **Top row:** pixies x, y, and z, randomly drawn from a semantic space $\mathcal{X}$. Their joint distribution is determined by the DMRS links. **Middle row:** each predicate c in the vocabulary V is randomly true or false for each pixie, according to the predicate's semantic function. **Bottom row:** for each pixie, we randomly generate one predicate, out of all predicates true of the pixie.

3.3 Denotations versus Truth-Conditional Functions

If individuals are atomic elements, without any further structure, then denotations and truth-conditional functions have almost identical representations. A denotation is a subset of the set of individuals, while a truth-conditional function is the indicator function for this subset: individuals in the denotation are mapped to 1, and other individuals to 0. Converting between these two representations is trivial.

However, if individuals are structured objects, denotations and truth-conditional functions may have rather different representations. To represent the structure of individuals, we assume we have a semantic space, where each point in the space represents a possible individual, including information about all its features. We will use the term 'pixie' to refer to a point in the semantic space, as it is intuitively a 'pixel' of the space. Note that E&C use the term 'entity' to refer to both individuals and pixies.

For example, consider a model with five individuals: two black cats, a white cat, a bowl of rice, and a carrot. If we use a semantic space, and represent these individuals with the features COLOUR (*black*, *white*, or *orange*) and ANIMACY ($+$ or $-$), then the denotation of the predicate for *cat* is a set of three individuals, whose pixies are {COLOUR: *black*, ANIMACY: $+$} (appearing twice) and {COLOUR: *white*, ANIMACY: $+$} (appearing once).[1] As a probability distribution, the denotation assigns a probability of ⅔ to the first pixie, ⅓ to the second, and 0 to all others. However, the truth-conditional function can be represented much more simply – it takes the value 1 if and only if the pixie is animate.

As can be seen in this example, we may have multiple individuals represented by the same pixie. This can be accounted for in the probabilistic model structure, by assigning higher probabilities to pixies that correspond to more individuals. Note that, technically, this means that we are not working directly with distributions over situations, but rather with distributions over equivalence classes of situations, where situations are equivalent if their individuals are indistinguishable in terms of their features.

3.4 Functional Distributional Semantics as Model-Theoretic Semantics

Now we have described the above probabilistic generalisation of a model structure, we explain how Functional Distributional Semantics can be seen as implementing such a generalised model structure.

E&C define a probabilistic graphical model to generate semantic dependency graphs like that in Fig. 1. The aim is to train the model in an unsupervised[2] way on a parsed corpus – that is, to optimise the model parameters to maximise the probability of generating the dependency graphs in the corpus. Furthermore, Dependency Minimal Recursion Semantics (DMRS) (Copestake, 2009) allows a logical

---

[1] We could add an 'ID' feature to distinguish otherwise identical individuals, but will not take this approach here.

[2] Following Ghahramani (2004), supervised learning requires both inputs and outputs, while unsupervised learning requires only inputs. The annotations in our training corpus are not desired outputs, so learning is unsupervised in this sense.

interpretation of the dependency graphs: each node represents a predicate, and the ARG links represent argument structure. The graphical model in Fig. 2 generates dependency graphs corresponding to transitive sentences – the predicates (p, q, r) can be seen at the bottom, and the dependency links (ARG1, ARG2) can be seen at the top. For example, p, q, and r might correspond to *pictures*, *tell*, and *stories*.

Rather than generating a dependency graph directly, the semantic function model assumes that it generated based on latent structure. We assume that for each observed predicate, there is an unobserved, latent pixie which the predicate is true of. These pixies are the orange nodes at the top of Fig. 2. Each pixie node is a random variable, taking values in the semantic space $\mathcal{X}$ of all possible pixies. We also assume that every predicate is either true or false of each pixie. These truth values are the purple nodes in the middle row of Fig. 2 (note that each node is repeated $|V|$ times, once for each predicate). They are random variables, with two possible values: true or false. While we know each observed predicate is true of its pixie, the truth values for all other predicates are latent variables.

The generative model proceeds from the top to the bottom of Fig. 2. First, we define a joint distribution over pixies, as an undirected graphical model – whenever a pair of pixie nodes is linked, the model determines how likely it is for specific values of those nodes to co-occur. This allows us to generate tuples of pixies. E&C implement this with a Cardinality Restricted Boltzmann Machine (CaRBM) (Swersky et al., 2012): pixies are sparse binary-valued vectors, with each dimension representing a different feature. Each dependency link determines how likely it is for specific features of the linked pixies to co-occur; this is encoded using one trainable parameter for each pair of dimensions.

Next, we define a semantic function for each predicate – this maps each pixie to the probability that the predicate is true of it. So, given a set of generated pixies, we can generate truth values for each pixie. E&C implement these functions with one-layer feedforward networks – by using a sigmoid activation, the output is in the range $[0, 1]$, so it can be interpreted as a probability. Finally, given the truth values for all predicates, we generate one predicate for each pixie, by choosing from the true predicates.

The above generative process was given by E&C. However, we can see the first two stages in this process as an instance of the probabilistic model structure discussed in §3.2. The linked pixies can together be viewed as a situation. The joint distribution over pixies then gives us a distribution over situations, which can be seen as our probabilistic generalisation of a set of situations in a model structure. Furthermore, as the semantic functions map from pixies to probabilities, they can be seen as generalised truth-conditional functions. So, we can view the semantic function model as generating dependency graphs based on a probabilistic model structure. In this model, a denotation can be represented by a probability distribution over the semantic space, while a truth-conditional function can be represented by a semantic function, mapping from the semantic space to $[0, 1]$.

However, we should note that this model only implements soft constraints on semantics – indeed, it would be difficult to learn hard constraints from corpus data alone. This means that, all our distributions over pixies have a non-zero probability for every pixie, and all our semantic functions assign a non-zero probability of truth to every pixie. By analogy with a traditional model structure, we might want to have zero values, to indicate that a certain pixie or situation is impossible, or that a certain predicate is definitely false. However, from a Bayesian point of view, zero probabilities are problematic – they would imply that, no matter what new evidence we observe, we cannot change our mind.

In practice, some probabilities will be vanishingly small. In fact, to make interesting predictions, this is necessary – for high-dimensional spaces, an interesting subspace (perhaps representing a domain, like rock-climbing or ballroom dancing) may be small. For example, suppose we have 1000 binary-valued dimensions, with only 40 active at once. This gives 10^{72} pixies. A subspace only using 200 dimensions has 10^{42} pixies, or one part in 10^{30} of the whole space! To define a distribution with most probability mass in this subspace, pixies in the subspace must be at least 10^{30} times more likely than outside.

Suppose a predicate is probably true in this subspace, and probably false outside. Given a uniform prior over the space, and observing the predicate to be true, we may expect the posterior to assign most probability mass to the subspace. For this to happen, the probability of truth in the subspace must be 10^{30} times larger than outside. So, for a semantic function to be useful, it must be close to a step function. This makes it look more like a traditional truth-conditional function with only 0 and 1 as values.

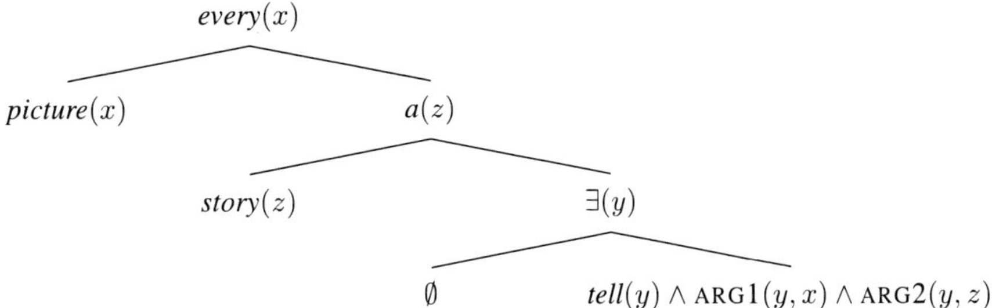

Figure 3: Fully scoped representation of the most likely reading of *Every picture tells a story*. Each non-terminal node is a quantifier, its left child its restriction, and its right child its body. We assume that event variables are existentially quantified with no constraints on the restriction.

3.5 Interpretation of Quantifiers

Interpreting the semantic function model as a probabilistic model structure, we can define quantification in a natural way. Unlike Herbelot and Vecchi (2015), we are not mapping from a distributional space to a model structure, but directly interpreting quantifiers in our distributional model.

To assign a truth value to DMRS graph, we must first convert it to a fully scoped representation, such as in Fig. 3. In cases of scope ambiguity, a single DMRS graph allows several scoped representations, and this conversion must resolve the ambiguity.[3]

In a complete structure, there is one quantifier for each MRS variable, and hence also for each pixie-valued random variable, as there is a one-to-one mapping between them. For each quantifier, we define a binary-valued random variable, representing whether the quantified expression is true (given any remaining free variables). We define distributions for these random variables recursively, bottom-up through the scope tree. At each stage, we marginalise out the quantified pixie variable. This is analogous to semantic composition in traditional models – truth values are calculated bottom-up, and evaluating a quantifier removes a free variable. At the root of the tree, we have a single probabilistic truth value.

Each quantifier depends on its restriction and body, each of which may be either[4] a predicate or a quantified expression – both are binary-valued random variables. In the classical theory of generalised quantifiers, the truth of a quantified expression depends on the cardinality of the restriction set, and the cardinality of the intersection of the restriction and body sets (Barwise and Cooper, 1981; Van Benthem, 1984). As explained in §3.3, our probabilistic model structure uses probabilities in place of cardinalities. Let the probabilistic truth values for the quantified expression, restriction, and body be Q, R, and B, respectively. It makes sense to consider the conditional probability $P(B|R)$, which naturally uses both of the classical sets, since $P(B|R) = \frac{P(R \cap B)}{P(R)}$. Intuitively, the truth of Q depends on how likely B is to be true, given that R is true.[5]

In a traditional logic, the truth value of a quantified expression is a function of all free variables. Analogously, each quantifier's random variable is conditionally dependent on all free variables. More precisely, if the set of free variables is V, let us define the function $q(V) = P(B|R, V)$. We can now consider different quantifiers, and define the probability of the quantified expression Q being true, in terms of the value of q: *every* is true iff $q = 1$, *some* is true iff $q > 0$, *most* is true iff $q > 1/2$, and so on. In these cases, the probability of truth is exactly 0 or 1, but by using intermediate probabilities, we can also naturally model 'fuzzy' quantifiers such as *few* and *many*, which do not have a sharp cutoff.

---

[3] A DMRS graph includes scopal constraints, specifying that nodes are the same place in the scope tree, or that one dominates another. These constraints were not used in the generative model in §3.4, akin to other simplified MRS-based dependency structures such as EDS (Oepen and Lønning, 2006), but they are necessary to specify the correct set of scope readings.

[4] More generally, we may have a set of predicates and quantified expressions. In this case, we can condition on all truth values in the set. We consider a single random truth value, for ease of exposition.

[5] This account does not cover cardinal quantifiers. However, the English Resource Grammar (ERG) represents numbers not as quantifiers, but as additional predicates. This is compatible with Link (2002)'s lattice-theoretic approach, which allows reference to plural individuals without quantification. For more information on the semantic analyses in the ERG, see the documentation produced by Flickinger et al. (2014), which is available here: http://www.delph-in.net/esd

4 From Conditional Dependence to Context Dependence

In the previous section, we saw how a model structure can be generalised using probability distributions. In this section, we show how this approach allows us to capture context-dependent meanings using conditional probabilities, in a natural way.

4.1 Occasion Meaning versus Standing Meaning

When discussing context dependence (a challenge for both formal semantics and vector-based semantics), it is helpful to distinguish two kinds of meaning, following Quine (1960): *standing* meaning refers to the fixed, unchanging meaning that a linguistic expression has in general; *occasion* meaning refers to the particular meaning that a linguistic expression has in a given context.

Searle (1980) discusses an interesting set of examples, noting how a gardener cutting grass involves a very different kind of cutting from a child cutting a cake. There is something common to both events, but they involve different tools and different physical motions. However, Searle also notes how there are also less obvious interpretations of these expressions. For a gardener who sells turf to people who need ready-grown lawns, cutting grass could also refer to cutting out an area of grass, including the soil.[6] This kind of cutting would more closely resemble cutting a cake. We can see from this example that while an expression may refer to quite different situations, some situations may be more likely than others.

This state of affairs can be modelled in our probabilistic version of model theory. We can say that an expression like *cut grass* has fixed truth conditions – it is true of both mowing a lawn and preparing a section of turf. However, we can also say that the former is much more probable than the latter. More precisely, our prior distribution over situations assigns a much higher probability to lawn-mowing situations than to turf-slicing situations; but the probabilistic truth-conditional functions for *cut* and *grass* assign high probabilities to their respective individuals in both of these types of situation.

While the expression *cut grass* could refer to different types of situation, in most contexts we can infer that it is likely to refer to a lawn-mowing situation. We can view this as performing Bayesian inference. We begin with a prior probability distribution over situations, where the situation includes (at least) two pixies y and z, with an ARG2 link from y to z (i.e. the situations with enough structure for *cut grass*, since *grass* is the ARG2 of *cut*). This prior distribution is given to us by our probabilistic model structure. Importantly, these situations are jointly distributed with truth values for the predicates for *cut* and *grass* (as well as all other predicates). On observing that the *cut* predicate is true of the pixie y, and the *grass* predicate is true of the pixie z (the ARG2 of y), we can form a posterior distribution over situations (i.e. a joint posterior over the pixies). This posterior should assign a high probability to lawn-mowing situations, a low probability to turf-slicing situations, and an extremely low probability to unrelated situations like baking a cake. If we receive information that makes a turf-slicing situation more likely (e.g. hearing about a person selling turf), we can update our posterior again, and assign a higher probability to such a situation. However, in the absence of such information, we effectively 'default' to the higher-probability lawn-mowing interpretation.

In summary, we can view truth-conditional functions as representing context-invariant standing meanings, and posterior distributions over situations as representing context-dependent occasion meanings.

4.2 Context Dependence in Functional Distributional Semantics

In Functional Distributional Semantics, the standing meaning of a predicate is its semantic function – a mapping from the semantic space to probabilities of truth. These are the arrows in Fig. 2 from the orange pixie nodes (top row) to the purple truth value nodes (middle row). These functions are implemented as feedforward neural networks – note that the meaning is not the input or output of a network, but rather the network itself.

The occasion meaning of a predicate is the posterior distribution over the semantic space, for the pixie the predicate is true of. The pixies are the orange nodes in Fig. 2, but these nodes do not directly

---

[6] There are yet other interpretations of *cut grass*, such as *adulterate marijuana*, but we focus on the two discussed by Searle.

stand for meanings – an occasion meaning is the posterior distribution of such a node, when conditioned on the truth of one or more predicates.

We should also note that, while we only consider specific kinds of linguistic contexts in this paper, this approach generalises to arbitrary contexts. As an occasion meaning is simply a posterior distribution, we could in principle condition on any kind of observation. For example, if we are dealing with a specific domain, and we know the kinds of pixies that are likely to appear in this domain, we can produce a domain-specific meaning, which we could then further condition on a linguistic context.

To calculate occasion meanings, we need to calculate posterior distributions over the semantic space, given some observed truth values. However, exactly calculating the posterior is generally intractable, as this requires summing over the entire semantic space. For a large number of dimensions, the space is simply too big. Sampling from the space using a Markov Chain Monte Carlo method, as described by E&C, is also computationally expensive.

To make calculating the posterior tractable, we can use a variational approximation – this involves specifying a restricted class of distributions which is easier to work with, and then finding the optimal distribution in this restricted class that approximates the posterior. In particular, we can use a mean field approximation, following Emerson and Copestake (2017) (henceforth E&C2) – we assume that each dimension (intuitively, each feature) has an independent probability of being active, and we optimise each of these probabilities based on the mean activations of all other dimensions. Under this approximation, an occasion meaning is represented by a mean field vector. Intuitively, we assign high probabilities to a dimension for two possible reasons: either it's connected with high weights to highly probable dimensions in other pixies, or activating this dimension makes it much more likely for an observed predicate to be true. If neither of these facts hold, we will assign a low probability – because we are enforcing sparsity on the pixie vectors, the dimensions are effectively competing with each other.

This mean field approximation gives us a tractable way to approximately calculate a posterior distribution over pixies. This allows us to construct vectors representing context-dependent meanings, which we can use as the basis for further calculations, as illustrated in the following sections.

4.3   Semantic Composition using Context-Dependent Meanings

Semantic composition involves taking semantic representations for multiple expressions, and combining them into a single representation for the whole expression. In vector space models, this involves mapping two or more vectors to a single vector. Intuitively, with a fixed number of dimensions, this loses information. As Mooney (2014) colourfully put it, "You can't cram the meaning of a whole %&!$# sentence into a single $&!#* vector!" More precisely, if nearby vectors represent similar meanings, only the first few significant digits of each dimension are important, which limits how much information a vector can contain. Even if we use sparse vectors, at some point we will have 'used up' all of the available dimensions. So, composing vectors is not viable in the general case – even proponents of vector space models would not suggest composing vectors to produce an accurate representation of an entire book.

Unlike vectors, the representations used in formal semantics are not bounded in size – logical formulae and semantic dependency graphs can be arbitrarily large. While it can be useful to summarise a large representation with a smaller one, we do not believe that a semantic theory should force composition to involve summarisation. Full and detailed semantic representations should also have their place.

In a semantic function model, we can use DMRS composition. Individual lexical items are associated with predicates, and these are composed to form a DMRS graph. However, the probabilistic framework gives us a new interpretation of the DMRS graphs. If we start from two DMRS graphs, we can consider the two posterior distributions over situations defined by those graphs. Once we compose these two graphs, we have a new posterior distribution, over larger situations. However, this posterior is not the same as naively combining the posteriors of the two subgraphs. As the pixie nodes of the two subgraphs are now linked together, we have a joint distribution for all the pixie nodes, which depends on all the observed predicates. This means that, as we build a composed DMRS graph, we modify the posterior distributions at every step. In this way, we can see semantic composition as simultaneously composing the logical structure and refining the context-dependent meanings.

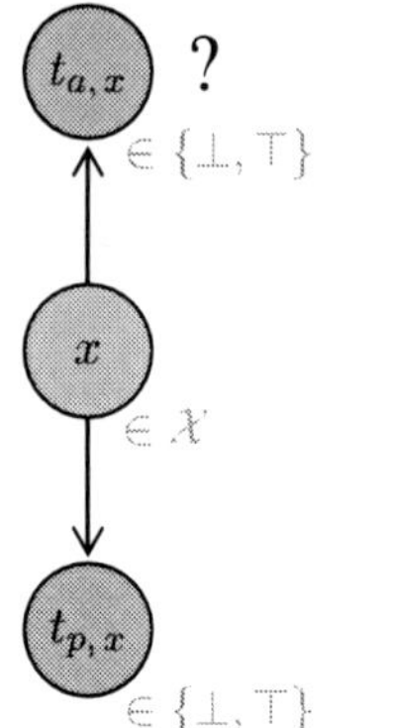
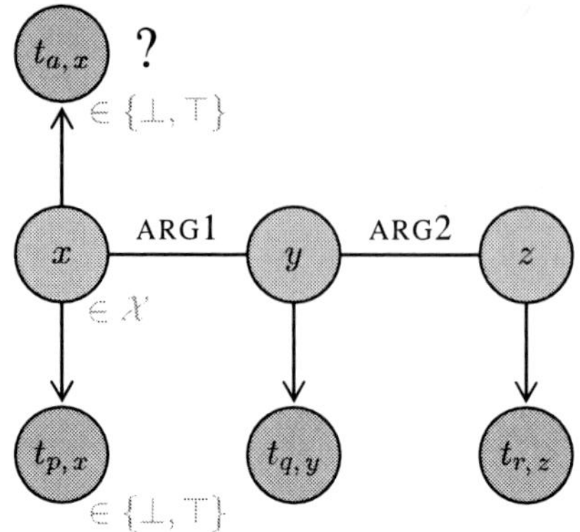

(a) Inferring if a is true of x, when there are no further pixies in the situation, and given the truth value for the predicate p.

(b) Inferring if a is true of x, when x is part of a larger situation, and given the truth value for one predicate for each pixie in the situation.

Figure 4: Examples of graphical models for inference. In both cases, we want to find the probability of the predicate a being true of a pixie x, given some other information about the situation.

4.4 Inference using Context-Dependent Meanings

A semantic function model includes a random variable for the truth of each predicate for each pixie. As noted by E&C2, these random variables allow us to convert certain logical propositions into statements about conditional probabilities. For example, we might be interested in whether one predicate implies another. For simplicity, we can first consider a situation containing only a single pixie x, as shown in Fig. 4a. Then, the proposition $\forall x \in \mathcal{X},\ p(x) \Rightarrow a(x)$ is equivalent to the statement $P(t_{a,x}|t_{p,x}) = 1$. Conditioning on $t_{p,x}$ means restricting to those pixies x for which the predicate p is true, and if the probability of $t_{a,x}$ being true is 1, then it is always true. Similarly, $\exists x \in \mathcal{X},\ a(x) \wedge b(x)$ is equivalent to $P(t_{a,x}|t_{p,x}) > 0$. This equivalence is discussed in more detail by E&C2.

In practice, the conditional probability $P(t_{a,x}|t_{p,x})$ will never be exactly 0 or 1, as discussed in §3.4. Nonetheless, this quantity represents the degree to which a implies b, in an intuitive sense: the higher the value, the closer we are to *every*; and the lower the value, the closer we are to *no*. We will use this quantity in §5.1 to measure semantic similarity.

To calculate $P(t_{a,x}|t_{p,x})$, we need to marginalise out x, because the model defines the joint probability $P(x, t_{p,x}, t_{a,x})$. This is analogous to the process of removing bound variables in §3.5, but note that here we do not have quantifiers to evaluate. Rather, we know certain facts about a situation, so we want to consider just those situations where those facts are true. Exactly marginalising out a pixie would require summing over the entire semantic space $\mathcal{X}$, which is intractable for a large number of dimensions. As explained in §4.2, the posterior for x given $t_{p,x}$ can be approximated using a mean field vector. This gives us a probability for each dimension of x, representing a 'typical' pixie for the observed truth values. Applying the semantic function for a to this mean field vector lets us approximately calculate $P(t_{a,x}|t_{p,x})$.

In the general case, we have more than one pixie in a situation, as shown in Fig. 4b. For example, if we know that a person is cutting grass, we could ask how likely it is that the person is also a gardener (likely), an artist (less likely), or a flowerpot (very unlikely). As before, we can answer this question by calculating a conditional probability: $P(t_{a,x}|t_{p,x}, t_{q,y}, t_{r,z})$. Because the truth values are connected via the latent pixies, the truth of one predicate depends on all the others. Inference requires marginalising out all pixies in the situation, so we first find the joint mean field distribution for all pixies, and then apply the semantic function for *gardener* to the mean field vector for the *person* pixie. Note how the context-dependent meaning of *person* (the mean field vector) is crucial to this calculation – although we are only applying applying the *gardener* function to the *person* vector, this vector depends on all predicates in the context.

5 Experimental Results

We trained our model using WikiWoods[7], a corpus providing DMRS graphs for 55m sentences of English (900m tokens). WikiWoods was produced by Flickinger et al. (2010) and Solberg (2012) from the July 2008 dump of the full English Wikipedia, using the English Resource Grammar (Flickinger, 2000, 2011) and the PET parser (Callmeier, 2001; Toutanova et al., 2005), with parse ranking trained on the manually treebanked subcorpus WeScience (Ytrestøl et al., 2009). It is distributed by DELPH-IN.

We extracted SVO triples (in a slight abuse of terminology), by which we mean DMRS subgraphs comprising a verbal predicate and nominal ARG1 and/or ARG2, discarding pronouns and named entities. This gives 10m full SVO triples, and a further 21m where one of the two arguments is missing. For further details, see E&C. To preprocess the corpus, we used the python packages pydelphin[8] (developed by Michael Goodman), and pydmrs[9] (Copestake et al., 2016). Our source code is available online.[10]

Carefully initialising the model parameters allows us to drastically reduce the necessary training time. We initialised the parameters of the semantic functions using random positive-only projections, a simple random-indexing technique introduced by QasemiZadeh and Kallmeyer (2016). The total number of dimensions is fixed, and each context predicate is randomly assigned to a context dimension (which means that many contexts will be randomly assigned to the same dimension). For each target predicate, we count how many times each context dimension appears. With these counts, we can calculate a standard PPMI vector. This method lets us initialise vectors in very little time, and we can use the same hyperparameters discussed by Levy et al. (2015). However, it should be noted that, because we are not using the vectors in the same way, the ideal hyperparameters are not the same. In particular, we found that, unlike for normal word vectors, it was unhelpful to use a negative offset for PPMI scores.

Once the semantic function parameters have been initialised, the CaRBM parameters can be initialised based on mean field vectors. Each semantic function defines a no-context mean field vector, as described in §4.4 for Fig. 4a. For each SVO triple in the training data, we can take the mean field vectors for the observed predicates, and for each link, we can calculate the mean field activation of each pair of dimensions of the linked pixies – this is simply the outer product of the mean field vectors for the linked pixies. We can then average these mean field activations across the whole training set, and calculate PPMI scores, which we can use to initialise the link's parameters. For an average mean field activation of f, the PPMI is $\log(f) - 2\log(\frac{C}{D})$, where D is the dimensionality and C the cardinality, since the expected activation of a pair of dimensions of two random vectors is $(\frac{C}{D})^2$.

We compare our model to two vector baselines. The first is a standard Word2Vec model (Mikolov et al., 2013), trained on the plain text version of the WikiWoods corpus. The second is the same Word2Vec algorithm, trained on the SVO triples we used to train our model: each triple was used to produce one 'sentence', where each 'token' is a predicate.

Finding a good evaluation task is far from obvious. Simple similarity tasks do not require semantic structure, while tasks like textual entailment require a level of coverage beyond the scope of this paper. We consider the SVO similarity and RELPRON datasets, described below, because they provide restricted tasks in which we can explore approaches to semantic composition. The results on RELPRON were also reported by E&C2, but we give further error analysis here. In future work, we plan to use the datasets produced by Herbelot and Vecchi (2016) and Herbelot (2013), where pairs of 'concepts' (such as *tricycle*) and 'features' (such as *is small*) are annotated with suitable quantifiers (out of these options: *all, most, some, few, no*). One challenge posed by these datasets is the syntactic variation in the features, such as *has 3 wheels* and *lives on coasts*. These datasets can be seen as a further stepping stone between this paper and general textual entailment.

---

[7] http://moin.delph-in.net/WikiWoods
[8] https://github.com/delph-in/pydelphin
[9] https://github.com/delph-in/pydmrs
[10] https://github.com/guyemerson/sem-func

Model	SL Noun	SL Verb	SimVerb	MEN	WS Sim	WS Rel
Word2Vec	.40	.23	.21	**.62**	**.69**	.46
SVO Word2Vec	.44	.18	.23	.60	.61	.24
Semantic Functions	**.46**	**.25**	**.26**	.52	.60	**.16**

Table 1: Spearman rank correlation with average annotator judgements, for SimLex-999 (SL) noun and verb subsets, SimVerb-3500, MEN, and WordSim-353 (WS) similarity and relatedness subsets. Note that we would like to have a *low* score for WS Rel (which measures relatedness, rather than similarity).

Model	GS2011	RELPRON Dev	RELPRON Test
Word2Vec, Addition	.12	.50	.47
SVO Word2Vec, Addition	.30	–	–
Semantic Functions	.25	.20	.16
(SVO) Word2Vec and Sem-Func Ensemble	**.32**	**.53**	**.49**

Table 2: Spearman rank correlation with average annotator judgements, on the GS2011 dataset, and mean average precision on the RELPRON development and test sets. For RELPRON, the Word2Vec model was trained on a larger training set, so that we can directly compare with Rimell et al.'s results. For GS2011, the ensemble model uses SVO Word2Vec, while for RELPRON, it uses normal Word2Vec.

5.1 Lexical Similarity

We evaluated our model on several lexical similarity datasets. Our aim is firstly to show that the performance of our model is competitive with state-of-the-art vector space models, and secondly to show that our model can specifically target *similarity* rather than *relatedness*. For example, while the predicates *painter* and *painting* are related, they are true of very different individuals.

We used SimLex-999 (Hill et al., 2015) and SimVerb-3500 (Gerz et al., 2016), which both aim to measure similarity, not relatedness; MEN (Bruni et al., 2014); and WordSim-353 (Finkelstein et al., 2001), which Agirre et al. (2009) split into similarity and relatedness subsets.

To calculate a similarity score in our model, we can use the conditional probability of one predicate being true, given that another predicate is true, as shown in Fig. 4a. To make this into a symmetric score, we can multiply the conditional probabilities in both directions. Results are shown in Table 1.[11]

We can see that the semantic function model is competitive with Word2Vec, but has qualitatively different behaviour, as it has very low correlation for the relatedness subset of WordSim-353. It has lower performance on MEN and the similarity subset of WordSim-353, but these two datasets were not annotated to target similarity, in the sense given above. For SimLex-999 and SimVerb-3500, which do target similarity, performance is higher than Word2Vec.

We note also that the performance of our model is higher than that reported in our previous work. This is due to better hyperparameter tuning. Using the initialisation method described above allowed for faster experiments and hence a greater exploration of the hyperparameter space. Using more datasets also allowed for more targeted tuning: hyperparameters for each dataset were tuned on the remaining datasets, except for SimVerb-3500, which has its own development set. Compared to E&C2's results, performance is much improved on the verb subset of SimLex-999, which was previously tuned on noun datasets only, indicating that the optimal settings for nouns and verbs differ considerably.

5.2 Similarity in Context

Grefenstette and Sadrzadeh (2011) produced a dataset of pairs of SVO triples, where only the verb varies in the pair. Each pair was annotated for similarity. For example, annotators had to judge the similarity

---

[11] Performance of Word2Vec on SimLex-999 is higher than reported by Hill et al. (2015). Despite correspondence with the authors, it is not clear why their figures are so low.

of the triples (*table, show, result*) and (*table, express, result*). In line with lexical similarity datasets, a system can be evaluated using the Spearman rank correlation between the system's scores and the average annotations.

For each triple, we calculated the mean field vector for the verb, conditioned on all three predicates. We then calculated the probability that the other verb's predicate is true of this mean field vector, similarly to Fig. 4b (the only difference being that we are interested in pixie y, not pixie x). To get a symmetric score, we multiplied the probabilities in both directions.

Results are given in the "GS2011" column of Table 2. The performance of our model (.25) matches the best model Grefenstette and Sadrzadeh consider. The performance of our ensemble (.32) matches the improved model of Grefenstette et al. (2013), despite using less training data. Furthermore, the fact that the ensemble outperforms both the semantic function model and the vector space model shows that the two models have learnt different kinds of information. This is not simply due to the combined model having a larger capacity – increasing the size of the individual models did not give this improvement.

5.3 Composition of Relative Clauses

The RELPRON dataset was produced by Rimell et al. (2016). It consists of a set of 'terms', each paired with up to ten 'properties'. Each property is a short phrase, consisting of a hypernym of the term, modified by a relative clause with a transitive verb. For example, a *telescope* is a *device that astronomers use*, and a *saw* is a *device that cuts wood*. The task is to identify the properties which apply to each term, construed as a retrieval task: given a single term, and the full set of properties, the aim is to rank the properties, with the correct properties at the top of the list. There are 65 terms and 518 properties in the development set, and 73 terms and 569 properties in the test set.

Since every property follows one of only two patterns (subject or object relative clause), this dataset lets us focus on evaluating semantics, rather than parsing. A model that uses relatedness can perform fairly well on this dataset – for example, *astronomer* can predict *telescope*, without knowing what relation there is between them. However, the dataset also includes lexical confounders – for example, a *document that has a balance* is a financial *account*, not the quality of *balance* (not falling over). The textual overlap means that a vector addition model is easily fooled by such confounders, and indeed the best three models that Rimell et al. tested all ranked this confounding property at the top.

We can represent each property as a situation of three pixies, as in Fig. 4b. Although they are syntactically noun phrases, the argument structure is the same as a transitive clause. For each property, we calculated the contextual mean field vectors, conditioned on all three predicates. To find the probability that the term's predicate is true, we apply the term's semantic function to the hypernym's mean-field vector. The difference between subject and object relative clauses is captured by whether this vector corresponds to the ARG1 pixie or the ARG2 pixie.

Results are given in the last two columns of Table 2. Our model performs worse than vector addition, perhaps as expected, since it does not capture relatedness, as explained in §5.1. However, the ensemble performs better than either model alone – just as argued in §5.2, this shows that our model has learnt different information from the vector space model. In particular, the ensemble improves performance on the lexical confounders. of which there are 27 in the test set. The vector space model places 17 of them in the top rank, and all of them in the top 4 ranks. The ensemble model, however, succeeds in moving 9 confounders out of the top 10 ranks. To our knowledge, this is the first system that manages to improve both overall performance as well as performance on the confounders.

6 Conclusion

We can interpret Functional Distributional Semantics as learning a probabilistic model structure, which gives us natural operations for composition, inference, and context dependence, with applications in both computational and formal semantics. Our experiments show that the additional structure of the model allows it to learn and use information that is not captured by vector space models.

Acknowledgements

We would like to thank Emily Bender, for helpful discussion and detailed feedback on an earlier draft. This work was supported by a Schiff Foundation studentship.

References

Agirre, E., E. Alfonseca, K. Hall, J. Kravalova, M. Paşca, and A. Soroa (2009). A study on similarity and relatedness using distributional and wordnet-based approaches. In *Proceedings of the 2009 Conference of the North American Chapter of the Association for Computational Linguistics*, pp. 19–27. Association for Computational Linguistics.

Allan, K. (2001). *Natural language semantics*. Blackwell Publishers.

Balkir, E., D. Kartsaklis, and M. Sadrzadeh (2016). Sentence entailment in compositional distributional semantics. In *Proceedings of the International Symposium on Artificial Intelligence and Mathematics (ISAIM)*.

Baroni, M., R. Bernardi, and R. Zamparelli (2014). Frege in space: A program of compositional distributional semantics. *Linguistic Issues in Language Technology 9*.

Barwise, J. and R. Cooper (1981). Generalized quantifiers and natural language. *Linguistics and Philosophy 4*(2), 159–219.

Barwise, J. and J. Perry (1983). *Situations and Attitudes*. MIT Press.

Beltagy, I., S. Roller, P. Cheng, K. Erk, and R. J. Mooney (2016). Representing meaning with a combination of logical and distributional models. *Computational Linguistics 42*(4), 763–808.

Bruni, E., N.-K. Tran, and M. Baroni (2014). Multimodal distributional semantics. *Journal of Artificial Intelligence Research (JAIR) 49*(2014), 1–47.

Callmeier, U. (2001). Efficient parsing with large-scale unification grammars. Master's thesis, Universität des Saarlandes, Saarbrücken, Germany.

Cann, R. (1993). *Formal semantics: an introduction*. Cambridge University Press.

Coecke, B., M. Sadrzadeh, and S. Clark (2010). Mathematical foundations for a compositional distributional model of meaning. *Linguistic Analysis 36*, 345–384.

Cooper, R. (2005). Austinian truth, attitudes and type theory. *Research on Language and Computation 3*(2-3), 333–362.

Cooper, R., S. Dobnik, S. Larsson, and S. Lappin (2015). Probabilistic type theory and natural language semantics. *LiLT (Linguistic Issues in Language Technology) 10*.

Copestake, A. (2009). Slacker semantics: Why superficiality, dependency and avoidance of commitment can be the right way to go. In *Proceedings of the 12th Conference of the European Chapter of the Association for Computational Linguistics*, pp. 1–9.

Copestake, A., G. Emerson, M. W. Goodman, M. Horvat, A. Kuhnle, and E. Muszyńska (2016). Resources for building applications with Dependency Minimal Recursion Semantics. In *Proceedings of the 10th International Conference on Language Resources and Evaluation (LREC)*. European Language Resources Association (ELRA).

Copestake, A., D. Flickinger, C. Pollard, and I. A. Sag (2005). Minimal Recursion Semantics: An introduction. *Research on Language and Computation 3*(2-3), 281–332.

Davidson, D. (1967). The logical form of action sentences. In N. Rescher (Ed.), *The Logic of Decision and Action*, Chapter 3, pp. 81–95. University of Pittsburgh Press.

Emerson, G. and A. Copestake (2016). Functional Distributional Semantics. In *Proceedings of the 1st Workshop on Representation Learning for NLP (RepL4NLP)*, pp. 40–52. Association for Computational Linguistics.

Emerson, G. and A. Copestake (2017). Variational inference for logical inference. In *Proceedings of the 2017 Workshop on Logic and Machine Learning for Natural Language (LaML)*.

Erk, K. (2016). What do you know about an alligator when you know the company it keeps? *Semantics and Pragmatics 9*, 17–1.

Erk, K. and S. Padó (2008). A structured vector space model for word meaning in context. In *Proceedings of the 13th Conference on Empirical Methods in Natural Language Processing*, pp. 897–906. Association for Computational Linguistics.

Erk, K. and S. Padó (2010). Exemplar-based models for word meaning in context. In *Proceedings of the 48th Annual Meeting of the Association for Computational Linguistics*, pp. 92–97.

Finkelstein, L., E. Gabrilovich, Y. Matias, E. Rivlin, Z. Solan, G. Wolfman, and E. Ruppin (2001). Placing search in context: The concept revisited. In *Proceedings of the 10th International Conference on the World Wide Web*, pp. 406–414. Association for Computing Machinery.

Flickinger, D. (2000). On building a more efficient grammar by exploiting types. *Natural Language Engineering 6*(1), 15–28.

Flickinger, D. (2011). Accuracy vs. robustness in grammar engineering. In E. M. Bender and J. E. Arnold (Eds.), *Language from a cognitive perspective: Grammar, usage, and processing*, pp. 31–50. CSLI Publications.

Flickinger, D., E. M. Bender, and S. Oepen (2014). Towards an encyclopedia of compositional semantics: Documenting the interface of the English Resource Grammar. In *Proceedings of the 9th International Conference on Language Resources and Evaluation (LREC)*, pp. 875–881. European Language Resources Association (ELRA).

Flickinger, D., S. Oepen, and G. Ytrestøl (2010). WikiWoods: Syntacto-semantic annotation for English Wikipedia. In *Proceedings of the 7th International Conference on Language Resources and Evaluation (LREC)*. European Language Resources Association (ELRA).

Garrette, D., K. Erk, and R. Mooney (2011). Integrating logical representations with probabilistic information using Markov logic. In *Proceedings of the 9th International Conference on Computational Semantics (IWCS)*, pp. 105–114. Association for Computational Linguistics.

Gerz, D., I. Vulić, F. Hill, R. Reichart, and A. Korhonen (2016). SimVerb-3500: A large-scale evaluation set of verb similarity. In *Proceedings of the 2016 Conference on Empirical Methods on Natural Language Processing*.

Ghahramani, Z. (2004). Unsupervised learning. In *Advanced Lectures on Machine Learning*. Springer.

Goodman, N. D. and D. Lassiter (2015). Probabilistic semantics and pragmatics: Uncertainty in language and thought. *The handbook of contemporary semantic theory, 2nd edition. Wiley-Blackwell.*

Grefenstette, E. (2013). Towards a formal distributional semantics: Simulating logical calculi with tensors. In *Proceedings of the 2nd Joint Conference on Lexical and Computational Semantics (*SEM)*, pp. 1–10.

Grefenstette, E., G. Dinu, Y.-Z. Zhang, M. Sadrzadeh, and M. Baroni (2013). Multi-step regression learning for compositional distributional semantics. In *Proceedings of the 10th International Conference on Computational Semantics (IWCS)*.

Grefenstette, E. and M. Sadrzadeh (2011). Experimental support for a categorical compositional distributional model of meaning. In *Proceedings of the 2011 Conference on Empirical Methods in Natural Language Processing*, pp. 1394–1404. Association for Computational Linguistics.

Herbelot, A. (2013). What is in a text, what isn't, and what this has to do with lexical semantics. In *Proceedings of the 10th International Conference on Computational Semantics (IWCS)*.

Herbelot, A. and E. M. Vecchi (2015). Building a shared world: mapping distributional to model-theoretic semantic spaces. In *Proceedings of the 2015 Conference on Empirical Methods on Natural Language Processing (EMNLP)*, pp. 22–32.

Herbelot, A. and E. M. Vecchi (2016). Many speakers, many worlds: Interannotator variations in the quantification of feature norms. *LiLT (Linguistic Issues in Language Technology) 13*.

Hill, F., R. Reichart, and A. Korhonen (2015). Simlex-999: Evaluating semantic models with (genuine) similarity estimation. *Computational Linguistics 41*(4), 665–695.

Kamp, H. and U. Reyle (2013). *From discourse to logic: Introduction to modeltheoretic semantics of natural language, formal logic and discourse representation theory*, Volume 42. Springer Science & Business Media.

Labov, W. (1973). The boundaries of words and their meanings. In C.-J. Bailey and R. W. Shuy (Eds.), *New Ways of Analyzing Variation in English*, pp. 340–371. Georgetown University Press.

Larsson, S. (2013). Formal semantics for perceptual classification. *Journal of Logic and Computation 25*(2), 335–369.

Levy, O., Y. Goldberg, and I. Dagan (2015). Improving distributional similarity with lessons learned from word embeddings. *Transactions of the Association for Computational Linguistics (TACL) 3*, 211–225.

Lewis, M. and M. Steedman (2013). Combining distributional and logical semantics. *Transactions of the Association for Computational Linguistics 1*, 179–192.

Link, G. (2002). The logical analysis of plurals and mass terms: A lattice-theoretical approach. In P. Portner and B. H. Partee (Eds.), *Formal semantics: The essential readings*, Chapter 4, pp. 127–146. Blackwell Publishers.

Lui, M., T. Baldwin, and D. McCarthy (2012). Unsupervised estimation of word usage similarity. In *Proceedings of the Australasian Language Technology Association Workshop*, pp. 33–41.

McMahan, B. and M. Stone (2015). A Bayesian model of grounded color semantics. *Transactions of the Association for Computational Linguistics 3*, 103–115.

Mikolov, T., K. Chen, G. Corrado, and J. Dean (2013). Efficient estimation of word representations in vector space. In *Proceedings of the 1st International Conference on Learning Representations*.

Mitchell, J. and M. Lapata (2010). Composition in distributional models of semantics. *Cognitive science 34*(8), 1388–1429.

Mooney, R. J. (2014). Semantic parsing: Past, present, and future. Invited Talk at the ACL 2014 Workshop on Semantic Parsing.

Oepen, S. and J. T. Lønning (2006). Discriminant-based MRS banking. In *Proceedings of the 5th International Conference on Language Resources and Evaluation (LREC)*, pp. 1250–1255. European Language Resources Association (ELRA).

Parsons, T. (1990). *Events in the Semantics of English: A Study in Subatomic Semantics*. Current Studies in Linguistics. MIT Press.

QasemiZadeh, B. and L. Kallmeyer (2016). Random positive-only projections: PPMI-enabled incremental semantic space construction. In *Proceedings of the 5th Joint Conference on Lexical and Computational Semantics (*SEM 2016)*, pp. 189–198.

Quine, W. V. O. (1960). *Word and Object*. MIT Press.

Rimell, L., J. Maillard, T. Polajnar, and S. Clark (2016). RELPRON: A relative clause evaluation dataset for compositional distributional semantics. *Computational Linguistics 42*(4), 661–701.

Schlangen, D., S. Zarrieß, and C. Kennington (2016). Resolving references to objects in photographs using the words-as-classifiers model. In *Proceedings of the 54th Annual Meeting of the Association for Computational Linguistics*, pp. 1213–1223.

Searle, J. R. (1980). The background of meaning. In J. R. Searle, F. Kiefer, and M. Bierwisch (Eds.), *Speech act theory and pragmatics*, pp. 221–232. Reidel.

Socher, R., C. D. Manning, and A. Y. Ng (2010). Learning continuous phrase representations and syntactic parsing with recursive neural networks. In *Proceedings of the NIPS-2010 Deep Learning and Unsupervised Feature Learning Workshop*, pp. 1–9.

Solberg, L. J. (2012). A corpus builder for Wikipedia. Master's thesis, University of Oslo.

Sutton, P. R. (2015). Towards a probabilistic semantics for vague adjectives. In *Bayesian Natural Language Semantics and Pragmatics*, pp. 221–246. Springer.

Sutton, P. R. (2017). Probabilistic approaches to vagueness and semantic competency. *Erkenntnis*, 1–30.

Swersky, K., I. Sutskever, D. Tarlow, R. S. Zemel, R. R. Salakhutdinov, and R. P. Adams (2012). Cardinality Restricted Boltzmann Machines. In *Advances in Neural Information Processing Systems 25 (NIPS)*, pp. 3293–3301.

Thater, S., H. Fürstenau, and M. Pinkal (2011). Word meaning in context: A simple and effective vector model. In *Proceedings of the 5th International Joint Conference on Natural Language Processing*, pp. 1134–1143.

Toutanova, K., C. D. Manning, and S. Oepen (2005). Stochastic HPSG parse selection using the Redwoods corpus. *Journal of Research on Language and Computation 3*(1), 83–105.

Turney, P. D. and P. Pantel (2010). From frequency to meaning: Vector space models of semantics. *Journal of Artificial Intelligence Research 37*, 141–188.

Van Benthem, J. (1984). Questions about quantifiers. *The Journal of Symbolic Logic 49*(2), 443–466.

Ytrestøl, G., , S. Oepen, and D. Flickinger (2009). Extracting and annotating Wikipedia sub-domains. In *Proceedings of the 7th International Workshop on Treebanks and Linguistic Theories*.

Zarrieß, S. and D. Schlangen (2017a). Is this a child, a girl or a car? Exploring the contribution of distributional similarity to learning referential word meanings. In *Proceedings of the 15th Annual Conference of the European Chapter of the Association for Computational Linguistics*, pp. 86–91.

Zarrieß, S. and D. Schlangen (2017b). Obtaining referential word meanings from visual and distributional information: Experiments on object naming. In *Proceedings of the 55th Annual Meeting of the Association for Computational Linguistics*.

Towards an Inferential Lexicon
of Event Selecting Predicates for French

Ingrid Falk and Fabienne Martin
Universität Stuttgart
`first.second@ling.uni-stuttgart.de`

Abstract

We present a manually constructed seed lexicon encoding the *inferential profiles* of French event selecting predicates across different uses. The inferential profile (Karttunen, 1971a) of a verb is designed to capture the inferences triggered by the use of this verb in context. It reflects the influence of the clause-embedding verb on the *factuality* of the event described by the embedded clause. The resource developed provides evidence for the following three hypotheses: (i) *French implicative verbs have an aspect dependent profile* (their inferential profile varies with outer aspect), while *factive verbs have an aspect independent profile* (they keep the same inferential profile with both imperfective and perfective aspect); (ii) *implicativity decreases with imperfective aspect*: the inferences triggered by French implicative verbs combined with perfective aspect are often weakened when the same verbs are combined with imperfective aspect; (iii) *implicativity decreases with an animate (deep) subject*: the inferences triggered by a verb which is implicative with an inanimate subject are weakened when the same verb is used with an animate subject. The resource additionally shows that verbs with different inferential profiles display clearly distinct sub-categorisation patterns. In particular, verbs that have both factive and implicative readings are shown to prefer infinitival clauses in their implicative reading, and tensed clauses in their factive reading.

1 Introduction

Texts not only describe events, but also encode information conveying whether the events described correspond to real situations in the world, or to uncertain, (im)probable or (im)possible situations. This level of information concerns *event factuality*. The factuality of an event expressed in a clause results from a complex interaction of many different linguistic aspects. It depends, among others, on the explicit polarity and modality markers, as well as on the syntactic and semantic properties of other expressions involved (among them verbal predicates). In this study, we are concerned with one of these parameters, namely the predicates selecting event-denoting arguments (e.g. *manage to P*), which contribute in a crucial way to *lexically* specify event factuality. Saurí and Pustejovsky (2012) call these verbs 'event selecting predicates', or ESPs. For example, in "Kim *failed to* reschedule the meeting", the ESP *fail to* turns the embedded reschedule-event into a counter-fact.

In previous work, Saurí and Pustejovsky (2012) encoded into a lexical resource the *inferential profile* of English ESPs, that is, their influence on the factuality of the embedded events, and showed that this resource could successfully be used to automatically assess the factuality of events in English newspaper texts.

Our long-term goal is the automatic detection of event factuality in French texts. Given that Saurí and Pustejovsky (2012)'s representation of event modality and their automatic factuality detection method is language independent, it can also be used for French event factuality detection. We plan to use this approach and describe here our efforts to bootstrap the required lexical ESP resource for French.

The lexical resource built by Saurí and Pustejovsky (2012) for English is not public, and therefore cannot be used as a starting point for a similar French lexicon. Additionally, Romance languages like French raise a further issue, for, as will be shown in Section 3, outer (grammatical) aspect interferes with the inferential profile of ESPs. To achieve our long-term goal, we therefore firstly need to build a lexical resource providing an inferential profile for French ESPs, starting from a seed set of suitable verbs. This resource should specify the inferences a predicate triggers about the event described in the embedded clause (henceforth *embedded event*). For example, it should specify that the perfective form of *échouer à P* 'fail to P' triggers the inference that the embedded event is a counter-fact under positive polarity, whereas the embedded event is entailed when the predicate is used under negative polarity.

One of the challenges raised by such a lexicon concerns the polysemy of ESPs and the fact that their inferential profile is likely to vary with each use and/or syntactic frame. For instance, *Peter didn't remember to P* and *Peter didn't remember **that** P* trigger very different inferences about the embedded event (a counter-fact in the former case, and a fact in the latter). In order to address this challenge, we collected each use for these verbs as they are delineated in available detailed syntactic-semantic valency lexicons for French, and calculated an inferential profile for each of them.[1] The additional advantage of this method is that we can make use of the detailed syntactic-semantic features encoded for each use in these lexicons. Also, it led to the interesting observation that verbs whose inferential profile varies with the reading selected (including its argument structure) are very pervasive among French ESPs, which confirms the need to distinguish between particular senses and/or syntactic frame combinations an ESP may instantiate. It also revealed interesting correlations between inferential profiles on one hand, and particular sets of syntactic/semantic properties on the other.

The paper is structured as follows. We first introduce in Section 2 the two strands of research on which our work is based. We then describe our data and experiments in Section 3 and discuss the resulting findings in Section 4.

2 Related Work

We rely on two important bodies of research. The first is centred around FactBank (Saurí and Puste-jovsky, 2009, 2012), a corpus of English newspaper texts annotated with information concerning the factuality of events. The second is a long standing research project on English predicates with sentential complements led at Stanford University (Karttunen, 1971b,a; Nairn et al., 2006; Karttunen, 2012; Karttunen et al., 2016). We briefly introduce these lines of research in the following subsections.

2.1 FactBank

The English FactBank is built on top of the English TimeBank corpus (Pustejovsky et al., 2005) by adding a level of semantic information. The factuality information encoded in TimeBank and relevant for our work is the ESPs projecting a factual value on the embedded event by means of subordination links (or SLINKs). In TimeBank, a total of 9 488 events across 208 newspaper texts have been manu-ally identified and annotated. FactBank assigns additional factuality information to these events. More specifically, it indicates for each event (i) whether its factuality is assessed by a source different from the text author (which is the case with e.g. *confirm P*, but not with *manage to P*) and (ii) the degree of factuality the new source and the text author attribute to the event (for instance, *Peter affirmed P* presents *P* as certain for Peter, but does not commit the text author to *P* in a specific way). Saurí and Pustejovsky (2009) distinguish six 'committed' factuality values (i.e. values to which a source is committed) and one 'uncommitted' value, which are shown in Table 1. Saurí and Pustejovsky (2012) present an algo-rithm, called *DeFacto*, which assigns to each TimeBank event a factuality profile consisting of (i) its factuality value, (ii) the source(s) assigning the factuality value to that event and (iii) the time at which the factuality value assignment takes place. The algorithm assumes that events and relevant sources are already identified and computes the factuality profile of events by modelling the effect of factuality relations across levels of syntactic embedding. It crucially relies on three lexical resources which the authors developed manually for English. The first is a list of negation particles (adverbs, determiners

---

[1]In this paper, we call *readings* of a verb the different verb-valence pairs *and/or* different senses delineated for a same lemma in these lexicons.

Contextual factuality												
	CT			PR			PS			U		
polarity	$+$	$-$	u	$+$	$-$	u	$+$	$-$	u	$+$	$-$	u
manage	CT+	CT−	CTu	PR+	PR−	PRu	PS+	PS−	PSu	Uu	Uu	Uu
fail	CT−	CT+	CTu	PR−	PR+	PRu	PS−	PS+	PSu	Uu	Uu	Uu

Table 1: Sample lexical entries for NSIPs. CT, PR and PS signify certain, probable and possible respectively, U (and/or u) unspecified (unknown or uncommitted)

	Polarity of ESP		Signatures		Sample
	$+$	$-$			predicate
2-way	$+$	$-$	$++\|--$	$1\|-1$	*manage to*
implicatives	$-$	$+$	$+-\|-+$	$-1\|1$	*fail to*
1-way	$+$	n	$++\|-n$	$1\|n$	*force to*
+implicatives	$-$	n	$+-\|-n$	$-1\|n$	*refuse to*
1-way	n	$-$	$+n\|--$	$n\|-1$	*attempt to*
-implicatives	n	$+$	$+n\|-+$	$n\|1$	*hesitate to*
factives	$+$	$+$	$++\|-+$	$1\|1$	*forget that*
counter-factives	$-$	$-$	$+-\|--$	$-1\|-1$	*pretend that*
Neutral	n	n	$+n\|-n$	$n\|n$	*want to*

Table 2: Semantic classification of clause-embedding verbs wrt. the effect of the polarity of the main clause (ESP, head row) on the factuality of the embedded clause (embedded event, subsequent rows). n stands for none.

and pronouns) which determine the *polarity* of the context while the second resource aims to capture the influence of epistemic *modality* on the event. The third resource is the most complex one and accounts for the influence on the event factuality value in cases where the event is embedded by an ESP. Saurí and Pustejovsky distinguish two kinds of ESPs: *Source Introducing Predicates (SIPs)* introduce a new source in discourse (e.g. *suspect/affirm*); *Non Source Introducing Predicates (NSIPs)* do not (e.g. *manage/fail*). As part of their lexical semantics, SIPs determine (i) the factuality value the new source (the 'cogniser') assigns to the event described by the embedded clause, and (ii) the factuality value assigned by the text author (i.e. the 'anchor') to the same event. NSIPs, on the other hand, determine event factuality wrt. a unique source, the anchor. In addition, the assessment of event factuality wrt. the relevant source(s) varies with the polarity and modality present in the context of the ESP. Table 1 illustrates the lexicon layout through sample entries for the NSIPs *manage* and *fail*.[2] Given the lexical entry for *fail to* shown in Table 1, the factuality of the *reschedule$_e$* event in "Kim *failed to* reschedule$_e$ the meeting" can be derived as follows. Since in the embedded clause, there are no polarity or modality particles which could influence its factuality, we assume that the contextual factuality of the embedded clause is CT+. The corresponding cell in the *fail to* row in Table 1 is CT−, i.e. the event is counter-factual.

2.2 The lexicon resource from the *Language and Natural Reasoning* group (Stanford)

Another strand of research is represented by Nairn et al. (2006). Those authors developed a semantic classification of English event selecting predicates, according to their effect on the factuality of their embedded clauses when used in positive or negative polarity. All those verbs are factive or implicative verbs, and therefore non source introducing predicates.[3] In many cases, a single lemma is assigned different entries varying with the syntactic type of the embedded clause (e.g. *remember that/remember to* are assigned two different entries). This classification is shown in Table 2. We illustrate how the table works through concrete examples.

In example (1), the ESP *fail to* has positive polarity. We obtain the factuality of the embedded event (*reschedule*) by retrieving from the polarity $+$ column in Table 2 the polarity value in the *fail to* row, which is '−', i.e. the meeting is not rescheduled (has factuality CT−). For (2), the factuality

---

[2]The lexicon layout for SIPs, less relevant for our study, is very similar except that an SIP lexicon entry must also provide factuality values for the cogniser source in addition to the anchor.

[3]Factives are predicates that trigger the same entailment under both positive and negative polarity. Implicatives are non-factive predicates that trigger an entailment under at least one polarity.

must be retrieved from the polarity − column resulting in '+', i.e. a factuality of CT+ (the meeting is rescheduled).

(1)   Kim *failed to* <u>reschedule</u> the meeting.

(2)   Kim did not *fail to* <u>reschedule</u> the meeting.

The effect of a predicate on the factuality of its embedded clause is represented more concisely through a "signature". For instance, the signature of factive verbs as *forget that* is '+ + | − +' and even more concisely '1|1' (Read: 'if positive polarity, event happens; if negative polarity, event happens').

Nairn et al. (2006) compiled a list of roughly 250 English verbs found to carry some kind of implication: a positive or negative entailment, a factive or a counter-factive presupposition[4]. The resource makes a difference between entailments (marked by '+' or '−'), and strong inferences (marked by '+*' or '−*'). More recently, Karttunen et al. (2016) refined the annotation further by using *probabilistic* signatures, allowing to reflect the strength of the inference in a more fine-grained way. Thus, for example, the predicate *be able* is assigned the signature $0.9| − 1$, in order to capture the fact that under positive polarity, it triggers a strong (but defeasible) inference rather than an entailment.[5] In Saurí and Pustejovsky's terms, probabilistic signatures convey less than certain factuality values.[6]

The signatures assigned in the lexical resource from the Stanford group are calculated for the verb combined with the simple past. This choice seems implicitly justified by the fact that for many ESPs, no alternative past tense form is available. For instance, it has been observed for implicative verbs that their progressive form is odd, see e.g. *?John was managing to eat the pizza* (cf. Bhatt, 1999). Also, many factive verbs are stative, and therefore equally odd with the progressive (*John was knowing the answer*).

For our experiments, we decided to start with the French counterparts of the English verbs in this resource, assuming that the inferential profile may be roughly extensible to French verbs under their perfective form. We then looked at the sentences in the French TimeBank using these French ESPs. We first briefly introduce the French TimeBank before describing our data, experiments and findings.

2.3   The French TimeBank

The French TimeBank (Bittar, 2010; Bittar et al., 2011) is built on the same principles as the English TimeBank, but introduces additional markup language to deal with linguistic phenomena not yet covered and specific to French. Most relevant to this study is the fact that most French ESPs can be fully inflected and fall within the scope of aspectual operators — most French modal auxiliaries, but also most implicative and factive verbs are fully acceptable in their perfective and imperfective forms. For instance, the French counterpart of *manage to*, namely *réussir à*, accepts both the perfective and the imperfective (see e.g. the example (4) below). Probably for this reason, all these verbs are also marked up as events in the French TimeBank; in particular, modal verbs are marked up as events of the 'modal' subclass (see Bittar et al. (2011), while in the English TimeBank, modal predicates are not marked up as events. Lastly, the TimeML schema was adapted to represent the grammatical tense/aspect system of French, and to account e.g. for the *imparfait* (the imperfective aspectual morphology), not grammaticalised in English. Since TimeBanks mark up events and (temporal) relations between them, the French TimeBank offers a sample of ESPs used in French newspaper texts, together with some typical embedded events.

Note that the French TimeBank as well as FactBank not only mark up events realised by VPs, but also events realised by NPs. For our experiments, we also annotated the way the verbs under investigation influence the factuality of events described by one of their event-denoting NP arguments. For instance, *Cela a garanti la survie des passagers* 'this ensured the survival of the passengers' and *Cela a garanti que les passagers survivent* 'This ensured that the passengers survived' both entail that the passengers survived, and the annotation aims to capture parallelisms of this type.

---

[4]These resources are available at `https://web.stanford.edu/group/csli_lnr/Lexical_Resources/`.

[5]Probabilistic signatures provided in Karttunen et al. (2016) are rough counts based on the inspection of a lot of examples found on the Internet and the COCA corpus (L. Karttunen, p.c.).

[6]However, while in Saurí and Pustejovsky's annotation, uncertainty is expressed through the two discrete values (PR and PS), probabilistic signatures represent uncertainty on a continuous scale between 0 and 1.

3 Towards an ESP lexicon

We started with the observation that the inferential classification developed by Nairn et al. (2006) and described in Section 2.2 can be used to bootstrap an English ESP lexicon. Based on the signature of a predicate and its polarity in a given sentence, we can determine the factuality of the embedded event in that sentence. The classification in Table 2 can be straightforwardly "plugged" into the ESP lexical resources illustrated in Table 1: For a given ESP for which a lexical entry has to be set up (*eg. fail to*), the factuality value conveyed on the embedded event can be retrieved from Table 2 whenever the corresponding table entry is not n (neutral). In case it is, this shows that the ESP has no effect on the factuality of the embedded event; its polarity value therefore remains unspecified.

3.1 Our Data

To build our seed lexicon, we started from the ESPs marked up in the French TimeBank. From these predicates, we selected those 49 verbs which occurred as translations of the English ESPs derived from the inferential classification of Nairn et al. (2006). This way, we could use the inferential information from the English classification, and compare it to the French counterparts of these English ESPs. We assigned inferential signatures to each reading of these French ESPs, and this with two research questions in mind:

    i. Does the inferential behaviour (the signature) vary with the animacy of the external argument and/or with outer aspect?

    ii. Can we differentiate the main sub-types of inferential signatures (factive, implicative, etc.) by specific subsets of semantic/syntactic properties?

Lexical entries. For the selected 49 verb types we extracted all readings from two French lexicons: "Les Verbes Français", henceforth LVF (François et al., 2007), and an electronic version of the Lexicon-Grammar tables, henceforth LGLEX (Tolone, 2011; Constant and Tolone, 2010). We chose these resources because they provide detailed morpho-syntactic and semantic descriptions for each reading of a verb rather than giving an (ambiguous) verb type based description. The LVF is based on a traditional French lexicon where the different lexical entries (called here readings, see fn 1) for a verb type have been assigned additional detailed and systematic morpho-syntactic, semantic and valency information. In LGLEX, each verb type is associated with one or more tables which represent its meaning and behaviour with respect to valency. We consider each such lemma-table association to represent a particular reading of the verb. For our seed lexicon, we extracted lexical entries from the LVF and lemma-table pairs from the LGLEX. We merged duplicate entries from the two lexicons. The remaining entries were aligned such that each entry in our lexicon represents a different reading.

Annotation. We obtained ≈ 930 readings, which we manually filtered, keeping only the ESP readings. The remaining ≈ 170 readings were manually assigned probabilistic signatures (gathered in a file available on line) by an expert (the second author of this paper).[7] The annotation was done on the basis of the sentences by which the LVF exemplifies each delineated use of a verb, and on the inspection of natural occurrences of the relevant form in the internet and corpora (such as Frantext).[8] When the exemplifying sentence contains elements that can affect the event factuality independently from the ESP itself (modal verbs, NPs biased towards a generic interpretation, etc.), these elements were abstracted away for the annotation. We chose probabilistic signatures, since we aimed to distinguish between entailments, graded inferences (strong vs. weak) and the absence of inference (neutral). We distinguished 4 intermediate positive values, namely 0.9 (very likely/almost certain), 0.8 (likely), 0.7 (very possible/almost likely) and 0.6 (quite possible), and 4 intermediate negative values (-0.9 for very unlikely, etc.). However, for the experiments, we only considered 0.9 to indicate a 'strong inference', and the values 0.6 to 0.8 were

---

[7] At `https://docs.google.com/spreadsheets/d/1sgDxfYSh91N0zI2hwfq2bG6TdA7EvusaH15irmWC2QE/edit?usp=sharing`

[8] The exemplifying sentences from the LVF can also be found online at `http://rali.iro.umontreal.ca/rali/?q=en/node/1238`

Pierre/cela a obligé Marie à partir.		
'Peter/something force-PAST-PFV.3SG Mary to go.'		
PFV+anim	PFV-anim	IMP
$0.9\|n$	$1\|n$	$n\|n$

Table 3: Assigned signatures for reading *obliger 02* ('force/oblige').

kept undistinguished from the neutral case (absence of inference).[9]

For Romance languages like French, it is known that inferential profiles vary with outer aspect (Hacquard, 2006). Also, cross-linguistic data tend to suggest that the inferential profile also varies with the animacy of the (deep) subject (Martin and Schäfer, 2012).[10] We therefore distinguished three cases: (i) perfective aspect, animate subject ; (ii) perfective aspect, inanimate subject; (iii) imperfective aspect. Distinguishing again between two types of subject for the imperfective was not justified, since most readings (around 80%) were only compatible with a single type of subject to begin with (either animate, or inanimate, but not both).[11] This reflects the fact that the LVF and the LGLEX often differentiate readings according to the (non)-animacy of the subject. This means that in practice, we typically assigned two signatures instead of three for each reading, namely one for the perfective, either with an animate subject, or with an inanimate one, and one for the imperfective. The third possible case was typically not applicable. So for instance, when a reading compulsorily selects for an animate subject, we assigned one signature for the 'animate perfective' context, and assigned none for the 'inanimate perfective' context (introducing the value NA, for 'not applicable'). In this case, if a signature is assigned for the 'imperfective' context, we know that this imperfective signature is calculated with an animate subject, too.

In the rare case where both types of subjects were possible for a single reading (16% of all readings), we tested the imperfective verb with the subject type that triggers the strongest entailment with the perfective, namely the inanimate subject. Typically, the effect of the subject type on the inference is neutralised with the imperfective.[12]

Table 3 shows the assigned signatures for the reading *02* of the verb *obliger* ('oblige, force') (as delineated in the LVF). We see that, under perfective aspect and with an animate subject, this predicate triggers, under positive polarity, a strong albeit defeasible inference (there is a high probability that the embedded event is a fact). Under negative polarity, no inference is triggered. Under perfective aspect with an inanimate subject, *obliger 02* entails the embedded event under positive polarity, and triggers no inference under negative polarity. Finally, when used with imperfective aspect, *obliger 02* is inferentially neutral, i.e. it triggers no inference about the embedded event (both with animate and inanimate subjects).

Figure 1 gives an overview of the inferences triggered by these 170 readings according to the assigned signatures in the three contexts delineated (PFV+anim: perfective aspect with animate subject; IMP: imperfective aspect with any kind of subject; PFV-anim: perfective aspect with inanimate subject). The figure shows a coloured box for each assigned signature. The columns in the matrix represent the annotated readings (in alphabetic order)[13] and the rows correspond to the aspectual and animacy values used when testing the triggered inferences, namely PFV+anim, IMP and PFV-anim. A white box indicates that the test was not applicable (e.g., the verb is inherently agentive under the relevant reading and

---

[9]In the future, we plan to develop guidelines and explore automatic methods that could assist and support the manual annotations. However, our manual annotations already sufficed to test interesting hypotheses about the impact of outer aspect, animacy and syntax on the inferential profile of ESPs, as we will see in the next section.

[10]The sentences tested were mostly active, but some of them were passive. It is the animacy of the external argument (deep subject) that has been shown to matter for the inferential profile of ESPs.

[11]131 out of 168 annotated readings were acceptable with either an animate or an inanimate subject (but not both) in the perfective. Only 27 (16%) of these 168 readings which were assigned a signature with the imperfective were acceptable with both an animate and an inanimate subject.

[12]See the examples (7)-(9) below for an illustration.

[13]In the readings labelled with a simple number (e.g. *aider 01*), the number is the one given in the LVF lexicon, accessible online at http://rali.iro.umontreal.ca/rali/?q=en/node/1238. When the readings are labelled as in *lemma_V_T_R*, they are extracted from the Lexicon-Grammar tables. *T* designates the table name and *R* the row the verb occurred in.

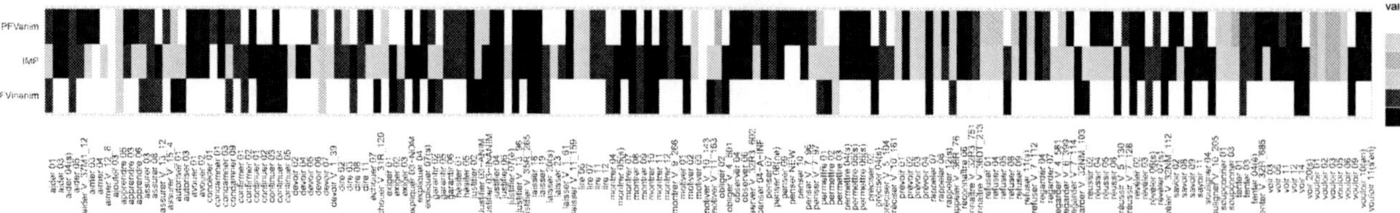

Figure 1: Inferences triggered by French readings when used with perfective aspect and animate or inanimate subject or with imperfective aspect.

col	description	sample sign.	#sign.	inferential classes
5	max inference	$1\|1, 1\| - 1$	177	(counter-)factives, 2-way implicatives
4	max under 1 polarity	$1\|n, 0.9\| - 1$	77	1-way implicatives
3	strong, not max, under 2 polarities	$0.9\| - 0.9$	9	2-way quasi implicatives
2	strong, not max, under 1 polarity	$0.9\|n, n\| - 0.9$	8	1-way quasi implicatives
1	neutral, no inference	$n\|n$	78	neutral
0	not applicable or not grammatical	NA or UNGR	161	

Table 4: Overview of mappings between colours, strength of inference, signature and inferential classes.

is therefore not annotated with an inanimate subject), or returns agrammaticality (e.g., the verbal reading combined with perfective aspect generates an ungrammatical sentence). As just mentioned above, a very large number of readings have either a signature for the PFV+anim context, or one for the PFV-anim one, but not for both. In the IMP contexts, almost all readings were assigned a signature, since we did not differentiate between subject types in this context. Interestingly, more signatures are assigned in the PFV+anim context than in the PFV-anim context, which suggests that a substantial number of ESPs tend to be inherently agentive.

The colours reflect the "strength" of the triggered inference. The strongest inference (value 5) is triggered whenever the signature shows a maximal (deterministic) inference (1 or -1) under both polarities (i.e. signatures of the type $x\|y$ with $|x| = |y| = 1$). These correspond to the classes of factives, counter-factives and 2-way implicatives displayed in Table 2. Weaker inferences (value 4) are reflected by signatures where there is a maximal inference (1 or -1) under at least one polarity (signatures $x\|y$ where $|x| = 1$ or $|y| = 1$, 1-way implicatives in Table 2). The next value (3) on the inference scale represent ('2-way quasi-implicative') signatures where there is a strong, albeit not maximal and thus defeasible, inference under both polarities ($|x| = |y| = 0.9$[14]). Even weaker inferences (value 2, '1-way quasi-implicative') are those where at least under one polarity the reading is associated with a strong inference ($|x| = 0.9$ or $|y| = 0.9$). Finally, the absence of inference (or neutral inference, value 1) is represented by n. Table 4 sums up the mapping between colours, strength of inference, signatures and inferential classes. As shown by the general colour pattern, inferences under perfective aspect tend to be stronger than those under imperfective (and this even for many implicative verbs), an observation confirmed by a closer look at the data, as we will see in Section 4.

4 Results and discussion

We first compared the signatures of the French predicates with their rough English counterparts classified by Nairn et al. (2006). We found that in many cases, the signatures of the English predicates matched those of their French counterparts under their perfective form. For example, the implicative signature '$1\| - 1$' of *manage to* is inherited by its translation *réussir à* combined with a past perfective

---

[14]We only distinguish between maximal, strong and neutral inferences, with signature values $|x| = 1$, $|x| = 0.9$ and $x = 0$ respectively. As mentioned before, the annotation has been performed also using intermediate values, which we aim to use in later work.

	with IMP PFV signature	IMP sign≠PFV sign
Factives under PFV	54	2 (4%)
Implic. under PFV	77	36 (48%)

Table 5: Influence of outer aspect on factivity.

morphology.[15] Second, we aimed to test three hypotheses about the semantic and syntactic properties that potentially contribute to drive the inferential profile of the readings:

1. *implicative verbs have an aspect dependent profile* (their inferential profile varies with outer aspect); *factive verbs have an aspect independent profile* (they keep the same inferential profile with both imperfective and perfective aspect);
2. *implicativity decreases with imperfective aspect*, i.e., the inferences triggered by a verb which is implicative combined with perfective aspect are weakened when the same verb combines with imperfective aspect;
3. *implicativity decreases with an animate subject*, i.e., the inferences triggered by a verb which is implicative with an inanimate subject are weakened when the same verb is used with an animate subject.

Based on counts, we could find evidence in our data supporting the three hypotheses.

Implicatives, but not factives, have an aspect dependent profile. Factive predicates are predicates that trigger the same entailment under both positive and negative polarity, i.e. these predicates have either signature $1|1$ or $-1|-1$. Implicatives are non-factive predicates that trigger an entailment under at least one polarity (among the potential implicative signatures, we find e.g. $1|-1$, $1|n$, $-0.7|-1$). Table 5 shows that of the 54 readings that were factive with perfective aspect, only 2 had a different signature with imperfective aspect. On the other hand, for the readings that were implicative with the perfective, almost half of them (36 out of 77 or 48%) had a different signature with the imperfective aspect (are only considered here readings for which a signature could be assigned with both perfective and imperfective aspect). In other words, outer aspect has virtually *no* influence on factivity. This is reflected in Fig. 1 by the fact that the cells with the darkest colour in the PFV+anim row keep this darkest colour in the IMP row. By contrast, the inferential profile of implicative verbs tends to change with aspect, supporting our hypothesis 1.

Implicativity decreases with imperfective aspect. For French, it is standardly assumed that implicative verbs keep their entailment with the perfective (see e.g. Hacquard 2006). Our data challenge this assumption, and support the alternative hypothesis that implicativity tends to decrease with imperfective aspect. This hypothesis is illustrated by the data in examples 3 and 4, with the verb *réussir* 'manage to', that has an implicative profile when combined with perfective aspect.[16] Recall that implicatives trigger a maximal inference under at least one polarity, i.e. at least under one polarity the signature is $max = 1$ or $max = -1$.[17]

(3)   *A ce moment-là, elle **a réussi** à s'enfuir. #Et pourtant, elle*
      at that moment she manage-**PST-PFV**.3SG to escape and nevertheless she
      ne s'est pas enfuie du tout.
      NEG escape-**PST-PFV**.3SG at all
      'At that moment, she managed to escape. And nevertheless, she didn't escape at all.'

(4)   *A ce moment-là, elle **réussissait** (encore) à s'enfuir. OK Et pourtant,*
      at that moment she manage-**IMP**.3SG (still) to escape and nevertheless,
      elle ne s'est pas enfuie du tout/ elle n'essayait même pas de le
      she NEG escape-**PST-PFV**.3SG at all she NEG try-**PST-IMP**.3SG even NEG to it

---

[15]Our translation approach raised additional issues detailed in Falk and Martin (2017).

[16]The examples are made up for illustration purposes. This use of *réussir* corresponds to the readings *05* and *06* in the LVF.

[17]Therefore, an implicative signature $max|x$ or $x|max$ describes a stronger inference than signatures $a|x$ or $x|a$ with $|a| < 1$ or $a = n$.

faire!
do

'At that moment, she 'was (still) managing' to escape. And nevertheless, she didn't escape at all/
she wasn't even trying to do so.'

In this example, the same predicate is used in two contexts that mainly differ by the aspect morphology
on the verb: perfective in (3) and imperfective in (4). However, in (3), *réussir* triggers an entailment,
whereas the inference triggered in (4) is defeasible (both through a perfective and an imperfective de-
nial).[18]

The sceptical reader could argue that in (4), the imperfective sentence is the consequent of an implicit
conditional (*A ce moment-là, il réussissait à s'enfuir s'il le voulait* 'At that moment, he manage-**PST-
IMP**.3SG to flee if he want-**PST-IMP**.3SG to'). The absence of entailment would then reflect the fact that
this implicit conditional is counter-factual, rather than the influence of aspect on the inferential profile
of *réussir*.[19] However, this objection does not apply to the example (6) below, where a conditional
antecedent cannot be felicitously added. Additionally, (6) contains a past progressive, which, contrary to
the imperfective, is not a necessary ingredient of counter-factuality (Iatridou, 2000, 257). The sentence
in (6) therefore contains a run-of-the-mill imperfective, and, again, the actuality entailment triggered
with the perfective in (5) is lost.

(5)   *Ana   a réussi   à   gagner   la   partie #quand   tout à coup,   son   rival*
      Ana   manage-**PST-PFV**.3SG to   win   the   game   when   all of a sudden   her   opponent
      l'a faite   échec   et   mat.
      her make**PST-PFV**.3SG chess   and   mat
      'Ana managed to win the game when all of a sudden, her opponent gave her checkmate.'

(6)   *Ana   était en train de réussir   à   gagner   la   partie quand   tout à coup,   son   rival*
      Ana   manage-**PST-PROG**.3SG to   win   the   game   when   all of a sudden   her   opponent
      l'a faite   échec   et   mat.
      her make-**PST-PFV**.3SG chess   and   mat
      'Ana 'was managing' to win the game when all of a sudden, her opponent checkmated her.'

As shown in Table 6, we found strong support in our data for the hypothesis that the inferential behaviour
of *réussir* follows a more general pattern. That is, in general, the inferences characteristic of implicative
readings are in fact conditional on the presence of perfective aspect in languages like French, and tend to
be weakened or even vanish with imperfective aspect.[20] In almost all cases (34 out of 36) where a reading
was implicative with a perfective and triggered a different inference with the imperfective, the inference
triggered with the imperfective was weaker than the one triggered with the perfective. Table 7 shows
some more examples (from the LVF) where the inferential profile varies with the aspect used. Also, the
examples below for the verb *refuser* 'to refuse' illustrate the general fact that even when the perfective

---

[18]Hacquard (2006, 71) claims that the imperfective form of *réussir* is implicative on the basis of the oddity of sentences
like *Darcy réussissait à soulever cette table, #mais il ne la soulevait pas.* ('Darcy manage-**PST-IMP**.3SG to lift this table, but
wasn't lifting it'). We agree with Hacquard's judgment, but we think that the problem partly comes from the absence of any
adverbial providing a reference time combined with the presence of the imperfective in the second clause. A sentence like *A
ce moment-là, Darcy réussissait clairement à soulever cette table. Et pourtant, il n'essayait même pas de la soulever* ('At that
moment, Darcy clearly manage-**PST-IMP**.3SG to lift to lift this table. And nevertheless, he wasn't even trying to do so.') is
completely acceptable.

[19]In French, counter-factual conditionals typically have the *conditionnel* in the consequent (and the *imparfait* in the antecedent). However, it is also possible to have an imparfait in both the antecedent and consequent, as also the case in Italian, cf.
Ippolito (2003).

[20]Among the 41 readings that remain implicative with imperfective aspect, most do not express what we call below the
actualisation of a causal factor for the truth of *p*, and are therefore not expected to lose their entailment with the imperfective.
This is for instance the case of *montrer 04, 09, 11, 12, V-9-266* 'show', *penser 07, 09, 09* 'think', *vouloir 09* 'want'. Also, quite
a few of these readings are reflexive (7), a factor that seems to interfere with the inferential profile, too.

IMP⤳weaker inference	IMP⤳stronger inference	no change
44.2% (34)	2.6% (2)	53.2% (41)

Table 6: Inferential behaviour of the 77 readings which are implicative with a perfective. For 34 of them (44.2%), the inference triggered with perfective aspect is stronger than with imperfective aspect.

reading	translation	ASPECT USED	
		PFV	IMP
assurer 03 (la victoire)	'ensure (the victory)'	$1|n$	$n|n$
échouer 07 (à persuader x)'	'fail (to persuade x)'	$-1|1$	$n|n$
motiver 03 (x à venir)	'motivate (x to come)'	$0.7|{-0.7}$	$n|n$
penser 04 (à divorcer)	'think (about divorcing)'	$-0.7|{-1}$	$n|n$

Table 7: Examples of verbs whose inferential profile varies with the outer aspect used.

verb triggers an entailment with an inanimate subject *only*, this entailment is lost in the IMP even when combined with such an inanimate subject.[21]

(7) *Pierre a refusé/refusait   que j'ouvre le tiroir, OK mais je*
    Pierre refuse-**PST-PFV/PST-IMP**.3SG that I open the drawer   but   I
    l'ai ouvert   quand même.
    it open-**PST-PFV**.1SG   nevertheless
    'Pierre refused to let me open the drawer, but I opened it nevertheless.'

(8) *Le tiroir   a refusé   de s'ouvrir,   #mais finalement, il*
    the drawer refuse-**PST-PFV**.3SG to REFL open but   at the end it
    s'est ouvert   quand même.
    REFL open-**PST-PFV**.3SG nevertheless
    'The drawer refused to open, but at the end, it opened nevertheless.'

(9) *Le tiroir   refusait   de s'ouvrir,   OK mais finalement, il*
    the drawer refuse-**PST-IMP**.3SG to REFL open   but at the end it
    s'est ouvert   quand même/ en forçant un peu Ana l'ouvrait
    REFL open-**PST-PFV**.3SG nevertheless in forcing a   bit Ana it open-**PST-IMP**.3SG
    sans   problème.
    without problem
    'The drawer 'was refusing' to open, but at the end, it opened nevertheless/by forcing a bit Ana was opening it without difficulty.'

Why do implicative verbs (contrary to factive verbs) lose their entailment when combined with IMP? Recent analyses of implicative verbs by Baglini and Francez (2016) and Nadathur (2016) can help to explain this observation. According to Baglini & Francez' analysis, a *manage p* statement *presupposes* familiarity with a causally necessary but insufficient condition A for the truth of p, and *asserts* that A actually caused the truth of p. Nadathur extends a modified version of this analysis to the whole class of implicative verbs. The important point for us is that under these analyses, implicative verbs have an at-issue component (and on this point, they drastically differ from the traditional analysis held e.g. by Karttunen (1971a), according to which implicative verbs like *manage to P* make no truth-conditional contribution beyond that of their embedded clause). Under these new analyses, implicative verbs assert what we propose to call an 'actualisation event', namely the obtaining/actualisation of the causal factor A for the truth of p. Given the 'imperfective paradox' (Dowty, 1977), the imperfective form of such verbs unsurprisingly *suspends* the actualisation event – similarly to what happens with the imperfective form

---

[21]The use of *refuser* with animate subject illustrated in (4) corresponds to the LVF reading *09*, and its use with inanimate subject illustrated in (8) corresponds to the LVF reading *08*.

of overtly causative verbs (e.g. *Trump was causing a new catastrophe when Pence stopped him* does not entail the occurrence of a new catastrophe).

On the other hand, factive verbs like *savoir que p* 'know that *p*' do not assert the obtaining of a causal factor for the truth of *p*, but rather a mental state having *p* as its object. We therefore do not expect aspect to interfere with their inferential profile.

Implicativity decreases with an animate subject. We showed through the example in Table 3 (*Pierre/-cela a obligé Marie à partir*/'Peter/something force-PFV-3SG Mary to go') that the inference triggered by the perfective form of *obliger 02* ('oblige/force') when used with an animate subject (signature $0.9|n$) is weaker than with an inanimate subject (signature $1|n$). This example also instantiates a more general pattern observed in our data. Firstly, if only coloured boxes in Fig. 1 are considered, the 'PFV-anim' row contains altogether darker colours (representing stronger inferences) than the 'PFV+anim'. This is reflected in the respective average inference value for these two contexts: 4,53 for PFV-anim v. 3,92 for PFV+anim. Secondly, the same pattern is confirmed when we look at particular verbs under their different readings. Among the 49 verbs in our inferential lexicon, 13 received a signature in both PFV+anim and PFV-anim contexts. For 8 of these 13 verbs, the readings with inanimate subjects were found to trigger stronger inferences than those with an animate subject.

Further evidence supporting this hypothesis is related to source introducing predicates (SIPs, defined in Section 2.1). SIPs typically trigger no or only weak inferences on the (non-)occurrence of the embedded event in the world of evaluation (for instance, *Peter believed that P* does not say much about whether *P* is a fact in the actual world — it mainly indicates that Peter believes *P* to be sure). Of the 13 predicates with SIP readings, 10 also had readings with an inanimate subject. Unsurprisingly, all of these 10 inanimate readings were not SIP readings anymore (since the inanimate subject cannot be a cogniser), but more interestingly, they have then an implicative or quasi-implicative reading. For example, in *Pierre a garanti le succès de l'affaire* 'Peter promised success for the business', *garantir 06* (with animate subject) introduces a new source and therefore tells us nothing about the embedded event in the actual world. On the other hand, in *Cela a garanti notre survie* 'This ensured our survival', *garantir 05* (with inanimate subject) is *not* an SIP reading, and is implicative.[22]

Differently from implicative verbs that often can take either an animate or inanimate subject, factive predicates seem to require an animate subject much more forcefully. Out of the 42 readings with a factive signature with an animate subject, only 9 readings are acceptable with an inanimate subject. This restriction imposed on the animacy of the subject by factive verbs probably simply reflects the fact that these predicates are inherently attitude verbs.

Syntactic type of embedded clauses. For English, it has often been pointed out that factives and implicatives show different sub-categorisation patterns. White (2014) mentions that for verbs that have both factive and implicative readings, the factive reading is often associated with a tensed (*that-*)clause (as e.g. *remember that*) whereas the implicative reading is associated with an infinitival clause (as e.g. *remember to*). For implicative verbs, it has often been observed (by e.g. Landau, 2001) that they typically do not take finite (*that-*) clauses (cf. e.g. **manage/dare that*), but often select infinitival (*to-*) clauses. However, to our knowledge, there is no study confirming these correlations by empirical evidence.

Given that similar correlations are expected to hold for French, we therefore looked at the type of embedded clauses associated with the readings in our French inferential lexicon. More specifically, we checked, for each reading, whether it can sub-categorise the infinitival and tensed clauses listed in Table 8. We firstly extracted this information from our two French valency lexicons. However, since the data collected this way was not completely reliable, we manually corrected the classification thus obtained.

In our data, 20 verbs had both factive (41) and implicative (45) readings. Figure 2 shows that there are very clear differences in the types of embedded clauses accepted by implicative vs. factive readings of these 'inferentially polysemous verbs': implicative readings tend to be associated with infinitival clauses and to reject tensed clauses, while factive readings show the inverse pattern.

---

[22]Examples taken from the LVF.

		example	**translation**
	aInf	Il *autorise* Pierre **à sortir**.	'He allows Pierre to go out.'
infinitival	**deInf**	Le tiroir *refuse* **de s'ouvrir**.	'The drawer refuses to open.'
	inf	Il *regarde* la pluie **tomber**.	'He watches the rain fall.'
finite	**que**	Il *pense* **que Pierre est sincère**.	'He thinks Peter is sincere.'

Table 8: Types of infinitival and finite embedded clauses for French observed for our data (sample phrases taken from LVF).

	implic. r. (45)	factive r. (41)
+INF	69%	37%
+QUE	22%	73%
+INF −QUE	55%	12%
−INF +QUE	9%	48%

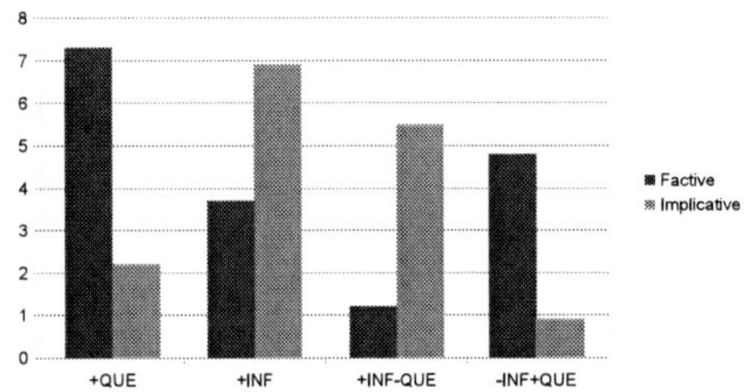

Figure 2: Factive and implicative verbs display different syntactic patterns with respect to the types of sub-categorised embedded clauses.

5 Conclusion and outlook

In this work, we developed a seed lexicon associating readings of French clause-embedding verbs with three different probabilistic inferential signatures, varying with outer aspect and the animacy of the subject. Through these inferential signatures, we concisely represent the inferences that can be drawn from the use of a clause-embedding predicate about the event expressed by the embedded clause given the polarity used. The experiments performed on the collected data support three hypotheses. Firstly, they show that in French where most ESPs have perfective and imperfective forms, implicativity, but not factivity, depends on perfective aspect. Interestingly, this hypothesis seems extendable to other Romance languages like Spanish, where implicative verbs also seem to lose the actuality entailment obtained with the perfective when they are used imperfectively, see the contrast below:

(10)   *Ana logró   ganar la   partida #cuando, de repente,   su   rival*
Ana manage-**PST-PFV**.3SG win   the game   when   all of a sudden her opponent
le   dio   jaque mate.
her give-**PST-PFV**.3SG chess mat
'Ana managed to win the game when all of a sudden, her opponent checkmated her.'

(11)   *Ana estaba logrando   ganar la   partida OK cuando, de repente,   su*
Ana manage-**PST-PROG**.3SG win   the game   when   all of a sudden her
rival   le   dio   jaque mate.
opponent her give-**PST-PFV**.3SG chess mat
'Ana 'was managing' to win the game when all of a sudden, her opponent checkmated her.'

Secondly, they show that implicativity, but not factivity, tends to decrease with the animacy of the subject. Thirdly, they indicate that verbs with both a factive and an implicative reading tend to accept infinitival clauses and to reject tensed clauses under their implicative readings, while they show the inverse pattern under their factive readings.

Acknowledgments

We are grateful to the anonymous IWCS reviewers for their detailed and constructive feedback, criticisms and suggestions. This work is part of the project B5 of the Collaborative Research Centre 732 hosted by the University of Stuttgart and financed by the *Deutsche Forschungsgemeinschaft*.

References

Baglini, R. and I. Francez (2016). The Implications of managing. *Journal of Semantics 33/3*, 541–560.

Bhatt, R. (1999). Ability modals and their actuality entailments. In *Proceedings of WCCFL*, Volume 17, pp. 17–34.

Bittar, A. (2010). *Building a TimeBank for French: a reference corpus annotated according to the ISO-TimeML standard.* Ph. D. thesis, Paris 7.

Bittar, A., P. Amsili, P. Denis, and L. Danlos (2011). French TimeBank: an ISO-TimeML annotated reference corpus. In *Proceedings of the 49th Annual Meeting of the Association for Computational Linguistics: Human Language Technologies: short papers-Volume 2*, pp. 130–134. Association for Computational Linguistics.

Constant, M. and E. Tolone (2010, April). A generic tool to generate a lexicon for NLP from Lexicon-Grammar tables. In M. D. Gioia (Ed.), *Proceedings of the 27th international congress on lexicon and grammar (L'Aquila, 10-13 september 2008)*, Volume 1 of *Lingue d'Europa e del Mediterraneo, Grammatica comparata*, pp. 79–93. Aracne.

Dowty, D. (1977). Toward a semantic analysis of verb aspect and the English 'imperfective' progressive. *Linguistics and Philosophy 1/1*, 45–77.

Falk, I. and F. Martin (2017). *Proceedings of the Workshop Computational Semantics Beyond Events and Roles*, Chapter Towards a lexicon of event-selecting predicates for a French FactBank, pp. 16–21. Association for Computational Linguistics.

François, J., D. Le Pesant, and D. Leeman (2007). Présentation de la classification des Verbes Français de Jean Dubois et Françoise Dubois-Charlier. *Langue française 153*(1), 3–19.

Hacquard, V. (2006). *Aspects of modality.* Ph. D. thesis, Massachusetts Institute of Technology.

Iatridou, S. (2000). The grammatical ingredients of counterfactuality. *Linguistic inquiry 31*(2), 231–270.

Ippolito, M. (2003). *A pragmatic analysis of Imperfect Conditionals*, pp. 133–150. John Benjamins.

Karttunen, L. (1971a). Implicative Verbs. *Language 47*(2), 340–358.

Karttunen, L. (1971b). *The logic of English predicate complement constructions*, Volume 4. Indiana University Linguistics Club Bloomington, Indiana.

Karttunen, L. (2012). Simple and phrasal implicatives. In *Proceedings of the First Joint Conference on Lexical and Computational Semantics-Volume 1: Proceedings of the main conference and the shared task, and Volume 2: Proceedings of the Sixth International Workshop on Semantic Evaluation*, pp. 124–131. Association for Computational Linguistics.

Karttunen, L., I. Cases, and G. Supaniratisai (2016). A Learning Corpus for Implicatives. Presentation at the Semantics and Pragmatics Group meeting.

Landau, I. (2001). *Elements of control: Structure and meaning in infinitival constructions*, Volume 51. Springer Science & Business Media.

Martin, F. and F. Schäfer (2012). The modality of offer and other defeasible causative verbs. In *Proceedings of the 30th West Coast Conference on Formal Linguistics, Somerville: Cascadilla Proceedings Project*, pp. 248–258.

Nadathur, P. (2016). Causal necessity and sufficiency in implicativity. In *Proceedings of Semantics and Linguistics Theory (SALT) 26*, pp. 1002–1021.

Nairn, R., C. Condoravdi, and L. Karttunen (2006). Computing relative polarity for textual inference. In *Proceedings of the Fifth International workshop on Inference in Computational Semantics (ICoS-5)*, pp. 20–21.

Pustejovsky, J., R. Knippen, J. Littman, and R. Saurí (2005). Temporal and event information in natural language text. *Language resources and evaluation 39*(2), 123–164.

Saurí, R. and J. Pustejovsky (2009). FactBank: a corpus annotated with event factuality. *Language resources and evaluation 43*(3), 227.

Saurí, R. and J. Pustejovsky (2012). Are you sure that this happened? assessing the factuality degree of events in text. *Computational Linguistics 38*(2), 261–299.

Tolone, E. (2011). *Syntactic analysis with tables of French Lexicon-Grammar*. Ph. D. thesis, Université Paris-Est.

White, A. S. (2014). Factive-implicatives and modalized complements. In *Proceedings of the 44th annual meeting of the North East Linguistic Society (NELS)*, pp. 267–278.

Learning to Compose Spatial Relations with Grounded Neural Language Models

Mehdi Ghanimifard
CLASP
University of Gothenburg, Sweden
mehdi.ghanimifard@gu.se

Simon Dobnik
CLASP
University of Gothenburg, Sweden
simon.dobnik@gu.se

Abstract

Language is compositional: we can generate and interpret novel sentences by having a notion of meaning of their individual parts. Spatial descriptions are grounded in perceptional representations but their meaning is also defined by what neighbouring words they co-occur with. In this paper we examine how language models conditioned on perceptual features can capture the semantics of composed phrases as well as of individual words. We generate a synthetic dataset of spatial descriptions referring to perceptual scenes and examine how grounded language models built with deep neural networks can account for compositionality of descriptions – by evaluating how the learned language models can deal with novel grounded composed descriptions and novel grounded decomposed descriptions, constituents previously not seen in isolation.

1 Introduction

Representing and reasoning with linguistic meaning is a central task in computational linguistics. Here two kinds of meaning representations are used: (i) *probabilistic language models* and (ii) *meaning representations grounded* in other, typically perceptual information. Recently, there have been several approaches in deep learning that deal with both, either independently or together.

The main goal of *probabilistic language models* is to estimate a probability distribution of sequences of words based on observable samples from language production, typically by estimating conditional probabilities of words with a categorical distribution. This gives language models means for representing words as sequences with a measure of likelihood for each sequence. Neural language models perform this objective by parametrising a probability density function with parametric representations of words and functions which compose words into phrases (Bengio et al., 2003; Mnih and Hinton, 2007; Mikolov et al., 2010). The gradient based learning in neural networks turns the modelling problem into an optimisation problem, minimising the error or distance between a model prediction and an observable data over a list of parameters:

1. parameters representing words with feature vectors known as *word embeddings*;

2. parameters of functions composing word features into a structure;

3. parameters of projections from final composed representations to categorical probabilities which in sequential models are the next word predictions.

There have been many attempts to show that the learned word embeddings in vector spaces are good representations of meaning. Basing the argument on the distributional hypothesis, if a probabilistic model of words is conditioned on their context words (i.e. skip-grams or bag-of-words), the word embeddings must encode semantic information by having learned distances in vector spaces which correspond to semantic similarity scores obtained through relatedness tests performed by native speakers. These representations were extended to word compositions by considering different compositional functions as vector manipulations (Mitchell and Lapata, 2010; Coecke et al., 2010; Baroni et al., 2014). Our notion of composition in a language model is broader than this: it involves (1) distributional models of words estimated from word sequences as well as (2) their grounding into representations of physical space. This extends the Montague's notion of compositionality. Lexical representations and their compositions are not dependent on meaning postulates and lexicalised constraints but rather perceptual evidence which is (probabilistically) associated with them.

Harnad (1990); Roy (2005) define language grounding as a process of relating words with an agent's perception. The ambiguity and vagueness of grounded meanings as well as of syntactic structures suggest that the connection between language and perception is gradient and therefore probabilistic. The main approaches to probabilistic models of grounded language are probabilistic learning of grounded language and grammar (Roy and Mukherjee, 2005; Matuszek et al., 2012), classifiers (Dobnik, 2009), and feature representations in perceptual space such as colour (McMahan and Stone, 2015). Our proposal is in line with all three approaches.

A *grounded language model* is a language model conditioned by perceptual representations that it refers to. Ideally, the model should capture how each constituent in the composed phrase relates to some perceptual representations. For example, in an image captioning task, a grounded language model estimates a conditional probability of a word sequence $w_{1:T}$ given some image feature c that the words refers to. A general way to model word sequences is to use the chain rule as follows. The model can generate phrases and sentences step-by-step by predicting the next word in a sequence:

$$Pr(w_{1:T}|c) = \prod_{t=1}^{T} Pr(w_t|w_{1:t}, c) \tag{1}$$

The parametrisation of vision and language is often done by combining word-embeddings with multimodal embeddings (Kiros et al., 2014; Socher et al., 2014). In the state of the art models for image captioning with encoder-decoder architecture, the encoder module is trained under the assumption that grounded words only denote features in subareas of an image, e.g bounding boxes (Karpathy and Fei-Fei, 2015) and pixel-wise mapping with attention models (Xu et al., 2015; Lu et al., 2016). Another example of a visually grounded language model is a model that is used to demonstrate the compositionality of colour descriptions in (Monroe et al., 2016) where linguistic descriptions are associated with areas of the colour space. Similar to (McMahan and Stone, 2015), each observed instance is a colour term paired with a colour code but instead of considering each description as a lexical entry, phrases are captured by a grounded language model as in Equation 1. The qualitative human evaluation of how newly composed colour words by this model refer to the colour space suggest that language models can capture compositionality through gradient learning used with neural networks.

In this paper, we follow up and extend the work of (Monroe et al., 2016). We focus on recurrent neural language models of sequences of words conditioned by encoded locations that these words refer to in visual scenes. Hence, we are interested in grounded semantic composition that is not only captured by probabilistic models of words given their context words, but also by models of their relatedness to perceptual representations. An important and novel question we investigate is *what these models are learning*: to what degree the representations of meaning (both collocational from vector spaces and grounded in perception) are interpretable and therefore *compositional* in the sense of (Montague, 1974). We focus on one domain of grounded meaning: spatial descriptions of various length and their grounding in spatial templates of Logan and Sadler (1996). In particular we try to answer the following questions: *(1)* To what extent are the language models that have been learned grounded in spatial representations? *(2)* Is it possible to generate new, previously unseen grounded composed spatial descriptions from observing their words only in other grounded composed phrases?

This paper is organised as follows. In Section 2 we describe the creation of an artificial dataset of composed spatial templates and the associated descriptions based on the experimental work of (Logan and Sadler, 1996). In Section 3 we describe our neural network model which we use for training our grounded language model. Section 4 describes an evaluation of the learned representations compared to the original representations the system was learning from. Finally, Section 5 points to conclusions and further work. The code and results are available at `https://github.com/GU-CLASP/`

`spatial-composition`.

2 The dataset

In order to train a grounded language model we require samples of language use paired with locations they are referring to. Considering the rationality of speakers and their observers (Grice, 1975), the frequency of each co-occurring utterance–location corresponds to the appropriateness of such utterance as a description of that location. One complication of judging the appropriateness of spatial terms this way is that they are not only depended on the location they describe but also on other properties of the situation such as the agreed frame of reference, object shape, and the function of the landmark and the target objects involved, etc. (Herskovits, 1986; Dobnik and Cooper, 2017). However, these properties will not be considered in the present study.

Logan and Sadler (1996) performed several psychological experiments related to the geometric apprehension of spatial relations. For example, they collected acceptability ratings (1–9) for a set of spatial relations per different locations of the target object in a 7×7 grid relative to the landmark object in the centre $(3, 3)$. The acceptability scores were collected from 32 informants through random presentation and then averaged per location. The matrix of average acceptability scores per description is called a *spatial template* and represents the appropriateness of each location in the process of interpreting that spatial relation (Logan and Sadler, 1996). They collect spatial templates for the following spatial relations: *right_of, left_of, below, under, over, above, near_to, next_to, far_from,* and *away_from* which we also apply in our work. Furthermore, in order to be able to explore the limits of the language models for learning compositions, we extend this vocabulary with a few additional words. We describe how we used them to synthesise the composed spatial templates for our training data in the following section.

2.1 Spatial templates as probabilities

As stated earlier, the spatial templates of Logan and Sadler (1996) give us the average acceptability scores on the scale 1–9 for each of $7 \times 7 - 1$ locations. In the process of grounding a description $(w_{1:T} = w_1 w_2 \ldots w_T)$, a vector of scores representing its spatial template is used to rank the description's acceptability across all possible locations:

$$T_{w_{1:T}} = \{Score(w_{1:T}, l)\}_{l \in L} \tag{2}$$

Our goal is to find such representation for any composed phrase $w_{1:T}$. We introduce the following assumption to convert the acceptability scores to probabilities. The acceptability scores are an indicator of a degree of belief (Ramsey, 1931) that a rational speaker would use a particular description $(w_{1:T})$ to describe the landmark object at a certain location $(c \in L)$. We therefore expect:

$$Score(w_{1:T}, c) \propto Pr(w_{1:T}, c) \tag{3}$$

where the $Pr(w_{1:T}, c)$ is the probability of observing a co-occurrence of a phrase $w_{1:T}$ and a location c. In order to be able to compare spatial templates generated by the learned neural language models and the original acceptability scores which were used to generate the training data, we assume that all locations are equally accessible, then:

$$\begin{aligned} Pr(w_{1:T}, c) &= Pr(w_{1:T}|c)Pr(c) \\ &\implies Score_{(w_{1:T}, c)} \propto Pr(w_{1:T}|c) \end{aligned} \tag{4}$$

We compare the generated probability scores by our neural language model, a vector of probabilities over all locations, for a particular description with its expected spatial template. We use a correlation coefficient to quantify the difference between a predicted and the "real" spatial template. A spatial template gives us information about the applicability of each location. When choosing a location given a description we would consider the ranking of locations by their applicability score. Hence, since we are not interested in the actual scores but their ranking, Spearman's rank correlation coefficient is a suitable measure for comparing spatial templates.

$$
\begin{aligned}
T_{w_{1:T}} &= \{Score_{w_{1:T},l}\}_{l \in L} \\
\hat{T}_{w_{1:T}} &= \{Pr(w_{1:T}|c)\}_{l \in L} \\
\rho(T_{w_{1:T}}, \hat{T}_{w_{1:T}}) &\quad \text{Spearman's rank correlation coefficient}
\end{aligned}
\tag{5}
$$

2.2   Synthesised data

Considering the assumptions from the previous section, using a simple min-max normalisation, the list of scores in a spatial template can be translated to a Bernoulli probability of events:

$$
Pr(w_{0:T}, c) \approx s_{w_{1:T},c} = \frac{Score(w_{1:T}, c) - 1}{9 - 1}
\tag{6}
$$

Using these probabilities, we synthesise instance events of locations and descriptions that make our training dataset using the same method as (Coventry et al., 2004). Having normalised acceptability ratings as probabilities, we can generate samples with a frequency corresponding to these probabilities.

$$
freq(w_{0:T}, c) = n \times Pr(w_{0:T}, c)
\tag{7}
$$

For example, by choosing $n = 5$, for a location with normalised scores 0.58 for *right_of*, 0.15 for *left_of* and 0.91 for *next_to*, we generate 2, 0, 4 instances for each respective description.

(Logan and Sadler, 1996) present acceptability scores for spatial descriptions obtained experimentally only for single-word spatial descriptions such as *left* and *above*. However, in our task we need their composed representations. We take the assumption that all spatial templates compose with some known function. For example for two spatial descriptions conjoined with an intersective *and* "{spatial_term1} and {spatial_term2}", Gapp (1994) discusses (but not experimentally evaluates) five compositional functions for grounding spatial templates. More recently, Dobnik and Åstbom (2017) show that taking a *geometric mean* over acceptability scores per location give highly correlated compositions with spatial templates of composed descriptions obtained experimentally. Another study on representing binary beliefs with beta distributions (Jøsang and McAnally, 2005), shows that the product of scores has the best approximation for conjoined opinions. We also take this as our compositional function to generate spatial templates for composite descriptions as in Figure 1, here further defined as:

$$
\begin{aligned}
g_\wedge &: \quad (v_i, v_j) \to [v_i, \text{"and"}, v_j] \\
\hat{s}_{g_\wedge(v_i,v_j),c} &= s_{v_i,c} \times s_{v_j,c}
\end{aligned}
\tag{8}
$$

Where $g_\wedge$ is a grammar rule for conjoined composition. Similarly, following (Jøsang and McAnally, 2005), logical OR-composition can be defined with co-multiplication:

$$
\begin{aligned}
g_\vee &: \quad (v_i, v_j) \to [\text{"either"}, v_i, \text{"or"}, v_j] \\
\hat{s}_{g_\vee(v_i,v_j),c} &= s_{v_i,c} + s_{v_j,c} - s_{v_i,c} \times s_{v_j,c}
\end{aligned}
\tag{9}
$$

For negation "not {spatial_term}" we take a complement of the acceptability scores as shown in Figure 1.

$$
\begin{aligned}
g_\neg &: \quad v \to [\text{"not"}, v] \\
\hat{s}_{g_\neg(v),c} &= 1 - s_{v,c}
\end{aligned}
\tag{10}
$$

The resulting compositions are shown in Figure 1. One might object to the usage of such synthetic data. It is important to note that the prime goal of this work is not to learn grounded models of spatial language that would best approximate human intuitions but to test to what degree grounded neural language models are capable of capturing grounded compositionality expressed as compositional functions of various complexities which have been confirmed in the previous literature to work well. Hence, we are interested in testing to what extent new machine learning models are capable of learning these functions.

We create two datasets. In the first dataset all descriptions are grounded in spatial templates as described above. In the second dataset additional words were added which we assume have no grounding

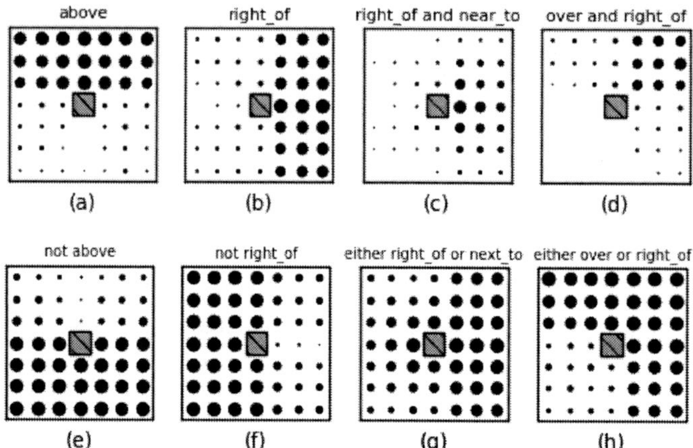

Figure 1: Spatial templates in a 7×7 grid: (a) and (b) are spatial templates for "above" and "right" from (Logan and Sadler, 1996) collected from human judgements. (c-h) are their synthetic compositions. (c) and (d) are intersective-AND compositions of two spatial templates using point-wise multiplication. (e) and (f) represent the negation of (a) and (b) using a complement operation. (g) and (h) are logical-OR compositions of two spatial templates using a point-wise co-multiplication.

in perception to test if the neural language model is able to distinguish them from the words sensitive to grounding. For example: "{the object | it | the ball} is {spatial_phrase} {the object | it | the box}". The following additional grammar rules were applied during the generation of the second dataset:

$$
\begin{aligned}
g_1 &: (v*) \rightarrow [v*] \\
g_2 &: (v*) \rightarrow [\text{``it''}, \text{``is''}, v*] \\
g_3 &: (v*) \rightarrow [\text{``it''}, \text{``is''}, v*, \text{``the''}, \text{``box''}] \\
g_4 &: (v*) \rightarrow [\text{``the''}, \text{``ball''}, \text{``is''}, v*, \text{``the''}, \text{``box''}] \\
g_5 &: (v*) \rightarrow [\text{``the''}, \text{``object''}, \text{``is''}, v*, \text{``the''}, \text{``box''}]
\end{aligned}
\tag{11}
$$

Algorithm 1 Synthetic generator

1: $n = 5$
2: $g_{compositional} = \{g_1, g_\neg, g_\wedge, g_\vee\}$
3: $g_{textual} = \{g_1, g_2, g_3, g_4, g_5\}$
4: **procedure** SYNTHETICGENERATOR($v*, c, g$)
5:     $freq \leftarrow n \times \hat{s}_{g(v*),c}$
6:     **for** 1 **to** $freq$ **do**
7:         $syntax \leftarrow \text{choose\_random}(g_{textual})$
8:         $text \leftarrow syntax(g(v*))$
9:         **Generate**($text, c$)

In the generated descriptions, words such as *and, not, the, box, ball, it, object,* and *is* are not grounded in locations individually but the phrases they occur in refer to locations on the map.

3 Neural network architecture

We use the Recurrent Neural Network (RNN) architecture for a language model (Graves, 2013) with Long-Short Term Memory (LSTM) (Hochreiter and Schmidhuber, 1997) and a decoder architecture from (Cho et al., 2014) which concatenates word-embeddings of each input word with an encoded location:

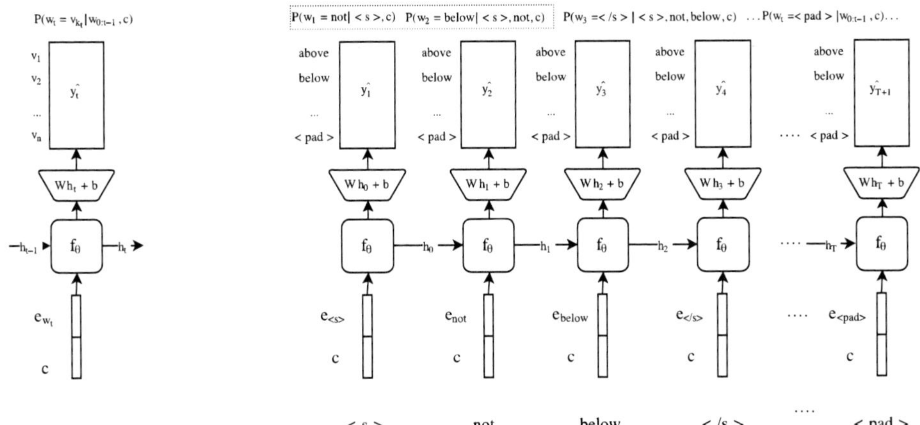

Figure 2: The diagram on the left illustrates the architecture of the model at word/time-step t using a vocabulary size n. On the right, there is an unfolded example how a phrase like "not below" is paired with a location c as in $(w_{1:T}, c)$ and fed as input to the LSTM decoder. In this setup, similar to (Graves, 2013), we train the model to predict the next word in a sequence and the chain of output probabilities is taken to estimate the final probability. The sequence can be cut before reaching the end tag $< /s >$.

$$
\begin{aligned}
y_t &= Pr(w_t|w_{1:t-1}, c) \\
\mathbf{h}_t &= f_\theta(\mathbf{e}_{w_{t-1}}; \mathbf{c}, \mathbf{h}_{t-1}) \\
\hat{\mathbf{y}}_t &= \text{softmax}(\mathbf{W}\mathbf{h}_t + \mathbf{b})
\end{aligned}
\tag{12}
$$

where $\hat{\mathbf{y}}_t$ is the expected categorical probability at time t, f is a recurrent cell with parameters θ, $\mathbf{e}_w$ is an embedding vector for a word w, and $\mathbf{c}$ is an encoded location as a one-hot vector as shown in Figure 2.

The training set in a batch are pairs of word sequences and their corresponding location codes: $\{(w^{(i)}_{1:T}, c^{(i)})\}_{i \in D}$ where D is our training dataset. The loss function used is the cross entropy distance between predicted distribution and targeted distribution or *log-loss*. The observed true output $\mathbf{y}^{(i)}_t$ is represented with one-hot encodings. The training process can be summarised as follows:

$$
\begin{aligned}
\mathbf{y}^{(i)}_t &= \delta_{w^{(i)}_t} \\
L^{(i)}(\Theta) &= -\sum_{t=1}^{T+1} \mathbf{y}^{T(i)}_t \log(\hat{\mathbf{y}}^{(i)}_t) \\
&= -\sum_{t=1}^{T+1} \log(\hat{\mathbf{y}}^{(i)}_t(w^{(i)}_t))
\end{aligned}
\tag{13}
$$

We train the network parameters with *Adam stochastic gradient descent* (Kingma and Ba, 2014) with batch normalisation implemented as an optimiser in Keras (Chollet, 2015). On each mini-batch update as $(\Theta_b \leftarrow \Theta_{b-1} + AdamSGD(\nabla_\Theta \mathcal{L}))$ the following parameters of the model (Θ) are updated:

$$
\begin{aligned}
&\{\mathbf{e}_w\}_{w \in V} && \text{Embedding vectors for all words} \\
&\theta && \text{Parameters of the RNN cell, composed feature vectors} \\
&\mathbf{W}, \mathbf{b} && \text{Parameters of the final dense layer}
\end{aligned}
\tag{14}
$$

3.1 Implementation

We implemented our model in Keras (Chollet, 2015) with TensorFlow (Abadi et al., 2015) as a back-end. All parameters were initialised randomly with Keras recommendations. In the current implementation, the size of the $\mathbf{h}_t$, the hidden unit of LSTM, is 15, and the parameters of the RNN cell have a dropout of 0.1. The dropout on embeddings is set to 0.3.

We left-padded descriptions $w_{1:T'}$ with a starting token $w_0 =< s >$ and right-padded them with a finishing token $w_{T'+1} =< /s >$ while the rest was padded with $< pad >$ up to the maximum description length of $T + 1$ as illustrated in Figure 2. The final y_{T+1} can be either $< pad >$ or $< /s >$. The length of the RNN chain has to be of the fixed size $T + 1$, the length of the longest possible sentence, in order to be used with Keras and its implementation on graphic cards.

During each experiment, we trained the model until it reached an over-fitting point with equal training and validation loss.

3.2 From the outputs of the RNN to probabilities of composed descriptions

The decoder architecture of RNNs is normally used as a generator which produces sequences of words or characters from an encoded sequence, e.g. (Cho et al., 2014; Graves, 2013). This can be achieved by applying Equation 1. The decoder predicts the most likely next word in a chain of softmax productions $\hat{y}_t$. The unfolded RNN in Figure 2 shows how for a sequence of words as input vectors, $\hat{y}_t$ are predicted which represent categorical probabilities for all possible following words at a time step t. For a given sequence, $w_{1:T} = v_{k_1:k_t}$, we estimate the probabilities using Equation 1 as follows:

$$
\begin{aligned}
Pr(w_t = v_{k_t} | w_{1:t-1} = v_{k_1:k_t}, c) &= \hat{y}_t(v_{k_t}) \\
Pr(w_{1:T} = v_{k_1:k_T} | c) &= \prod_{t=1}^{T} \hat{y}_t(v_{k_t})
\end{aligned}
\tag{15}
$$

The estimated probability is then used to generate spatial templates as in Equation 5. The probabilities over all possible locations on the map L for a given composition of words can be aggregated as follows:

$$
\hat{T}_{v_{k_1:k_{T'}}} = \{Pr(w_{1:T'} = v_{k_1:k_{T'}} | c)\}_{c \in L}
\tag{16}
$$

4   Evaluation

We evaluate the learning of composed grounded phrases by examining to what degree the spatial templates produced by the learned model correspond to the original spatial templates that were used in generating the training data, how successful is the learning with different kinds of compositions, and what is the effect of adding distractor words. We ran two experiments, (1) on a simple synthetic dataset containing short phrases where all words are grounded in locations, and (2) on a synthetic dataset generated with five additional grammar rules from Equation 11, introducing words without spatial grounding or distractor words. We test the learning of compositional phrases by training a language model on phrases produced by individual composition types as well as all composition types in both synthetic datasets. A comparison of the predicted spatial templates with the original spatial templates with Spearman's rank correlation coefficient (Equation 5) in Table 1 shows that there is high correlation between them. We report the average Spearman's ρ and their median p-values for statistical significance.

	Simple phrases	With distractors	Untrained
AND-phrases	0.87	0.85	-0.00
NEG-phrases	0.72	0.82	0.03
OR-phrases	0.79	0.80	-0.03
SINGLE-word	0.92	0.91	-0.05
All previous	0.83	0.83	-0.01
All previous + distractors	NaN	0.84	-0.03

Table 1: For each type of compositional phrases we calculate the average Spearman's rank correlation coefficient (ρ) between the predicted spatial templates and the templates used to generate the training data. The median p-value of ρ of all trained models is < 0.001. The column *Untrained* indicates the performance of the model with a random initialisation of weights.

For both Experiment 1 and 2 we created two variations: (1) learning of novel grounded compositions, where different proportions of AND-phrases and OR-phrases are omitted from the dataset and therefore hidden from the learner; (2) learning of novel single words from grounded compositions, where proportions of single-word instances are omitted from the dataset and their representations can only be learned from their occurrence in composed phrases with other words.

In all experiments we hold out 10% of the dataset for validation. In Experiment 1 we iterated the training over 64 epochs using a batch size 8. In Experiment 2, using a batch size 256, we stopped learning iterations before 1024 epochs if the validation loss became equal to the training loss.

4.1 Experiment 1: Learning composition of short phrases

In this experiment the training data is generated for single spatial words, AND-compositions, OR-compositions, and negated phrases without additional distractor words save "and", "either", "or", and "not".

4.1.1 Learning of novel grounded compositions

The training data contains synthesised samples of all single words and their negations. However, different proportions of AND-phrases and OR-phrases are removed from the training set to test if the model can learn unseen composed phrases. Table 2 shows the average of Spearman's ρ correlation coefficient for different portions of held-out phrases. Figure 3 illustrates some predicted novel grounded compositions where 50% of complex phrases were held out. The ρ scores lower than 0.6 may not be trustworthy, e.g. "above and left_of" with $\rho = 0.5$ in Figure 3.

Proportions of 90 combinations	10%	20%	30%	40%	50%	60%	70%	80%	90%	100%
AND-phrases	0.84	0.8	0.78	0.76	0.71	0.67	0.64	0.53	0.45	0.29
OR-phrases	0.74	0.73	0.69	0.67	0.56	0.57	0.54	0.38	0.23	-0.23

Table 2: Spearman's ρ for held-out proportions of phrases up to 80% have a median p-value < 0.001 and p-value > 0.05 for higher proportions.

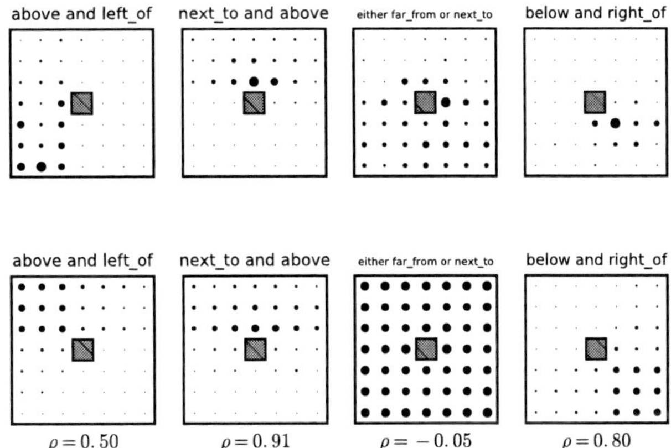

Figure 3: The predicted spatial templates are shown on the top and the original spatial templates in the bottom.

The results indicate that the model can produce spatial templates for novel compositions. However, the learning of composed phrases is dependent on the size and the variety of training instances. Some phrases are more difficult to train than others. For example, OR phrases correspond to regions that are more spread out across the 48 locations which makes them more difficult to learn, e.g. an extreme case such as "either far from or next to".

	10%	20%	30%	40%
AND-phrases	0.86	0.8	0.77	0.81
NEG-phrases	0.83	0.64	0.59	0.43
OR-phrases	0.73	0.78	0.68	0.69
SINGLE-word	0.9	0.9	0.84	0.87

Figure 4: The average Spearman's ρ for different proportions of unseen examples.

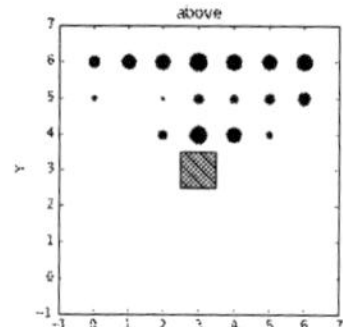
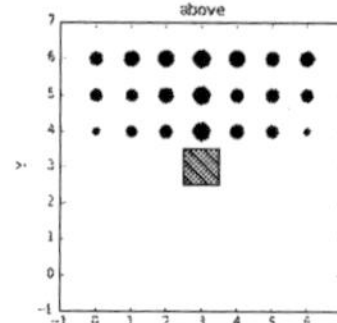

Figure 5: The predicted and the original spatial template.

4.1.2 Learning of novel single words from grounded compositions

In this experiment we omit identical proportions of all description types, thus also single word descriptions and negated descriptions. In this case, the predicted novel spatial templates are learned solely based on observing these words in combination with other words. As before, we conduct the test with different sizes of held-out data. The results are shown in Figure 4. When omitting up to 4 single descriptions (*right_of, over, far_from* and *under*) the average ρ on grounded SINGLE-word descriptions decreases only by 0.05 (from 0.92, Table 1). This means that their grounding is successfully learned from grounded composed expressions. Figure 5 shows a novel learned spatial template for "above".

4.1.3 Qualitative observations

A qualitative examination of the predicted spatial templates shows that spatial templates with the lowest ρ are those with no points in space ("right_of and left_of") or those with a uniform spread of points across space ("either far_from or next_to") which in our scenario includes a number of training instances as rules from Section 2.2 were applied to all combinations of spatial templates. We get the highest ρ with compositions such as "over and above", possibly because the two spatial templates overlap and result in a simplified composed representation.

4.2 Experiment 2: Adding distractor words with no spatial grounding

In Experiment 2 we train and measure the performance of the model on grounded descriptions which also include non-grounded distractor words, for example: "the ball is not left_of the box" or "it is above and right_of the object". The words such as "ball", "object", "box", "it" and "is" provide no contribution to the grounded meaning (location). In this dataset the number of possible composed phrases increases from 200 to 1,000. Algorithm 1 in Section 2.2 ensures that in the 1,000 possible phrases the same number of instances is generated as before, now per each of the five permutation rules introducing distractors. The held-out proportions of spatial descriptions are created before Algorithm 1 is applied so permutations including these are not generated.

4.2.1 Learning of novel grounded compositions

Although now the training data includes longer sequences and several distractors which make these compositions harder to learn, the results are only slightly weaker than in Experiment 1 as shown by a comparison of Table 3 with Table 2.

Proportions of 90 combinations	10%	20%	30%	40%	50%	60%	70%	80%
AND-phrases	0.82	0.79	0.75	0.78	0.73	0.69	0.66	0.45
OR-phrases	0.78	0.69	0.67	0.66	0.59	0.59	0.44	0.33

Table 3: The average Spearman's ρ with the median p-value of < 0.001. After 80% of held-out phrase types the ρ values are not statistically significant.

	10%	20%	30%	40%
AND-phrases	0.82	0.60	0.71	0.81
NEG-phrases	0.75	0.66	0.45	0.30
OR-phrases	0.76	0.76	0.71	0.64
SINGLE-word	0.88	0.43	0.73	0.84

Figure 6: The average Spearman's correlations decomposition task Experiment 2.

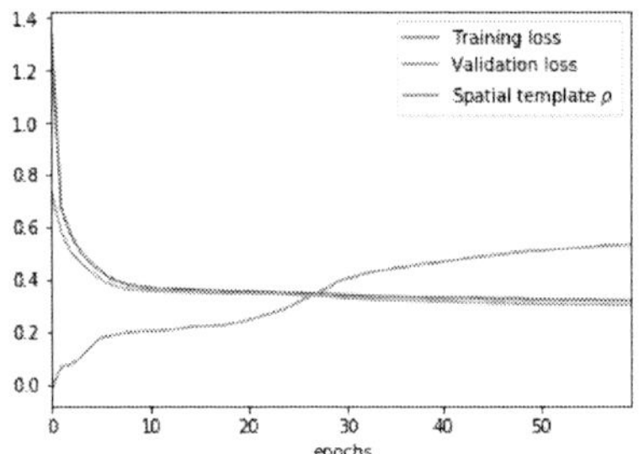

Figure 7: The learning curve for Experiment 3.

4.2.2 Learning of novel single words from grounded compositions

The results of this task on the dataset from Experiment 2 are shown in Figure 6. The ρ are nearly identical or only slightly lower for SINGLE-words compared to Experiment 1 (Figure 4). There is an unusual drop in ρ at 20% of held-out descriptions which requires further investigation. Overall, we can conclude that the system successfully learned omitted single words from their grounded compositions even with distractor words.

4.3 Experiment 3: How much grounding?

In Experiment 3, we examine how the amount of training corresponds to the groundedness of expressions in spatial templates. In particular, we examine the learning curve across several epochs at which more of the same data is presented incrementally to the learner and how well does the currently learned model corresponds to the target spatial templates. Typically, the performance of the learner at each epoch is estimated by a loss function, here the cross-entropy (log-loss). We compare the loss at each epoch with the average Spearman's ρ between the predicted templates and the original templates for 110 possible combinations of descriptions from Experiment 1 (excluding OR-phrases). Here, we only run the experiment with 20% omission of the dataset. Figure 7 shows how average ρ corresponds to the learning progress. The figure shows that even after the training and the validation loss are only slightly decreasing between epochs the groundedness is increasing at a higher rate. This can be explained by the fact that the network is not only predicting locations but also sequences of descriptions which adds a further complexity to learning which is reflected in the loss.

5 Conclusion and future work

We have presented a grounded language model with recurrent deep neural networks. The objective of our task was to examine to what extent our neural network architecture can learn a grounded language model that generated the training data and whether a word that is grounded as a part of a phrase can "carry over" its grounding to another phrase not observed in the training data. In our view this is the ultimate test that grounding is compositional. We conduct two learning experiments. In the first experiment we learn a grounded language model where all descriptions in a sequence are grounded. In the subsequent sub-experiments we test the success of the grounded language models where some word compositions are omitted from training. We show that the model is capable of grounding novel compositions and also predicting grounding of single words while only learning from compositions. However, the degree of success, while on overall high, is dependent on the amount of the absent information and the coverage of the training instances. In the second experiment, we add words to our grounded language model that have no grounding and test whether the system is able to learn different grounding sensitivities of different words. We show that our language model is capable of recognising the contribution of each constituent to the meaning of the entire grounded composition. Finally, in the third experiment we examine grounding related to the log-loss success rate of learning. Overall, we conclude that our deep neural architecture successfully learns grounded spatial descriptions in a way that the learned functions are similar to the ones that generated the data. This is a useful result which points towards the fact that language is compositional both at the level of word sequences and the portions of scenes that they refer to, thus confirming the result in (Dobnik and Åstbom, 2017). In the future work we will focus on the effects of the varying dataset sizes on the rate of learning and test the learning setup on more complex perceptual representations (in terms of the expected irregularities) such as images.

References

Abadi, M., A. Agarwal, P. Barham, E. Brevdo, Z. Chen, C. Citro, G. S. Corrado, A. Davis, J. Dean, M. Devin, S. Ghemawat, I. Goodfellow, A. Harp, G. Irving, M. Isard, Y. Jia, R. Jozefowicz, L. Kaiser, M. Kudlur, J. Levenberg, D. Mané, R. Monga, S. Moore, D. Murray, C. Olah, M. Schuster, J. Shlens, B. Steiner, I. Sutskever, K. Talwar, P. Tucker, V. Vanhoucke, V. Vasudevan, F. Viégas, O. Vinyals, P. Warden, M. Wattenberg, M. Wicke, Y. Yu, and X. Zheng (2015). TensorFlow: Large-scale machine learning on heterogeneous systems. Software available from tensorflow.org.

Baroni, M., R. Bernardi, and R. Zamparelli (2014). Frege in space: A program of compositional distributional semantics. *LiLT (Linguistic Issues in Language Technology) 9*.

Bengio, Y., R. Ducharme, P. Vincent, and C. Jauvin (2003). A neural probabilistic language model. *journal of machine learning research 3*(Feb), 1137–1155.

Cho, K., B. Van Merriënboer, C. Gulcehre, D. Bahdanau, F. Bougares, H. Schwenk, and Y. Bengio (2014). Learning phrase representations using rnn encoder-decoder for statistical machine translation. *arXiv preprint arXiv:1406.1078*.

Chollet, F. (2015). Keras. `https://github.com/fchollet/keras`.

Coecke, B., M. Sadrzadeh, and S. Clark (2010). Mathematical foundations for a compositional distributional model of meaning. *arXiv preprint arXiv:1003.4394*.

Coventry, K. R., A. Cangelosi, R. Rajapakse, A. Bacon, S. Newstead, D. Joyce, and L. V. Richards (2004). Spatial prepositions and vague quantifiers: Implementing the functional geometric framework. In *International Conference on Spatial Cognition*, pp. 98–110. Springer.

Dobnik, S. (2009, September 4). *Teaching mobile robots to use spatial words*. Ph. D. thesis, University of Oxford: Faculty of Linguistics, Philology and Phonetics and The Queen's College, Oxford, United Kingdom.

Dobnik, S. and A. Åstbom (2017, August 15–17). (Perceptual) grounding as interaction. In V. Petukhova and Y. Tian (Eds.), *Proceedings of Saardial – Semdial 2017: The 21st Workshop on the Semantics and Pragmatics of Dialogue*, Saarbrücken, Germany, pp. 17–26.

Dobnik, S. and R. Cooper (2017). Interfacing language, spatial perception and cognition in Type Theory with Records. *Accepted for Journal of Language Modelling n*(n), 1–30.

Gapp, K.-P. (1994, 12-14 September). A computational model of the basic meanings of graded composite spatial relations in 3D space. In *Advanced geographic data modelling. Spatial data modelling and query languages for 2D and 3D applications (Proceedings of the AGDM'94)*, Publications on Geodesy 40, pp. 66–79. Netherlands Geodetic Commission.

Graves, A. (2013). Generating sequences with recurrent neural networks. *arXiv preprint arXiv:1308.0850*.

Grice, H. P. (1975). Logic and conversation. In P. Cole and J. Morgan (Eds.), *Syntax and Semantics: Speech Acts*, Volume 3, pp. 41–58. Academic Press.

Harnad, S. (1990). The symbol grounding problem. *Physica D: Nonlinear Phenomena 42*(1-3), 335–346.

Herskovits, A. (1986). *Language and spatial cognition: an interdisciplinary study of the prepositions in English*. Cambridge: Cambridge University Press.

Hochreiter, S. and J. Schmidhuber (1997). Long short-term memory. *Neural computation 9*(8), 1735–1780.

Jøsang, A. and D. McAnally (2005). Multiplication and comultiplication of beliefs. *International Journal of Approximate Reasoning 38*(1), 19–51.

Karpathy, A. and L. Fei-Fei (2015). Deep visual-semantic alignments for generating image descriptions. In *Proceedings of the IEEE Conference on Computer Vision and Pattern Recognition*, pp. 3128–3137.

Kingma, D. and J. Ba (2014). Adam: A method for stochastic optimization. *arXiv preprint arXiv:1412.6980*.

Kiros, R., R. Salakhutdinov, and R. S. Zemel (2014). Unifying visual-semantic embeddings with multimodal neural language models. *arXiv preprint arXiv:1411.2539*.

Logan, G. D. and D. D. Sadler (1996). A computational analysis of the apprehension of spatial relations. In P. Bloom, M. A. Peterson, L. Nadel, and M. F. Garrett (Eds.), *Language and Space*, pp. 493–530. Cambridge, MA: MIT Press.

Lu, J., C. Xiong, D. Parikh, and R. Socher (2016). Knowing when to look: Adaptive attention via a visual sentinel for image captioning. *arXiv preprint arXiv:1612.01887*.

Matuszek, C., N. FitzGerald, L. Zettlemoyer, L. Bo, and D. Fox (2012). A joint model of language and perception for grounded attribute learning. *arXiv preprint arXiv:1206.6423*.

McMahan, B. and M. Stone (2015). A bayesian model of grounded color semantics. *Transactions of the Association for Computational Linguistics 3*, 103–115.

Mikolov, T., M. Karafiát, L. Burget, J. Cernockỳ, and S. Khudanpur (2010). Recurrent neural network based language model. In *Interspeech*, Volume 2, pp. 3.

Mitchell, J. and M. Lapata (2010). Composition in distributional models of semantics. *Cognitive science 34*(8), 1388–1429.

Mnih, A. and G. Hinton (2007). Three new graphical models for statistical language modelling. In *Proceedings of the 24th international conference on Machine learning*, pp. 641–648. ACM.

Monroe, W., N. D. Goodman, and C. Potts (2016). Learning to generate compositional color descriptions. *arXiv preprint arXiv:1606.03821*.

Montague, R. (1974). *Formal Philosophy: Selected Papers of Richard Montague*. New Haven: Yale University Press.

Ramsey, F. P. (1931). Truth and probability (1926). *The foundations of mathematics and other logical essays*, 156–198.

Roy, D. (2005). Semiotic schemas: A framework for grounding language in action and perception. *Artificial Intelligence 167*(1-2), 170–205.

Roy, D. and N. Mukherjee (2005). Towards situated speech understanding: Visual context priming of language models. *Computer Speech & Language 19*(2), 227–248.

Socher, R., A. Karpathy, Q. V. Le, C. D. Manning, and A. Y. Ng (2014). Grounded compositional semantics for finding and describing images with sentences. *Transactions of the Association for Computational Linguistics 2*, 207–218.

Xu, K., J. Ba, R. Kiros, K. Cho, A. C. Courville, R. Salakhutdinov, R. S. Zemel, and Y. Bengio (2015). Show, attend and tell: Neural image caption generation with visual attention. In *ICML*, Volume 14, pp. 77–81.

If Sentences Could See: Investigating Visual Information for Semantic Textual Similarity

Goran Glavaš[1], Ivan Vulić[2], and Simone Paolo Ponzetto[1]

[1]Data and Web Science Group
University of Mannheim
`{goran, simone}@informatik.uni-mannheim.de`

[2]Language Technology Lab
University of Cambridge
`iv250@cam.ac.uk`

Abstract

We investigate the effects of incorporating visual signal from images into unsupervised Semantic Textual Similarity (STS) measures. STS measures exploiting visual signal alone are shown to outperform, in some settings, linguistic-only measures by a wide margin, whereas multi-modal measures yield further performance gains. We also show that selective inclusion of visual information may further boost performance in the multi-modal setup.

1   Introduction

Semantic textual similarity (Agirre et al., 2012, 2015, *inter alia*) measures the degree of semantic equivalence between short texts, usually pairs of sentences. Despite the obvious applicability to sentence alignment for machine translation (MT) (Resnik and Smith, 2003; Aziz and Specia, 2011) or plagiarism detection (Potthast et al., 2011; Franco-Salvador et al., 2013), cross-lingual STS models were proposed only recently (Agirre et al., 2016; Brychcín and Svoboda, 2016; Jimenez, 2016). These are, however, essentially monolingual STS models coupled with full-blown MT systems that translate sentences to English.

Although research in cognitive science (e.g., Lakoff and Johnson (1999); Louwerse (2011)) shows that our meaning representations are grounded in perceptual system, the existing STS models (monolingual and cross-lingual alike) exploit only linguistic signals, despite the fact that models using perceptual information outperform uni-modal linguistic models on tasks like detecting conceptual association and word similarity (Silberer and Lapata, 2012; Bruni et al., 2014; Kiela and Bottou, 2014), predicting phrase compositionality (Roller and Schulte Im Walde, 2013), recognizing lexical entailment (Kiela et al., 2015), and metaphor detection (Shutova et al., 2016). While still predominantly applied in monolingual settings, representations originating from the visual modality are inherently language-invariable (Bergsma and Durme, 2011; Kiela et al., 2015). As such, they could serve as a natural cross-language bridge in cross-lingual STS.

In this work, we investigate unsupervised multi-modal and cross-lingual STS models that leverage visual information from images alongside linguistic information from textual corpora. We feed images retrieved for textual queries to the deep convolutional network (CNN) for image classification and use the CNN's abstract image features as visual semantic representations of words and sentences.

We implement models that combine linguistic and visual information at different levels of granularity – *early fusion* (word level), *middle fusion* (sentence level), and *late fusion* (fusing similarity scores). Results of an evaluation on two cross-lingual STS datasets (mutually very different in terms of text genre and average sentence length) show that (1) the proposed multi-modal STS models outperform uni-modal models relying only on visual or linguistic input and (2) in several experimental runs, purely visual STS models outperform purely linguistic STS models. We obtain further performance gains by selectively exploiting visual information, conditioned on the dispersion of retrieved images.

2 Related Work

We provide an overview of two different lines of research: (1) existing STS methods, which exploit linguistic information only and (2) multi-modal semantic representations used in other applications.

Semantic Textual Similarity. Despite the existence of earlier models (Islam and Inkpen, 2008; Oliva et al., 2011), the true explosion of STS research efforts is credited to the SemEval-2012 Pilot on Semantic Textual Similarity (Agirre et al., 2012). The most successful systems (Bär et al., 2012; Šarić et al., 2012) were methodologically similar – they employed a supervised regression model to learn the optimal combination of many different sentence-comparison features.

Subsequent STS shared tasks witnessed successful unsupervised STS models, based on aligning words between sentences and counting the number of aligned pairs. Han et al. (2013) use LSA-based and WordNet-based measures of word similarity to find the pairs of semantically aligned words. Sultan et al. (2014) further employ NER and dependency parsing to better align the words between the sentences. These models depend on language-specific resources and tools, which are fairly expensive to build and exist only for a handful of languages.

The cross-lingual STS has been tackled only in the most recent edition of the SemEval STS shared task (Agirre et al., 2016). The best performing systems (Brychcín and Svoboda, 2016; Jimenez, 2016), with over 90% correlation with human similarity scores, directly employ full-blown MT systems and next apply monolingual STS measures. Besides being as resource-intensive as monolingual

STS models, the applicability of this methodology is limited to language pairs for which a robust MT model exists.

The multi-modal STS measures proposed in this work are resource-light and do not require any language-specific resources and tools. For a given language, our models require only (1) reasonably large corpora to obtain linguistic representations (i.e., word embeddings) and (2) an image-retrieval system to obtain visual representations (i.e., image embeddings). In the cross-lingual STS setting, the models additionally require a reasonably small set of word translation pairs to learn a shared cross-lingual vector space (Mikolov et al., 2013).

Multi-modal semantics. While research in cognitive science clearly suggests that human meaning representations are grounded in our perceptual system and sensori-motor experience (Harnad, 1990; Lakoff and Johnson, 1999; Louwerse, 2011, *inter alia*), previous STS models relied exclusively on linguistic processing and textual information. To the best of our knowledge, there has not yet been an STS method that leveraged visual information and combined linguistic and visual input into a visually-informed multi-modal STS system. However, such visually-informed models have been successfully used in other tasks such as selectional preferences (Bergsma and Goebel, 2011), detecting semantic similarity and relatedness (Silberer and Lapata, 2012; Bruni et al., 2014; Kiela and Bottou, 2014), recognizing lexical entailment (Kiela et al., 2015), and metaphor detection (Shutova et al., 2016), to name only a few.

Another important property of visual data is their expected language invariance,[1] exploited in recent work on multi-modal modeling in cross-lingual settings (Bergsma and Durme, 2011; Kiela et al., 2015; Vulić et al., 2016; Specia et al., 2016). Supported by these findings, in this work we show that our multi-modal STS framework may be straightforwardly extended to cross-lingual settings.

3 Multi-Modal Concept Representations

Our multi-modal STS measures combine – at different fusion levels – linguistic and visual concept representations. We obtain linguistic and visual representations for unigrams and then derive sentence representations by aggregating unigram representations. This was a pragmatic decision, as we were unable to consistently retrieve images for whole sentences as queries.

3.1 Linguistic Representations

We use the ubiquitous word embeddings as the linguistic representations of words. Aiming to make our approach language-independent, we opted for embedding models that require nothing but the large corpora as input. Due to the common

---

[1] Using a simple example from Vulić et al. (2016), bicycles resemble each other irrespective of whether we call them *bicycle, vélo, fiets, bicicletta,* or *Fahrrad*; see also Fig. 1

usage, we chose the Skip-Gram (Mikolov et al., 2013) and GloVe (Pennington et al., 2014) embeddings.

For the cross-lingual STS setting, the words of the two languages have to be projected to the same embedding space. To achieve this, we employ the translation matrix model of Mikolov et al. (2013), who have shown that the linear mapping can be established between independently trained embedding spaces. Given a set of translation pairs $\{s_i, t_i\}_{i=1}^{n}$, $s_i \in \mathbb{R}^{d_s}$, $t_i \in \mathbb{R}^{d_t}$ (with d_s and d_t being the sizes of source and target embeddings, respectively), we obtain the translation matrix $M \in \mathbb{R}^{d_s \times d_t}$ by minimizing the sum:

$$\sum_{i=1}^{n} \|s_i M - t_i\|_2$$

Once learned, the matrix M is used to project the embeddings of the whole source language vocabulary to the embedding space of the target language.

3.2 Visual Representations

Image embeddings. We use a standard procedure to obtain visual representations for words, e.g., (Kiela et al., 2015, 2016): we first retrieve n images for the word via Bing image search ($n = 20$ in all experiments).[2] Example images for the four languages we consider in our experiments (cf. Section 5) are shown in Figure 1.

We next run a deep convolutional neural network (CNN) pre-trained on the ImageNet classification task (Russakovsky et al., 2015) and extract the 4096-dimensional vector from the pre-softmax layer to represent each image. We opt for the VGG network (Simonyan and Zisserman, 2014) which, according to Kiela et al. (2016), has a slight edge on the two other alternatives – AlexNet (Krizhevsky et al., 2012) and GoogLeNet (Szegedy et al., 2015). We used the MMFeat toolkit (Kiela, 2016) to facilitate the process of image retrieval and CNN-based feature extraction.

Visual similarity. Because we retrieve more than one image per word, our visual representation of the word is a set of image embedding vectors. This allows for different visual similarity measures taking as input two sets of image embeddings (Kiela et al., 2015), given in Table 1.

3.3 Multi-Modal Representations

In order to compute multi-modal STS scores, one can combine linguistic and visual embeddings of words and sentences in a number of ways. Here, we explore three different levels of combining visual and linguistic representations, to which we refer as *early fusion*, *middle fusion*, and *late fusion*. We also experiment with selective

---

[2]Our choices were based on the findings from a recent systematic study on visual representation for multi-modal semantics (Kiela et al., 2016): (1) Visual representations from images obtained via Google and Bing image search are of similar quality. We opted for Bing for logistic reasons; (2) The performance of multi-modal models in semantic tasks typically saturates for n in the interval $[10, 20]$.

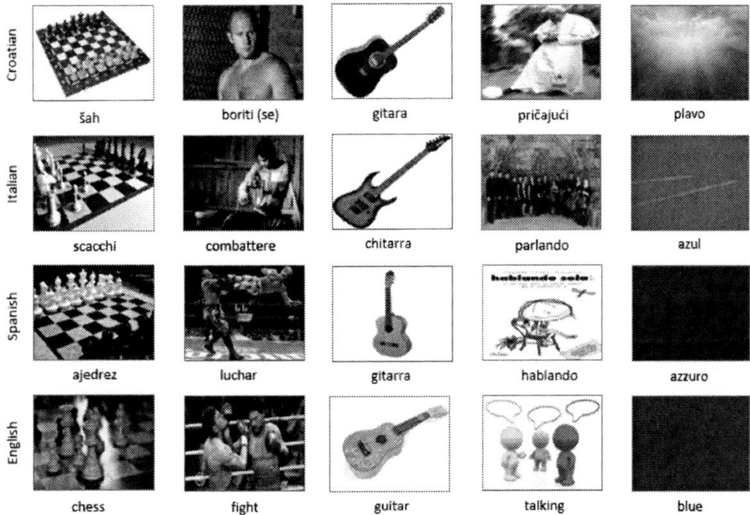

Figure 1: Example images (Bing image search)

Measure	Computation
AVG-MAX	$\frac{1}{n} \sum_{e_i \in \mathcal{I}(w_i)} \max_{e_j \in \mathcal{I}(w_j)} \cos(e_i, e_j)$
MAX-MAX	$\max_{e_i \in \mathcal{I}(w_i)} \max_{e_j \in \mathcal{I}(w_j)} \cos(e_i, e_j)$
SIM-AVG	$\cos\left(\frac{1}{n} \sum_{e_i \in \mathcal{I}(w_i)} e_i, \frac{1}{n} \sum_{e_j \in \mathcal{I}(w_j)} e_j \right)$
SIM-MAX	$\cos\left(\max_{el} \mathcal{I}(w_i), \max_{el} \mathcal{I}(w_j) \right)$

Table 1: Visual similarity measures for two sets of n images. $\mathcal{I}(w)$ is the set of image embeddings of word w. Function $\max_{el}$ computes the single element-wise maximum of the input vectors.

inclusion of visual information into the multi-modal representations, based on the measure of image dispersion.

Early fusion. This type of fusion concatenates ($\|$) the visual and linguistic embeddings of words:

$$e_{ef}(w) = e_v(w) \| e_t(w) \tag{1}$$

where $e_v(w)$ is the visual embedding of the word w, computed either by averaging or element-wise maxing of word's image embeddings, and $e_t(w)$ is the linguistic embedding of the word w. The similarity of two words is then simply computed as the cosine similarity of their fused multi-modal vectors.

Middle fusion. This type of fusion is performed at the sentence level. We first independently compute the aggregate linguistic representation and the aggregate visual representation for the whole sentence by averaging linguistic embeddings and visual embeddings of its words, respectively. The middle-fusion sentence representation is then the concatenation of the aggregated linguistic and visual representations. Let S be the set of words of a sentence. The middle-fusion sentence representation is then given as follows:

$$e_{mf}(S) = \left(\frac{1}{|S|} \sum_{w \in S} e_v(w) \right) \| \left(\frac{1}{|S|} \sum_{w \in S} e_t(w) \right) \qquad (2)$$

Note that the middle-fusion representation of each sentence equals to averaging the early-fusion representations of its constituent words.

Late fusion. The late fusion combines the visual and linguistic signal at the level of similarity scores rather than at the embedding level. Thus, it may be applied both for computing word and sentence similarities. Let sim_v be the similarity measure (cf. Section 4) for two words or sentences computed using their visual representations, and let sim_t be their similarity computed using their linguistic representations. The late-fusion similarity is then computed as the linear combination of the uni-modal similarities, i.e., as $a \cdot sim_v + b \cdot sim_t$. The default late-fusion model uses $a = b = 0.5$.

Selective inclusion of visual information. Previous studies (Hill et al., 2013; Kiela et al., 2014) show that visual signal does not improve the semantic representation equally for all concepts. In fact, the inclusion of visual information deteriorates semantic representations for abstract concepts (e.g., *honesty, love, freedom*). In order to selectively include the visual information, we need a measure reflecting the quality of the visual signal. To this end, we use the *image dispersion* score (Kiela et al., 2014). A concept's image dispersion is the cosine distance between image embeddings, averaged over all pairs of images obtained for the concept w:

$$id(w) = \frac{1}{\binom{\mathcal{I}(w)}{2}} \sum_{\substack{e_i, e_j \in \mathcal{I}(w) \\ i \neq j}} 1 - \cos(e_i, e_j) \qquad (3)$$

High image dispersion indicates that the images obtained for the concept are diverse. This means that the concept does not have a standard visual representation due to, e.g., its abstractness or its inherent polysemous nature.

We extend our middle-fusion and late-fusion models with selective inclusion of visual information. For the middle fusion, we measure the average image dispersion of all the words in a sentence. If the larger of the image dispersions of sentences in comparison scores above treshold τ,[3] we compare only the linguistic sentence embeddings. Otherwise, we compare the "middle-fused" multi-modal embeddings of the two sentences. For the late fusion, we compute the linear combination coefficients a and b as functions of image dispersions (the formula is given for words, but we also apply it to sentences in an analogous manner):

$$
\begin{aligned}
sim_{lf}(w_i, w_j) = {} & (1 - id(w_i, w_j)) \cdot sim_v(w_i, w_j) \\
& + id(w_i, w_j) \cdot sim_t(w_i, w_j)
\end{aligned}
\tag{4}
$$

where $id(w_i, w_j)$ represents the larger of the image dispersions of the words w_i and w_j.[4]

4 Unsupervised STS Measures

In the previous section we explained the different levels at which we may combine visual and linguistic representations. However, we still have to define the actual STS measures that compute similarity scores for given pairs of sentences. We propose two simple unsupervised scores for measuring textual similarity. Both scores are agnostic of the actual modality used: this means that we can swap linguistic, visual, and multi-modal vectors as desired without altering the actual STS measure.

Optimal aligment similarity. Following the ideas from successful unsupervised STS models (Han et al., 2013; Sultan et al., 2014), we aim to align words between the two sentences at hand. Aiming to devise language-independent STS models (i.e., language-specific tools that could help better align the words are off-limits), we can resort to word similarity measures as the sole information source guiding the alignment process. This STS measure is based on the optimal alignment between the words of the two input sentences. Given the similarity scores for all pairs of words between the sentences S_1 and S_2, we are looking for an alignment $\{(w_{S_1}^i, w_{S_2}^i)\}_{i=1}^{N}$ (N is the number of aligned pairs, equal to the number of words in the shorter of the sentences) that maximizes the sum of the pairwise similarities, i.e.:

$$
\max_{\{w_{S_1}^i, w_{S_2}^i\}_{i=1}^{N}} \sum_{i=1}^{N} sim(w_{S_1}^i, w_{S_2}^i)
\tag{5}
$$

As this is a prototypical assignment problem, we find the optimal word alignment using the Hungarian algorithm (Kuhn, 1955), which provides the solution in polynomial time.[5] Because pairs of longer sentences will be assigned larger similarity scores on the account of more aligned word pairs simply due to length, we normalize the above sum of similarities with the length of each of the two input sentences,

---

[3] In all experiments, we set the treshold to the middle of the image dispersion range, i.e., $\tau = 0.5$.

[4] We also experimented with $b = 1$, but it yielded inferior performance. This implies that the contribution of the "useful" (i.e., non-dispersed) visual signal should outweigh the linguistic signal.

[5] The time complexity of the algorithm, also known as the Kuhn-Munkres algorithm, is $\mathcal{O}(n^3)$.

respectively. Finally, the optimal alignment similarity is the average of these two length-normalized similarity scores.

Aggregation similarity.   In order to compute the aggregation similarity, we first compute the aggregate vector representation for each of the two sentences and then compare these aggregate sentence vectors. The aggregate vector representation of the sentence S is computed simply as the mean of the vectors of its words, i.e., $e(S) = \frac{1}{|S|} \sum_{w \in S} e(w)$. The aggregation similarity score is then computed as the cosine similarity between the aggregate vector representations of the two sentences, i.e., $sim_{agg} = \cos(e(S_1), e(S_2))$. Note that, for multi-modal STS models, the aggregation similarity based on early-fusion word vectors is equivalent to the similarity of middle-fused sentence representations.

5   Evaluation

In this section, we provide all details relevant to the evaluation of our unsupervised multi-modal STS models, from the description of datasets to the discussion of the experimental results.

Datasets.   We use two different STS datasets to evaluate all models: we opt for very different STS datasets to gain more insight about the effectiveness of visually-informed STS models in different settings. The first dataset is the evaluation portion of the Microsoft Research video captions dataset (MSRVID) from the SemEval 2012 STS challenge Agirre et al. (2012). MSRVID consists of 750 pairs of short English sentences containing rather concrete concepts (people and animals performing simple actions, e.g., *"A woman is slicing onions"*). We couple the MSRVID dataset with the cross-lingual English-Spanish STS dataset (NEWS-16) from the SemEval 2016 STS shared task Agirre et al. (2016). NEWS-16 comprises 301 pairs of long sentences taken from news stories.

Considering (1) that MSRVID is a monolingual English dataset and NEWS-16 considers only one language pair and (2) that we aim to evaluate cross-lingual STS models on several language pairs, we derived other cross-lingual versions of these datasets. In addition to the standard monolingual English evaluation on the MSRVID dataset, we perform cross-lingual evaluations for three different language pairs: English-Spanish (EN-ES), English-Italian (EN-IT), and English-Croatian (EN-HR). We selected Spanish because of a readily available ES-EN NEWS-16 dataset and Italian because we had access to native speakers.

To test the claim that the proposed approach is language-independent, we also include an under-resourced language in the evaluation. As for Italian, we chose Croatian because we had access to a native speaker of that language. We created the additional cross-lingual datasets (all three language pairs for MSRVID; EN-IT and EN-HR for NEWS-16) by: (1) translating one of the sentences from each pair

	MSRVID		NEWS-16	
Language	ASL	AID	ASL	AID
English	3.42	0.51	17.0	0.68
Spanish	3.59	0.58	17.2	0.65
Italian	4.66	0.66	20.9	0.70
Croatian	3.54	0.70	17.7	0.71

Table 2: Statistics of the STS evaluation datasets.

to another language via Google translate and (2) having native speakers fix the machine translation errors.[6]

We depict the differences between the datasets in terms of the average sentence length in number of words (ASL) and the average image dispersion of words (AID) in Table 2, for all four languages. The average image dispersion is much lower on the MSRVID dataset (especially for English), which implies that the NEWS-16 dataset has larger portion of concepts that simply do not have a standardized visual representation. A closer manual inspection of the two datasets revealed that NEWS-16, besides having more abstract concepts than MSRVID, contains also a much larger number of polysemous words. This is not surprising considering the news-story origin of the sentences in NEWS-16. The differences in average image dispersion between the languages on the MSRVID dataset imply that Bing image search does not perform equally well for all languages.

Linguistic embeddings. We used the readily available word vectors for English (200-dimensional GloVe vectors trained on 6B tokens corpus), Spanish (300-dimensional Skip-Gram vectors trained on a 1.5B tokens corpus), and Italian (300-dimensional Skip-Gram vectors trained on a 2B tokens corpus). For Croatian, we trained 200-dimensional Skip-Gram embedding vectors on the 1.2B token version of the hrWaC corpus (Ljubešić and Erjavec, 2011).

To train the translation matrices, we selected the 4200 most frequent English words and translated them to the other three languages via Google translate, as done in prior work (Mikolov et al., 2013; Vulić et al., 2016). Native speakers of target languages fixed incorrect machine translations. We learned the optimal values of the translation matrices stochastically with the Adam algorithm (Kingma and Ba, 2014) on the 4000 word translation pairs. The obtained results of the evaluation of the translation quality on the remaining 200 test pairs – 58.8% P@5 for EN-ES, 56.3% for EN-IT, and 56.2% for EN-HR – are comparable to those reported in the original study from Mikolov et al. (2013).

STS Models in Evaluation. Our general approach includes several methods for measuring visual similarity (Table 1), different types of multi-modal information

---

[6]We make the STS datasets and the multi-modal STS code freely available at `http://tinyurl.com/jc8rd57`.

Model	MSRVID				NEWS-16		
	EN-EN	EN-ES	EN-IT	EN-HR	EN-ES	EN-IT	EN-HR
Linguistic-only							
TXT-OA	74.9	57.3	50.6	55.3	82.7	79.2	78.8
TXT-AGG	74.7	54.9	42.9	51.1	57.3	48.1	54.5
Visual-only							
VIS-OA-AVG-MAX	76.5	70.4	63.1	45.0	56.9	57.5	47.7
VIS-AGG-SIM-AVG	77.6	71.8	63.1	38.2	18.0	12.4	4.4
Multi-modal							
EF-OA-AVG	77.0	71.5	59.7	33.3	52.8	48.9	41.7
MF-AVG	77.8	72.0	63.8	38.9	19.1	14.8	1.3
LF-WORD-OA	76.6	67.9	60.9	58.3	78.1	74.9	71.0
LF-SENT	80.8	**73.1**	**65.4**	59.2	78.0	74.0	71.3
Multi-modal with selective inclusion of visual information							
MF-AVG-ID	78.1	70.6	50.0	53.9	57.4	50.2	54.5
LF-WORD-OA-ID	77.3	64.3	56.9	58.8	82.7	79.3	78.6
LF-SENT-ID	**81.0**	71.8	63.4	**61.0**	**83.1**	**79.6**	**79.5**

Table 3: STS performance on the MSRVID and NEWS-16 datasets (Pearson ρ).

fusion (Section 2) and two STS measures (Section 4). For brevity, we present results only for the following models:

i) Linguistic-only models employ linguistic embeddings with optimal alignment or aggregation similarity (TXT-OA and TXT-AGG);

ii) Visual-only models use optimal alignment or aggregation similarity with the visual similarities from Table 1 that yield the best performance (VIS-OA-AVG-MAX and VIS-AGG-SIM-AVG);

iii) Multi-modal models exploit both the linguistic and visual signal by combining early or middle fusion with the averaged image embedding (EF-OA-AVG and MF-AVG). Additionally, LF-WORD-OA performs the late fusion at the word level with optimal alignment similarity, whereas LF-SENT model computes the average of the similarity scores produced by the best-performing linguistic-only model and the best-performing visual-only model on the respective dataset. For the last three models we also evaluate variants with image dispersion-based weighting (MF-AVG-ID, LF-WORD-OA-ID and LF-SENT-ID).

Results and Discussion. Results using Pearson correlation between human and automatic similarity scores are shown in Table 3.

i) Multi-modal vs. uni-modal.   The visual-only models tend to outperform the linguistic-only models on MSRVID. The multi-modal models further improve the performance of the visual-only models. We believe that this is the result of good visual representations we are able to obtain for concrete concepts, which are abundant in MSRVID. In the multi-modal landscape, the late fusion at the level of similarity scores (i.e., the LF-SENT model) seems to be the best way to combine visual and linguistic information.

The performance of the visual-only models on NEWS-16 is, however, much lower than the performance of the linguistic-only models. We believe that this is the direct consequence of obtaining rather noisy visual signal for the majority of concepts in this dataset. We observe that only 17.9% of English words from NEWS-16 have the image dispersion score below 0.5 (the statistics is 38.7% on MSRVID). The number is even lower for the other three languages. Therefore, the direct multi-modal models (i.e., without the selective inclusion of visual information) also perform worse than the linguistic-only models.

Aggregation-based models (TXT-OA, VIS-AGG-AVG, and MF-AVG) perform comparably to their respective optimal alignment counterparts (TXT-OA, VIS-OA-AVGMAX, and EF-OA-AVG) on MSRVID, but display drastically lower performances on NEWS-16. The explanation for this is rather intuitive – it is harder to aggregate the meaning of a sentence from the meaning of its words for long than for short sentences. On the other hand, by aligning pairs of words and accounting for the number of alignments, the optimal alignment similarity is not affected by the sentence length.

ii) Monolingual vs. cross-lingual.   The performance gap on MSRVID in favor of visual-only and multi-modal models is significantly larger in the cross-lingual settings than in the monolingual English setting. On one hand, the cross-lingual linguistic-only models suffer from the imperfect mappings between monolingual embedding spaces. On the other hand, the visual signal seems not to deteriorate as much in quality for other languages. The performance of visual-only and multi-modal models is naturally lower for language pairs with languages for which more dispersed visual signals are used (IT and HR, see the scores in Table 2).

iii) Selective inclusion of visual information.   The models that selectively include visual information do not consistently improve the results of the direct multi-modal models on MSRVID. Since the impact of the visual signal is scaled according to the the larger of the image dispersions, the selection model might discard useful visual information for a word/sentence on one side, because of the poor visual information on the other side. On the other hand, we have less informative visual representations across the board on NEWS-16: here, a selective inclusion of visual information in the similarity-level late fusion model (LF-SENT-ID) has a slight edge on the linguistic-only model (TXTOA). This improvement is small due to a shortage of concepts with sufficiently coherent visual representations in NEWS-16. This suggests that more sophisticated image extraction and content selection methods are required in future work.

iv) Comparison with state-of-the-art. For the monolingual English MSRVID dataset and the cross-lingual EN-ES NEWS-16 dataset, we also compare our results with the best-performing systems from the corresponding SemEval shared tasks. Šarić et al. (2012) reach 88% correlation on MSRVID, which is 7% better than our LF-SENT-ID model. The system of Brychcín and Svoboda (2016) achieves the correlation score of 91% on the EN-ES NEWS-16, 8% above the performance of LF-SENT-ID. We find these gaps in performance to be reasonably low, given that both state-of-the-art systems use a set of expensive language-specific tools (e.g., dependency parsers, NER). Moreover, the system of Šarić et al. (2012) is supervised, whereas the Brychcín and Svoboda (2016) require a full-blown MT system.

6 Conclusion

Semantic representations of meaning that combine signals from visual and linguistic input tend to outperform uni-modal models exploiting only linguistic information across a variety of semantic tasks. In this work, we have investigated the effects of leveraging visual information in measuring semantic textual similarity (STS) of short texts. We have retrieved images for single-word concepts and extracted visual embeddings via a transferred deep CNN (VGG). We fused visual and linguistic signals at three different levels of granularity and plugged the variety of representations (linguistic, visual, multi-modal) into two simple unsupervised STS measures. In addition, we investigated the selective inclusion of visual information in multi-modal STS models based on image dispersion.

Experimental results suggest that the visual-only models outperform the linguistic-only models by a wide margin on datasets containing a large number of concrete concepts, especially in the cross-lingual setting. Moreover, the multi-modal STS models with selective inclusion of visual information seem to provide a performance boost even for the dataset for which the visual signal is dispersed.

The experiments show that the performance of visual-only and multi-modal models highly depends on the quality (dispersion) of images obtained for the concepts. Our future efforts will thus aim to devise methods for extracting and selecting better visual representations for visually dispersed concepts (e.g., by clustering the retrieved images by similarity and considering only images from the largest cluster).

References

Agirre, E., C. Banea, C. Cardiec, D. Cerd, M. Diabe, A. Gonzalez-Agirrea, W. Guof, I. Lopez-Gazpioa, M. Maritxalara, R. Mihalcea, et al. (2015). Semeval-2015 Task 2: Semantic textual similarity, English, Spanish and pilot on interpretability. In *SemEval*, pp. 252–263.

Agirre, E., C. Banea, D. Cer, M. Diab, A. Gonzalez-Agirre, R. Mihalcea, G. Rigau, and J. Wiebe (2016). Semeval-2016 Task 1: Semantic textual similarity, monolingual and cross-lingual evaluation. In *SemEval*, pp. 497–511.

Agirre, E., M. Diab, D. Cer, and A. Gonzalez-Agirre (2012). Semeval-2012 Task 6: A pilot on semantic textual similarity. In *SemEval*, pp. 385–393.

Aziz, W. and L. Specia (2011). Fully automatic compilation of Portuguese-English and Portuguese-Spanish parallel corpora. In *STIL*, pp. 234–238.

Bär, D., C. Biemann, I. Gurevych, and T. Zesch (2012). UKP: Computing semantic textual similarity by combining multiple content similarity measures. In **SEM*, pp. 435–440.

Bergsma, S. and B. V. Durme (2011). Learning bilingual lexicons using the visual similarity of labeled web images. In *IJCAI*, pp. 1764–1769.

Bergsma, S. and R. Goebel (2011). Using visual information to predict lexical preference. In *RANLP*, pp. 399–405.

Bruni, E., N. Tran, and M. Baroni (2014). Multimodal distributional semantics. *Journal of Artiifical Intelligence Research 49*, 1–47.

Brychcín, T. and L. Svoboda (2016). UWB at SemEval-2016 Task 1: Semantic textual similarity using lexical, syntactic, and semantic information. In *SemEval*, pp. 588–594.

Franco-Salvador, M., P. Gupta, and P. Rosso (2013). Cross-language plagiarism detection using a multilingual semantic network. In *ECIR*, pp. 710–713.

Han, L., A. Kashyap, T. Finin, J. Mayfield, and J. Weese (2013). UMBC EBIQUITY-CORE: Semantic textual similarity systems. In *SemEval*, pp. 44–52.

Harnad, S. (1990). The symbol grounding problem. *Physica D: Nonlinear Phenomena 42*(1-3), 335–346.

Hill, F., D. Kiela, and A. Korhonen (2013). Concreteness and corpora: A theoretical and practical analysis. In *Proceedings of the Workshop on Cognitive Modeling and Computational Linguistics*, pp. 75–83.

Islam, A. and D. Inkpen (2008). Semantic text similarity using corpus-based word similarity and string similarity. *ACM Transactions on Knowledge Discovery from Data (TKDD) 2*(2), 10.

Jimenez, S. (2016). SERGIOJIMENEZ at SemEval-2016 Task 1: Effectively combining paraphrase database, string matching, WordNet, and word embedding for semantic textual similarity. In *SemEval*, pp. 749–757.

Kiela, D. (2016). MMFeat: A toolkit for extracting multi-modal features. In *ACL (Demos)*, pp. 55–60.

Kiela, D. and L. Bottou (2014). Learning image embeddings using convolutional neural networks for improved multi-modal semantics. In *EMNLP*, pp. 36–45.

Kiela, D., F. Hill, A. Korhonen, and S. Clark (2014). Improving multi-modal representations using image dispersion: Why less is sometimes mor. In *ACL*, pp. 835–841.

Kiela, D., L. Rimell, I. Vulić, and S. Clark (2015). Exploiting image generality for lexical entailment detection. In *ACL*, pp. 119–124.

Kiela, D., A. L. Verő, and S. Clark (2016). Comparing Data Sources and Architectures for Deep Visual Representation Learning in Semantics. In *EMNLP (to appear)*.

Kiela, D., I. Vulić, and S. Clark (2015). Visual bilingual lexicon induction with transferred ConvNet features. In *EMNLP*, pp. 148–158.

Kingma, D. and J. Ba (2014). Adam: A method for stochastic optimization. *arXiv preprint arXiv:1412.6980*.

Krizhevsky, A., I. Sutskever, and G. E. Hinton (2012). ImageNet classification with deep convolutional neural networks. In *NIPS*, pp. 1097–1105.

Kuhn, H. W. (1955). The hungarian method for the assignment problem. *Naval Research Logistics Quarterly 2*(1-2), 83–97.

Lakoff, G. and M. Johnson (1999). *Philosophy in the flesh: The embodied mind and its challenge to Western thought.*

Ljubešić, N. and T. Erjavec (2011). hrWaC and siWaC: Compiling Web corpora for Croatian and Slovene. In *TSD*, pp. 395–402.

Louwerse, M. M. (2011). Symbol interdependency in symbolic and embodied cognition. *Topics in Cognitive Science 59*(1), 617–645.

Mikolov, T., Q. V. Le, and I. Sutskever (2013). Exploiting similarities among languages for machine translation. *CoRR abs/1309.4168*.

Mikolov, T., I. Sutskever, K. Chen, G. S. Corrado, and J. Dean (2013). Distributed representations of words and phrases and their compositionality. In *NIPS*, pp. 3111–3119.

Oliva, J., J. I. Serrano, M. D. del Castillo, and Á. Iglesias (2011). Symss: A syntax-based measure for short-text semantic similarity. *Data & Knowledge Engineering 70*(4), 390–405.

Pennington, J., R. Socher, and C. D. Manning (2014). Glove: Global vectors for word representation. In *EMNLP*, pp. 1532–1543.

Potthast, M., A. Barrón-Cedeño, B. Stein, and P. Rosso (2011). Cross-language plagiarism detection. *Language Resources and Evaluation 45*(1), 45–62.

Resnik, P. and N. A. Smith (2003). The Web as a parallel corpus. *Computational Linguistics 29*(3), 349–380.

Roller, S. and S. Schulte Im Walde (2013). A multimodal LDA model integrating textual, cognitive and visual modalities. In *EMNLP*, pp. 1146–1157.

Russakovsky, O., J. Deng, H. Su, J. Krause, S. Satheesh, S. Ma, Z. Huang, A. Karpathy, A. Khosla, M. Bernstein, et al. (2015). ImageNet large scale visual recognition challenge. *International Journal of Computer Vision 115*(3), 211–252.

Šarić, F., G. Glavaš, M. Karan, J. Šnajder, and B. D. Bašić (2012). Takelab: Systems for measuring semantic text similarity. In *SemEval*, pp. 441–448.

Shutova, E., D. Kiela, and J. Maillard (2016). Black holes and white rabbits: Metaphor identification with visual features. In *NAACL-HLT*, pp. 160–170.

Silberer, C. and M. Lapata (2012). Grounded models of semantic representation. In *EMNLP*, pp. 1423–1433.

Simonyan, K. and A. Zisserman (2014). Very deep convolutional networks for large-scale image recognition. *arXiv preprint arXiv:1409.1556*.

Specia, L., S. Frank, K. Sima'an, and D. Elliott (2016). A shared task on multimodal machine translation and crosslingual image description. In *WMT*, pp. 543–553.

Sultan, M. A., S. Bethard, and T. Sumner (2014). DLS@CU: Sentence similarity from word alignment. In *SemEval*, pp. 241–246.

Szegedy, C., W. Liu, Y. Jia, P. Sermanet, S. Reed, D. Anguelov, D. Erhan, V. Vanhoucke, and A. Rabinovich (2015). Going deeper with convolutions. In *CVPR*, pp. 1–9.

Vulić, I., D. Kiela, S. Clark, and M.-F. Moens (2016). Multi-modal representations for improved bilingual lexicon learning. In *ACL*, pp. 188–194.

A constrained graph algebra for semantic parsing with AMRs

Jonas Groschwitz[*†]   Meaghan Fowlie[*]   Mark Johnson[†]   Alexander Koller[*]
[*] Saarland University, Saarbrücken, Germany   [†] Macquarie University, Sydney, Australia
`jonasg|mfowlie|koller@coli.uni-saarland.de`
`mark.johnson@mq.edu.au`

Abstract

When learning grammars that map from sentences to abstract meaning representations (AMRs), one faces the challenge that an AMR can be described in a huge number of different ways using traditional graph algebras. We introduce a new algebra for building graphs from smaller parts, using linguistically motivated operations for combining a head with a complement or a modifier. Using this algebra, we can reduce the number of analyses per AMR graph dramatically; at the same time, we show that challenging linguistic constructions can still be handled correctly.

1 Introduction

Semantic parsers are systems which map natural-language expressions to formal semantic representations, in a way that is learned from data. Much research on semantic parsing has focused on mapping sentences to Abstract Meaning Representations (AMRs), graphs which represent the predicate-argument structure of the sentences. Such work builds upon the AMRBank (Banarescu et al., 2013), a corpus in which each sentence has been manually annotated with an AMR.

The training instances in the AMRBank are annotated only with the AMRs themselves, not with the structure of a compositional derivation of the AMR. This poses a challenge for semantic parsing, especially for approaches which induce a grammar from the data and thus must make this compositional structure explicit in order to learn rules (Jones et al., 2012, 2013; Artzi et al., 2015; Peng et al., 2015). In general, the number of ways in which an AMR graph can be built from its atomic parts, e.g. using the generic graph-combining operations of the HR algebra (Courcelle, 1993), is huge (Groschwitz et al., 2015). This makes grammar induction computationally expensive and undermines its ability to discover grammatical structures that can be shared across multiple instances. Existing approaches therefore resort to heuristics that constrain the space of possible analyses, often with limited regard to the linguistic reality of these heuristics.

We propose a novel method to generate a constrained set of derivations directly from an AMR, but without losing linguistically significant phenomena and parses. To this end we present an *apply-modify (AM) graph algebra* for combining graphs using operations that reflect the way linguistic predicates combine with complements and adjuncts. By equipping graphs with annotations that encode argument sharing, AM algebra derivations can model phenomena such as control, raising, and coordination straightforwardly. We describe a method to generate the AM algebra for an AMR in practice, and demonstrate its effectiveness: e.g. for graphs with five nodes, our method reduces the number of candidate terms from 10^{17} to just 21 on average.

The paper is structured as follows. Section 2 reviews some related work and sets the stage for the rest of the paper. Section 3 briefly reviews the HR algebra and its problems for grammar induction, and then defines the AM algebra. In Section 4, we discuss a number of challenging linguistic phenomena and demonstrate that AM algebra derivations can capture the intended compositional derivations of the resulting AMRs. We explain how to obtain AM algebra derivations for graphs in the AMRBank in Section 5. Finally, we show that in practice, we can indeed reduce the set of derivations while achieving high coverage in Section 6.

2   Related work

This paper is concerned with finding the hidden compositional structure of AMRs, the semantic representations annotated in the AMRBank (Banarescu et al., 2013). AMRs are directed, acyclic, rooted graphs with node labels indicating semantic concepts and edge labels indicating semantic roles, such as arguments ARG0, ARG1, ... and modifiers, such as manner and time.

An example is shown in Fig. 1.[1] Here, *snake* is an ARG0 of both *chew* and *swallow*, and *prey* is an ARG1 of *swallow*. Nodes can fill argument positions of multiple predicate nodes, not just because of grammatical phenomena such as control, but also because of coreference (***its** prey*), or because they are pragmatically implied arguments (edge from *chew* to *prey*). An AMR's root represents a "focus" in the graph; the root is often the main predicate of the sentence. In Fig. 1, the root is the *swallow* node. AMRs are "abstract" because they gloss over certain details of the syntactic realization. For example, *destruction of Rome* and *Rome was destroyed* have the same AMR; among others, tense and determiners are dropped.

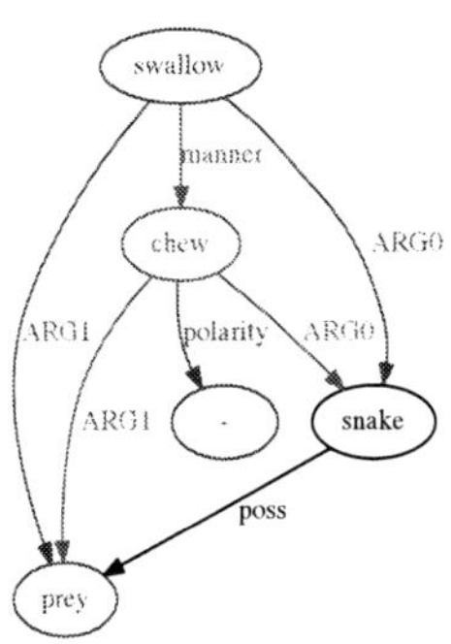

Figure 1: AMR of *The snake swallows its prey without chewing.*

The availability of the AMRBank has spawned much research on semantic parsing into AMR representations. The work in this paper is most obviously connected to research that models the compositional mapping from strings to AMRs with grammars – using either synchronous grammars (Jones et al., 2012; Peng et al., 2015) or CCG (Artzi et al., 2015; Misra and Artzi, 2016). Not all AMR parsers learn explicit grammars (Flanigan et al., 2014; Peng et al., 2017). However, we believe that these, too, may benefit from access to the compositional structure of the AMRs, which the algebra we present makes easier to compute.

The operations our algebra uses to combine semantic representations are closely related to those of the "semantic algebra" of Copestake et al. (2001), which was intended to reflect universal semantic combination operations for large-scale handwritten HPSG grammars. More distantly, the ability of our semantic representations to select the type of its arguments echoes the use of types in Montague Grammar and in CCG (Steedman, 2001), applied to graphs.

3   Algebras for constructing graphs

We start by reviewing the HR algebra and discussing some of its shortcomings in the context of grammar induction. Then we introduce the apply-modify graph algebra, which tackles these shortcomings in a linguistically adequate way.

Notation: For a given (partial) function $f : A \rightarrow B$, we write $\mathcal{D}(f) \subseteq A$ for the set of values on which f is defined and $\mathcal{I}(f) \subseteq B$ for its image. When convenient, we read functions as sets of input-output pairs, so that e.g. $\emptyset$ denotes the partial function that is undefined everywhere. If f, g are (partial) functions, we write $f \circ g$ for the function h such that $h(a) = f(g(a))$ for all a. If f is injective, we write f^{-1} for its inverse (partial) function. We write $\overline{f}$ for the total function such that $\overline{f}(a) = f(a)$ if $f(a)$ is defined and $\overline{f}(a) = a$ otherwise. Finally, for an input value $x \in \mathcal{D}(f)$, we write $f \setminus x$ for the function that is equal to f except that it is undefined on x.

A Σ-*algebra* $\mathbb{A} = \langle \mathcal{A}, (\mathsf{f})_{\mathsf{F} \in \Sigma} \rangle$ is a structure in which terms over a *signature* Σ can be evaluated as elements from the algebra's *domain* $\mathcal{A}$. Here, Σ is a *ranked signature*; that is, a set of symbols $\mathsf{F} \in \Sigma$, each of which is equipped with a *rank* $\in \mathbb{N}$. Symbols of rank 0 are called *constants*. For each $\mathsf{F} \in \Sigma$ of rank k, the algebra defines a function $\mathsf{f} : \mathcal{A}^k \rightarrow \mathcal{A}$; in particular, constants are interpreted as elements of $\mathcal{A}$. The functions may be partial; then $\mathbb{A}$ is called a *partial* algebra. We define the *terms* over Σ, T_Σ, recursively: all constants are terms, and if $\mathsf{F} \in \Sigma$ has rank n and $t_1, \ldots, t_n \in T_\Sigma$, then $\mathsf{F}(t_1, \ldots, t_n)$ is

---

[1] Originally, AMR represents labels on nodes as labelled leaves, i.e. edges of cardinality 1. For readability, we write the labels directly in the nodes, and refer to them as *node labels* in text. We also drop the predicate senses that AMR draws from the OntoNotes project: In reality, e.g. the *swallow* node would be labelled *swallow-01*

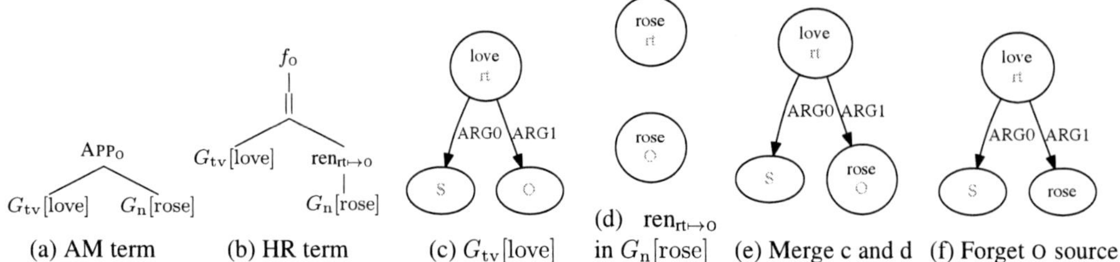

(a) AM term   (b) HR term   (c) $G_{\mathrm{tv}}[\text{love}]$ (d) $\text{ren}_{\mathrm{rt}\mapsto\mathrm{o}}$ in $G_{\mathrm{n}}[\text{rose}]$ (e) Merge c and d   (f) Forget O source

Figure 2: HR algebra derivation of *loves a rose*.

also a term. Such a term *evaluates* recursively to the value $[\![t]\!] = \mathsf{f}([\![t_1]\!], \ldots, [\![t_n]\!]) \in \mathcal{A}$. Approaching graphs algebraically allows us to examine the compositionality of graphs – how graphs can be built from smaller graphs. For example, the terms in Figures 2a and 2b both describe the combining of the graphs in Figures 2c and 2d to form the graph in Fig. 2f. We describe the operations used in these terms in the following subsections.

Convention: To increase readability and since in this paper we focus on the functions and rarely refer to a symbol itself, we will denote a function corresponding to a symbol with the symbol itself. I.e. we will use the same notation for both symbol and associated function, not making the distinction between F and f as in the definition above. But as a general principle in this paper, this common notation always refers to the function in text and definitions, and to the symbol in terms such as in Figures 2a and 2b.

3.1 S-graphs and the HR algebra

A standard algebra for the theoretical literature for describing graphs is the *HR algebra* of Courcelle (1993). It is very closely related to hyperedge replacement grammars (Drewes et al., 1997), which have been used extensively for grammars of AMR languages (Chiang et al., 2013; Peng et al., 2015), and Koller (2015) showed explicitly how to do compositional semantic construction using the HR algebra.

The objects of the HR algebra are *s-graphs* $G = (g, S)$, consisting of a graph g (here, directed and with node and edge labels) and a partial function $S : S \rightsquigarrow V$, which maps *sources* from a fixed finite set S of source names to nodes of g. Sources thus serve as external, interpretable names for some of the nodes. If we have $S(a) = v$, then we call v an *a-source* of G. An example of an s-graph with a root-source (rt) and a subject-source (s) is shown in Fig. 2f. Sources are marked in diagrams as red node labels.

The HR-algebra serves as a compositional algebra for graphs because it includes an operation *merge* which connects two graphs at the nodes that share source names. The algebra evaluates terms from a signature which, in addition to constants for s-graphs, contains three further types of function symbols. The *merge* operation $||$, of rank two, combines two s-graphs G_1 and G_2 into a new s-graph G' that contains all the nodes and edges of G_1 and G_2. If G_1 has an *a*-source u and G_2 has an *a*-source v, for some source name a, then u and v will be mapped to the same node in G', taking with it all the edges into and out of u and v. We will usually write $||$ in infix notation. The *rename* operation $\text{ren}_{\{a_1\mapsto b_1,\ldots,a_n\mapsto b_n\}}$, of rank one, renames the sources of an s-graph; if the node u was an a_i-source before the rename, it becomes a b_i-source. Finally, the *forget* operation f_a, of rank 1, removes the entry for source a from S, i.e. the resulting s-graph no longer has an *a*-source.

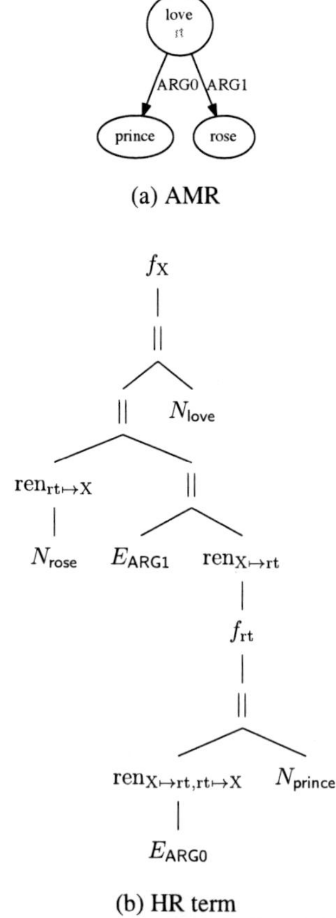

(a) AMR

(b) HR term

Figure 3: AMR generated by linguistically bizarre HR term

An example for a term of the HR algebra is shown in Fig. 2b. This term uses the constants $G_{\mathrm{tv}}[\text{love}]$ (Fig. 2c) and $G_{\mathrm{n}}[\text{rose}]$, which are evaluated by replacing the node label "**" in the graphs G_{tv} and G_{n} in

122

Fig. 4 with "love" and "rose", respectively. The term *renames* the rt-source of $G_n[\text{rose}]$ to an O-source (Fig. 2d). Thus when the result is *merged* with $G_{tv}[\text{love}]$, the "rose" label is inserted into the object position of the verb (Fig. 2e). Finally, we *forget* the O-source, yielding the s-graph in Fig. 2f.

The operations of the HR algebra are rather fine-grained, and can be combined flexibly. This is an advantage when developing grammars using the HR algebra by hand (Koller, 2015), but makes the automatic induction of grammars from the AMRBank expensive and error-prone. Groschwitz et al. (2015) show that with more than three sources, the problem becomes quite extreme, and that with such few sources available, one must use constants of only one or two nodes. Following the experimental setup of Groschwitz et al. (2015), N_{rose}, N_{prince} and N_{love} in Figure 3b evaluate to labelled nodes with a rt-source, and E_{ARG0} and E_{ARG1} evaluate to single edges with a rt-source at their source and an X-source at their target. Using these constants and just the two sources rt and X, there are already 3584 terms over the HR algebra which evaluate to the (quite small) s-graph in Fig. 3a.

This set of terms is riddled with spurious ambiguity and linguistically bizarre analyses, such as the term shown in Fig. 3b. Two strange aspects of this example are: one, *prince* becomes an X-source by first switching X and rt and then switching them back; this step is unnecessary and inconsistent with the corresponding process for *rose* here. Two, *prince* and *rose* are combined with empty argument connectors before *love* finally is inserted as the predicate, despite these roles being originally defined in *love*'s semantic frame.

Not only does this make graph parsing computationally expensive (Chiang et al., 2013; Groschwitz et al., 2015), it also makes grammar induction difficult. For example, Bayesian algorithms sample random terms from the AMRBank and attempt to discover grammatical structures that are shared across different training instances. When the number of possible terms is huge, the chance that no two rules share any grammatical structure increases, undermining the grammar induction process. Existing systems therefore apply heuristics to constrain the space of allowable HR terms. However, these heuristics are typically ad-hoc, and not motivated on linguistic grounds. Thus there is a risk that the linguistically correct compositional derivation of an AMR is accidentally excluded.

3.2   The apply-modify graph algebra

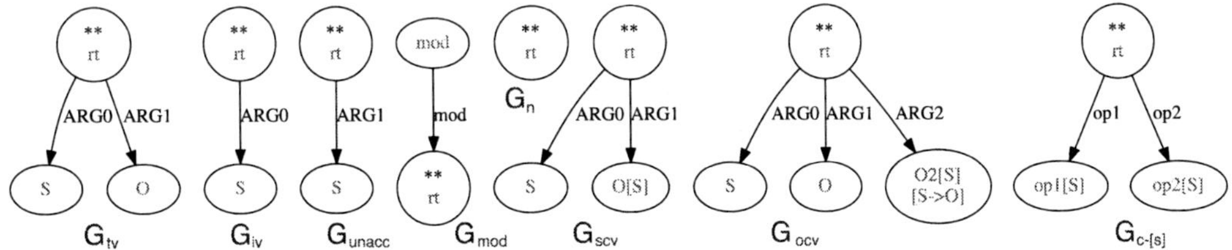

Figure 4: Lexicon. ** can be replaced by a label of the right category. Examples: G_{tv}: love, G_{iv}: sleep; G_{unacc}: relax; G_{mod}: red; G_n: prince,rose,sheep,pilot; G_{scv}: want; G_{ocv}: persuade; $G_{c-[s]}$: and (seeking operands of type [s]). rt stands for *root*, s for *subject*, O for *object*, and mod for *modifier*.

Upon closer reflection, the structure of the HR term in Fig. 2b is not arbitrary. Many semantic theories assume that two key operations in combining semantic representations compositionally are *application* (i.e., the combination of a predicate with a complement) and *modification*. The term in Fig. 2b simply spells out application for the O-argument of "love": The root of "rose" is inserted into the O-argument-slot, and afterwards we forget the O-source since the slot has been filled. Here we define the *apply-modify (AM) graph algebra*, which replaces the rename-merge-forget operation sequences of the HR algebra with operations that directly model application and modification. In this way, we constrain the set of possible terms for each graph, while preserving linguistically motivated compositional structures. For instance, there will be no equivalent for the term in Fig. 3b.

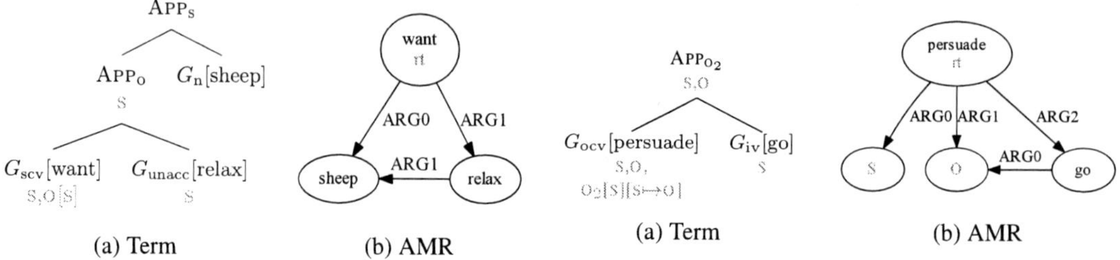

<table>
<tr><td>(a) Term</td><td>(b) AMR</td><td>(a) Term</td><td>(b) AMR</td></tr>
</table>

Figure 5: Subject control *The sheep wants to relax*

Figure 6: Object control: *persuade __ to go*

3.2.1 Application

We first define the *apply* operation APP_α, where α is a source name. In the simple case of Fig. 2a, APP_O renames the rt-source of its second argument G_2 to O, merges the result with the first argument G_1, and then forgets O – just as in the HR term in Fig. 2b, but with a single algebra operation.

In this simple case, G_2 was complete; its only source was rt. However, in certain cases, we want to combine a predicate with an argument that is itself still looking for arguments. Take the graph in Fig. 5b for example, corresponding to the sentence "the sheep wants to relax", where the sheep is both the wanter and the relaxer. For the subject control verb *want*, we use the lexicon entry $G_\text{scv}[\text{want}]$ of Fig. 4. Its O source is *annotated* with the *argument type* S (written O[S]). This means that $G_\text{scv}[\text{want}]$ requires its object argument to contain an S-source; during application this node is merged with the S-source of $G_\text{scv}[\text{want}]$ itself. This yields a graph with an (undirected) cycle, that is, a graph that is not a tree.

We also allow annotations for *renaming* sources, in order to model phenomena such as object control verbs, as in "the prince persuaded the sheep to sleep" (see Fig. 6a-b). Here, *sheep* is both the subject of *sleep* and the object of *persuade*. We can handle this with the graph for $G_\text{ocv}[\text{persuade}]$ in Fig. 4, that features an O_2-source which is annotated as $\text{O}_2[\text{S}][\text{S}\mapsto\text{O}]$. This O_2-source must be filled by a graph G_2 that still has an S-source, which is renamed to an O-source during application, and thus merged with the O-source of persuade. This yields the structure shown in Fig. 6b. To capture these intuitions formally, we present the following definitions.

Definition 3.1 (Graph types (TY)). A *graph type* is a pair $\tau = (T, R)$ of a function $T : S \to \text{TY}$, where $S \subseteq \mathcal{S}$ is a set of source names, that assigns a graph type to each source, and a function $R : S \to \{r : S \rightsquigarrow S \mid r \text{ partial, injective}\}$ that annotates each source with a renaming function. R may only rename sources T requires , i.e. we demand $\forall T(\alpha) = \langle T', R'\rangle$, $\mathcal{D}(R(\alpha)) \subseteq \mathcal{D}(T')$. We say that S is the *domain* of τ. Intuitively, the graph type τ provides annotations for all source names in S.

Definition 3.2 (Annotated s-graph (as-graph)). An *annotated s-graph (as-graph)* is a pair $\mathcal{G} = \langle G, \tau\rangle$ of an s-graph $G = (g, S)$ that contains a "root" source (i.e. rt $\in \mathcal{D}(S)$) and a *graph type* $\tau \in \text{TY}$ with domain $S \setminus \{\text{rt}\}$. We write $\mathcal{AS}$ for the set of all as-graphs.

Our notation, as seen in the above examples, follows the pattern $\alpha[T(\alpha)][R(\alpha)]$ for a source α and its annotation, but we simplify it and drop empty types and functions. For example, the notation O in $G_\text{tv}[\text{love}]$ indicates that $T(\text{O}) = (\emptyset, \emptyset)$ and $R(\text{O}) = \emptyset$. The notation O[S] in $G_\text{scv}[\text{want}]$ indicates that $T(\text{O}) = (\{\text{S} \mapsto (\emptyset, \emptyset)\}, \{\text{S} \mapsto \emptyset\})$ and $R(\text{O}) = \emptyset$. That is, we require the argument to have an S-source that itself is not further annotated, and we do not rename it. Finally, the notation $\text{O}_2[\text{S}][\text{S}\mapsto\text{O}]$ in $G_\text{ocv}[\text{persuade}]$ indicates that similarly $T(\text{O}_2) = (\{\text{S} \mapsto (\emptyset, \emptyset)\}, \{\text{S} \mapsto \emptyset\})$, but now $R(\text{O}_2) = \{\text{S} \mapsto \text{O}\}$, signalling the rename.

Definition 3.3 (Apply operation (APP)). Let $\mathcal{G}_1 = ((g_1, S_1), (T_1, R_1))$, $\mathcal{G}_2 = ((g_2, S_2), (T_2, R_2))$ be as-graphs. Then we let $\text{APP}_\alpha(\mathcal{G}_1, \mathcal{G}_2) = ((g', S'), (T', R'))$ such that

$$(g', S') = f_\alpha((g_1, S_1) \parallel \text{ren}_{\{\text{rt}\to\alpha\}}(\text{ren}_{R_1(\alpha)}((g_2, S_2))))$$
$$T' = (T_1 \setminus \{\alpha\}) \cup (T_2 \circ \overline{R_1(\alpha)^{-1}})$$
$$R' = (R_1 \setminus \{\alpha\}) \cup (R_2 \circ \overline{R_1(\alpha)^{-1}})$$

if and only if

1. $\mathcal{G}_1$ actually has an α-source to fill, i.e. $\alpha \in \mathcal{D}(T_1)$,
2. $\mathcal{G}_2$ has the type α is looking for, i.e. $T_1(\alpha) = (T_2, R_2)$, and
3. T', R' are well-defined (partial) functions;

otherwise $\text{APP}_\alpha(\mathcal{G}_1, \mathcal{G}_2)$ is undefined.

The interpretation is just as discussed at the start of Section 3.2 above: we apply all renamings required by R_1 to (g_2, S_2), we rename the root to α, we merge the graphs, and then we forget α. The type of the output graph, (T', R'), is defined such that the source we just filled, α, is removed, and the renaming function of $\mathcal{G}_1$ at α is applied to the domains of T_2 and R_2, so that any requirements $\mathcal{G}_2$ had on its arguments are properly carried over into the new renamed graph. Conditions 1 and 2 ensure that the operation matches the intuition behind the source annotations. Condition 3 guarantees that there are no conflicts in the remaining source annotations of the two graphs. Note that since $T_1(\alpha)$ equals the type (T_2, R_2) if Condition 2 holds, the type (T_1, R_1) can then alone guarantee Condition 3. Observe that the term in Fig. 2a generates the as-graph in Fig. 2f; in both Figures 5 and 6, the term in (a) generates the graph in (b).

3.2.2 Modification

We further define a *modify* operation MOD_α, which models modification of its first argument G_1 by its second argument G_2. An example of using MOD_{MOD} to construct an as-graph for "red rose" is shown in Fig. 7, where the modify operation captures the HR term in Fig. 7b: We forget the rt-source of the as-graph $G_{\text{mod}}[\text{red}]$; rename its MOD-source to rt; and then merge it with $G_n[\text{rose}]$. That is, we shift the rt-source of the modifer G_2 to the unlabelled MOD-source and attach it at the root of G_1. This yields the AMR in Fig. 7c. Unlike in the apply case, we can repeat this modification operation as many times as we like: no sources of G_1 are forgotten.

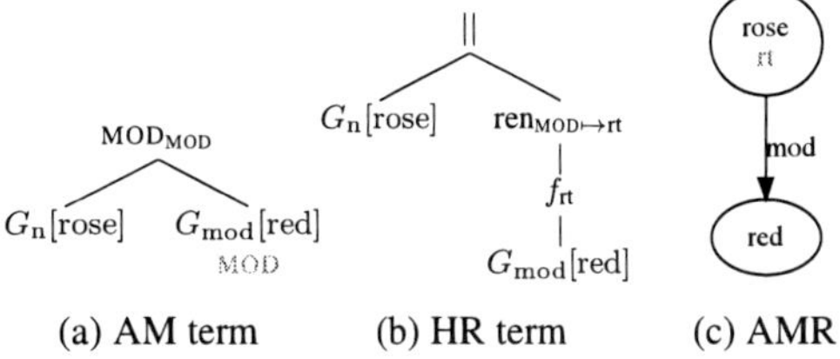

(a) AM term   (b) HR term   (c) AMR

Figure 7: Modification: *a red rose*

Definition 3.4 (Modify operation (MOD)). In general, we define the *modify operation* for a source α as follows. Again, let $\mathcal{G}_1 = ((g_1, S_1), (T_1, R_1))$, $\mathcal{G}_2 = ((g_2, S_2), (T_2, R_2))$ be as-graphs. Then we let $\text{MOD}_\alpha(\mathcal{G}_1, \mathcal{G}_2) = ((g', S'), (T_1, R_1))$ such that

$$(g', S') = (g_1, S_1) \,\|\, \text{ren}_{\{\alpha \mapsto \text{rt}\}}(f_{\text{rt}}((g_2, S_2)))$$

if and only if
1. $\alpha \in \mathcal{D}(\tau_2)$, i.e. $\mathcal{G}_2$ has an α source,
2. $T_2(\alpha) = (\emptyset, \emptyset)$, i.e. $\mathcal{G}_2$ does not have complex expectations at α, and
3. $T_2 \setminus \alpha \subseteq T_1$ and $R_2 \setminus \alpha \subseteq R_1$, i.e. any remaining sources and annotations in $\mathcal{G}_2$ are already in $\mathcal{G}_1$;

otherwise it is undefined.

Again, the s-graph evaluation and Condition 1 are straightforward. Modification is more restricted then application, and we demand that the modifier does not change the modifiee's type (Condition 3). We do however allow additional sources in $\mathcal{G}_2$ to merge with existing ones of $\mathcal{G}_1$. For example, when *chew* would modify *swallow* to create the graph in Fig. 1 ("without chewing"), their subject and object would merge. Condition 2 avoids using e.g. the control structure of $G_{\text{scv}}[\text{want}]$ for modification.

We conclude this section by defining the *apply-modify graph algebra (AM algebra)* as an algebra whose domain is the set of all as-graphs. In addition to constants (which evaluate to as-graphs), the AM algebra's signature contains the symbols APP_α (of rank 2) and MOD_α (of rank 2). The associated functions are the ones just defined.

4 Linguistic Discussion

The AM algebra restricts the derivations for a given AMR. The danger, then, is that we could lose all derivations for an AMR, making it unparseable, or that the terms we are left with are not linguistically reasonable. In this section, we show we find reasonable terms for a range of challenging examples. A quantitative analysis of the amount of graphs in the AMRBank for which we can find a decomposition is provided in Section 6.

We have already seen how to derive simple argument application, modification, and control constructions. APP is designed explicitly to parallel for example beta-reduction in lambda calculus, and syntactic operations such as forward and backward application in categorial grammars or endocentric context-free rules. The two arguments of the function combine in such a way that one is in a sense inserted into the other, and the operation is only permitted if the types are correct. In an AM-algebra, APP_α is only allowed if the first argument's type includes the source α, and the second argument's type is $T_1(\alpha)$, and the result is a graph in which the first argument keeps its original root, and the second graph is inside the first. MOD is designed to parallel for example modification of phrases by phrases in a context-free grammar, or modification as X/X categories in categorial grammars: the type of the modifier is a subset of the modified graph, so that modification has no effect on the type of the modified graph, and the modification happens at the root. Modification can also derive control in *secondary predicates* that modify the verb phrase and link an argument to an argument of the verb. For example, to derive (1), the graph for *without dreaming* modifies $G_{\text{iv}}[\text{sleep}]$ while both have an open S-source.

(1)   The prince$_i$ slept [without [__$_i$ dreaming]]

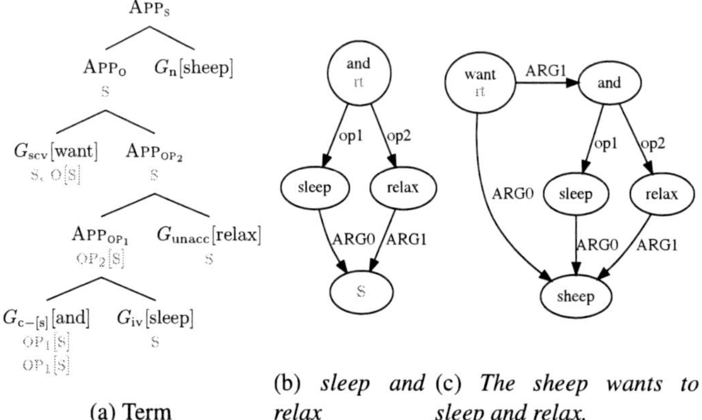

(a) Term   (b) *sleep and relax*   (c) *The sheep wants to sleep and relax.*

Figure 8: Conjoining intransitive verbs

4.1 Coordination

Coordination is a source of re-entrancies in AMRs. For example, when two verb phrases are conjoined, as in (2-a), their subjects must co-refer. Objects can also co-refer in English, as in (2-b). Control verbs, which already have re-entrancies of their own, can be conjoined, as in (2-c). Even subject- and object-control verbs can be conjoined if the object control verb is in the passive (2-d).

(2)   a.   The prince$_i$ __$_i$ sang and __$_i$ danced
        b.   The prince$_i$ __$_i$ grew __$_j$ and __$_i$ loved __$_j$ a rose$_j$
        c.   The sheep$_i$ __$_i$ wanted and __$_i$ needed __$_i$ to relax
        d.   The prince$_j$ wanted __$_j$ to go$_v$, or __$_j$ was persuaded __$_j$ to __$_v$.
        e.   The rose$_i$ [asked __$_j$ __$_v$] and __$_i$ [persuaded the Prince$_j$ to stay$_v$].

Coordination is generally observed to be between like things; for us this mean the arguments have the same type. For example, in Fig. 8, we choose an *and* that chooses arguments that are missing their subject – it has annotated sources $\text{OP}_i[\text{S}]$. When $G_{\text{iv}}[\text{sleep}]$ and $G_{\text{unacc}}[\text{relax}]$ merge, so do their subjects. In this way, the graph for *sleep and relax* can be selected by a control verb, $G_{\text{scv}}[\text{want}]$, merging its subject with theirs. Similarly, for example (2-e), *ask* and *persuade* are conjoined by a conjunction *and* which is looking for two object-control verbs; that is, *and* has type $\{\text{OP}_1[\text{S},\text{O},\text{O}_2[\text{S}][\text{S}\mapsto\text{O}]], \text{OP}_2[\text{S},\text{O},\text{O}_2[\text{S}][\text{S}\mapsto\text{O}]]\}$.

There is nothing in the algebra that principally prevents coordination of graphs with different types; however, we restrict our lexicon to constants for coordination nodes that expect like types in their arguments – we do this in our implementation in Section 5.

4.2 Relative Clauses

Relative clauses are unusual in that one of the arguments of a modifier is the very thing it is modifying. For example, in (3-a), the relative clause *that relaxed* has *sheep* as the subject of *relax*, and *that relaxed* modifies *sheep*. To capture this, we include MOD_S and MOD_O in our repertoire. For a subject relative we make the subject into the root and use it to modify *sheep*, as in Figure 9.

(3) a. [The sheep$_i$ [that —$_i$ relaxed]] —$_i$ slept
     b. [The asteroid$_i$ that the pilot thought the prince visited —$_i$] is tiny

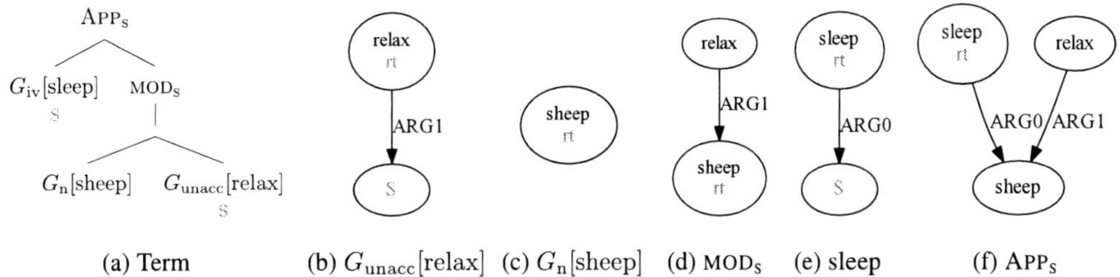

(a) Term   (b) $G_\text{unacc}[\text{relax}]$ (c) $G_\text{n}[\text{sheep}]$ (d) MOD_S (e) sleep   (f) APP_S

Figure 9: Relative Clause: *The sheep that relaxed slept*

An unboundedly embedded argument can be relativised on, as in (3-b). We handle these the same way they are handled in Tree Adjoining Grammars: by relativising on the clausal argument slot (Fig.10).

5 Decomposing AMRs with the AM algebra

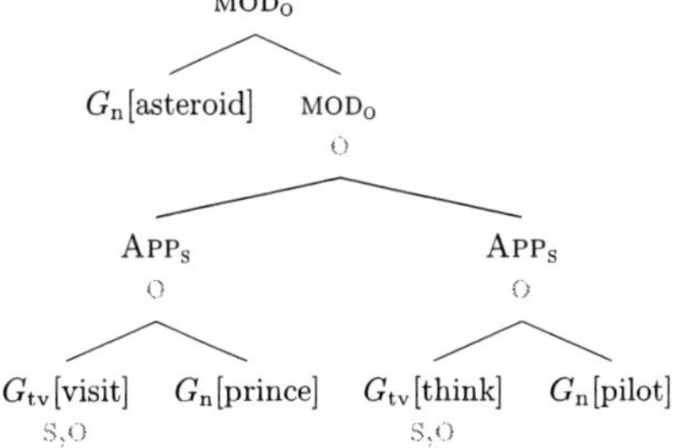

Figure 10: *the asteroid the pilot thinks the prince visited —*

At this point, we have defined the AM algebra – as a more constrained algebra of graphs than the HR algebra – and shown the adequacy of the apply and modify operations for a number of nontrivial linguistic examples. We will now show how to enumerate AM terms that evaluate to a given graph, e.g. an AMR in the AMRBank. As indicated above, this is a crucial ingredient for grammar induction.

The first step in decomposing a graph G in this way is to select the constants for as-graphs that we will use in the AM algebra – i.e., "atomic" as-graphs such as those in Fig. 4. During grammar induction, we have no grammar or lexicon to draw from, so we will use heuristic methods to extract constants from G. Throughout, we assume that G is an AMR, and we will use a fixed set of sources $S = \{\text{rt}, \text{S}, \text{O}, \text{O}_2, \ldots, \text{O}_9, \text{MOD}, \text{POSS}, \text{DOMAIN}\} \cup \{\text{OP}_x \mid \text{op}_x \text{ edge label occurs in the corpus}\}$.

5.1 Constants and their types

We start by cutting G up into the subgraphs that will serve as graph backbones of the constants. We do this by splitting G into *blobs*. A blob consists of a main labeled node and its *blob edges*, which are the node's outgoing edges with an

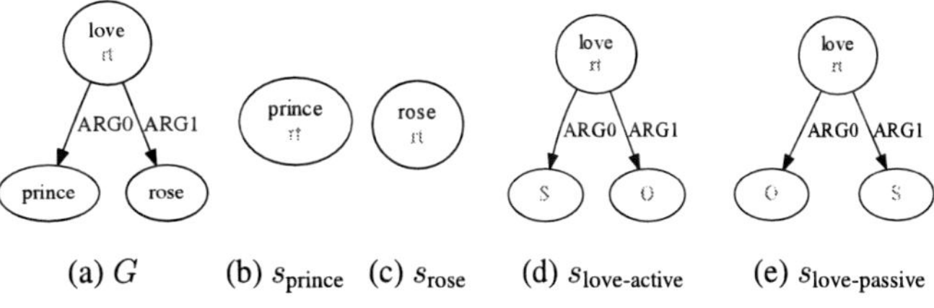

(a) G (b) s_prince (c) s_rose (d) $s_\text{love-active}$ (e) $s_\text{love-passive}$

Figure 11: (a) An AMR G; (b)-(e) the constants we obtain

ARG_x, op_x, snt_x ($x \in \mathbb{N}$), domain, poss or part label, and its incoming edges with any other label. Blobs defined in this way uniquely partition an AMR's edge set. An example of an AMR's blobs is shown in Fig. 1, where the blobs are distinguished by colour. For example, the *chew* blob is the red subgraph, including unlabelled nodes where ever a red edge touches a non-red node. These unlabelled endpoints are its *blob-targets*. We will construct a set of constants for each blob, such that the value of each constant is an as-graph whose graph component is the blob. The main node of the blob will be the rt-source. It remains to assign source names to the blob-targets and annotate them with types and renaming functions. The different choices of annotated source names constitute the different constants for this blob.

5.1.1 Source names

We heuristically assign (syntactic) source names from S to the blob-target nodes based on the edge label of their adjacent edge in the blob. Let v be a node. Canonically, we use the following edge-to-source mapping E2S to determine sources for v's blob-targets: For most nodes v, E2S maps ARG0 to S; ARG1 to O and other ARG_x to O_x; poss and part to POSS; snt_x, op_x and domain to themselves; and all other edges to MOD. Exceptionally, if v has a node label that is a conjunction[2] and at least two outgoing ARG_x edges, we map ARG_x to OP_x instead. E2S determines the canonical *target-to-source mapping* b_v, which assigns a source to each blob-target u: if the edge between v and u has label e, $b_v(u) = \text{E2S}(e)$. When decomposing the graph in Figure 11a, looking at the *love* node as v, this gives us the constant in Figure 11d.

A given blob may generate more than one constant, each with different sources on different nodes; accordingly, for each node v in G, we collect a *set* $B(v)$ of such target-to-source mappings. $B(v)$ contains the canonical mapping b_v, and we generate further target-to-source mappings by applying a fixed set of lexical rules to b_v. The *passive* rule switches S with any O, and *object promotion* maps O_i to O_{i-1} (let $\text{O}_0=\text{O}$). We allow all results of such mappings with at most one use of *passive* that have no duplicate source names. For example, the constant in Figure 11e is a result of the passive rule. For each mapping in $B(v)$, we create a constant with the respective sources and trivial types.

5.1.2 Annotations

We can also use these target-to-source mappings to extract constants that have sources with non-trivial argument types and renaming functions. Consider the subject-control AMR in Fig. 5b in section 3.2.1 above. So far, we obtain the constant in Fig. 12a, but we also want to generate the constant $G_{\text{scv}}[\text{want}]$ in Fig. 12b; i.e. determine the S entry in $T(\text{O})$. Writing v_{want}, v_{sheep}, and v_{relax} for the *want*, *sheep*, and *relax* nodes of the graph in 5b, note that it is the ARG1 edge from v_{relax} to v_{sheep} that signals the control structure. That is, v_{want} has a blob-target

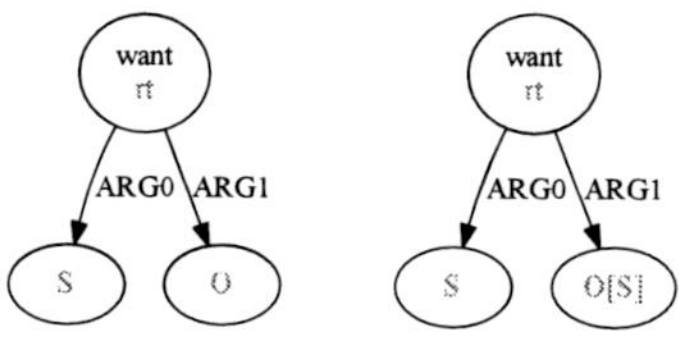

(a) trivial types   (b) non-trivial types

Figure 12: Possible source assignments for the *want* constant for the graph in Figure 5b.

v_{relax}, and the two share a *common* blob-target v_{sheep}. For such a triangle structure, we consider any target-to-source mappings $m_w \in B(v_{\text{want}})$ and $m_r \in B(v_{\text{relax}})$. We then add a constant for v_{want} which as before uses the source names of m_w, but now the annotation of $m_w(v_{\text{relax}})$ has an entry for $m_r(v_{\text{sheep}})$, anticipating the open source coming from the v_{relax} constant. We add a rename annotation $[m_r(v_{\text{sheep}}){\mapsto}m_w(v_{\text{sheep}})]$ if necessary. That is, we set up the annotation in the v_{want} constant such that when we apply it to a v_{relax} constant that has sources according to m_r, we obtain the structure we found in the graph. Take for example $m_w = \{v_{\text{relax}} \mapsto \text{O}, v_{\text{sheep}} \mapsto \text{S}\}$ and $m_r = \{v_{\text{sheep}} \mapsto \text{S}\}$.[3] In this case, $m_w(v_{\text{sheep}}) = m_r(v_{\text{sheep}}) = \text{S}$, therefore no rename is necessary and we obtain the constant of Figure 12b. If we choose $m_r = \{v_{\text{sheep}} \mapsto \text{O}\}$ instead, we obtain a constant for the v_{want} blob where the O source is annotated O[O][O$\mapsto$S]. In this graph, this is not particularly meaningful from a linguistic perspective, but in other graphs this principle allows us to generate e.g. the object control structure of

---

[2]According to the AMR documentation, these are *and, or, contrast-01, either* and *neither*.

[3]Since *relax* is an unaccusative verb, its sole argument is semantically an object (ARG1) but we can treat it as a syntactic subject by choosing the passive mapping, which promotes the object to subject.

$G_{\mathrm{ocv}}[\text{persuade}]$. To ensure that we recover the correct constant, we simply add constants for all choices of $m_w \in B(v_{\mathsf{want}})$ and $m_r \in B(v_{\mathsf{relax}})$.

Let us now find the constants for the *and* node in Fig. 8b. Our algorithm restricts constants to coordination of like types. In the intended AM term, shown in Fig. 8a, we first coordinate *relax* and *sleep* before we apply the result to the common argument *sheep*. To generate the constant for *and*, we consider maps $m_s \in B(v_{\mathsf{sleep}})$ and $m_r \in B(v_{\mathsf{relax}})$, where v_{sleep} and v_{relax} are the nodes labelled *sleep* and *relax* respectively. The *sheep* node v_{sheep} is a blob-target of both v_{sleep} and v_{relax}. If additionally the target-to-source maps agree, e.g. $m_s(v_{\mathsf{sheep}}) = m_r(v_{\mathsf{sheep}}) = \mathsf{S}$, we add a new constant for the *and* blob where both $T(\mathrm{OP}_1)$ and $T(\mathrm{OP}_2)$ have an S entry. This yields $G_{\mathrm{c-[s]}}[\text{and}]$ as depicted in Fig. 4. For the case where $m_s(v_{\mathsf{sheep}}) = \mathsf{S}$ but $m_r(v_{\mathsf{sheep}}) = \mathsf{O}$, we do not create a new constant. Again, we take all combinations of choices for m_s and m_r into account. We never rename for coordination.

Similar patterns allow us to find possible raised subjects for raising constructions, and to handle coordination of control verbs. Using these patterns recursively, we can handle nested control, coordination and raising constructions. For example in Fig. 8c, finding the *sheep* node as a common target in coordination allows us to generate $G_{\mathrm{scv}}[\text{want}]$ analogously to Fig. 5b.

In sum, we obtain types and renaming functions that cover a variety of phenomena, in particular the ones described in Section 4.

5.2 Coreference

In the AMRBank annotations, the same node can become the argument of multiple predicates in two very different ways: because the grammar specifies it (as with control, (4-b)), and through accidental coreference (4-a).

(4) a. Mary$_i$ thinks she$_{i/j}$'s a genius
     b. Mary$_i$ wants ___$_i$ to be a genius

Because accidental coreference is not a compositional phenomenon, we add an extra mechanism for handling it. We follow Koller (2015) in introducing special sources COREF1, COREF2,...,COREFn for some maximal $n \in \mathbb{N}$. We add variants of the previously found constants with a COREF source at their root. We further add constants consisting of a single unlabelled node, which is both a rt-source and a COREF-source. The COREF sources are never annotated and are ignored in the types. They are never forgotten, and each can therefore be used only on one node in the derivation. Two COREF sources with the same index will be automatically merged together during the usual APP and MOD operations, due to the semantics of the underlying merge operation of the HR algebra.

COREF sources increase runtimes and the number of possible terms per graph significantly (see Section 6), and thus we limit the number of COREF sources to zero to two in practice.

5.3 Obtaining the set of terms

We can compactly represent the set of all AM terms that evaluate to a given AMR G in a *decomposition automaton* (Koller and Kuhlmann, 2011), a chart-like data structure in which shared subterms are represented only once. We can enumerate the terms from this automaton.

To enumerate all rules of the decomposition automaton, we explore it bottom-up, with Algorithm 1. We first find all constants for G in Line 2, as described in Section 5.1, and then repeatedly apply APP and MOD operations (Lines 3 onward; the set $\mathcal{O}$ contains all relevant APP and MOD operations). The constants and the successful operation applications are stored as rules in the automaton.

To ensure that the resulting terms evaluate to the input graph G, we use subgraphs of G as states – like one uses spans in string parsing. This is paired with additional constraints, for example in $\mathrm{APP}_\alpha(s, s')$, the root of s' must be the same node of G as the α-source node in s. These additional constraints are as described in Groschwitz et al. (2015), when interpreting the AM operations as terms of the HR algebra (c.f. Section 3.2); plus the constraint that a rt-source at the root node of G may not be renamed or forgotten. These constraints are the analogue of only combining neighbouring spans in string parsing.

Let us decompose the graph G in Figure 11a as an example. Let us call the nodes labelled "love", "prince", and "rose" v_{love}, v_{prince} and v_{rose} respectively. In Line 2, we add the subgraphs of Fig. 11(b-e) to the agenda. Say we first pull s_{rose} from the agenda – since the chart is empty at this point, no operation is applicable. Say we pull $s_{\text{love-active}}$ next, and try to combine it with the items in the chart – just s_{rose} at this point. If we try to apply APP_S, we realize that this tries to fill the node v_{prince} of $s_{\text{love-active}}$, but the root of s_{rose} is v_{rose}. Thus, the operation fails. (Trying APP_S with s_{rose} as the left and $s_{\text{love-active}}$ as the right child fails immediately since s_{rose} has no S-source). MOD_S fails similarly. However, APP_O succeeds – both the O-source in $s_{\text{love-active}}$ and the rt-source in s_{rose} are at v_{rose} – and produces the graph in Fig. 2f. MOD_O fails, since it would involve forgetting rt at v_{love}, and the root of the full graph must be preserved. We therefore add the result of APP_O to the agenda and move on.

To explore the possibilities for combining as-graphs efficiently, we do not iterate over all graphs in Line 6, but for each operation use an indexing structure based on source nodes and types.

Note that the operations in the automaton are restricted by the AM algebra's type system. Therefore, selecting the correct constants as in Section 5.1 is critical to obtaining the desired derivations. We do obtain all the terms in the examples in this paper in practice.

Algorithm 1 Agenda-chart-algorithm

1: init chart, agenda empty
2: add constants to agenda
3: **while** agenda not empty **do**
4: pull subgraph s from agenda
5:   **for** operation $o \in \mathcal{O}$ **do**
6:    **for** subgraph s' in chart **do**
7:     **if** $o(s, s')$ allowed **then**
8:      add $o(s, s')$ to agenda
9:     **end if**
10:     **if** $o(s', s)$ allowed **then**
11:      add $o(s', s)$ to agenda
12:     **end if**
13:    **end for**
14:   **end for**
15:   add s to chart
16: **end while**

---

6 Evaluation

We conclude by analyzing whether the AM algebra achieves our goal of reducing the number of possible terms for a given AMR, compared to the HR algebra. Both algorithms are implemented and available in the Alto framework[4]. For the HR algebra, we use the setup of Groschwitz et al. (2015): Constants consist of single labeled nodes and single edges, and they are combined using the operations of the HR algebra. We use an HR algebra with two source names (HR-S2) and one with three source names (HR-S3); this has an impact on the set of graphs that can be analyzed and on the runtime complexity. For the AM algebra, we use the method of Section 5 with different numbers of allowed COREF sources (AM-C0, AM-C1, AM-C2 for 0, 1, 2 COREF sources respectively). We use all graphs of the LDC2016E25 training corpus with up to 50 nodes, for a total of 35685 graphs.

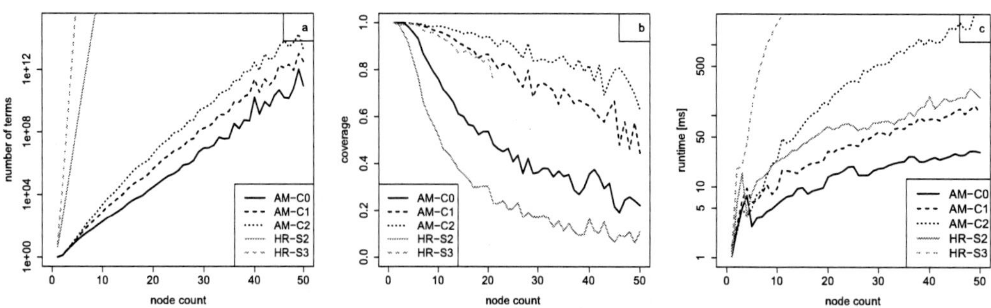

Figure 13: Number of terms per AMR (a), coverage (b) and runtimes (c).

Coverage. Consider first the *coverage* of the different graph algebras, i.e. the proportion of graphs of a given size for which we find at least one term, shown in Fig. 13b as a function of the graph size. As expected, coverage goes up as the number of source nodes (for HR) and COREF nodes (for AM)

---

[4]`bitbucket.org/tclup/alto`

increases. The coverage of AM-C0 is higher than that of HR-S2 because HR-S2 can only analyze graphs of treewidth 1, i.e. without (undirected) cycles, whereas AM-C0 can handle local re-entrancies e.g. from control constructions through the type annotations. For example, the AMRs in Fig. 5b,6b can be decomposed by AM-C0 and HR-S3, but not HR-S2. The highest coverage is achieved by AM-C2.

Number of terms. We now turn to the (geometric) mean number of terms each algebra assigns to those graphs of a given size that it can analyze (Fig. 13a). We find that the AM algebras achieve a dramatic reduction in the number of terms, compared to the HR algebras: Even the high-coverage AM-C2 has much fewer terms than the very low-coverage HR-S2 (note the log-scale on the vertical axis). As an example, switching from HR-S2 to AM-C0 reduces the number of terms for the graph in Fig. 3a from 3584 to 4 (they differ in active vs passive, and order of application). For 5 nodes, the average for HR-S3 is 10^{17} terms, and for AM-C2 just 21. This reduction has multiple reasons: we can use larger constants in the AM algebra, and the graph-combining operations of the AM algebra are much more constrained. Further, the type system and carefully chosen set of constants restrict application and modification.

Note that just because an algebra can find *some* term for an AMR does not necessarily mean that it makes sense from a linguistic perspective (cf. Fig. 3b). Conversely, by reducing the set of possible terms, there is a risk that we might throw out the linguistically correct analysis. By choosing the operations of the AM algebra to match linguistic intuitions about predicate-argument structure, we have reduced this risk. We leave a precise quantitative analysis, e.g. in the context of grammar induction, for future work.

Runtime. We finish by measuring the mean runtimes to compute the decomposition automata (Fig. 13c). Once again, we find that the AM algebra solidly outperforms the HR algebra. The runtimes of HR-S3 are too slow to be useful in practice, whereas even the highest-coverage algebra AM-C2 decomposes even large graphs in seconds. Moreover, the runtimes for AM-C1 are faster than even for the very low-coverage HR-S2 algebra.

The previously fastest parser for graphs using hyperedge replacement grammars was the one of Groschwitz et al. (2016), which used Interpreted Regular Tree Grammars (IRTGs) (Koller and Kuhlmann, 2011) together with the HR algebra. Because we have seen how to compute decomposition automata for the AM algebra in Section 5, we can do graph parsing with IRTGs over the AM algebra instead. The fact that decomposition automata for the AM algebra are smaller and faster to compute promises a further speed-up for graph parsing as well, making wide-coverage graph parsing for large graphs feasible.

7 Conclusion

In this paper, we have introduced the apply-modify (AM) algebra for graphs. The AM algebra replaces the general-purpose, low-level operations of the HR algebra by high-level operations that are specifically designed to combine semantic representations of syntactic heads with arguments and modifiers. We have demonstrated that the AM algebra dramatically reduces the number of terms for given AMR graphs, while supporting natural analyses of a number of challenging linguistic phenomena.

With this work we have laid the foundation for automatically inducing grammars that can map compositionally between strings and AMRs while using linguistically meaningful graph-combining operations. Our immediate next step will be to use the AM algebra for this purpose. On a more theoretical level, while the algebra objects differ greatly, the similarity of the *signature* of the AM algebra with that of the "semantic algebra" of Copestake et al. (2001) is striking. We will explore this connection, and investigate whether a universal signature for a semantic construction algebra can be defined.

8 Acknowledgements

We thank the anonymous reviewers for their comments. We would also like to thank Christoph Teichmann, Antoine Venant and Mark Steedman for helpful discussions. This work was supported by the DFG grant KO 2916/2-1, and a Macquarie University Research Excellence Scholarship for Jonas Groschwitz.

References

Artzi, Y., K. Lee, and L. Zettlemoyer (2015). Broad-coverage ccg semantic parsing with amr. In *Proceedings of the 2015 Conference on Empirical Methods in Natural Language Processing*, pp. 1699–1710.

Banarescu, L., C. Bonial, S. Cai, M. Georgescu, K. Griffitt, U. Hermjakob, K. Knight, P. Koehn, M. Palmer, and N. Schneider (2013). Abstract Meaning Representation for sembanking. In *Proceedings of the 7th Linguistic Annotation Workshop and Interoperability with Discourse*.

Chiang, D., J. Andreas, D. Bauer, K. M. Hermann, B. Jones, and K. Knight (2013). Parsing graphs with hyperedge replacement grammars. In *Proceedings of the 51st Annual Meeting of the Association for Computational Linguistics*.

Copestake, A., A. Lascarides, and D. Flickinger (2001). An algebra for semantic construction in constraint-based grammars. In *Proceedings of the 39th ACL*.

Courcelle, B. (1993). Graph grammars, monadic second-order logic and the theory of graph minors. In N. Robertson and P. Seymour (Eds.), *Graph Structure Theory*, pp. 565—590. AMS.

Drewes, F., H.-J. Kreowski, and A. Habel (1997). Hyperedge replacement graph grammars. pp. 95–162.

Flanigan, J., S. Thomson, J. Carbonell, C. Dyer, and N. A. Smith (2014). A discriminative graph-based parser for the abstract meaning representation. In *Proceedings of the 52nd Annual Meeting of the Association for Computational Linguistics (Volume 1: Long Papers)*, pp. 1426–1436.

Groschwitz, J., A. Koller, and M. Johnson (2016). Efficient techniques for parsing with tree automata. In *Proceedings of the 54th Annual Meeting of the Association for Computational Linguistics*.

Groschwitz, J., A. Koller, and C. Teichmann (2015). Graph parsing with S-graph Grammars. In *Proceedings of the 53rd Annual Meeting of the Association for Computational Linguistics and the 7th International Joint Conference on Natural Language Processing*.

Jones, B., J. Andreas, D. Bauer, K.-M. Hermann, and K. Knight (2012). Semantics-based machine translation with hyperedge replacement grammars. In *Proceedings of COLING*.

Jones, B. K., S. Goldwater, and M. Johnson (2013). Modeling graph languages with grammars extracted via tree decompositions. In *Proceedings of the 11th International Conference on Finite State Methods and Natural Language Processing*, pp. 54–62.

Koller, A. (2015). Semantic construction with graph grammars. In *Proceedings of the 11th International Conference on Computational Semantics*, pp. 228–238.

Koller, A. and M. Kuhlmann (2011). A generalized view on parsing and translation. In *Proceedings of the 12th International Conference on Parsing Technologies*.

Misra, D. K. and Y. Artzi (2016). Neural shift-reduce ccg semantic parsing. In *Proceedings of the 2016 Conference on Empirical Methods in Natural Language Processing*.

Peng, X., L. Song, and D. Gildea (2015). A synchronous hyperedge replacement grammar based approach for amr parsing. In *Proceedings of the 19th Conference on Computational Language Learning*, pp. 32–41.

Peng, X., C. Wang, D. Gildea, and N. Xue (2017). Addressing the data sparsity issue in neural AMR parsing. In *Proceedings of the 15th EACL*.

Steedman, M. (2001). *The Syntactic Process*. Cambridge, MA: MIT Press.

Coarse Semantic Classification of Rare Nouns Using Cross-Lingual Data and Recurrent Neural Networks

Oliver Hellwig
Düsseldorf University, SFB 991
ohellwig@
phil-fak.uni-duesseldorf.de

Abstract

The paper presents a method for WordNet supersense tagging of Sanskrit, an ancient Indian language with a corpus grown over four millenia. The proposed method merges lexical information from Sanskrit texts with lexicographic definitions from Sanskrit-English dictionaries, and compares the performance of two machine learning methods for this task. Evaluation concentrates on Vedic, the oldest layer of Sanskrit. This level of Sanskrit contains numerous rare words that are no longer used in the later language and whose word senses can, therefore, not be induced from their occurrences in other texts. The paper studies how to efficiently transfer knowledge from later forms of Sanskrit and from modern Western dictionaries for this special task of supersense disambiguation.

1 Introduction

The paper discusses experiments in coarse-grained word semantic disambiguation (WSD) for Classical (CS) and Vedic Sanskrit (VS).[1] These experiments are part of a project that deals with the verb-argument labeling of Vedic texts. The project is based on a manual annotation of all 27,104 verbal forms and their main arguments found in the Ṛgveda (RV), the core text of the Vedic corpus (Hettrich, 2007).[2] Apart from relating arguments to their governing verbs, the annotation disambiguates case semantic functions such as time or location for the locative, and it assigns a basic word semantic class to each argument (refer to the sample annotation in Fig. 1). The word semantic annotations differentiate between eight classes that include, among others, abstract concepts, humans, and animals. We are planning to use the annotation of the RV as training corpus for building a verb-argument labeler that can be applied to other texts of the Vedic corpus.

Several publications on argument and role labeling use word semantic classes or distributional representations of words for modeling selectional preferences of verbs (Wilks, 1975; Che et al., 2010; Yu et al., 2010; Roth and Lapata, 2015). Following this work, we are going to employ WordNet supersenses (WNSS; Ciaramita and Johnson, 2003) of Vedic words as an additional prior in our argument labeling pipeline, both for detecting arguments in unlabeled texts (see the semantic coherence criterion in Laparra and Rigau (2013)), and for assigning appropriate word semantic classes to arguments.

The paper interprets WSD as a sentence classification task, where definitions from bilingual Sanskrit-English dictionaries and sentential contexts serve for predicting word semantic classes of Sanskrit nouns. The paper concentrates on rare nouns, because the vocabulary of Vedic texts contains numerous lemmata that have disappeared in later Classical Sanskrit, so their distributional properties cannot be estimated

---

[1]Sanskrit can be divided into two historical layers, whose relationship resembles that of Homeric and Classical Ancient Greek, or even the later *koine*. Vedic Sanskrit is one of the oldest Indo-European languages. Its earliest parts may have been composed in the second millenium BCE (Witzel, 1995). Around 350 BCE, the grammarian Pāṇini compiled the grammar Aṣṭādhyāyī, a linguistic overview of a late form of VS, which became the prescriptive standard for CS (Scharfe, 1977). Although the vast majority of Sanskrit texts is written in CS, VS also has produced a sizeable corpus of several million words.

[2]The annotation was performed by a H. Hettrich, and parts of it were later inspected randomly by linguists; personal communication by H. Hettrich.

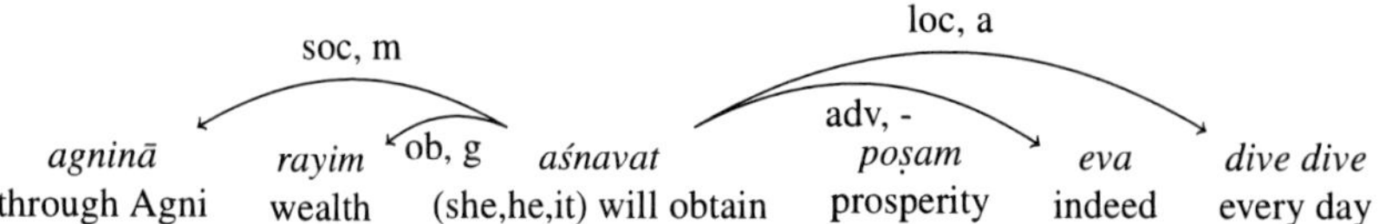

Figure 1: Verb-argument annotation of Ṛgveda 1.1.3 ("He will obtain wealth [and] prosperity through Agni every day."). Labels on the arcs indicate the syntactic functions (soc[iative], ob[ject], loc[ation]) and coarse word semantic classes (m = human, g = object, a = generic expression) of the arguments. If more than one word fits into an argument class, only the first one is annotated.

reliably from the later corpus. We will compare the efficiency of different machine learning models for this task. In addition, the paper pays special attention to the philological setting of WSD. While most NLP studies work with huge, contemporaneous corpora from closed domains (newspapers, Twitter), and can rely on richly annotated data sets, WSD for Vedic and Classical Sanskrit lacks most of these prerequisites. As a consequence, transfer of knowledge between languages (English definitions to Sanskrit word senses) and between different historical domains of Sanskrit literature plays an important role in our research.

While there is, in principle, no lack of Sanskrit texts,[3] the language is nevertheless under-resourced from the perspective of NLP. First, large parts of the literature have not yet been digitized. This applies to the Sanskrit source texts and to their translations into modern languages, and complicates unsupervised knowlegde acquisition from large (parallel) corpora as, for instance, proposed by Prochasson and Fung (2011). Second, the rich morphology, especially of VS, the lack of reliable punctuation marks[4], and the phonetic phenomenon of Sandhi ("combination [of phonemes]") make linguistic analysis a hard task for NLP. Due to these features, standard token-based NLP pipelines cannot be applied to Sanskrit, as becomes apparent for a short phrase such as *saitatpaśyatītyuktvā*. This string is formed by phonetically merging the five inflected tokens *sā*, *etad*, *paśyati*, *iti*, and *uktvā* (tiny "equations" give the operative Sandhi rules):

sā [ā+e=ai]   *etad* [d+p=tp]   *paśyati* [i+i=ī]   *iti* [i+u=yu]   *uktvā*
she:N.SG.   this:A.SG.   see:3.sg., pr.   thus:ind.   say:abs.
... having said: 'She sees this' ...

Apart from the correct analysis given above, this string has at least seven further readings that are lexically valid, though semantically meaningless. Because the valid tokenization of a Sanskrit text requires a full morphological and lexical analysis, the methods described in this paper operate with fully disambiguated lemmata, instead of tokenized strings as is usually done in NLP of English.

In order to mitigate the problems introduced by size and structure of the corpus, we use bilingual information for WSD. Sanskrit has a rich history of philological research both in India and in the West. Part of this history are comprehensive Sanskrit-English dictionaries, which are also available in digital form.[5] These dictionaries provide English definitions for Sanskrit lemmata, and the definitions are ordered following lexicographic considerations. We will use the lexical definitions and their lexicographic order along with Sanskrit context words for WNSS classification in VS and CS. This setting may remind

---

[3] The size of Sanskrit literature can not be estimated reliably. Wujastyk (2014) considers that there exists a total of 30,000,000 Indian manuscripts, a substantial number of which may contain Sanskrit works. Several thousand Sanskrit texts have been edited and printed in the last 200 years, and a few hundred of them are available in digital form.

[4] Sanskrit texts are structured by *daṇḍas* 'sticks' (|). These symbols indicate the end of metrical sequences, which are quite frequently not identical with sentence boundaries (Hellwig, 2016). Sentence internal structuring symbols such as commata and colons are missing completely. When applied to a Sanskrit text, the term 'sentence' refers to *daṇḍa*-delimited sequences of words in the rest of the paper.

[5] http://www.sanskrit-lexicon.uni-koeln.de/

of knowledge based approaches to WSD. However, it should be noted that the proposed method does not calculate the lexical overlap between the Sanskrit text and dictionary glosses for determining the best fitting word sense, as proposed by Lesk (1986) and later authors. Moreover, it does not use the graph structure of OpenCyc for WSD (Agirre and Soroa (2009) et al.). On the technical side, the paper will compare the efficiency of Maximum Entropy and of recurrent neural network models, both of which are regularly applied to WSD.

The rest of the paper is organized as follows. After an overview of related research in Section 2, Section 3 introduces the corpus and describes its semantic annotation layer. Section 4 describes how features for WSD are created, and which models are applied to the task. Section 5 compares the performance of the models and gives a short error analysis. Section 6 summarizes the paper.

2   Related Research

Although there exists a Sanskrit WordNet (Kulkarni et al., 2010), Sanskrit WSD has found little attention in research. While Kulkarni et al. (2010) and Bhingardive and Bhattacharyya (2017) concentrate on (broad) sense induction for Hindi and other modern Indian languages, Hellwig (2012) reports quantitative results only for a few ambiguous Sanskrit lemmata. Some recent studies have dealt with WSD for other classical languages such as Old English (Wunderlich et al., 2015) or Latin (Aguilar et al., 2016; Bamman and Crane, 2011). The methodology described in the last two papers (structured prediction for WSD, knowledge acquisition from parallel bilingual corpora) cannot be transferred to Sanskrit WSD, because corpora with contiguous word semantic annotations and large parallel corpora are largely missing. Similarly, diachronic WSD using word embeddings (Hamilton et al., 2016) or graphical models (Wijaya and Yeniterzi, 2011; Frermann and Lapata, 2016) cannot be applied due to the limited size of the digital Sanskrit corpus and the uncertainties in its historical stratification.

Ciaramita and Johnson (2003) introduced the task of Wordnet supersense (WNSS) classification by mapping fine-grained WordNet senses to the titles of the containing lexicographer files. The authors report accuracy rates of 52.3% on the type and 53.4% on the token level for words contained in WordNet 1.71, but not found in WordNet 1.6. This work was continued by Curran (2005), who discusses linguistic and lexicographic challenges in WNSS definition and assignment, and achieves an overall accuracy of 68% using a multi-class perceptron. Similar approaches are reported in Ciaramita and Altun (2006) and Schneider and Smith (2015). Johannsen et al. (2014) study supersense tagging for English Twitter data, using structured prediction and pretrained word embeddings. Flekova and Gurevych (2016) co-train word and supersense embeddings using the word2vec model, and construct a supersense tagger for English by feeding these embeddings along with further hand-crafted features into a multi-layer neural network. The authors obtain a classifier that performs close to the state of the art.

To sum up, the present paper is, to the best of our knowledge, the first attempt to develop a WNSS tagger for Sanskrit. Contrary to many proposed methods for WNSS of English, it relies heavily on cross-lingual information, and cannot make use of Lesk-style measures of text-gloss overlap, because texts and glosses are composed in different languages.

3   WordNet Supersenses for Sanskrit

We perform WSD with the 26 WordNet supersenses of nouns introduced in Ciaramita and Johnson (2003). WNSS are generated from the word semantic annotation layer of the Digital Corpus of Sanskrit (DCS; Hellwig, 2015). This corpus contains 4,170,064 word tokens (85,431 lexical types) with manually validated morphological and lexical annotations from all periods of Sanskrit literature, but with a strong focus on CS. 491,119 out of these 4,170,064 tokens are additionally annotated with fine-grained word semantic labels by a single annotator, using the OpenCyc (Lenat, 1995) sense inventory as starting point. Relying on the results of a single annotator is far from ideal, because there is no control of the error level, and no baseline for disagreement of human annotators can be calculated. However, as in the case of the verb-argument labelings themselves (see p. 1), other large scale annotations are not available at the

Word class	Tokens	Types
Nouns	294,506	20,307
Adjectives	67,958	3,521
Verbs	71,942	2,798
Particles, indeclinables	56,713	396

Table 1: Size of the word semantic annotation layer in the DCS: Number of lexical tokens and types with word semantic annotations, split by word classes

moment. Table 1 shows that the majority of annotated lemmata, both on token and type level, are nouns. These 294,506 sense annotated noun tokens serve for training and testing the WSD models in this paper.

Concepts not found in the original version of OpenCyc were added to the sense inventory during annotation of texts. A total of 18,804 distinct concepts were annotated in the DCS, 10,065 of which were not contained in the original OpenCyc inventory. Translations between OpenCyc concepts and WNSS were generated by first mapping OpenCyc concepts onto the English Wordnet. For finding corresponding entries, we compared the terms and the string based overlap of their definitions in OpenCyc and Wordnet. Based on this information, supersenses were retrieved from the WordNet lexicographer files. Newly created concepts, for which this mapping provides no WNSS, were labeled with the WNSS of their parent concept.[6]

While parts of the alchemical literature ($\geq$ 1300 CE) and the Bhagavadgītā (100-300 CE?) were sense annotated completely in the DCS, many semantic annotations were added to single, "philologically interesting" words; this means either to frequent words with an unusual meaning, or to rare words. The majority of these words are nouns and refer to concrete entities. The bias introduced by this annotation mode is aggravated by the text-historical composition of the DCS, because scientific (medical, alchemical) and epic texts such as the Mahābhārata (300 BCE - 500 CE?) are strongly overrepresented. The dominance of the scientific subcorpus is particularly relevant for WSD, because its vocabulary contains numerous rare technical terms denoting plants, diseases, body parts, and medical or alchemical procedures. As a consequence, senses denoting concrete entities and acts are overrepresented.

The semantic classification targets Vedic and rare nouns, and it cannot be taken for granted that these nouns show the same distribution of WNSS as frequent ones. In addition, WNSS were originally designed for modern Western texts, so that they may not cover the conceptual space of ancient Indian texts in an appropriate way. In order to understand the distribution of supersenses over noun frequency classes, we annotated three additional data sets S_{1-3} of 400 tokens each with WNSS. S_1 simulates the distribution of hapax legomena in a medium-sized corpus, and corresponds to the evaluation setting **Rare nouns** (see Sec. 5). The complete DCS is split into 20 subcorpora of approximately 200,000 tokens, respectively.[7] From each subcorpus, we randomly drew 20 tokens that are hapax legomena in their respective subcorpus. S_2 contains 400 randomly drawn hapax legomena from the Vedic layer of the DCS, and corresponds to the evaluation setting **Vedic nouns** in Sec. 5. S_3 consists of 400 randomly drawn tokens from the complete DCS, which must not be hapax legomena. S_3 is intended for simulating the composition of the training set.

The frequency distribution of supersenses in the three samples displayed in Table 2 allows several interesting insights. First, few supersenses are frequent in all three samples. When considering the nature of the Sanskrit texts and the annotation mode, high frequencies could be expected for concrete supersenses such as *'artifact'*, *'person'*, *'plant'*, and *'substance'*. Because most instances of *'substance'* and

---

[6]OpenCyc is not structured in a strictly hierarchical manner. The parent concept P of a given concept C is obtained by selecting the most frequently annotated item for which a subclass relation between P and C is recorded; if such a record does not exist, P is set to the most frequently annotated item, for which an instance or member relation is recorded.

[7]We chose this size because it comes close to that of the Ṛgveda.

	S_1	S_2	S_3	N	P
person	25.25	29.84	24.26	247	26.45
act	13.13	14.4	7.35	117	11.63
comm.	4.8	17.02	2.94	88	8.25
substance	9.34	2.62	14.71	67	8.89
artifact	5.56	6.28	7.35	56	6.4
plant	10.1	1.83	3.68	52	5.2
state	3.54	5.76	2.94	40	4.08
cognition	2.53	2.09	8.82	30	4.48
attribute	3.54	2.88	2.94	29	3.12
location	3.79	1.83	5.15	29	3.59
body	3.28	2.36	3.68	27	3.11
feeling	2.53	1.57	2.21	19	2.1
animal	1.77	2.09	2.21	18	2.02
group	2.02	1.57	0.74	15	1.44
time	0.51	1.83	4.41	15	2.25
object	1.52	1.31	1.47	13	1.43
process	1.77	1.31	0.74	13	1.27
quantity	1.01	0.26	2.94	9	1.4
event	0.76	0.79	0.74	7	0.76
phen.	1.01	0.79	0	7	0.6
poss.	0.76	0.52	0.74	6	0.67
shape	0.51	0.52	0	4	0.34
food	0.25	0.52	0	3	0.26
relation	0.76	0	0	3	0.25

Table 2: Proportions of WNSS in three manually annotated samples of 400 lexical tokens; S_1: hapax legomena in 200,00 token subcorpora; S_2: hapax legomena in late Vedic texts; S_3: random tokens from the full DCS. – Rows are ordered by summed absolute frequencies (N) of supersenses in the three samples (P: proportions in the three samples). Differences to the sum of 3×400 indicate that some samples could not be labeled.

'*plant*' occur in the late medical and alchemical subcorpora, these two supersenses have low proportions in the sample from old literature (S_2). '*cognition*', '*time*', and '*quantity*' are more frequent in S_3 than in the hapax legomena samples, because they comprise generic terms such as *samaya* '(right) moment', *jñāna* 'knowledge', and number words, which are frequent, but have few synonyms.

The supersenses '*act*' and '*communication*' show a somehow opposite distribution. These supersenses are more frequent in S_1 and S_2 than in S_3 and, therefore, relevant for the main task of this paper. While '*act*' often denotes special procedures in medicine and ritual such as *mahāśānti* 'an expiatory observance and recitation', tokens annotated as '*communication*' in S_2 mostly denote special types of Vedic hymns mentioned in theoretical passages.[8] It is important to keep in mind that the RGVEDA, whose verb-argument annotation basically motivates this paper, comes from a different text genre than the other Vedic texts. While it also deals with the invocation of deities, it puts no emphasis on the theoretical reflection of the involved speech acts, but takes its imagery from battle, mythology, and daily life.

4   Models and Features

Classification cannot benefit from structured prediction, because the majority of annotations is attached to isolated words (Sec. 4). Therefore, we perform WSD of single words using a Maximum Entropy model

---

[8]The ritual handbooks called Brāhmaṇas and the Upaniṣads constitute the major part of the old layer in the DCS, from which S_2 is drawn. These texts discuss the ritual and especially ritual formulae and hymns by drawing analogies between these texts and the outer world (Hillebrandt, 1897).

(ME) and an ensemble of recurrent neural networks (RNN). This section describes the architecture of these classifiers and the features used to train them.

4.1 Maximum Entropy

We use two types of features for training the ME model (Berger et al., 1996). **Definitions** are extracted from the English glosses provided by Monier-Williams (1899). Each definition is parsed using the Stanford NLP parser (Manning et al., 2014)[9], and the syntactic root ("head") and all other nouns, adjectives, and verbs are extracted ("context"). The lexicographic definitions contain many entries of the form "a kind of plant" or "name of a warrior", where the direct syntactic dependent of the root better indicates the semantic class of the lemma than the actual root ("a kind of plant" primarily denotes a plant). These definitions are detected using the string pattern *a* (name|kind|class) of.** The dependent of the syntactic root is extracted from the parse tree of the definition, and selected as the head word of the definition. As an example, the lexicographic definition "any cry or noise" (for *ruta*) produces "cry" as head and "noise" as context word, while the definition "a particular class of gods under the Manu Tāmasa" yields the head "god" (being the direct dependent of the syntactic root "class") and the context words "particular", "class", "Manu", and "Tāmasa".

Head and context words are weighted by their lexicographic ranks in Monier-Williams (1899), because the dictionary orders the defininitions mainly, though not fully consistently by their importance.[10] Let N denote the number of definitions of a Sanskrit lemma, and r_i the 1-based rank of a single definition i, head and context words extracted from this definition are weighted with a factor w_{lex}:

$$w_{lex} = \frac{N - r_i + 1}{\sum_{j=1}^{N}(N - r_j + 1)}$$

The feature type *definitions* is generated for the target word itself, and for the two words directly preceding resp. following the target in the Sanskrit sentence.[11] Heads and context words for targets and surrounding lemmata are distinguished with prefixes.

The second type of features is the lexical context provided by the Sanskrit lemmata that surround the target word in a sentence and that are not function words (**lex_context**). Lemmata are weighted with their inverse distances to the target for ME.

The ME model is trained with limited-memory BFGS and L2 regularization of 0.5. We use the implementation from `http://www.logos.ic.i.u-tokyo.ac.jp/~tsuruoka/maxent/`.

4.2 Baseline

We use the WNSS of the first head of the first definition of a lemma as a baseline for WSD. As an example, the first definition of the lemma *viṣṇu* is given as "name of one of the principal Hindū deities". The head word of this definition according to 4.1 is "deity", which is mapped to the WNSS *'person'* as baseline prediction. If WordNet contains more than one synset containing the head word, the supersense of the first synset is chosen as prediction. If the head is not contained in WordNet, the baseline predicts the UNK tag.

4.3 Recurrent Neural Network Model

The RNN model is an extension of the architecture proposed by Tang et al. (2015) for sentiment classification. We test this kind of architecture, because we try to predict a WNSS on the basis of sentences (Sanskrit context) and phrases (English definitions). Both feature types are strictly ordered by sentence

---

[9]Package version 3.6.0; we use the pipeline "tokenize, ssplit, pos, lemma, parse".

[10]Much of the material contained in Monier-Williams (1899) is translated from Böhtlingk and Roth (1875), and the lexicographic order of this source influences the order in Monier-Williams (1899); see Zgusta (1988).

[11]Pre-tests with larger contexts showed no increase of accuracy.

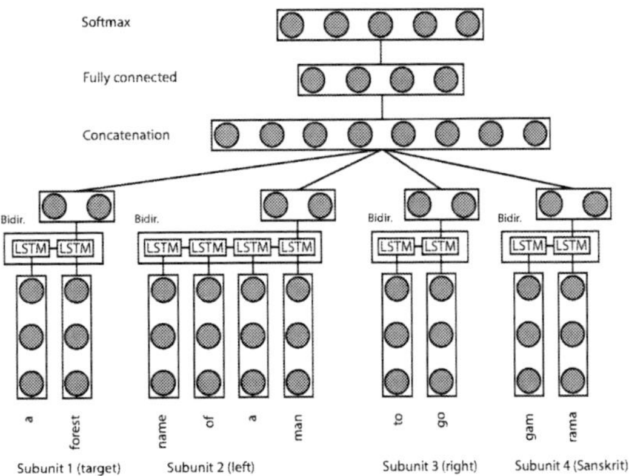

Figure 2: RNN architecture for joint training of English definitions and Sanskrit lemmata, illustrated for disambiguating the central word *vana* 'forest' in the dummy sentence *rāmo vanaṃ gacchati* 'Rāma goes into the forest'; definitions: *rāma* → "name of a man", *vana* → "a forest", *gam* → "to go".

structure ("city of god" $\neq$ "god of the city") and the lexicographic order of definitions. Choosing a recurrent architecture seemed appropriate for capturing this order. In addition, the RNN produces fixed-size numeric representations of the dictionary definitions, and thereby facilitates the transition from phrasal to lexical semantics (Hill et al., 2016).

The RNN consists of four subunits. The first three subunits receive concatenated dictionary definitions, while the fourth subunit processes the Sanskrit lemmata in the source sentence. Each subunit consists of an embedding layer of dimensions $d \times |V|$, with d denoting the embedding dimension and $|V|$ the size of the vocabulary, a bidirectional LSTM layer (Hochreiter and Schmidhuber, 1997; Graves et al., 2005) with 100 hidden units, and a dropout layer (Hinton et al., 2012) with a dropout rate of 25%. The outputs of the subunits at the last time step are concatenated and further processed with a fully connected and a softmax layer (Fig. 2). The RNN is trained with cross-entropy error as loss function, backpropagation, and a constant learning rate of 0.005 for 30 iterations.

The input for the three dictionary subunits consists of the definitions provided by Monier-Williams (1899) for the target (first subunit) and its left and right context words (second and third subunits, respectively). Definitions for each word are concatenated in their lexicographic order. Assume, for example, that Monier-Williams (1899) provides the two definitions "name of a man" and "a town" for the target word. The first subunit will receive the concatenated string "name of a man a town" in this case. The Sanskrit subunit receives the lemmata of the full sentence, where the target lemma is replaced by the UNK symbol.

The embeddings of the English words (subunits 1–3) are initialized with the pretrained vectors from the GloVe database (Pennington et al., 2014).[12] Embeddings of unknown English words are initialized with random values, and trained together with the other embeddings. In this way, words not contained in the GloVe database such as Sanskrit terms in IAST transliteration ("Śiva", "Viṣṇu"; found as "shiva" and "vishnu" in GloVe), or orthographic variants ("sun-flower") are integrated into the feature space. Embeddings of Sanskrit lemmata are pretrained using the `word2vec` tool (Mikolov et al., 2011).[13]

---

[12]Wikipedia 2014 + Gigaword 5 embeddings; embedding size: 50

[13]Settings: BOW, window size: 8, 5 iterations, minimal frequency of a lemma: 3, embedding size: 50. – Mixing embeddings trained with different algorithms may not be a good idea, because the choice of the training algorithm may influence how well the produced embeddings perform in specific linguistic tasks (Schnabel et al., 2015).

Rare nouns				
Classifier	Metrics	P	R	F
baseline	mi	58.46	34.82	43.64
	ma	40.43	41.71	41.06
ME	mi	76.5	76.5	76.5
	ma	53.53	53.55	53.54
RNN	mi	**77.68**	**77.68**	**77.68**
	ma	**56.19**	**55.25**	**55.71**

Vedic nouns				
Classifier	Metrics	P	R	F
baseline	mi	55.7	47.16	51.08
	ma	42.73	38.46	40.48
ME	mi	56.82	56.82	56.82
	ma	47.7	41.02	44.11
RNN	mi	**63**	**62.88**	**62.94**
	ma	**53.74**	**51.09**	**52.38**

Table 3: Results in terms of mi(cro-) and ma(cro-average) p(recision), r(ecall), and F-score; details in Table 4.

5 Experiments and Results

The models are evaluated in two settings:

Rare nouns uses the 2,809 sense annotated noun tokens whose lemmata occur less than three times in the complete DCS as test set, and the remaining sense annotated noun tokens as training set.

Vedic nouns uses the 528 sense annotated noun tokens whose lemmata occur only in the Vedic layer of the DCS as test set, and the remaining sense annotated noun tokens as training set. This setting simulates knowledge transfer from CS to VS. Note that lemmata in the test set are not required to be rare, contrary to the *rare nouns* settings.

Table 3 presents micro- and macro-averaged precision, recall, and F-scores for the two settings, while Table 4 breaks up these numbers by WNSS. Although the historical structure of the Sanskrit corpus, the annotation mode (Sec. 3), and the classifier types do not allow direct comparison with the results reported by Curran (2005) and Ciaramita and Altun (2006), Table 3 shows that ME and RNN achieve good performance, especially for *rare nouns*. Both classifiers clearly improve over the baseline. Low recall rates of the baseline indicate problems with WordNet coverage, while its low precision is caused by the interaction between high semantic ambiguity of Sanskrit nouns and lexicographic arrangement (refer to Fn. 10). For the word *aurabhra*, for example, Monier-Williams (1899) provides the definitions "a coarse woollen blanket" and "name of a physician". Although the first meaning occurs only in indigenous monolingual dictionaries, Monier-Williams (1899) places it at first position, because it may be the etymologically older meaning (*urabhra* 'sheep' $\gg$ *aurabhra*). The baseline can, therefore, never access the second, correct solution.

Details in Tab. 4 demonstrate that ME and RNN have problems with nouns denoting abstract concepts.[14] While ME and RNN obtain accuracy rates of 81.7% and 83.5% for concrete nouns in the setting *rare nouns*, they only achieve 56.0% and 54.7% for abstract ones in the same setting. The higher error rate for abstract nouns can partly be explained by missing specialization of the English dictionary. In

[14]The supersenses "animal", "artifact", "body", "food", "location", "object", "person", "plant", "substance" constitute the set of concrete nouns. All other supersenses are counted as abstract.

the medical text Suśrutasaṃhitā, Cik. 11.3, for example, the term *parisaraṇa* denotes a symptom of the urinary disease called *prameha*, as a patient suffering from *prameha* "gets the habit of *parisaraṇa*." Monier-Williams (1899) glosses the hapax legomenon *parisaraṇa* as "running or moving about", which is a direct translation of the meaning "Umherlaufen" in Böhtlingk and Roth (1875). Both dictionaries were obviously not aware that the term has a medical meaning in this passage, and can best be translated as "restlessness". This translation was actually chosen as the word semantic annotation of *parisaraṇa*, and was connected with the synset "restlessness (inability to rest or relax or be still)" in OpenCyc. While the WNSS of "restlessness" is "attribute", both ME and RNN classify this occurrence of *parisaraṇa* as an "act" – a meaningful proposal given the limited amount of information available in Monier-Williams (1899) and Böhtlingk and Roth (1875).

Other misclassified instances of the WNSS "attribute" point to the problems inherent in annotating ancient languages, as in the case of the hapax legomenon *anavekṣā* mentioned in the juridicial treatise Manusmṛti (Manusmṛti, 7.111):

mohād   rājā   sva-rāṣṭraṃ   yaḥ   karṣayaty   anavekṣayā
folly:AB.   king:N.   own-realm:A.   who:N.   oppress:3.sg.   carelessness:I.
When a king in his folly oppresses his own realm indiscriminately, ... (Olivelle, 2005, 160)

The word was annotated with the OpenCyc concept "carelessness (the quality of not being careful or taking pains)" (WNSS: "attribute"), but labeled as "act" by ME, and as "state" by RNN. All three solutions can be justified semantically in the given textual context. While the gold annotation "attribute" fits well into the scientific character of the text, which draws a systematic picture of the ideal king, the solution "act" would highlight the voluntary negligence of royal duties. Interestingly, the semantic ambiguity is reflected, and even increased by the Sanskrit commentaries of the text. The commentary of Medhātithi seems to support a reading as an "act", because he paraphrases the term with the clause "when the king has not performed the considerations described above" (Mandlik (1886, 890); *yastu rājā pūrvoktavivekam akṛtvā* ...). On the other hand, the commentators Kullūka ("through bad teachings and lack of knowledge", *duṣṭaśiṣṭājñānena*) and Rāmacandra ("through lack of consideration", *avicāreṇa*) interpret *anavekṣā* rather as a cognitive feature or process. If their interpretation is accepted, the term should have been labeled as "cognition" in the given context. Apart from emphasizing the problem of missing adjudication (Sec. 3), this example shows the limits of semantic differentiability when interpreting ancient texts, whose languages are not spoken anymore.

ME and RNN consistently perform better for rare than for Vedic nouns. This behavior points to the problems inherent in transfering word semantic knowledge over long distances in time, and supports the conclusions reached by Sukhareva and Chiarcos (2014) for projecting parser annotations. The vast majority of training records in both settings comes from CS, so that classifiers are biased towards this form of Sanskrit. The composition of the test sets, on the other hand, shows clear differences: Out of the 2,809 words in the test set of *rare nouns*, 1,363 belong to the medical and alchemical subcorpus, 574 to the epic literature, and 247 to the poetic and narrative subcorpus, while only 118 are from the Vedic period (106 of them from the Ṛgveda). The training set of *rare words* provides plenty of data for disambiguating the WNSS of nouns from the later subcorpora, because the alchemical and the epic subcorpora are more densely annotated than other parts of the DCS (refer to page 4). These properties are not met for the setting *Vedic nouns*.

Although the ME is trained with preprocessed English definitions, the RNN produces better overall results in both experimental settings. This conclusion holds for frequent and for rare WNSS, as is evidenced by the macro-average values in Table 3 and the F-scores of rare WNSS in Table 4. We hypothesize that the ME is not able to integrate context features appropriately in several cases. In the medical passage Suśrutasaṃhitā, Nidānasthāna 9.16, for example, the word *vegāghāta* 'constipation' is correctly labeled as '*state*' by the RNN, but as '*act*' by the ME, although the head word "constipation" receives the highest coefficient of 1.529 for the label '*state*'. The misclassification of this token is caused by context features such as the Sanskrit lemma *vyāyāma* 'exertion', whose linear combination produces the final decision for '*act*'. On the other hand, performance of the RNN model drops sharply, when randomly

Rare nouns

WNSS	N	Baseline			ME			RNN		
		P	R	F	P	R	F	P	R	F
act	124	25.42	24.19	24.79	53.1	**48.39**	**50.63**	**63.24**	34.68	44.79
animal	52	**66.00**	63.46	64.71	64.44	55.77	59.79	63.79	**71.15**	**67.27**
artifact	404	60.52	34.9	44.27	**75.00**	70.54	72.7	73.85	**75.50**	**74.66**
attribute	33	24.49	**36.36**	29.27	28.21	33.33	30.56	**33.33**	30.3	**31.75**
body	44	48.78	45.45	47.06	47.73	47.73	47.73	**59.26**	**72.73**	**65.31**
cognition	14	19.23	35.71	25	**25.00**	**50.00**	**33.33**	14.29	7.14	9.52
communication	111	30.99	19.82	24.18	**73.33**	69.37	71.3	70.8	**72.07**	**71.43**
event	23	16.22	26.09	20	**50.00**	30.43	37.84	47.06	**34.78**	**40.00**
feeling	3	**30.00**	**100.00**	**46.15**	20	33.33	25	28.57	66.67	40
food	58	61.11	18.97	28.95	61.7	50	55.24	**73.17**	**51.72**	**60.61**
group	10	9.76	40	15.69	55.56	**50.00**	**52.63**	**100.00**	10	18.18
location	101	65.85	26.73	38.03	75.21	**87.13**	**80.73**	**76.15**	82.18	79.05
object	172	74.35	82.56	78.24	85.47	**85.47**	85.47	**90.74**	85.47	**88.02**
person	834	89.29	35.97	51.28	90.25	**92.09**	91.16	**93.62**	91.49	**92.54**
phenomenon	7	25	**57.14**	34.78	**50.00**	28.57	**36.36**	50	28.57	36.36
plant	196	52.27	11.73	19.17	**79.80**	80.61	**80.20**	71.25	**87.24**	78.44
possession	11	21.62	72.73	33.33	**75.00**	**81.82**	**78.26**	60	81.82	69.23
process	83	**66.67**	2.41	4.65	55.41	49.4	52.23	63.01	**55.42**	**58.97**
quantity	20	13.51	25	17.54	**52.17**	60	**55.81**	34.15	**70.00**	45.9
relation	2	0	0		0	0		0	0	
shape	1	12.5	**100.00**	22.22	0	0			0	
state	113	67.61	42.48	52.17	**68.97**	70.8	69.87	64.03	**78.76**	70.63
substance	378	77.99	32.8	46.18	78.61	**80.69**	**79.63**	**79.27**	79.89	79.58
time	12	29.41	41.67	34.48	**40.00**	50	44.44	38.89	**58.33**	**46.67**
Tops	3	22.22	**66.67**	33.33	**33.33**	33.33	33.33	0	0	

Vedic nouns

WNSS	N	Baseline			ME			RNN		
		P	R	F	P	R	F	P	R	F
act	51	**62.96**	33.33	43.59	62.26	**64.71**	**63.46**	57.69	58.82	58.25
animal	24	76.47	54.17	63.41	87.5	**58.33**	70	**93.33**	58.33	**71.79**
artifact	35	**66.67**	51.43	58.06	51.28	57.14	54.05	57.5	**65.71**	**61.33**
attribute	37	**57.50**	**62.16**	**59.74**	37.84	37.84	37.84	54.55	32.43	40.68
body	21	**63.16**	57.14	**60.00**	55.56	47.62	51.28	57.14	57.14	57.14
cognition	8	10	**12.50**	11.11	12.5	12.5	12.5	**14.29**	12.5	**13.33**
communication	32	41.94	40.62	41.27	**64.00**	50	56.14	60	**65.62**	**62.69**
event	10	18.18	**20.00**	19.05	**66.67**	20	**30.77**	14.29	10	11.76
feeling	11	43.75	**63.64**	**51.85**	20	9.09	12.5	**44.44**	36.36	40
food	3	**50.00**	33.33	**40.00**	18.18	**66.67**	28.57	16.67	66.67	26.67
group	13	16.67	**15.38**	16	**50.00**	15.38	**23.53**	33.33	7.69	12.5
location	20	**63.64**	**35.00**	**45.16**	33.33	30	31.58	46.67	35	40
object	14	46.15	42.86	44.44	26.09	42.86	32.43	**58.82**	**71.43**	**64.52**
person	163	**87.13**	53.99	66.67	70.85	86.5	77.9	76.72	**88.96**	**82.39**
phenomenon	15	42.86	40	41.38	**60.00**	20	30	42.86	**60.00**	**50.00**
plant	4	0	0		57.14	**100.00**	72.73	**60.00**	75	66.67
possession	7	60	**85.71**	**70.59**	33.33	42.86	37.5	**75.00**	42.86	54.55
process	5		0		0	0		100	**40.00**	57.14
quantity	7	0	0		50	14.29	22.22	**77.78**	**100.00**	87.5
shape	1	0	0			0			0	
state	21	61.54	**76.19**	**68.09**	50	33.33	40	**62.50**	47.62	54.05
substance	14	**77.78**	50	60.87	47.62	**71.43**	57.14	76.92	71.43	**74.07**
time	7	36.36	57.14	44.44	42.86	42.86	42.86	**55.56**	**71.43**	**62.50**
Tops	5	0	0		**100.00**	20.00	33.33	0	0	

Table 4: P(recision), r(ecall) and F-score for rare (upper subtable) and Vedic nouns (lower subtable). Row-wise maxima are printed bold.

initialized English and Sanskrit word embeddings are used instead of pretrained ones (macro-averaged
P: 32.40, R: 34.44, F: 33.39, for the *Vedic nouns* settings; compare with Tab. 3). This finding underlines
the importance of using appropriate pretrained embeddings in downstream tasks (Schnabel et al., 2015).

6   Conclusion

The paper has demonstrated that definitions from modern Western dictionaries and the lemmatized sentence context provide enough information for an efficient supersense disambiguation of rare and Vedic
nouns. We would like to argue that gold information on the lemmatization level is crucial for this task,
and compensates for the lack of large Sanskrit corpora to a certain degree. This indirect form of supervision is especially relevant for a morphologically rich language such as (Vedic) Sanskrit, where nouns
and adjectives regularly occur in 24 case forms, and a single verbal root can produce more than 100
inflected forms. It should be noted that lemmatization not only disambiguates the Sanskrit words in the
sentence context, but is equally relevant for retrieving the correct dictionary definitions of a word, which
are appended to the lemma in the database of the DCS.

Future work in this area will follow two tracks. First, sense tagging was performed without using
lemma information of the target word as a feature. The paper ignores the target lemma, because lemmata
are by definition not useful for semantically disambiguating rare words and especially hapax legomena.
It can, however, be expected that the lemma feature will clearly improve the accuracy of unrestricted
Sanskrit WSD. Second, we will try to include derivational information as an additional feature in WSD
of rare and Vedic nouns. Numerous Sanskrit nouns are derived from verbs or other nouns through
derivational morphology, as described in Pāṇini's Aṣṭādhyāyī, or by compounding. Such derivational
processes are recorded in Böhtlingk and Roth (1875) and Wackernagel and Debrunner (1954), but can
also be detected using probabilistic models such as Morfessor (Creutz and Lagus, 2007). Since derivation
can provide important semantic cues for the human reader, its inclusion may also improve automatic
supersense disambiguation of Sanskrit nouns.

Acknowledgments

We are grateful to the anonymous reviewers for their comments. Research for this paper was supported
by the Cluster of Excellence "Multimodal computing and interaction" (EXC 284, University of Saarbrücken), funded by DFG.

References

Agirre, E. and A. Soroa (2009). Personalizing PageRank for word sense disambiguation. In *Proceedings
of the 12th Conference of the EACL*, pp. 33–41.

Aguilar, S. T., X. Tannier, and P. Chastang (2016). Named entity recognition applied on a data base of
Medieval Latin charters. The case of chartae burgundiae. In *Proceedings of the 3rd HistoInformatics
Workshop*.

Bamman, D. and G. Crane (2011). Measuring historical word sense variation. In *Proceedings of the 11th
Annual International ACM/IEEE Joint Conference on Digital Libraries*, pp. 1–10.

Berger, A., S. D. Pietra, and V. D. Pietra (1996). A maximum entropy approach to Natural Language
Processing. *Computational Linguistics 22*(1), 39–71.

Bhingardive, S. and P. Bhattacharyya (2017). Word sense disambiguation using IndoWordNet. In N. S.
Dash, P. Bhattacharyya, and J. D. Pawar (Eds.), *The WordNet in Indian Languages*, pp. 243–260.
Singapore: Springer.

Böhtlingk, O. and R. Roth (1875). *Sanskrit-Wörterbuch.* St. Petersburg: Kaiserliche Akademie der Wissenschaften.

Che, W., T. Liu, and Y. Li (2010). Improving semantic role labeling with word sense. In *Human Language Technologies: The 2010 Annual Conference of the NAACL,* pp. 246–249.

Ciaramita, M. and Y. Altun (2006). Broad-coverage sense disambiguation and information extraction with a supersense sequence tagger. In *Proceedings of the 2006 Conference on EMNLP,* pp. 594–602.

Ciaramita, M. and M. Johnson (2003). Supersense tagging of unknown nouns in WordNet. In *Proceedings of the EMNLP,* pp. 168–175. Association for Computational Linguistics.

Creutz, M. and K. Lagus (2007, January). Unsupervised models for morpheme segmentation and morphology learning. *ACM Transactions on Speech and Language Processing 4*(1).

Curran, J. R. (2005). Supersense tagging of unknown nouns using semantic similarity. In *Proceedings of the 43rd Annual Meeting on ACL,* pp. 26–33.

Flekova, L. and I. Gurevych (2016). Supersense embeddings: A unified model for supersense interpretation, prediction, and utilization. In *Proceedings of the ACL,* pp. 2029–2041.

Frermann, L. and M. Lapata (2016). A Bayesian model of diachronic meaning change. *Transactions of the Association for Computational Linguistics 4,* 31–45.

Graves, A., S. Fernández, and J. Schmidhuber (2005). *Bidirectional LSTM Networks for Improved Phoneme Classification and Recognition,* pp. 799–804. Berlin, Heidelberg: Springer.

Hamilton, W. L., J. Leskovec, and D. Jurafsky (2016). Diachronic word embeddings reveal statistical laws of semantic change. In *Proceedings of the 54th Annual Meeting of the ACL,* pp. 1489–1501.

Hellwig, O. (2012). ratha = "warrior" or "chariot"? Computational Approaches to Polysemy in Sanskrit. In *Proceedings of the World Sanskrit Conference 2012.*

Hellwig, O. (2015). Morphological disambiguation of Classical Sanskrit. In C. Mahlow and M. Piotrowski (Eds.), *Systems and Frameworks for Computational Morphology,* Cham, pp. 41–59. Springer.

Hellwig, O. (2016). Detecting sentence boundaries in Sanskrit texts. In *Proceedings of the COLING,* pp. 288–297.

Hettrich, H. (2007). *Materialien zu einer Kasussyntax des Ṛgveda.* Würzburg: Universität Würzburg.

Hill, F., K. Cho, A. Korhonen, and Y. Bengio (2016). Learning to understand phrases by embedding the dictionary. *Transactions of the ACL 4,* 17–30.

Hillebrandt, A. (1897). *Ritual-Litteratur. Vedische Opfer und Zauber.* Grundriss der Indo-Arischen Philologie und Altertumskunde, III. Band, 2. Heft. Strassburg: Verlag von Karl J. Trübner.

Hinton, G. E., N. Srivastava, A. Krizhevsky, I. Sutskever, and R. R. Salakhutdinov (2012). Improving neural networks by preventing co-adaptation of feature detectors. *arXiv preprint arXiv:1207.0580.*

Hochreiter, S. and J. Schmidhuber (1997). Long Short-Term Memory. *Neural Computation 9*(8), 1735–1780.

Johannsen, A., D. Hovy, H. M. Alonso, B. Plank, and A. Søgaard (2014). More or less supervised supersense tagging of Twitter. In *Proceedings of the Third Joint Conference on Lexical and Computational Semantics,* pp. 1–11.

Kulkarni, M., C. Dangarikar, I. Kulkarni, A. Nanda, and P. Bhattacharyya (2010). Introducing Sanskrit Wordnet. In *Proceedings on the 5th Global Wordnet Conference,* pp. 287–294.

Kulkarni, M., I. Kulkarni, C. Dangarikar, and P. Bhattacharyya (2010). Gloss in Sanskrit Wordnet. In *Sanskrit Computational Linguistics*, pp. 190–197. Springer.

Laparra, E. and G. Rigau (2013). Impar: A deterministic algorithm for implicit semantic role labelling. In *Proceedings of the ACL*, pp. 1180–1189.

Lenat, D. B. (1995). CYC: A large-scale investment in knowledge infrastructure. *Communications of the ACM 38*(11), 33–38.

Lesk, M. (1986). Automatic sense disambiguation using machine readable dictionaries: How to tell a pine cone from an ice cream cone. In *Proceedings of the 5th Annual International Conference on Systems Documentation*, pp. 24–26.

Mandlik, V. N. (Ed.) (1886). *Mānava-Dharma Śāstra. With the commentaries of Medhātithi et al.* Bombay: Ganpat Krishnaji's Press.

Manning, C. D., M. Surdeanu, J. Bauer, J. Finkel, S. J. Bethard, and D. McClosky (2014). The Stanford CoreNLP natural language processing toolkit. In *Association for Computational Linguistics (ACL) System Demonstrations*, pp. 55–60.

Mikolov, T., A. Deoras, D. Povey, L. Burget, and J. Černocký (2011). Strategies for training large scale neural network language models. In *2011 IEEE Workshop on Automatic Speech Recognition and Understanding (ASRU)*, pp. 196–201.

Monier-Williams, M. (1899). *Sanskṛit-English Dictionary*. New Delhi: Munshiram Manoharlal Publishers Pvt. Ltd. (3rd edition, 1988).

Olivelle, P. (2005). *Manu's Code of Law. A Critical Edition and Translation of the Mānava-Dharmaśāstra*. Oxford: Oxford University Press.

Pennington, J., R. Socher, and C. D. Manning (2014). GloVe: Global vectors for word representation. In *Proceedings of the 2014 EMNLP*, pp. 1532–1543.

Prochasson, E. and P. Fung (2011). Rare word translation extraction from aligned comparable documents. In *Proceedings of the 49th Annual Meeting of the ACL: Human Language Technologies-Volume 1*, pp. 1327–1335. Association for Computational Linguistics.

Roth, M. and M. Lapata (2015). Context-aware frame-semantic role labeling. *Transactions of the Association for Computational Linguistics 3*, 449–460.

Scharfe, H. (1977). *Grammatical Literature*. A History of Indian Literature, Volume 5, Fasc. 2. Wiesbaden: Otto Harrassowitz.

Schnabel, T., I. Labutov, D. M. Mimno, and T. Joachims (2015). Evaluation methods for unsupervised word embeddings. In *Proceedings of the 2015 Conference on EMNLP*, pp. 298–307.

Schneider, N. and N. A. Smith (2015). A corpus and model integrating multiword expressions and supersenses. In *Proceedings of the NAACL*.

Sukhareva, M. and C. Chiarcos (2014). Diachronic proximity vs. data sparsity in cross-lingual parser projection. A case study on Germanic. In *Proceedings of the COLING*, pp. 11–20.

Tang, D., B. Qin, and T. Liu (2015). Document modeling with gated recurrent neural network for sentiment classification. In *Proceedings of the 2015 Conference on EMNLP*, pp. 1422–1432.

Wackernagel, J. and A. Debrunner (1954). *Altindische Grammatik. II, 2: Die Nominalsuffixes*. Göttingen: Vandenhoeck & Ruprecht.

Wijaya, D. T. and R. Yeniterzi (2011). Understanding semantic change of words over centuries. In *Proceedings of the 2011 International Workshop on Detecting and Exploiting Cultural diversity on the Social Web*, pp. 35–40.

Wilks, Y. (1975). A preferential, pattern-seeking, semantics for natural language inference. *Artificial Intelligence 6*(1), 53–74.

Witzel, M. (1995). Early Indian history: Linguistic and textual parametres. In G. Erdosy (Ed.), *The Indo-Aryans of Ancient South Asia. Language, Material Culture and Ethnicity*, Volume 1, pp. 85–125. Berlin, New York: Walter de Gruyter.

Wujastyk, D. (2014). Indian manuscripts. In *Manuscript Cultures: Mapping the Field*, pp. 159–182. Berlin: De Gruyter.

Wunderlich, M., A. Fraser, and P. Langeslag (2015). "GodWat Þæt Ic Eom God" – An exploratory investigation into word sense disambiguation in Old English. In *Proceedings of the GSCL*, pp. 39–48.

Yu, L.-C., C.-H. Wu, and J.-F. Yeh (2010). Word sense disambiguation using multiple contextual features. *Computational Linguistics and Chinese Language Processing 15*(3-4), 181–192.

Zgusta, L. (1988). Copying in lexicography: Monier-William's Sanskrit Dictionary and other cases (dvaikośyam). *Lexicographica 4*, 145–173.

Extracting hypernym relations from Wikipedia disambiguation pages: comparing symbolic and machine learning approaches

Mouna Kamel[1], Cassia Trojahn[1], Adel Ghamnia[1,2], Nathalie Aussenac-Gilles[1], Cécile Fabre[2]

[1] Institut de Recherche en Informatique de Toulouse, Toulouse, France

{mouna.kamel,cassia.trojahn,adel.ghamnia,nathalie.aussenac-gilles}@irit.fr

[2] Laboratoire CLLE, équipe ERSS, Toulouse, France

cecile.fabre@univ-tlse2.fr

Abstract

Extracting hypernym relations from text is one of the key steps in the construction and enrichment of semantic resources. Several methods have been exploited in a variety of propositions in the literature. However, the strengths of each approach on a same corpus are still poorly identified in order to better take advantage of their complementarity. In this paper, we study how complementary two approaches of different nature are when identifying hypernym relations on a structured corpus containing both well-written text and syntactically poor formulations, together with a rich formatting. A symbolic approach based on lexico-syntactic patterns and a statistical approach using a supervised learning method are applied to a sub-corpus of Wikipedia in French, composed of disambiguation pages. These pages, particularly rich in hypernym relations, contain both kinks of formulations. We compared the results of each approach independently of each other and compared the performance when combining together their individual results. We obtain the best results in the latter case, with an F-measure of 0.75. In addition, 55% of the identified relations, with respect to a reference corpus, are not expressed in the French DBPedia and could be used to enrich this resource.

1 Introduction

In many fields such as artificial intelligence, semantic web, software engineering or information retrieval, applications require a strong reasoning ability, based on semantic resources that describe concepts and the relations between them. These resources can be manually designed. They are of good quality, however due to the high cost of their design, they offer a limited domain coverage. With the increasing amount of textual documents available in digital format, NLP processing chains offer a good support to design such resources from text. In this context, the task of automatically extracting relations from text is a crucial step (Buitelaar et al., 2005). Numerous studies have attempted to extract hypernym relations, as they allow for expressing the backbone structure of such resources and for assigning types to entities.

While symbolic approaches usually rely on manually defined lexico-syntactic patterns identifying clues of relations between terms (Hearst, 1992), statistical approaches, which are nowadays predominant, are generally based on supervised (Pantel and Pennacchiotti, 2008) or unsupervised (Banko et al., 2007) learning methods, or on distributional spaces (Lenci and Benotto, 2012). These methods of different nature answer to the need of exploiting corpora with different specificities (e.g. domain granularity, nature of the corpus, language, target semantic resource, etc.) and which express the hypernym relation in different forms. For giving some examples, this kind of relation can be expressed by the lexicon and the syntactic structure as in the sentence *sand is a sedimentary rock*, by a lexical inclusion as in *domestic pigeon* (implied *domestic pigeon is a pigeon*), or by using punctuation or layout features that replace lexical markers like the comma in *Trojan horse, a Greek myth* or even the disposition in enumerative structures.

The study we conduct in this paper aims to show the interest of applying several approaches on a same corpus in order to identify hypernym relations through their various forms of expression. We are particularly interested in exploiting a corpus containing both well-written text (i.e., sentences expressed with a complete syntactic structure) and syntactically poor formulations (i.e., sentences with syntactic holes), together with a rich formatting. We analyze the complementarity of a symbolic approach based on lexico-syntactic patterns and a statistical approach based on supervised learning. We applied these two approaches to a corpus of Wikipedia disambiguation pages, which are very rich in hypernym relations differently expressed, as these pages contain both well-written text and poorly-written text.

Our proposal focuses on the combination of the individual results rather than on the combination of the approaches themselves (e.g., by learning patterns). Indeed, combining patterns with machine learning usually relies on path-based methods (Snow et al., 2004) (Snow et al., 2006) (Riedel et al., 2013). However, dependency parsers have proven to perform worse on poorly-written text. Although our approach is naive in that sense, it proves to provide good results, in particular, in terms of F-measure.

This work is part of the SemPedia[1] project that aims at enriching the semantic resource DBPedia for French (semantic resources targeting this language are scarce), by proposing a new Wikipedia extractors dedicated to the hypernym relation. Hence, we evaluate how the extracted relations could potentially enrich such kind of resource.

The paper is organized as follows. Section 2 outlines the main work related to our proposal. Section 3 presents the materials and methods used in our study, namely the description of the training and reference corpus, their pre-processing, and the extraction approaches. The results obtained are presented and discussed in Section 4. Finally, Section 5 concludes the paper and presents future directions.

2   Related work

In the field of relation extraction, the pioneering work of the symbolic methods is that of Hearst (Hearst, 1992) which defined a set of lexico-syntactic patterns specific to the hypernym relation for English. This work has been adapted and extended to French for the hypernym relation (Morin and Jacquemin, 2004), for the meronymic relation (Berland and Charniak, 1999), and for different types of relations (Séguéla and Aussenac-Gilles, 1999), by progressively integrating learning techniques.

With respect to statistical approaches and, in particular, those based on machine learning, which are specially required when dealing with large corpus, Snow and colleagues (Snow et al., 2004) and Bunescu and Mooney (Bunescu and Mooney, 2005) apply supervised learning methods to a set of manually anno-tated examples. While the cost of manual annotation is the main limitation of supervised learning, distant supervision method consists in building the set of examples using an external resource to automatically annotate the learning examples (Mintz et al., 2009). Another way to avoid manual annotation is the semi-supervised learning method called bootstrapping which uses a selection of patterns to construct the set of examples (Brin, 1998). Agichtein and Gravano (Agichtein and Gravano, 2000), and Etzioni and colleagues (Etzioni et al., 2004) have used this method by adding semantic features to identify relations between named entities. Unsupervised learning, based on clustering techniques, was implemented by Yates and colleagues (Yates et al., 2007) and Fader and colleagues (Fader et al., 2011) which used syn-tactic features to train their classifiers relations between named entities. Some of these works are also based on distributional analyses (Kotlerman et al., 2010) (Lenci and Benotto, 2012) (Fabre et al., 2014). In the work of Kotlerman and colleagues (Kotlerman et al., 2010), they quantify distributional feature inclusion, where the contexts of a hyponym are expected to be largely included in those of its hypernym. Lenci and Benotto (Lenci and Benotto, 2012) explore the possibility of identifying hypernyms using a directional similarity measure that takes into account not only the inclusion of the features of u in v, but also the non-inclusion of the features v in u. The hypothesis from Santus and colleagues (Santus et al., 2014) is that most typical linguistic contexts of a hypernym are less informative than those of its hyponyms.

Beyond these works, which evaluate approaches independently of each other, few results have been reported on the respective contributions and the complementarity of methods. Granada (Granada, 2015) compared the performance of different methods (patterns-based, head-modifier, and distributional ones)

---

[1]http://www.irit.fr/Sempedia

for the task of hypernym relation extraction in different languages, by defining several metrics such that density and depth of hierarchies. The evaluation was carried out on different types of corpus but does not take into account the learning approaches. Yap and Baldwin (Yap and Baldwin, 2009) study the impact of the corpus and the size of training sets on the performance of similar supervised methods, on the extraction of several types of relation (hypernym, synonymy and antonymy), whereas Abacha and Zweigenbaum (Ben Abacha and Zweigenbaum, 2011) combine patterns and a statistical learning method based on the SVM classifier for extracting relations between specific entities (disease and treatment) from a biomedical corpus. In the same line, we exploit methods of different nature, focusing on the specific hypernym relation.

In particular, with respect to the approaches combining patterns and distributional methods, most of them rely on path-based methods. It is the case, for instance, of the learning approach of Snow and colleagues (Snow et al., 2004), which automatically learned pattern spaces based on syntactic dependency paths. These paths represent the relationship between hypernym/hyponym word pairs from WordNet and are used as features in a logistic regression classifier. Variations of this method have been applied in different tasks, such as hypernym extraction (Snow et al., 2006) (Riedel et al., 2013) and extraction of definitions (Navigli and Velardi, 2010). However, as stated in (Kotlerman et al., 2010), one major limitation in relying on lexico-syntactic paths is the sparsity of the feature space, since similar paths may somewhat vary at the lexical level. In (Nakashole et al., 2012), generalizing such variations into more abstract paths proved to improve the results, in particular recall. On the other hand, while those approaches mostly rely on dependency trees extracted from well-written text, the performance of dependency parsers has proven to be very low on poorly-written corpus. In that sense, our focus here is to exploit strategies fitting a corpus rich in poorly-written text and where the polysemous occurs frequently (for instance, for the term "Didier Porte", "porte" is tagged as a verb instead of a noun). It is one of the reasons we focus here on the complementarity of the approaches rather than on their combination.

Finally, with respect to the enrichment of DBPedia knowledge base, several tools, called "extractors" have been developed to extract relations from the different elements present in the Wikipedia pages. Morsey and colleagues (Morsey et al., 2012) developed 19 extractors for analyzing abstract, images, infobox, etc. Other works focus on the hypernym relation. For example, Suchanek and colleagues (Suchanek et al., 2007) used the 'Category' part of Wikipedia pages to build the knowledge base, Yago, Kazama and Torisawa (Kazama and Torisawa, 2007) which exploited the 'Definition' part, and finally Sumida and Torisawa (Sumida and Torisawa, 2008) who were interested in the menu items. We can see that the DBPedia knowledge base is built essentially from the structural elements of the Wikipedia pages. Works targeting relation extraction from text have been exploited in a lesser extend (Rodriguez-Ferreira et al., 2016), which means that most of the knowledge in these pages remains under-exploited. Our aim here is to measure the degree of enrichment of semantic resources when exploiting this kind of relation extraction approach.

3 Material and methods

In this section, we describe the Wikipedia sub-corpus we used, its pre-processing, and the extraction methods we have considered.

3.1 Corpus

Different types of pages can be identified within the Wikipedia encyclopedia. Among them, the *disambiguation pages* list the articles whose title is polysemous, giving a definition of all the accepted meanings for this title, which refer to as many entities. Thanks to the Wikipedia's charter guidelines, which recommend the use of templates (for instance, *Toponyms*, *Patronyms*, etc.), these pages present editorial as well as formatting regularities for presenting the different meanings of the term on the page. For each meaning, a definition and a link to the corresponding page are provided. In fact, the definitions are textual objects in which the hypernym relation is often present (Malaisé et al., 2004) (Rebeyrolle and Tanguy, 2000). Furthermore, on these pages, the definitions take varied but predictable forms. For instance, the following excerpt (Figure 1) which comes from the *Mercure* disambiguation page[2] shows different hypernym relations, expressed thanks to the lexicon (*le mercure est un élément chimique*), with the help of punctuations (the comma in *le Mercure, un fleuve du sud de l'Italie*), taking benefit from the lexical inclusion (*appareil de mesure*, implying that *appareil de mesure* is an *appareil*), or using dispositional and typographical characters (the structure substitutes the lack of complete syntax and expresses a good part of the text meaning) especially when expressing enumerative structure (*la diode à vapeur de mercure est un appareil de mesure, la pile au mercure est un appareil de mesure*, etc.).

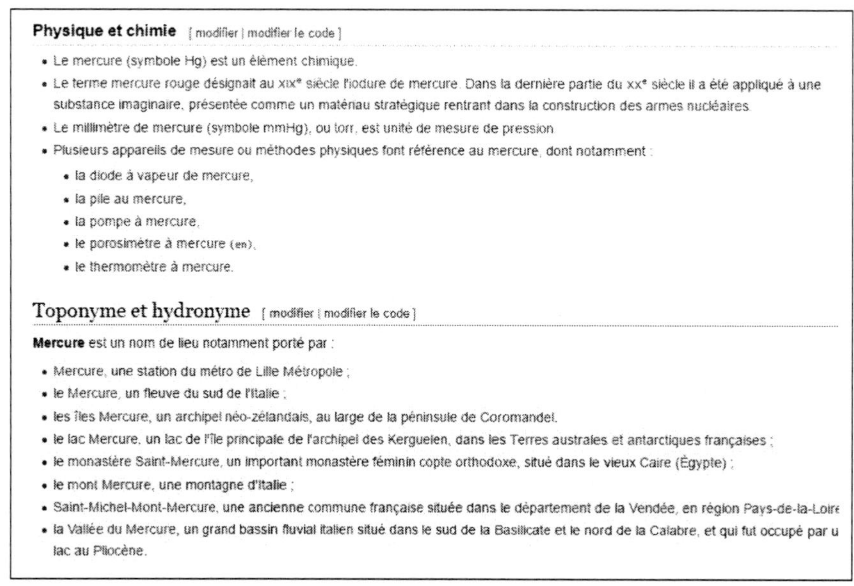

Figure 1: Fragment of the disambiguation page *Mercure*.

We have compiled a corpus made of 5924 French disambiguation pages (XML version of the 2016 Wikipedia dump). From this corpus were extracted two sub-corpora:

- 20 randomly selected disambiguation pages form the *reference corpus*. In these pages, hypernymy relations were manually annotated, marking the terms referring to the related entities and the zone of the text where the relations were identified. This sub-corpus is used to qualitatively evaluate our approach and to evaluate the potential enrichment of DBPedia (Section 4.3);

- the remaining pages form the *training corpus*, which is intended to train and evaluate our learning model (Section 3.3.2).

3.2 Pre-processing

The content of each page has been labeled with morpho-syntactic tags, POS and lemma, using TreeTagger[3]. For identifying the expression of semantic relations, the text is also annotated using terms, namely syntagms, usually nominal, that may designate entities or conceptual classes. For example, *Mercure, système solaire, planète* (*Mercury, solar system, planet*) are some of the terms in Figure 1. The terms can therefore be included in each other (e.g., *system* in *solar system*). Rather than using a term extractor, we chose to construct *a priori* two lists of terms:

---

[2]https://fr.wikipedia.org/wiki/Mercure

[3]http://www.cis.uni-muenchen.de/schmid/tools/TreeTagger

- LBabel contains the list of terms retrieved from the French labels of concepts present in the semantic resource BabelNet[4]. This list will serve to train the learning system, as detailed in Section 3.3.2;

- LCorpus contains the list composed of the manually annotated terms from the reference corpus (Section 4).

These lists are then respectively projected on the pre-processed learning and reference corpora. In fact, the annotation of the corpus by terms derived from a shared semantic source ensures the validity of the learning model. This also prevents the identification of terms biasing the relation extraction process.

3.3 Relation extraction approaches

As already stated before, we have chosen two approaches of different nature which are often opposed by the cost of their implementation and by the precision and recall they provide: a symbolic approach based on lexical-syntactic patterns, and a statistical approach based on supervised learning using the distant supervision principle. While patterns represent recurring language patterns expressed through lexicon, syntactic and punctuation elements, automatic learning allows for combining features of different natures (morphological, syntactic, semantic or shaping) and for capturing the properties of contexts in a more global way. These approaches are detailed below.

3.3.1 Lexico-syntactic patterns

A lexico-syntactic pattern is a regular expression composed of words, grammatical or semantic categories, and symbols aiming to identify textual segments which match this expression. In the context of relation identification, the pattern characterizes a set of linguistic forms whose the interpretation is relatively stable and which corresponds to a semantic relation between terms (Rebeyrolle and Tanguy, 2000). Patterns are in fact very efficient, particularly in terms of precision, as they are adapted to the corpus. However, since their development is cost-expensive, it is conventional to implement generic patterns such as those of Hearst (Hearst, 1992). Here, we use a more complete list of 30 patterns from the work of Jacques and Aussenac (Jacques and Aussenac-Gilles, 2006)[5]. We have also extended this set of patterns with more specific (ad-hoc) patterns which better fit the template structure of disambiguation pages (Ghamnia, 2016). This set of enriched patterns are the one used in our experiments.

3.3.2 Distant supervision learning

We have chosen to use the principle of distant supervision proposed by Mintz and colleagues (Mintz et al., 2009). This approach consists in aligning an external knowledge base to a corpus and in using this alignment to learn relations. The learning ground is based on the hypothesis that "if two entities participate in a relation, all sentences that mention these two entities express that relation". Although this hypothesis seems too strong, Riedel and colleagues (Riedel et al., 2010) have showed that it makes sense when the knowledge base used to annotate the corpus is derived from the corpus itself.

As with any supervised learning method, it is necessary to create a set of examples, to train a statistical model on these examples, and to evaluate the model on a test set or by cross-validation. The originality of this approach refers to the fact that the learning examples are automatically built with the help of a semantic resource: the class associated to a pair of terms present in a same sentence, corresponds to the the relation (if it exists) that binds these terms in the external resource. Once trained from the learning examples, a multi-class classification algorithm makes it possible to associate a class (and therefore a relation) with each example of a new corpus.

We have adapted this method by focusing on the hypernym relation, and proceeding to a binary classification. A pair of terms is classified as a positive (negative) example if the two terms denoting two concepts that exist in the semantic resource are linked (are not linked) with the hypernymy relation

---

[4] http://babelnet.org/

[5] A JAPE implementation of these two types of patterns is available on https://github.com/aghamnia/SemPediaPatterns

in this resource. In all other cases, the term pair is not an example of learning. Our learning examples are constructed with reference to the semantic resource BabelNet which has the advantage of integrating various knowledge bases including DBPedia, the semantic resource that we want to enrich in a long term. In addition, the hypernymy relation is more straightforward expressed in BabelNet than in DBPedia.

Each example is built from a context which encompasses the two terms that are possibly linked by a relation. A context (or window) consists in n (n being the size of the window) tokens preceding, following and separating the two terms. The features are then extracted from that context. These features are described in Table 1.

Scope	Features	Signification	Type
Token	POS	Part Of Speech	string
	lemma	Lemmatized form of the token	string
Window	distT1	Number of tokens between the token and Term1	integer
	distT2	Number of tokens between the token and Term2	integer
	nbMotsFenître	Number of tokens in the window	integer
	distT1T2	Number of tokens between Term1 and Term2	integer
Sentence	nbMotsPhrase	Number of tokens in the sentence	integer
	presVerbe	Presence of a verbal form	boolean

Table 1: Features set.

Although the features we use here do not take into account more sophisticated structures, as dependency trees (as discussed in Section 2), they provide quite good results, as discussed in the next sections.

We illustrate the content of a feature vector with the following example where the length of the window is fixed to 3 (we have evaluated windows of dimensions 1, 3 and 5, the optimum being obtained for length 3):

"Lime ou citron vert, le fruit des limettiers : Citrus aurantiifolia et Citrus latifolia"

Mapping the list of terms leads to annotate the sentence with terms `Lime`, `citron`, `citron vert`, `vert`, `fruit`. Let us consider the pair <`Lime`, `fruit`> randomly chosen by the system: Term1=`Lime` and Term2=`fruit`.

The system thus extracts:

```
Terme1 ou citron vert, le Terme2 des limettiers :
```

where tokens corresponding to terms have been replaced with Term1 and Term2. TreeTagger annotation allows to replace the exact form of tokens by their part of speach followed by their lemma:

```
Terme1 KON/ou NOM/citron ADJ/vert PUN/, DET:ART/le Terme2

PRP:det/du NOM/limettier PUN/:
```

Finally, feature functions give distances (in number of tokens) between a token and the annotated terms in the form of the pair of values, the number of tokens between Term1 and Term2 (here 5) and the number of tokens in the whole sentence (here 16). The last feature indicates the presence of a verbal form to discriminate poorly-written text from well-written text.

```
(1,-5) (2,-4) (3,-3) (4,-2) (5,-1) (7,1) (8,2) (9,3) 5 16 true
```

The entire example leads to the following representation:

```
Terme1 KON/ou NOM/citron ADJ/vert PUN/, DET:ART/le Terme2

PRP:det/du NOM/limettier PUN/:

(1,-5) (2,-4) (3,-3) (4,-2) (5,-1) (7,1) (8,2) (9,3) 5 16 true
```

This example is a positive one as a hypernym link between *lime* and *fruit* exists in BabelNet.

From the whole set of examples produced according to the process described above, we randomly selected 3000 positive examples and 3000 negative examples (from a total of 84169 examples). From these 6000 examples, 4000 are used as the set of training examples and 2000 form for the test set (with a rate of 50% of positive examples, for both training and test sets). We are aware that the strategy we follow to split the set of examples may affect the results. Although alternative strategies consider, for instance, the zero-lexical overlapping, as adopted by Weeds and colleagues (Weeds et al., 2014) and Levy and colleagues (Levy et al., 2015), we can not follow this kind of strategy here due to the nature of the corpus, where each sentence of a page corresponds to a characterization or a definition of the entity described by this page.

We have trained a binary logistic regression algorithm, the Maximum Entropy classifier MaxEnt (Berger et al., 1996) on the training set. When applying this algorithm on the test set, we obtained a recall of 0.63 and an accuracy of 0.71.

4   Results and discussion

In the following, we discus the results of the approaches described above and we evaluate their complementarity, as well as the advantage of combining their results.

4.1   Results

The quantitative evaluation we present in this section is not intended to measure the performance of the approaches in absolute terms, but rather to know the order of magnitude of the number of relations found by each of them, whether they are common or specific. This evaluation is based on the reference corpus. The set of examples from the reference corpus contains 688 true positive examples (TP) and 267 true negative examples (TN). We consider the relations extracted by each of the approaches as well as the intersection and the union of the set of relations. Table 2 provides the results in terms of precision, recall, F-measure and accuracy. We can observe that we obtain the best values of F-measure when combining both the results of patterns and MaxEnt.

	Patterns	MaxEnt	Patterns inter MaxEnt	Patterns union MaxEnt
Precision	0.81	0.71	0.75	0.73
Recall	0.46	0.63	0.32	0.77
F-measure	0.53	0.67	0.45	0.75
Accuracy	0.54	0.55	0.43	0.63

Table 2: Evaluation of the approaches.

As we will better discuss in the next section, the two approaches do not often find the same relations, what corroborates their complementarity.

4.2   Discussion

We have carried out an analysis of the nature of the differences in the set of extracted relations from both approaches. We first counted the number of relations found by each approach individually, by both of them, or by none of the two (Table 3), with respect to the true positive relations extracted from the reference corpus.

Among the 221 TP relations found by the two approaches, few of them (9 relations) are expressed by the verb *to be*, as for instance, between the terms *macédoine* (*macedonia*) and *salade de fruits* (*fruit salad*) in the sentence "La macédoine est une salade de fruits ou de légumes" (*Macedonia is a salad of fruit or of vegetables*). Almost all other relations correspond to the pattern "X, Y" as in the sentence "Le cheval de Troie, un mythe grec" (*The Trojan horse, a Greek myth*).

	Number TP
Found by patterns AND MaxEnt	221
Found by patterns AND NOT by MaxEnt	96
Found by MaxEnt AND NOT by patterns	210
Found neither by MaxEnt nor by patterns	161

Table 3: Number of true positives (TP) found by the approaches.

From the 96 relations found by patterns and which were not identified by MaxEnt, 19 of them are expressed with the help of the verb *to be*, in particular when the relation is not expressed at the beginning of the sentence, as the relation between *Babel fish* and *espèce imaginaire* (*imaginary species*) in the sentence "Le poisson Babel ou Babel fish est une espèce imaginaire" (*Babel fish or Babel fish is an imaginary species*). Most of the remaining relations match again the pattern "X, Y". We observe as well that the cause of the silence of MaxEnt in this case may be some specific syntactic variations, such as the presence of dates between parentheses, different punctuation, etc. Indeed, our learning model is sensitive to these variations as sentences are very short and present strong regularities.

Among the 210 relations found by MaxEnt, and not found by patterns, we can observe that (i) many relations are expressed with the help of a lexical inclusion, as for instance in the noun phrase *gare de Paris Bastille* (*Paris Bastille railway station*) used to identify the relation *gare de Paris Bastille* (*Paris Bastille railway station*) is a *gare* (*railway station*); (ii) some relations are expressed with the help of a state verb, as for the relation between *aigle* (*eagle*) and *oiseaux* (*birds*) in the sentence "Aigle désigne en fran{cais certains grands oiseaux rapaces" (*Eagle designates some large birds*). We can notice as well that MaxEnt is able to identify the relations expressed in textual units containing a coordination, as the relation between *poisson Babel* (*Babel fish*) and *espèce imaginaire* (*imaginary specie*) in the sentence "Le poisson Babel ou Babel fish est une espèce imaginaire", or between *Louis Babel* and *explorateur* (*explorer*) in the sentence "Louis Babel, prêtre-missionnaire oblat et explorateur" (*Louis Babel, oblate missionary priest and explorer*). Finally, MaxEnt is also able to identify the relations within the text using formatting as in the relation between *arête* (*ridge*) and *barbe de l'épi* (*beard of the ear*) in the sentence "Arête, "barbe de l'épi"" (*Ridge, 'beard of the ear'*) or between *Aigle* and *chasseur de mines* (*mine hunter*) in the sentence "Aigle (M647), chasseur de mines" (*Eagle (M647), mine hunter*).

From the 161 true positive relations missed by both patterns and MaxEnt, 64 are expressed in sentences that contain parenthetical clauses which separate two terms, as in the sentence "Un Appelant (jansénisme) est, au XVIIIe siècle, un ecclésiastique qui appelle ... (*An Appellant (jansenism) is, during the XVIIIth century, an ecclesiastic who calls ...*) where the relation *Appelant* (*Appellant*) is a *ecclésiastique* (*ecclesiastic*) is not found. 55 of them correspond to the relations expressed by head modifier. We could not precisely identify the silence of MaxEnt in this case. The remaining 42 cases concern forms of expression not supported by the patterns and too scarce to be learned by MaxEnt, such as "X such as Y".

Furthermore, we could also observe that patterns were able to identify relations between common names, rather than between named entities, whereas MaxEnt mainly finds relations between named entities. The reason is that some patterns identify phrases that may not be annotated with the LCorpus terms.

In summary, these results corroborate the gain brought by the combination of complementary methods on the same corpus. Firstly, we could notice that MaxtEnt is able to identify hypernym relations within complex phrases or textual structures, such as vertical item lists, provided they appear with a minimal frequency. Secondly, the different occurrences of relations within the same sentence are identified by the two methods, as seen above through the example "Le poisson Babel ou Babel fish est une espèce imaginaire". In these experiments, patterns and MaxEnt are complementary in a proportion of ˜1/3 vs. 2/3.

4.3 DBPedia enrichment

In a last stage, we evaluated how much our approach could enrich DBPedia with the extracted relations. To do so, we manually checked their presence/absence in DBPedia. This verification had to be manual because the annotated terms come from LCorpus and may differ from the labels in DBPedia. We queried DBPedia to check if entities with labels close to *Term1* and *Term2* were linked by a path made of *rdf:type* and *rdf:subclassOf* relations. We set to 3 the maximum path length.

From the 688 TP in the reference corpus, 199 relations were not expressed in DBPedia. 103 of these 199 relations were identified by the learning approach and 42 of them were found by patterns. Considering the union of the results of the two approaches, 125 identified relations were not in DBPedia (20 relations belonging to the intersection of the individual results). Table 4 presents the rate of enrichment of DBPedia with respect to the relations identified by each approach and the union of their results. These figures confirm that the Wikipedia text, which is under-exploited by Wikipedia extractors, contains hypernym relations other than those found in structured elements (infobox, categories, etc.).

Method	Enrichment rate
Patterns	21%
MaxEnt	51%
Pattern union MaxEnt	63%

Table 4: DBPedia enrichment rate.

5 Conclusion and perspectives

The study reported in this paper led us to set up a methodology to compare two relation extraction approaches, in order to analyze their complementarity. The first results are encouraging and converge with the work of (Malaisé et al., 2004) (Granada, 2015) (Buitelaar et al., 2005). We plan to push this research further on in several directions. We want to integrate other methods, taking into account other textual elements, for example the system of (Kamel and Trojahn, 2016) that deals with vertical and regular enumerative structures, or the tools developed in (Granada, 2015). For improving the performance of each method, in addition to a better pattern encoding, we plan to add new features to the learning process. Moreover, the method will have to be tested on another corpus including other types of Wikipedia pages.

Ultimately, our ambition is to cross the methods so that the results of some serve as richer inputs to others, and thus improve their performance. The first step in this direction would be to annotate the corpus using patterns and tag it to signal whether a pattern is (or is not) recognized in the context of two terms, which would be a strong sign of the presence of the relation. This type of feature would allow the classifier to recognize several types of relations in addition to hypernymy.

Acknowledgement

The authors would like the Midi-Pyrénées (now Occitanie Pyrénées-Méditerranée) Region who funded the SemPedia project and Adel Ghamnia's Ph.D. grant.

References

Agichtein, E. and L. Gravano (2000). Snowball: Extracting relations from large plain-text collections. In *Proceedings of the 5th ACM conference on Digital libraries*, pp. 85–94. ACM.

Banko, M., M. J. Cafarella, S. Soderland, M. Broadhead, and O. Etzioni (2007). Open information extraction from the web. In *IJCAI*, Volume 7, pp. 2670–2676.

Ben Abacha, A. and P. Zweigenbaum (2011). A Hybrid Approach for the Extraction of Semantic Relations from MEDLINE Abstracts. In A. Gelbukh (Ed.), *Proceedings of the 12th International Conference on Computational Linguistics and Intelligent Text Processing, Tokyo, Japan, February 20-26*, pp. 139–150. Springer Berlin Heidelberg.

Berger, A. L., V. J. Della Pietra, and S. A. Della Pietra (1996). A maximum entropy approach to natural language processing. *Computational linguistics 22*(1), 39–71.

Berland, M. and E. Charniak (1999). Finding parts in very large corpora. In *Proceedings of the 37th annual meeting of the Association for Computational Linguistics on Computational Linguistics*, pp. 57–64. Association for Computational Linguistics.

Brin, S. (1998). Extracting patterns and relations from the world wide web. In *International Workshop on The World Wide Web and Databases*, pp. 172–183. Springer.

Buitelaar, P., P. Cimiano, and B. Magnini (2005). Ontology learning from text: An overview. In *Ontology Learning from Text: Methods, Evaluation and Applications*, pp. 3–12. IOS Press.

Bunescu, R. C. and R. J. Mooney (2005). A shortest path dependency kernel for relation extraction. In *Proceedings of the conference on human language technology and empirical methods in natural language processing*, pp. 724–731. Association for Computational Linguistics.

Etzioni, O., M. Cafarella, D. Downey, S. Kok, A.-M. Popescu, T. Shaked, S. Soderland, D. S. Weld, and A. Yates (2004). Web-scale information extraction in knowitall:(preliminary results). In *Proceedings of the 13th international conference on World Wide Web*, pp. 100–110. ACM.

Fabre, C., N. Hathout, L.-M. Ho-Dac, F. Morlane-Hondère, P. Muller, F. Sajous, L. Tanguy, and T. Van De Cruys (2014, June). Présentation de l'atelier SemDis 2014 : sémantique distributionnelle pour la substitution lexicale et l'exploration de corpus spécialisés. In *21e Conférence sur le Traitement Automatique des Langues Naturelles (TALN 2014)*, Marseille, France, pp. 196–205.

Fader, A., S. Soderland, and O. Etzioni (2011). Identifying relations for open information extraction. In *Proceedings of the Conference on Empirical Methods in Natural Language Processing*, pp. 1535–1545. Association for Computational Linguistics.

Ghamnia, A. (2016). Extraction de relations dhyperonymie partir de wikipdia. In *Actes de la confrence conjointe JEP-TALN-RECITAL 2016.*

Granada, R. L. (2015). *Evaluation of methods for taxonomic relation extraction from text*. Ph. D. thesis, Pontifícia Universidade Católica do Rio Grande do Sul.

Hearst, M. A. (1992). Automatic acquisition of hyponyms from large text corpora. In *Proceedings of the 14th Conference on Computational Linguistics - Volume 2*, COLING '92, Stroudsburg, PA, USA, pp. 539–545. Association for Computational Linguistics.

Jacques, M.-P. and N. Aussenac-Gilles (2006). Variabilité des performances des outils de TAL et genre textuel. Cas des patrons lexico-syntaxiques. *Traitement Automatique des Langues, Non Thmatique 47*(1).

Kamel, M. and C. Trojahn (2016). Exploiter la structure discursive du texte pour valider les relations candidates d'hyperonymie issues de structures énumératives parallèles. In *IC 2016 : 27es Journées francophones d'Ingénierie des Connaissances, Montpellier, France, June 6-10, 2016.*, pp. 111–122.

Kazama, J. and K. Torisawa (2007). Exploiting wikipedia as external knowledge for named entity recognition. In *Proceedings of the 2007 Joint Conference on Empirical Methods in Natural Language Processing and Computational Natural Language Learning*, pp. 698–707.

Kotlerman, L., I. Dagan, I. Szpektor, and M. Zhitomirsky-geffet (2010, October). Directional distributional similarity for lexical inference. *Nat. Lang. Eng. 16*(4).

Lenci, A. and G. Benotto (2012). Identifying hypernyms in distributional semantic spaces. In *Proceedings of the First Joint Conference on Lexical and Computational Semantics-Volume 1: Proceedings of the main conference and the shared task, and Volume 2: Proceedings of the Sixth International Workshop on Semantic Evaluation*, pp. 75–79. Association for Computational Linguistics.

Levy, O., S. Remus, C. Biemann, and I. Dagan (2015). Do supervised distributional methods really learn lexical inference relations? In *HLT-NAACL*.

Malaisé, V., P. Zweigenbaum, and B. Bachimont (2004). Detecting semantic relations between terms in definitions. In *COLING 2004 CompuTerm 2004: 3rd International Workshop on Computational Terminology*, pp. 55–62. COLING.

Mintz, M., S. Bills, R. Snow, and D. Jurafsky (2009). Distant supervision for relation extraction without labeled data. In *Proceedings of the Joint Conference of the 47th Annual Meeting of the ACL and the 4th International Joint Conference on Natural Language Processing of the AFNLP: Volume 2-Volume 2*, pp. 1003–1011. Association for Computational Linguistics.

Morin, E. and C. Jacquemin (2004). Automatic acquisition and expansion of hypernym links. *Computers and the Humanities 38*(4), 363–396.

Morsey, M., J. Lehmann, S. Auer, C. Stadler, and S. Hellmann (2012). Dbpedia and the live extraction of structured data from wikipedia. *Program 46*(2), 157–181.

Nakashole, N., G. Weikum, and F. Suchanek (2012). Patty: A taxonomy of relational patterns with semantic types. In *Proceedings of the 2012 Joint Conference on Empirical Methods in Natural Language Processing and Computational Natural Language Learning*, EMNLP-CoNLL '12, Stroudsburg, PA, USA, pp. 1135–1145. Association for Computational Linguistics.

Navigli, R. and P. Velardi (2010). Learning word-class lattices for definition and hypernym extraction. In *Proceedings of the 48th Annual Meeting of the Association for Computational Linguistics*, ACL '10, Stroudsburg, PA, USA, pp. 1318–1327. Association for Computational Linguistics.

Pantel, P. and M. Pennacchiotti (2008). Automatically harvesting and ontologizing semantic relations. *Ontology learning and population: Bridging the gap between text and knowledge*, 171–198.

Rebeyrolle, J. and L. Tanguy (2000). Repérage automatique de structures linguistiques en corpus : le cas des énoncés définitoires. *Cahiers de Grammaire 25*, 153–174.

Riedel, S., L. Yao, and A. McCallum (2010). Modeling relations and their mentions without labeled text. In *Proceedings of the 2010 European Conference on Machine Learning and Knowledge Discovery in Databases*, pp. 148–163.

Riedel, S., L. Yao, A. Mccallum, and B. M Marlin (2013). Relation extraction with matrix factorization and universal schemas. In *Proceedings of NAACL-HLT 2013*.

Rodriguez-Ferreira, T., A. Rabadan, R. Hervas, and A. Diaz (2016, may). Improving Information Extraction from Wikipedia Texts using Basic English. In *Proceedings of the Tenth International Conference on Language Resources and Evaluation (LREC 2016)*.

Santus, E., A. Lenci, Q. Lu, and S. Schulte im Walde (2014). Chasing hypernyms in vector spaces with entropy. In *Proceedings of the 14th Conference of the European Chapter of the Association for Computational Linguistics, volume 2: Short Papers*, pp. 38–42. Association for Computational Linguistics.

Séguéla, P. and N. Aussenac-Gilles (1999). Extraction de relations sémantiques entre termes et enrichissement de modèles du domaine. In *Conférence ingénierie des connaissances*, pp. 79–88.

Snow, R., D. Jurafsky, and A. Y. Ng (2004). Learning syntactic patterns for automatic hypernym discovery. *Advances in Neural Information Processing Systems 17*.

Snow, R., D. Jurafsky, and A. Y. Ng (2006). Semantic taxonomy induction from heterogenous evidence. In *Proceedings of the 21st International Conference on Computational Linguistics and the 44th Annual Meeting of the Association for Computational Linguistics*, ACL-44, pp. 801–808.

Suchanek, F. M., G. Kasneci, and G. Weikum (2007). Yago: A core of semantic knowledge unifying wordnet and wikipedia. In *Proceedings of the 16th International Conference on World Wide Web*, WWW '07, pp. 697–706.

Sumida, A. and K. Torisawa (2008). Hacking wikipedia for hyponymy relation acquisition. In *IJCNLP*, Volume 8, pp. 883–888.

Weeds, J., D. Clarke, J. Reffin, D. J. Weir, and B. Keller (2014). Learning to distinguish hypernyms and co-hyponyms. In *COLING 2014, 25th International Conference on Computational Linguistics, Proceedings of the Conference: Technical Papers, August 23-29, 2014, Dublin, Ireland*, pp. 2249–2259.

Yap, W. and T. Baldwin (2009). Experiments on pattern-based relation learning. In *Proceedings of the 18th ACM Conference on Information and Knowledge Management*, pp. 1657–1660. ACM.

Yates, A., M. Cafarella, M. Banko, O. Etzioni, M. Broadhead, and S. Soderland (2007). Textrunner: open information extraction on the web. In *Proceedings of Human Language Technologies: The Annual Conference of the North American Chapter of the Association for Computational Linguistics: Demonstrations*, pp. 25–26. Association for Computational Linguistics.

A Geometric Method for Detecting Semantic Coercion

Stephen McGregor
Queen Mary University of London
s.e.mcgregor@qmul.ac.uk

Elisabetta Jezek
University of Pavia
jezek@unipv.it

Matthew Purver
Queen Mary University of London
m.purver@qmul.ac.uk

Geraint Wiggins
Queen Mary University of London
geraint.wiggins@qmul.ac.uk

Abstract

In this paper we present state-of-the-art results on the computational classification of semantic type coercion, accomplished using a novel geometric method which is both context-sensitive and generalisable. We show that this method improves accuracy on a SemEval dataset over previous work, and gives promising results on a new more challenging experimental setup involving the same data. In addition to a description of our distributional semantic methodology and the results obtained on an established dataset, we offer an overview of the linguistic phenomenon of coercion and an analysis of the geometric features by which our results are achieved.

1 Introduction: Computers and Language in Context

Computers are notoriously literal devices. Provided that communication remains grounded in straightforward propositional expressions about named entities with categorical properties involved in unambiguously labelled processes, a computer has some hope of tracking the development of a linguistic exchange. In the pragmatic domain of natural language, however, we are never far from a slide into the webs of implication and inference that characterise communication between environmentally situated agents, capable of resorting to assumptions of isomorphic conceptual schemes in order to optimise the *quality*, *efficiency*, and *relevance* of linguistic constructs (Grice, 1975; Wilson and Sperber, 2012).

The computational representation of contextual shifts in lexical semantics presents a particularly significant challenge, in that it, at first glance, requires the establishment of a rule-based system for indicating the open-ended ways in which rules may be broken. Approaches have typically relied on the construction, in some way or another, of categorical conceptual representations – ontologies – designed for the transfer of properties between classes. So, for instance, motivated by the cognitive linguistic *conceptual metaphor* model of Lakoff and Johnson (1980), Shutova (2013) uses clustering techniques to define classes based on a statistical analysis of dependency relationship in a parsed corpus, and then uses class transgressions in verb-noun relationships to detect metaphor. Alternatively, Veale and Hao (2008) draw inspiration from the *conceptual blending* work of Fauconnier and Turner (2003) in their description of a system that combines information extracted from the WordNet knowledge base with statistical corpus analysis in order to treat metaphor as the porting of categorical information between conceptual domains. Of particular relevance to the research presented here is the work of Shutova et al. (2013), who likewise use a combination of corpus analysis and knowledge base extraction to predict classes of words in order to identify instances of logical metonymy.

Notwithstanding the impressive results generated by these and other similar models, they tend to require a certain degree of preprocessing, annotation, or often direct access to an existing knowledge base in order to achieve effective semantic extrapolation and are prone to falling short of the truly exponential compositionality that characterises natural language. As an alternative, we propose a method for building geometric semantic representations which, in their infinitely adaptable spatial situation, mirror the versatility of language in use. Our method offers three crucial features. First, it is context sensitive, in that it dynamically generates a subspace and a corresponding array of semantic relationships in response to online linguistic input, including the words being modelled as well as their sentential context where available. Second, it is generalisable, in that a straightforward classification model built on a relatively small training set can subsequently be applied to any given linguistic input, regardless of whether any of the words involved were observed in the training data. Third, it is built on unannotated raw textual data, extrapolating semantic relationships using distributional semantic techniques (see Clark, 2015, for an overview). In particular we have refrained from adorning our representations with information derived from, for instance, dependency parsing, allowing us to present a model that avoids downstream commitments regarding the cognitive role of grammatical class (Langacker, 1991).

We apply our method to a task involving the classification of semantic type coercion, a linguistic phenomenon which will be described in detail in the next section. The section following that will present our methodology for building a base space of co-occurrence dimensions from unlabelled data and then selectively projecting subspaces of these dimensions in order to contextually analyse the semantic relationships between words. Section 4 will describe the results of a logistic regression model applied to the geometric features generated by our subspace projection technique, trained on the labelled coercion data described in Section 2. Section 5 will analyse these results, examining the way that the typical geometry of semantic relationships shift as they move from selectional to coerced uses.

2 Background: Coercive Verbs, Susceptible Nouns

Coercion as a theoretical tool has been used in linguistic studies to account for several kinds of semantic shifts occurring in different linguistic structures. For example, *aspectual type coercion* (Moens and Steedman, 1988) identifies the shift occurring when a predicate denoting an event type is coerced to a different type by contextual triggers, as in (1a), where the punctual adverb *suddenly* coerces the predicate *know* from State to Transition. *Grinding* in the nominal domain (Copestake and Briscoe, 1995) consists of a mass construal of a count noun, as for *pillow* in (1b), which is coerced to mass by the quantifier *some*. Finally, *coercion by construction* (Michaelis, 2004) identifies a shift in the meaning of a verb as a result of its insertion in a specific construction, as in the causative construction in (1c).

(1) a. She suddenly knew it.
    b. Give me some pillow.
    c. He barked them back to work.

In this paper, we focus on semantic coercion in predicate-argument combination, intended as the compositional mechanisms that resolves an apparent mismatch between the semantic type expected by a predicate for a specific argument position (in one or more of its specific senses, should the predicate be polysemous) and the semantic type of the argument filler, by adjusting the type of the argument to satisfy the type requirement of the function (*argument type coercion*; Pustejovsky, 1991). An example is (2), where *wine* is coerced to an Activity (drinking) as a result of the semantic requirements the predicate imposes on its object, i.e. *finish* applies to an activity.[1]

(2) When they finished the wine, he stood up. (drinking)

In predicate-argument composition, the semantics of the argument plays a crucial role in two ways. First, it provides the semantic purport on which selection or coercion may apply;[2] second, in the presence of a coercion environment, it constrains the resulting interpretation. While the default interpretation of (2) is "drinking", the one in (3) is "eating"; in other words, different nouns grant privileged access to different activities, particularly those which are most frequently performed with the entities they denote.

---

[1]Such cases of coercion to event are referred to as *logical metonymies* (see Verspoor, 1997, and Lapata and Lascarides, 2003).

[2]Coercions are not always successful; that is, some predicate-argument combinations are not interpretable. Constraints on interpretability are clearly related to cognition and the way we conceptualize entities and relations among them, an aspect we will return to later in the paper.

(3) They finished their cake. (*drinking, eating)

It has been noted, however, that linguistic and situational contexts play a crucial role in the interpretation of coercions: for example, in the corpus fragment in (4), taken from the EnTenTen corpus, the context triggers a different interpretation for wine (preparing, making) as object of *finish*. In other words, the "reconstructed hidden event" may be assigned contextually.

(4) So unless the winemakers add tannin by finishing the wine in oak ...

Extensive corpus work on both English and Italian data (Pustejovsky and Jezek, 2008; Jezek and Quochi, 2010, *inter alia*) has shown that coercion in predicate-argument composition is particularly frequent with certain verb classes, including event-selecting verbs (attend, cancel, organize) of which aspectual verbs constitutes a subclass (finish, interrupt, start, continue), perception verbs (hear, listen), communication verbs (announce, inform), directed motion verbs (arrive, reach), and verbs indicating motion performed using a vehicle (land).

Data on mismatches between expected type and argument type offer several options of linguistic modelling. Pustejovsky (2011) for example proposes a two-layered coercion mechanism: *coercion by exploitation* takes an available part of the argument's type (modelled as *quale* to the type) to satisfy the function, whereas *coercion by introduction* wraps the argument with the type required by the function (for example, in "the passengers read the walls of the subway", read wraps the walls with an informational content, which is present in the selecting type but absent in the argument type). Asher (2011), on the other hand, acknowledging the role played by discourse context in the interpretation of mismatches, uses dependent types to model coercion. Both authors assume, in addition to the Montague types, e and t, a richer subtyping over the entity domain than is typically assumed in type theory, including complex types such as the one associated with *book*, which comprises a physical as well as an informational component.

Coercion detection has been addressed as a specific NLP task in the context of SemEval 2010[3], with the goal of testing the ability of computational models to identify whether the type that a verb selects is satisfied directly by the argument (selection), or whether the argument must change type to satisfy the verb typing (coercion), and classify it accordingly.[4] A dataset was produced for both English and Italian, using the methodology described by Pustejovsky et al. (2010).[5] First, five coercive verbs that impose semantic typing on one of their arguments in at least one of their senses (*arrive, cancel, deny, finish,* and *hear*) were selected by examining the data from the BNC, using the Sketch Engine corpus query tool. Sense inventories were compiled for each verb using OntoNotes as a reference. For each sense, a set of type templates was identified following the Corpus Pattern Analysis (CPA) technique (Pustejovsky et al., 2004; Hanks, 2013): every argument in the syntactic pattern associated with a given sense was assigned a type specification. The coercive senses of the chosen verbs were associated with type templates. Type templates and senses for the five verbs are summarized below:

(5) a. HUMAN arrive at LOCATION (reach a destination or goal)
    b. HUMAN cancel EVENT (call off)
    c. HUMAN deny PROPOSITION (maintain that something is untrue)
    d. HUMAN finish EVENT (complete an activity)
    e. HUMAN hear SOUND (perceive physical sound)

A set of sentences was randomly extracted for each target verb from the BNC. The extracted sentences were parsed automatically, and organized according to the grammatical relation the target verb was involved in. Word sense disambiguation of the predicate was performed manually on each extracted sentence, matching it against the sense inventory and the corresponding type template. The appropriate senses were then saved into the database along with the associated type template. The sentences containing coercive senses of the verbs were annotated for selection or coercion in the specified grammatical

---

[3] A metonymy resolution task not focused on verb-argument composition is described in Markert and Nissim (2009).

[4] Complex types and the distinction between exploitation and introduction as described above are not included in the task.

[5] For the purposes of this paper, we focus on the English data set in the following.

Source Type	Target Type	Verb	Train	Test
event	location	arrive	38	37
artifact	event	cancel	35	35
		finish	91	92
event	proposition	deny	56	54
artifact	sound	hear	28	30
event	sound	hear	24	26
document	event	finish	39	40

Table 1: Coercion Shifts in the English SemEval data set

relation (object). Only the six most recurrent coercion types were selected; these are reported in Table 1. Examples of annotated data tagged as coercions are given in (6).

(6) a. Mr Templeton said that when he arrived at the *fire* after 10 pm ... (Event → Location)
    b. Her *milk* and *newspapers* will have to be cancelled. (Artifact → Event)
    c. I can hear that *car* like it is just going past here. (Artifact → Sound)

The distribution of selectional and coercive instances were skewed to increase the number of coercions. The final English data set contains about 30% coercions. The data set was randomly split in half into a training set and a test set. The training data has 1032 instances, 311 of which are coercions, whereas the test data has 1039 instances, 314 of which are coercions. Of the 1992 sentences used in our tests (see Section 4), there were 20 unique surface forms for the 5 verbs analysed and 697 objects.

3 Methodology: Projecting Semantic Context

In this section, we describe a method for projecting distributional semantic subspaces based on contextual input in the form of a word or groups of words. Our hypothesis is that there should be a way to classify the coerciveness in a verb-object pairing in terms of the absolute and relative geometric features of the corresponding word-vectors in a subspace delineated in terms of a set of co-occurrence dimensions salient to the context in which the pairing arises. The intuition underlying this hypothesis is that there should be a distinction between the co-occurrence profiles of verbs and objects selected by the verb's argument class (expressed in the form of type specification) versus objects coerced by the same verb's expected argument class, and that this distinction should be particularly evident in the context of co-occurrences relevant to the conceptual domain indicated by the word pairing.

The particular methodology we propose has been developed from work originally described by Agres et al. (2015) and McGregor et al. (2015), and early versions of the subspace selection techniques outlined here have been applied by Agres et al. (2016) to a metaphoricity rating task. We begin by building a base space of word co-occurrence statistics, using a typical pointwise mutual information metric for representing the expectedness of observing a co-occurrence term c within n words of a target word w. This results in a co-occurrence matrix where the dimension corresponding to c for word-vector $\vec{w}$ is determined as follows:

$$PMI_{w,c} = \log_2 \left(\frac{f_{w,c} \times W}{f_w \times (f_c + a)} + 1 \right) \tag{1}$$

Here, $f_{w,c}$ is the number of times w and c are observed to co-occur, f_w is the independent frequency of w, f_c is the frequency of c, W is the total count of word tokens in the corpus, and a is a smoothing constant to avoid the proliferation of obscure dimensions in our dimension selection process, set here at 10,000. The ratio is incremented by 1 to ensure that all values are positive: a PMI score of 0 then corresponds to no observed co-occurrences between w and c.

This base matrix is very large – for the model applied here, in which 200,000 vocabulary word-vectors were extrapolated from an analysis of the English language component of Wikipedia, there are approximately 7.5 million unique co-occurrence types and corresponding dimensions – and very sparse

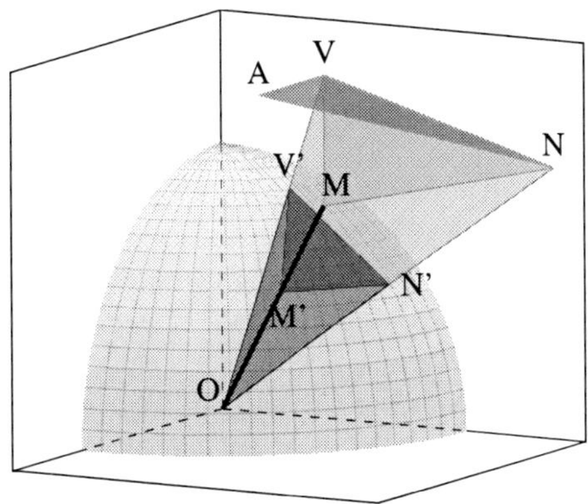

Figure 1: Semantics in Space: Verb-object pairs are projected into a subspace in which the geometric features of the relationship between the word-vectors, the origin, and salient points in the subspace are expected to collectively indicate semantic relationships such as coerciveness.

due to the long tail of relatively rare word types. From this base matrix, we project subspaces based on an analysis of the word-vectors corresponding to a group of input terms. Our objective is to discover a mechanism for identifying a set of co-occurrence features which is in some sense salient to these input terms, the idea being that semantic properties of relevant words should be apparent in their geometric situation in such a subspace. For the purposes of the experiments reported here, we explore three different subspace selection techniques:

Joint For input terms T, select the k co-occurrence dimensions that have non-zero values for all terms and the highest mean PMI values across all terms;

Indy For each term in T, select the $k/|T|$ dimensions that have the highest value for each term independent of other terms and combine them to form a k dimensional subspace;

Zipped From the subset of dimensions with non-zero values for all terms in T, select the $k/|T|$ terms with the highest value for each term, again combining for a k dimensional subspace.

For the purposes of the experiments described in this paper, we analyse the geometric relationship between word-pairs in a projection in order to determine the properties of each word-vector's situation in a space which correspond to instances of coercion. The geometric features we explore are illustrated in Figure 1, where V represents the position of the verb in a subspace and N the noun, M is the point representing the mean value for all non-zero word-vectors on each dimension, and A is the point representing the maximum value found on each dimension in the subspace. V', N', and M' are normalised vectors of V, N, and M respectively, and thus sit on the surface of a hypersphere emanating from the origin O. The features we examine are the lengths of $\overline{VO}$ and $\overline{NO}$ (the norms of each word-vector in the pair), the distances $\overline{VN}$ and $\overline{V'N'}$, the mean values of the pairs $(\overline{VO}, \overline{NO})$, $(\overline{V'M'}, \overline{N'M'})$, $(\overline{VM}, \overline{NM})$, and $(\overline{VA}, \overline{NA})$, as well as the ratios of the elements of each of those pairs, dividing the smaller constituent by the larger. We also examine the angles $\angle VON$, $\angle V'M'N'$, $\angle VMN$, and $\angle VAN$.

Our objective is to establish mechanisms for systematically gauging the geometric relationships between the word-vectors corresponding to word-pairs, as well as the relative relationships between these word-vectors and some anchor points within a given subspace. With regard to these anchor points, it is important to note that, unlike typical distributional semantic methods which build normalised spaces through either the factorisation of a matrix of co-occurrence statistics (Baroni and Lenci, 2010; Pennington et al., 2014) or the application of neural networks for the learning of abstract word-vectors across iterations of a corpus (Mikolov et al., 2013), our spaces are not normalised, and so there may be considerable variance in terms of the distribution of values across different dimensions. Our case is that, in non-normalised context-specific subspaces, we should be able to find a richer range of geometric features with which to analyse various semantic properties of words relevant to the specific context determining a given projection.

In fact, the contextually indifferent nature of co-occurrence based models subjected to principal component analysis (Lebret and Collobert, 2014), the aforementioned neural network models, and hybrid models applying both word counting and neural network techniques (Pennington et al., 2014) are a motivation for the model we describe in this paper. While these established methodologies have achieved impressive results on a variety of language processing tasks, the representations composing them are static and abstract, and are therefore not susceptible to the online influence of contextual factors at play in our dimension selection techniques. Our case is that, for a phenomenon such as coercion, we require, as Pustejovsky (1995) has put it, "a model of meaning in language that captures the means by which words can assume a potentially infinite number of senses in context, while limiting the number of senses actually stored in the lexicon," (ibid, p. 104). As a point of comparison, we will also present results from the `word2vec` model of Mikolov et al. (2013) trained on the same underlying corpus as our models. We also test models derived from a principal component analysis of one of our base co-occurrence spaces, applying a version of the standard singular value decomposition technique in order to build a matrix of abstract dimensions optimally capturing the statistical variance between features of word-vectors.

4   Results: Detecting Coercion in a SemEval Dataset

We train a model for the identification of coercion based on a logistic regression of features of the subspaces described in the previous section. We generate JOINT, INDY, and ZIPPED type subspaces for each verb-object pair in the training portion of the dataset described in Section 2 (Pustejovsky et al., 2010), extracting the 16 geometric features identified in Section 3, illustrated in Figure 1, and enumerated again in Table 5 in Section 5. We also experiment with three other feature extraction techniques:

Verb Select only the k co-occurrence dimensions with the highest values for the verb's word-vector;

Object Select only the k co-occurrence dimensions with the highest value for the object's word-vector;

Merged Take the average feature values for the VERB and OBJECT methods.

In the case of each subspace selection technique, we generate a 993 x 16 matrix, expressing 16 geometric features for each sentence in the training data (38 examples were withheld because the targeted argument was a multi-word token, and at this point our model has only been trained for single words). We perform mean-zero, std-one normalisation on this matrix, and then perform a logistic regression trained to classify selectionality versus coerciveness. We apply L2 regularisation to the regression coefficients, with a relatively strong regularisation strength of 1.67, determined experimentally.[6] We then similarly extract data from the testing data (here 40 examples are withheld), in this case, crucially, normalising the data reusing the mean and standard deviation from the training data in order to test the generality of this method and our ability to apply it arbitrarily to any given input. We apply the model learned from the training data to the normalised test matrix, evaluating each verb-object pair as either coercive or non-coercive. We experiment with models based on co-occurrence windows of both 2 and 5 words on either side of a vocabulary word as observed in the underlying corpus (Wikipedia), and with projected subspaces consisting of 20 and 200 dimensions.

Results for these experiments are reported in Table 2, with the 200 dimensional subspaces outperforming the 20 dimensional subspaces across the board, and the 5x5 word co-occurrence window models generally doing better, but only slightly better, than the 2x2 window models. The INDY subspace selection technique outperforms all other techniques, and its strong performance is particularly pronounced in terms of f-scores, indicating that this method, in addition to learning that most instance of word-pairs are not coercive, is also learning something about when to positively indicate coercion. The stronger performance of higher dimensional spaces suggests that significant information is available across a wider

---

[6]We implement the regression using the `scikit-learn` LogisticRegression module for python.

	JOINT	INDY	ZIPPED	VERB	OBJECT	MERGED
2x2, 20	0.484/0.761	0.564/0.776	0.464/0.753	0.546/0.764	0.494/0.752	0.539/0.766
2x2, 200	0.537/0.793	0.631/0.795	0.524/0.778	0.630/0.800	0.598/0.789	0.632/0.801
5x5, 20	0.463/0.763	0.536/0.765	0.519/0.776	0.571/0.775	0.482/0.755	0.521/0.765
5x5, 200	0.577/0.801	0.652/0.804	0.556/0.786	0.623/0.799	0.543/0.764	0.626/0.802

Table 2: F-score/accuracy results for coercion classification using various subspace selection techniques, adjusting parameters for co-occurrence window size (2x2 and 5x5) and subspace dimensionality (20 and 200). Baseline scores and scores from other studies are reported in Table 3.

range of co-occurrence profiles for a given target word, and inclusion of this information is desirable, but it's also interesting to note this dimensional gain deteriorates for smaller co-occurrence windows as information in our base matrix becomes sparser. We use the top performing 5x5 co-occurrence window, 200 dimensional subspaces in the rest of our experiments below.

In order to test the hypothesis that coercion is always ultimately contextually determined, we add information about the sentential context of the examples provided in the data. We do this by parsing each sentence in the data and then creating two additional sets of features: we generate new subspaces based on the other words in the sentence, and then extract features of the verb/object vector geometry as above; we do this first using only content words (other verbs, nouns, adjectives, and adverbs in the sentence), and then using only function words. We extract the geometric features from these spaces as described above, normalise them, and then concatenate them with the original features extracted using the corresponding technique. In the rare instances where no appropriate sentential analysis is available, we concatenate a feature vector of zeros, reasoning that, given the application of zero-mean normalisation, this should have relatively little impact on our model while maintaining the shape of the data. Results for the logistic regression experiment run on this enhanced data are reported in Table 3. The results from the INDY type space in particular are notable in that they outperform a number of other methods which we will now describe, and moreover return an improvement in accuracy on the non-contextual results of 0.014 and in f-score of 0.021. More generally, while accuracy scores don't admit significant improvement, f-scores are generally up in the range of about 0.040 points, indicating a particular increase in the models' abilities to detect coercion with increased contextual data.

We report a minority class baseline where all verb-object pairs are classified as coercive and a majority class where all are considered non-coercive. We also test an *example based learning* method in which we learn a single rule for each surface form of the five verb stems found in the data, and discover that fairly good results can be achieved by simply assuming a given verb is either coercive or not. (In practice, all verbs other than *finish* are observed to be typically non-coercive in the training data.) Because many of the objects also occur multiple times in both the training and testing data, we can learn an object-based rule for guessing coercion, resorting to the verb-based rule in cases where we encounter an object which hasn't been observed in the training data. The very strong results achieved using this method, designated EBL* in Table 3, which take tagged observations of word combinations into account, can be thought of as something of a ceiling for models such as ours: where the EBL and EBL* methods learn to predict semantic relationships between priorly observed words based on the actual identity of the words, our method simply learns something about the geometry that indicates a particular semantic relationship.

We also report results from two models defined by static lexical representations: a principle component model built using singular value decomposition,[7] and a model constructed using the skip-gram methodology described by Mikolov et al. (2013).[8] In the case of the former, we factorised our 5x5 word co-occurrence window base space and extrapolated a 200 dimensional matrix in which each dimension is orthogonal, capturing an optimal degree of variance between word-vectors (see Deerwester et al., 1990, for a classic overview of this approach). For the latter, we built a likewise 200 dimensional space of word-vectors derived over 10 traversals of our corpus, applying negative sampling at a rate of 10. In

---

[7]Implemented through the python scikit-learn `TruncatedSVD` module, `http://scikit-learn.org/stable/modules/generated/sklearn.decomposition.TruncatedSVD.html`.

[8]Implemented using the `gensim` package for python, `https://radimrehurek.com/gensim/`.

	prec	rec	f-score	acc		prec	rec	f-score	acc
JOINT	0.687	0.562	0.619	0.794	MINORITY	0.297	1.000	0.458	0.297
INDY	0.727	0.626	0.673	0.819	MAJORITY	0.000	0.000	0.000	0.703
ZIPPED	0.672	0.532	0.594	0.784	EBL	*0.630*	*0.498*	*0.556*	*0.764*
VERB	0.694	0.572	0.627	0.798	EBL*	*0.833*	*0.690*	*0.755*	*0.871*
OBJECT	0.636	0.529	0.577	0.770	R&H 2010	-	-	-	*0.961*
MERGED	0.708	0.562	0.627	0.801	R&H 2011	-	-	-	0.812
SVD	0.673	0.253	0.368	0.740	SKIP-GRAM	0.682	0.511	0.584	0.781

Table 3: Coercion identification scores on test data, based on a logistic regression on various dimension selection techniques in a 5x5 word co-occurrence window, 200 dimensional model built from training data, as well as scores for baselines. Methods using information about the identity of words priorly observed in selectional or coercive relationships are reported in italics.

both cases, we consider cosine distance between the word-vectors in the spaces as the singular metric of relationships between words, in line with results reported through the NLP literature.

The method described by Roberts and Harabagiu (2010) learns classes for nouns based on analysis of entailment relationships within WordNet. Combined with a statistical analysis of word and named entity co-occurrences, this approach essentially seeks to recapitulate the semantic class information available in knowledge bases in order to identify instances where coercion is indicated by verb-object class mismatches. We take as our main point of comparison the results reported on this dataset by Roberts and Harabagiu (2011), who develop a probabilistic model for coercion detection based within the latent Dirichlet allocation paradigm (Blei et al., 2003). In this later work the authors establish probability distributions for classes that can be taken as an argument by a verb V, and likewise for classes that can be assigned to an object N, and then calculate the summation of the joint probabilities of V taking a word of the same class as N as an argument, learning a threshold below which the value of this summation indicates coercion. The distributions themselves are learned through observations of predicate-argument pairings in a large-scale textual corpus, and so one might argue that here, again, there is an element of example based learning.

To briefly compare our different dimension selection techniques, the INDY technique seems to do the best job of capturing the semantic interaction between verb-object pair under analysis: the way that these terms intermingle across independently salient co-occurrence dimensions is most predictive of the alignment of semantic classes, while delineating subspaces based on joint or semi-joint co-occurrence profiles through the JOINT and ZIPPED techniques is less informative. In general the tendency towards stronger precision versus recall results indicates a tendency of our regression model to learn caution in predicting the minority class, an observation which may indicate future directions for experimenting with modelling techniques. It's also interesting to note that the VERB technique, focusing on the co-occurrence profile of the predicate in a sentence, outperforms the argument-oriented OBJECT technique, arguably supporting the hypothesis outlined in Section 2 that certain verbs tend to be more coercive than others. In terms of comparison with results from elsewhere, we significantly outperform baselines and event the EBL technique on all counts, and do slightly better than Roberts and Harabagiu (2011) on accuracy (f-scores weren't provided by those authors).

In terms of comparing with the fully recorded statistics for the abstract distributional approaches, it is interesting to note that, like with our context sensitive models, the static models also achieve higher precision than recall. In fact, the effect is even more obvious here, leading to relatively low f-scores as lower recall drags down the harmonic mean of model performance: combined with fairly high accuracy scores, this suggests that these models are learning a conservative strategy of favouring the more likely classification of selection over coercion. The stronger performance of the neural network skip-gram model over the SVD model is in line with the impressive results the word2vec paradigm has achieved in tests across the field, though Levy and Goldberg (2014) have made an interesting case for the commensurability of neural network and matrix factorisation techniques, attributing apparent differences in performance to the effects of the tuning of the many parameters associated with these types of models.

	prec	rec	f-score	acc
INDY 5X5 200	0.689	0.561	0.618	0.716
MINORITY	0.410	1.000	0.582	0.410
MAJORITY	0.000	0.000	0.000	0.590

Table 4: Coercion identification scores based on a logistic regression on the INDY selection technique in a 5x5 word co-occurrence window, 200 dimensional model, as well as scores for baselines, when the model was tested on words which were never seen in the training phase.

Regardless, the results of our experiment present context sensitive approaches in a relatively favourable light compared to two other general approaches to lexical semantic modelling.

Testing on Unseen Examples In order to test the generalisability of our approach, we reshuffled the data in such a way that the model could be trained on one set of verb-object pairs and then could be tested on a different set of word pairs where neither the verbs nor the objects had been observed in any of the pairings throughout the training data. The new arrangement of the data would be uninterpretable to the EBL techniques and the method of Roberts and Harabagiu (2010), all of which rely on prior observations of the words being analysed tagged for either selection or coercion. We found that by taking all objects paired with forms of the verbs *arrive, cancel,* and *deny* that weren't also paired with forms of the verbs *finish* and *hear* as training data, and then considering all pairings involving *cancel* and *deny* as test data, we could reshuffle the data such that we have 895 training sentences, 191 of which are instances of coercion, and 865 test sentences, 355 of which are instances of coercion. In order to maintain the generality of our results, we once again normalise the test data based on the mean and standard deviation of the training data.

Results for this version of the test are reported in Table 4. Accuracy scores are affected negatively by this data reshuffling, though this decrease should be understood in the context of the new balance of non-coercion and coercion in the data, likewise reflected in the new baselines—and in fact the improvement from our method over the majority class accuracy score is at least as substantial here. More notably, f-scores are also negatively impacted, but the effect here is considerably more marginal. From this we can infer that, in the case of classifying data on completely unseen word pairs, the model to some extent learns to usually err on the side of guessing for the majority class of argument type selection over coercion, but the gains in identifying coercion over the minority class baseline are still significant, and accuracy is likewise substantially improved from both baselines. In other words, in the case of the INDY subspace projection technique, the model seems to generalise very nicely.

5 Analysis: Interpreting the Geometry from Selection to Coercion

Table 5 presents the coefficients corresponding to geometric features learned by our logistic regression on the 5x5 co-occurrence window, 200 dimensional projections using the INDY method to analyse verb-object pair input, in this case without taking sentential context into account, as concatenating different contexts would complicate the visual analysis of the geometry of the subspace. An examination of these coefficients reveals the geometric tendencies that correspond to the slide from selection to coercion. One interesting outcome of the projection of coercion classification onto a logistic curve is the implication that coercion is a gradable as opposed to a binary phenomenon, something which is not necessarily taken for granted in the theoretical literature. Our regression is modelled to associate coercion with positive values and selection with negative values, so a positive coefficient indicates a positive correlation with the tendency towards coercion in a given subspace. The angular values used in the model are cosines, so a positive correlation here indicates a move towards coercion as the angle between two vectors becomes smaller.

The mean of the distances from the verb and object word-vectors to the maximal point (ie, the average length of $\overline{VA}$ and $\overline{NA}$) has a strong negative correlation with coercion, which, along with the positive

DISTANCES & ANGLES				MEANS & RATIOS			
$\overline{VN}$	$\overline{V'N'}$	$\overline{VO}$	$\overline{NO}$	$\mu(\overline{VO}, \overline{NO})$	$\mu(\overline{V'M'}, \overline{N'M'})$	$\mu(\overline{VM}, \overline{NM})$	$\mu(\overline{VA}, \overline{NA})$
-0.131	0.757	0.090	0.594	0.558	0.680	0.032	-0.949
$\angle VON$	$\angle V'M'N'$	$\angle VMN$	$\angle VAN$	$\overline{VO} : \overline{NO}$	$V'M' : \overline{N'M'}$	$\overline{VM} : \overline{NM}$	$\overline{VA} : \overline{NA}$
-0.594	-0.824	-0.018	0.980	0.379	0.298	0.367	-0.191

Table 5: Coefficients assigned to various geometric features based on a logistic regression of a 5x5 word co-occurrence window, 200 dimensional INDY type space.

correlation with the cosine of $\angle VAN$, suggests a tendency for the verb and object word-vectors to move outwards and away from each other even as N moves towards M in increasingly coercive contexts. This trend suggests something about the overall dimensional profiles selected in more coercive cases: as M moves away from the central region of the space and the distance of N from the origin increases, we get a picture of a set of co-occurrence dimensions with less aligned distributions between verbs and objects, indicating lower overall frequencies and a propensity for co-occurrence with other likewise less frequent terms. In other words, in the case of nouns in particular, we find that less frequent, less ambiguous, more specialised nouns are also more prone to coercion.

There is, conversely, a strongly positive correlation between the cosine of the normalised word-vectors at the vertex of the mean vector $\angle V'M'N'$, accompanied by a positive correlation with the distance $\overline{V'N'}$ and, at the same time, the average values of $\overline{V'M'}$ and $\overline{N'M'}$, indicating a broadening and a move again away from one another and also in this case away from the mean-adjusted centre of the subspace as the semantic context of the usage becomes more coercive. These statistics regarding effectively angular relationships between normalised vectors suggest a dimension-by-dimension divergence in the relative values of the analysed word-vectors as the INDY method selects increasingly uncorrelated dimensions for increasingly coercive semantic relationships, without necessarily saying anything about the overall trend of the length of the word-vectors in the overall subspace.

The negative correlation with the cosine $\angle VON$ tells a similar story: more coercive words tend to select co-occurrence subspaces in which the orientation of the corresponding word-vectors are less aligned. It is interesting to note, however, a likewise negative, albeit relatively minor, correlation with the actual distance between the vectors $\overline{VN}$. The immediate implication of an angle between vectors increasing even as the distance between them decreases is that the lengths of the word-vectors are shrinking, but this assumption is actually contradicted by the positive correlation with $\mu(\overline{VO}, \overline{NO})$, the average length of the word-vectors. Instead, it appears that the relative lengths of the word-vectors are actually growing closer to one another in coercive instances, moving towards a point where one vector is more optimally close to the other for a given angle. This suggests that more coercive subspaces are actually defined by dimensions for which the words in question have more distinctive profiles, and once again implies that nouns more susceptible to coercion tend to be more specialised and less ambiguous, in turn contributing a set of dimensions that are more conceptually specific, with a sparser distribution of higher PMI values by way of their half of the INDY dimensional selection process.[9]

Figure 2 illustrates cases from three points along the spectrum from selection to coercion, based on an analysis of just the verb-object pair modelled in a 5x5 co-occurrence window 200 dimensional space. Each of the subfigures shows each word-vector concerned projected into a three-dimensional space, along with the intersects of the normalised word vectors, V' and N', in their relationship to the normalised mean point M' and the maximal point A. These examples are extracted from the testing data based on the logistic regression method described above, and the geometries and the figures above have been projected to preserve the most predictive relationships $\angle VAN$, $\mu(\overline{VA}, \overline{NA})$, and $\angle V'M'N'$ while also maintaining the distances of V, N, and A from the origin, taking M' as central to the space.

The example where coercion is considered to be absent, the pairing *heard sound*, is unambiguously

---

[9]It should be noted that there could also be a degree of collinearity at play here, and there is grounds for experimenting with regularisation strengths and techniques in future work, as well as the application of a feature selection process involving something like a variance inflation factor (O'Brien, 2007).

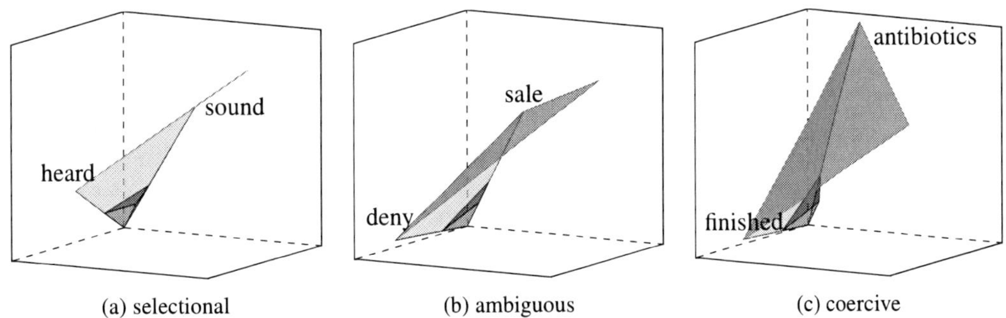

Figure 2: Spectrum of Coercion: Verb-object pairs deemed most selectional, ambiguous, and coercive are projected into subspaces using the INDY technique, with key geometric features preserved here.

an instance of a sound verb selecting a sound argument. Other instances at this end of the spectrum as construed by our model include the likewise straightforward *finished event* and *arrived port*. In the neutral area, effectively defined as the pairs whose geometric features are closest to 0.5 when passed through the softmax function, we observe the pairing *deny sale*, and note that *deny* here has an ambiguous interpretation: it could indicate the refutation of the information associated with the event of a sale, or it could alternatively denote the prevention of the same event. In this region of the model's output we also find instances where the object in the pairing offers an ambiguous interpretation, such as *heard chink* (is a *chink* a sound or a small gap?), *arrived flat* (flat could actually be interpreted as an adjunct), and *cancel classes* (*class* is in itself a very ambiguous noun, though arguably somewhat specified by the context of *cancel* in this case). Finally, at the coercive end of the model's output, we have examples such as *finished antibiotics*, *hears vowel*, and *denies rift* where the object is clearly taking on the type of the argument implied by the verb (and it's notable that the highly coercive verb *finish* figures prominently in this region of the output).

Geometrically speaking, what we observe as we move from the selectional to the coercive is first a broadening of the region defined by our model, and then a gradual listing as the noun typically becomes prevalent through the co-occurrence dimensions it contributes to the projection. We can detect a move into a less semantically coherent subspace as we discover less overlap between the dimensions that are salient to each of the terms under analysis. The decrease in the angle at the vertex of the maximal point A, and the corresponding increase in the angle at the normalised mean point M', is a perhaps slightly surprising but also rewarding and ultimately understandable feature of this approach. Another point of note is the relative lack of correlation with the actual distance $\overline{VN}$ between the word-vectors and coercion, which, in conjunction with the somewhat strong negative correlation between $\angle VON$ and coerciveness, suggests that the actual Euclidean relationship of the word-vectors is less semantically indicative than various other geometric features of these subspaces. It's also worth mentioning that the length of the object vector tends to increase towards coercion, indicating an increasing dominance of the argument over semantically contextualised subspaces, whereas the length of the verb is somewhat neutral across the spectrum.

6 Conclusion: Strong Results Using Minimal Data

We have proposed a new approach to the identification of semantic type coercion, achieving state-of-the-art results by using the context of both verb-object pairs and their sentential situation to projection semantically productive geometries. Moreover, we have demonstrated the generalisability of this approach, applying it to a more challenging experimental set-up based on a reshuffling of the data provided for the original task.

The work presented here is clearly an introduction to a novel approach to distributional semantics, motivated by theoretical insight. There are a variety of model parameters which merit further exploration:

the dimensionality of our subspaces, for instance, and the co-occurrence window size used to build our base space, not to mention the fundamental issue of corpus selection. There is also the question of the statistics which we use to calculate the scalars of our base spaces. PMI is a well known option, with the variant presented here being adapted to the fit the selectional requirements of our approach, but there are other methods worth considering as well (Bullinaria and Levy, 2007, offer an overview). Following on this is the question of the calculations used to make our dimensional selections. While we have made the assumption that dimensions with high PMI values for either or both terms being analysed will be good candidates for defining a subspace in which to compare the semantic relationship between the terms, it may be the case that some more subtle aspect of the relationship between the terms along a given dimension – their relative situation in relation to the mean value of the dimension, for instance – could indicate an even more productive projection from our base spaces. Indeed, it could turn out that there are features of dimensions themselves, such as variance, the clustering of values, of just the number of non-zero values, that might suggest a dimension is simply *ibso facto* better suited for providing a basis for a geometric analysis.

Returning to the theoretical overview of coercion offered in Section 2, we can now posit that there are interactions between the co-occurrence profiles of verbs, their arguments, and the overall sentential context in which they occur that induce geometries relating to the match or mismatch in the semantic class of the words being modelled. The tendency towards coercion can be captured in terms of a general widening and decentralising of the region of points associated with the words and the overall statistical features of the dimensions that they select. We have not attempted to make any headway on the interpretation of coercive usage through the identification of specific classes here, but the groundwork for a geometric, computational approach to this more involved semantic analysis has been laid.

We also note that our methodology does not make use of the identification of dependency relationships between the words in the sentences used for training and testing, or on any sort of parsing of the underlying corpus used to build our base model. It would be reasonable to conjecture that such steps might further enhance the models' already strong performances, as we would be building precisely the type of information used for the identification of the selected semantic class into the models' processes. But on the other hand, we argue that the fact that we can extrapolate such semantically productive geometries from such basic data indicates the power of this approach, not only in terms of its generalisability beyond the data observed in the process of training for coercion identification, but also potentially towards a wider range of semantic tasks involving more generally ambiguous language and compositionality.

Acknowledgement

Stephen McGregor's research has been supported by EPSRC grant EP/L50483X/1.

References

Agres, K., S. McGregor, M. Purver, and G. Wiggins (2015). Conceptualising creativity: From distributional semantics to conceptual spaces. In *Proceedings of the 6th International Conference on Computational Creativity*, Park City, UT.

Agres, K. R., S. McGregor, K. Rataj, M. Purver, and G. A. Wiggins (2016). Modeling metaphor perception with distributional semantics vector space models. In *Proceedings of the Workshop on Computational Creativity, Concept Invention, and General Intelligence*.

Asher, N. (2011). *Lexical meaning in context: A web of words*. Cambridge University Press.

Baroni, M. and A. Lenci (2010). Distributional memory: A general framework for distributional semantics. *Computational Linguistics 36*(4).

Blei, D. M., A. Y. Ng, and M. I. Jordan (2003). Latent Dirichlet allocation. *Journal of Machine Learning Research 3*, 993–1022.

Bullinaria, J. A. and J. P. Levy (2007). Extracting semantic representations from word co-occurrence statistics: A computational study. *Behavior Research Methods 39*(3), 510–526.

Clark, S. (2015). Vector space models of lexical meaning. In S. Lappin and C. Fox (Eds.), *The Handbook of Contemporary Semantic Theory*. Wiley-Blackwell.

Copestake, A. and T. Briscoe (1995). Semi-productive polysemy and sense extension. *Journal of semantics 12*(1), 15–67.

Deerwester, S., S. T. Dumais, G. W. Furnas, T. K. Landauer, and R. Harshman (1990). Indexing by latent semantic analysis. *Journal for the American Society for Information Science 41*(6), 391–407.

Fauconnier, G. and M. Turner (2003). *The Way We Think: Conceptual Blending and the Mind's Hidden Complexities*. New York, NY: BasicBooks.

Grice, H. P. (1975). Logic and conversation. In P. Cole and J. L. Morgan (Eds.), *Syntax and Semantics Volume 3: Speech Acts*, pp. 41–58. New York: Academic Press.

Hanks, P. (2013). *Lexical analysis: Norms and exploitations*. The MIT Press.

Jezek, E. and V. Quochi (2010). Capturing coercions in texts: a first annotation exercise. In *Proceedings of the Seventh conference on International Language Resources and Evaluation (LREC 2010)*, pp. 1464–1471.

Lakoff, G. and M. Johnson (1980). *Metaphors We Live By*. University of Chicago Press.

Langacker, R. (1991). *Concept, Image, and Symbol: The Cognitive Basis of Grammar*. Berlin: Mouton de Gruyter.

Lapata, M. and A. Lascarides (2003). A probabilistic account of logical metonymy. *Computational Linguistics 29*(2), 261–315.

Lebret, R. and R. Collobert (2014). Word embeddings through hellinger pca. In *Proceedings of the 14th Conference of the European Chapter of the Association for Computational Linguistics*, pp. 482–490.

Levy, O. and Y. Goldberg (2014). Neural word embedding as implicit matrix factorization. In Z. Ghahramani, M. Welling, C. Cortes, N. D. Lawrence, and K. Q. Weinberger (Eds.), *Advances in Neural Information Processing Systems 27*, pp. 2177–2185. Curran Associates, Inc.

Markert, K. and M. Nissim (2009). Data and models for metonymy resolution. *Language Resources and Evaluation 43*(2), 123–138.

McGregor, S., K. Agres, M. Purver, and G. Wiggins (2015). From distributional semantics to conceptual spaces: A novel computational method for concept creation. *Journal of Artificial General Intelligence*.

Michaelis, L. A. (2004). Type shifting in construction grammar: An integrated approach to aspectual coercion. *Cognitive linguistics 15*(1), 1–68.

Mikolov, T., K. Chen, G. Corrado, and J. Dean (2013). Efficient estimation of word representations in vector space. In *Proceedings of ICLR Workshop*.

Moens, M. and M. Steedman (1988). Temporal ontology and temporal reference. *Computational linguistics 14*(2), 15–28.

O'Brien, R. M. (2007). A caution regarding rules of thumb for variance inflation factors. *Quality & Quantity 41*(5), 673–690.

Pennington, J., R. Socher, and C. D. Manning (2014). Glove: Global vectors for word representation. In *Conference on Empirical Methods in Natural Language Processing*.

Pustejovsky, J. (1991). The generative lexicon. *Computational linguistics 17*(4), 409–441.

Pustejovsky, J. (1995). *The Generative Lexicon.* Cambridge, MA: MIT Press.

Pustejovsky, J. (2011). Coercion in a general theory of argument selection. *Linguistics 49*(6), 1401–1431.

Pustejovsky, J., P. Hanks, and A. Rumshisky (2004). Automated induction of sense in context. In *Proceedings of the 20th international conference on Computational Linguistics*, pp. 924–931.

Pustejovsky, J. and E. Jezek (2008). Semantic coercion in language: Beyond distributional analysis. *Italian Journal of Linguistics 20*(1), 175–208.

Pustejovsky, J., A. Rumshisky, A. Plotnick, E. Jezek, O. Batiukova, and V. Quochi (2010). Semeval-2010 task 7: Argument selection and coercion. In *Proceedings of the 5th International Workshop on Semantic Evaluation*, pp. 27–32.

Roberts, K. and S. M. Harabagiu (2010). UTDMet: Combining WordNet and corpus data for argument coercion detection. In *Proceedings of the 5th International Workshop on Semantic Evaluation*, pp. 252–255.

Roberts, K. and S. M. Harabagiu (2011). Unsupervised learning of selectional restrictions and detection of argument coercions. In *Proceedings of the Conference on Empirical Methods in Natural Language Processing*, EMNLP '11, pp. 980–990.

Shutova, E. (2013). Metaphor identification as interpretation. In *Proceedings of *SEM 2013*.

Shutova, E., J. Kaplan, S. Teufel, and A. Korhonen (2013, July). A computational model of logical metonymy. *ACM Trans. Speech Lang. Process. 10*(3), 11:1–11:28.

Veale, T. and Y. Hao (2008). A fluid knowledge representation for understanding and generating creative metaphors. In *Proceedings of the 22Nd International Conference on Computational Linguistics - Volume 1*, pp. 945–952.

Verspoor, C. M. (1997). *Contextually-dependent lexical semantics.* University of Edinburgh.

Wilson, D. and D. Sperber (2012). *Meaning and Relevance.* Cambridge University Press.

Exploring Substitutability through Discourse Adverbials and Multiple Judgments

Hannah Rohde
University of Edinburgh
`Hannah.Rohde@ed.ac.uk`

Anna Dickinson
University of Edinburgh
`Anna.Y.Dickinson@gmail.com`

Nathan Schneider
Georgetown University
`nathan.schneider@georgetown.edu`

Annie Louis
University of Edinburgh
`alouis@inf.ed.ac.uk`

Bonnie Webber
University of Edinburgh
`Bonnie.Webber@ed.ac.uk`

Abstract

In his systematic analysis of discourse connectives, Knott (1996) introduced the notion of *substitutability* and the conditions under which one connective (e.g., *when*) can substitute for another (e.g., *if*) to express the same meaning. Knott only uses examples which he constructed and judged himself. This paper describes a new multi-judgment study on naturally occurring passages, on which substitutability claims can be tested. While some of our findings support Knott's claims, other pairs of connectives that Knott predicts to be *exclusive* are in fact judged to substitute felicitously for one another. These findings show that discourse adverbials in the immediate context play a role in connective choice.

1 Introduction

The question of how different discourse connectives are used to realize particular types of coherence relations remains unresolved. While some connectives show nearly one-to-one mappings with individual coherence relations, other connectives permit much more flexible usage across contexts.

One early enterprise targeting the above question was Alistair Knott's systematic assessment of the conditions that permit one connective to *substitute* for another (Knott, 1996). *Substitutability*, along with categories of coherence relations, then predicts the behavior of individual connectives. Another such enterprise is our own (Rohde et al., 2015, 2016, 2017) on implicit connectives in the context of explicit discourse adverbials. Using naturally occurring passages, we have gathered judgments from multiple participants as to what connective, if any, they could insert into a particular passage immediately before an existing discourse adverbial, to make explicit the author's intended message. For example, when shown the passage *It's too far to walk. Instead let's take the bus.*, a participant might insert *so* to express what she takes to be the intended causal reading.

Our findings show variation across participant responses. Such divergence in judgments could pose a puzzle for Knott's substitutability claims – Do they reflect (1) merely different interpretations of the passage or (2) genuine substitutability between the connectives selected? This paper reports a new study to address this puzzle. In the study, participants are asked to identify not only the connective that best expresses the intended meaning of a passage, but also *what other connectives* they could use to express the same meaning. The study makes three contributions: (1) It sheds light on our earlier data on divergences in participants' judgments; (2) it serves as a large-scale test of some of Knott's *substitutability* claims; and (3) it provides more evidence *against* the common assumption that an explicit discourse connective between two clauses marks the coherence relation that holds between them and that no additional pragmatic inference is used to establish coherence between them (cf. Section 5). Correcting this assumption can improve modelling in computational semantics and the technology that depends on it, provide a more realistic account of translational divergences, and enable more effective design and interpretation of psycholinguistic experiments. As far as we are aware, the work presented here is the first to examine Knott's claims on the basis of large-scale experiments on naturally occurring data.

2 Background

2.1 Exploring discourse connectives through substitutability

In an innovative PhD thesis at the University of Edinburgh, Alistair Knott (1996) investigated what could be learned about discourse connectives through their possible substitutability relations. Informally, *substitutability* specifies the circumstances in which an author would be prepared to substitute one cue phrase for another in a passage of text (possibly with some reorganization of the passage and/or a change of style). So two cue phrases x and y may be *always* substitutable if wherever y appears, x is substitutable for y; *sometimes* substitutable if x is substitutable for y in some contexts in which y appears, but not all of them; or *never* substitutable if wherever y appears, x is not substitutable for y. His methodology involved: (1) Gathering a set of discourse connectives (which Knott called *cue phrases*); (2) defining a small set of *substitutability* relations which correspond to the contexts in which one cue phrase can substitute for another, with the same meaning being conveyed; (3) establishing the particular substitutability relations that hold between pairs of cue phrases; (4) using substitutability relations to define taxonomies of cue phrases; and (5) positing a set of semantic features that can be said to be intrinsic to cue phrases, such that subsumption relations between these features can explain the data-driven taxonomy of connectives based on substitutability.

The following three basic substitutability relations allow Knott to define four composite relations between cue phrases x and y, that underpin the rest of the thesis:

- SYNONYMOUS(x,y) if *always*(x,y) and *always*(y,x);

- EXCLUSIVE(x,y) if *never*(x,y) and *never*(y,x);

- HYPONYM(x,y) if *sometimes*(x,y) and *always*(y,x);

- CONTINGENTLY-SUBSTITUTABLE(x,y) if *sometimes*(x,y) and *sometimes*(y,x).

For example, SYNONYMOUS(*to begin with, to start with*) holds because in every context in which *to begin with* can be used as a cue phrase, so can *to start with*, with the same meaning being conveyed. In contrast, Knott claims EXCLUSIVE(*first, for one thing*) because there are no contexts in which *first* can substitute for *for one thing* and no contexts in which *for one thing* can substitute for *first*.

For the HYPONYM relation, Knott claims that HYPONYM(*for one thing, firstly*) holds because one can use *firstly* to start a sequence in any context, while one can only use *for one thing* to start a sequence in an argumentative context. Finally, the CONTINGENTLY-SUBSTITUTABLE relation is illustrated in (Knott and Mellish, 1996, p. 147) with *and* and *but* because there are some contexts in which *and* and *but* can both be used (Ex. 1), some contexts in which *and* can be used, but not *but* (Ex. 2), and some contexts in which *but* can be used, but not *and* (Ex. 3).

(1) Bill's a liar. He said he can run a mile in three minutes, [and, but] that's impossible.

(2) I'm very tired, [and, #but] I don't want to be disturbed.

(3) Don't be too harsh on Bob. He arrived late, [#and, but] he's usually very punctual.

Knott's analysis of cue phrases makes a further division of sense relations into ten sense *categories*: SEQUENCE, CAUSE, RESULT, RESTATEMENT, TEMPORAL, HYPOTHETICAL, SIMILARITY, DIGRESSION, ADDITIONAL INFORMATION and NEGATIVE POLARITY. Knott assigns some cue phrases to a single category (when their only sense belongs to that category) and other cue phrases (e.g., *since*, *and*, *or*) to multiple categories (when they can be used to express more than one sense). Since *substitutability* of connectives within the same sentence requires the sentence to retain the same meaning, we assume that when two cue phrases do not share a single category in common, Knott would take them to be EX-CLUSIVE. (While Spooren (1997) has posited specificity relations between sense categories, such that a CAUSAL relation can sometimes be conveyed by a TEMPORAL connective, our analysis here is based solely on Knott's empirical analysis involving *substitutability*.)

Knott's thesis incorporates ≈150 cue phrases into *substitutability* diagrams, which is a significant achievement. However, all examples in the thesis were ones he constructed, and all judgments, ones made by him alone. Knott recognized the need to carry out large-scale experiments using naturally occurring data to support his conclusions, but lacked the opportunity to do so.

Finally, as noted in point 5 above, while Knott posited a theoretical basis for substitutability in a set of binary-valued features intrinsic to the meaning of a cue phrase (or the sense of a cue phrase, for ones that belong to multiple categories), this paper just refers to Knott's claims about substitutability based on empirical judgments, and not to his later theoretical basis for the claims.

2.2 Collecting multiple judgments on discourse connectives

Our larger project addresses the common, but incorrect, assumption that only when explicit discourse connectives are absent or ambiguous is inference used to establish coherence between sentences and/or clauses. We have collected multiple judgments on connectives in naturally occurring text in order to understand and characterize implicit coherence relations that hold at the same time as coherence relations associated with explicit discourse adverbials. For example, while Ex. 4a contains only the explicit adverbial *instead*, it conveys the same meaning as Ex. 4b, in which the inferred causal relation has been made explicit.

(4) a. It's too far to walk. <u>Instead</u> let's take the bus.

    b. It's too far to walk. <u>So instead</u> let's take the bus.

Both versions convey that we should take the bus as an alternative to walking because it's too far to walk.

Because judgments on discourse connectives can vary in unexpected ways, we have collected data on a large number of adverbials in a large number of passages from a large number of participants – one experiment using 20 discourse adverbials, aimed at understanding the extent of variability across adverbials, and another using 37 discourse adverbials, aimed at exploring adverbials in terms of their common paired-connective distribution.

2.2.1 Dataset of connective insertions

Our first study (Rohde et al., 2016) involved 28 naive participants, all native English speakers engaged through Amazon Mechanical Turk. We showed them passages with discourse adverbials and asked them to identify which of several given connectives (if any) could appear in the position before the adverbial, to explicitly signal their interpretation of the passage.

The target passages shown to participants (minimally, a sentence and maximally, a short paragraph) were selected from the *New York Times Annotated Corpus* (Sandhaus, 2008). Each target passage consisted of two spans of text, the second beginning with a discourse adverbial. Half the passages (*explicit passages*) originally contained a conjunction before the adverbial, which we excised and replaced with a gap. The other half lacked a conjunction before the adverbial (*implicit passages*). With these, we simply inserted a gap before the adverbial, so that all passages had the following structure (also see Figure 2a):

(5) *Bruce, who was in Edinburgh at the time, was in the audience on the opening night ____ afterwards the Director invited Bruce to join him and some members of the cast for a drink in a pub in the Grassmarket.*

For each of the 20 adverbials used in the study, participants saw 25 *explicit passages* and 25 *implicit passages*, with the exception of *however*, which rarely occurs immediately after a conjunction. For *however*, we were only able to include 25 implicit passages and 1 explicit passage in the study. (Note that passages from one or more of our studies are given in italics. Examples which simply illustrate a point are presented in standard font.)

As for results, responses on *explicit passages* showed that participants selected the authors' original conjunctions 57% of the time. If we take participant BUT as substitutable for author AND in the context of the passage (and likewise, participant SO and author AND), agreement increases to 70%. Divergences with authors' original conjunctions provide evidence of certain adverbials having a preference for certain conjunctions, although it is neither the case that all adverbials co-occur with the same preferred conjunction, nor the case that each adverbial has a single preferred conjunction. However, responses to the *implicit passages* also demonstrate patterns that are unique to certain adverbials.

As with *explicit passages*, no single conjunction is preferred across the board with *implicit passages*, nor a single conjunction preferred uniformly for a given adverbial. Despite this non-determinism, pockets of systematicity arise. In some cases, similar adverbials show similar preferences: e.g., the pairs *nevertheless/nonetheless* and *therefore/thus* show a preference for the conjunction BUT and SO respectively. The variability that emerges is often passage-specific: e.g., some passages with *instead* favored BUT, while others lent themselves to the inference of BECAUSE. Further information and discussion can be found in (Rohde et al., 2016).

The second study, described in (Rohde et al., 2017), covered 37 discourse adverbials and used participants (N=28) recruited locally rather than via Amazon Mechanical Turk (AMT), so as to better ensure participants would complete the study. To ensure there was no dramatic difference between the AMT participants in the first study and local participants in the second, we carried out a pre-trial test on thirty-six passages from the first study: 18 passages where most AMT participants chose the same response (*strong signal*) and 18 passages on which their' responses spanned more than one response (*divided signal*).

We found that local participants agreed with AMT participants on the *strong signal* passages; on the *divided signal* passages, responses of local participants also varied, although not necessarily showing the exact same response pattern. A comparison across all 36 passages showed the response profiles of all items to be highly correlated across the two participant groups. So we concluded that the results of the two studies would be comparable, even with the new participant pool.

In addition, to reduce the prevalence of ambiguous and/or less informative responses (that is, AND and the no-conjunction response NONE), we offered these two possibilities as options only if a participant chose the response OTHER. This did indeed reduce the frequency with which AND and NONE were used.

As for results, for explicit passages, agreement with the author's original choice is comparable to the first study at 53%, rising to ≈70% if AND is taken to be *conditionally substitutable* for BUT and for SO. For the implicit passages, we see striking differences between adverbials. Some favor a conjunction that conveys a similar sense: e.g., *consequently, as a result, accordingly*, and *hence* all favor SO. Other preferences reflect usage rather than semantics. For example, *for one thing, first*, and *after all*, together with their context of use, favor the conjunction BECAUSE. From this, it is possible to see that adverbials must be characterized in terms of both their own semantics and their use in context.

2.2.2 Competition between (substitutable?) connectives

Of particular relevance to the current study (Section 3) is that participants showed strong biases about which conjunction(s) they saw as best expressing their interpretation. This can be seen in how frequent the top choice and second choice is for each passage in the second study: Figures 1(a) and 1(b) show that the top choice is typically favored by more than half the participants, whereas the second choice is favored by fewer than half. If all choices were near equi-probable, the top choice would have only achieved a plurality rather than a majority. If the selections that differed from the favored one were just noise, we would have expected to see the histogram pushed much farther to the left in Figure 1(b). However, the second choice frequently receives 5-10 votes, suggesting that when a passage permits multiple conjunctions to be selected across participants, there is consistency in those additional selections. This raises the

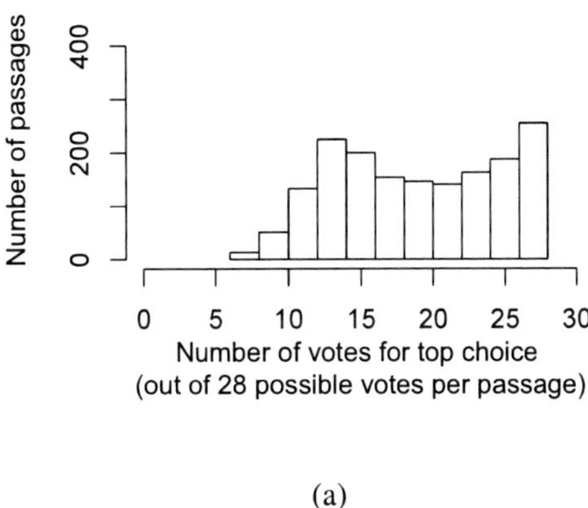

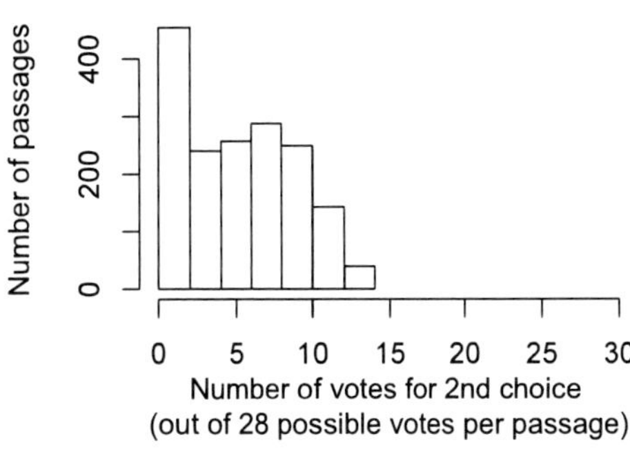

(a)   (b)

Figure 1: (a) Across passages, how many participants (out of 28) favored top choice? Histogram of the number of votes received by the favored conjunction in each passage. (b) Across passages, how many participants favored second choice? Histogram of number of votes given to second conjunction choice

question of what patterns underlie the pairings of the top-choice and runner-up connectives for a given passage and whether those pairings reflect distinct interpretations of the passage or the substitutability of those connectives in that context.

3 Substitutability Study

An important question raised by the earlier studies in this project is whether differences in participant choices indicate differences in understanding (*alternative interpretation*) or simply differences in how best to express otherwise shared understanding (*alternative preferences*). To answer this question, we devised a task to explicitly elicit participant judgments on all candidate connectives that could express their understanding of the passage.

3.1 Participants

Participation in the task was limited to participants from the second study (Section 2.2), who would thereby be familiar with the connective insertion task. Of the original 28 participants, we were able to collect data from 16 (11 female; ages 19-69 (mean 35); highest education: 5 high school, 6 undergraduate degree, 3 masters, 2 PhD).

3.2 Materials

We selected 67 passages for the task from passages used earlier; predominantly, but not exclusively, passages used in the first (Amazon Mechanical Turk) study. Both explicit and implicit passages were included, based on whether earlier responses to a passage would help explore whether divergent connective preferences reflected divergent readings or substitutability. For example, Ex. 6 (an implicit passage, with no connective adjacent to *therefore*) had earlier received responses split between AND and SO, whereas Ex. 7 (an explicit passage with author BECAUSE) had received responses split between BECAUSE and BUT.

(6) *Neocons pushed for this war ____ therefore they deserve the blame for its failure or the credit for its success.*

(7) *"Nervous? No, my leg's not shaking," said Griffey, who caused everyone to laugh ____ indeed his right foot was shaking.*

We speculated that the response pattern to passages like Ex. 6 might simply reflect participants choosing their preferred conjunction from two essentially substitutable options (AND and SO), while the response pattern to passages like Ex. 7 might reflect different interpretations, with BECAUSE linking the final segment to "caused everyone to laugh", and BUT contrasting it with "... my leg's not shaking". This would be in line with Knott's predictions: AND and SO are contingent substitutable, in which case participants asked to select conjunctions with the same meaning might select both AND and SO for Ex 6. On the other hand, with BUT and BECAUSE, participants would be unlikely to select both as expressing the same meaning.

Of the 67 passages, 46 were selected to test two of Knott's contingent substitutability claims (see breakdown in Figure 2b). The substitutability of AND and SO was tested with passages containing the discourse adverbials *for example, therefore, afterwards* or *then*, while the substitutability of AND and BUT was tested with passages containing *in fact, in general, (more) specifically* or *meanwhile*.

We also targeted connective combinations which are not substitutable under Knott's analysis and hence would be predicted to yield *exclusive* response patterns. These included 6 passages that had previously shown a combination of BECAUSE and BUT responses (with the discourse adverbials *after all, previously,* and *indeed*); 3 that had previously shown a combination of BECAUSE and OR responses (with the adverbials *otherwise* (2) and *hence* (1)); and 2 that had previously shown a combination of SO and OR responses (with adverbial *in other words*). These were to be contrasted with one passage that had previously received almost uniform BECAUSE responses (with adverbial *in fact*).

A further 8 passages targeted the insertion of no connective. These passages had received frequent NONE responses in our previous work and were included here so that not all passages would necessarily require the insertion of any/many connectives. Finally, we also included two "catch trials" in the form of constructed examples for which there was logically only one answer (e.g. OR for *David weighs more than Alice _____ Alice weighs more than David*).

3.3 Procedure

Participants were shown two text spans and asked to select the conjunction that best described the relationship between the spans. There were five available conjunctions: AND, BECAUSE, BUT, OR, and SO. *None at all* was also an option. After selecting their best choice, participants were shown a list of sentences with the gap replaced by each of the remaining conjunctions, and told: "Next thing to do is to decide if any of the other options could mean the same as the one you chose." Next to each sentence were two radio buttons: "Means the same", and "Does not mean the same". Participants had to select one of the buttons for each sentence before they could proceed to the next question. The screenshot in Figure 2a shows the layout of the interface. The order of candidate connectives and of passages was pseudo-randomized to control for order effects.

4 Results

For each passage, we assessed each of the 16 participants' response profiles and categorized them as responding with only one connective (e.g., "only SO") or a best plus other choice(s) (e.g., "SO:AND") or a best plus other choices that did *not* include some other relevant connective (e.g., "SO:¬AND"). This evaluation allows us to see which passages were dominated by which response profiles.

For example, in (Ex. 6), only one participant rejected the full substitutability of AND/SO. The 16 participants' response profiles consisted of 11 "SO:AND", 4 "AND:SO", and 1 "only SO". In (Ex. 7), as predicted, BECAUSE/BUT substitution was rare. The response profiles consisted of 11 "only BECAUSE", 1 "only BUT", 3 "BECAUSE:AND", and 1 "BECAUSE:AND,BUT".

(N.B. Our two catch-trials showed only one participant selecting an incorrect response. Since this participant's responses on target trials were in line with the other participants, their data was not excluded.)

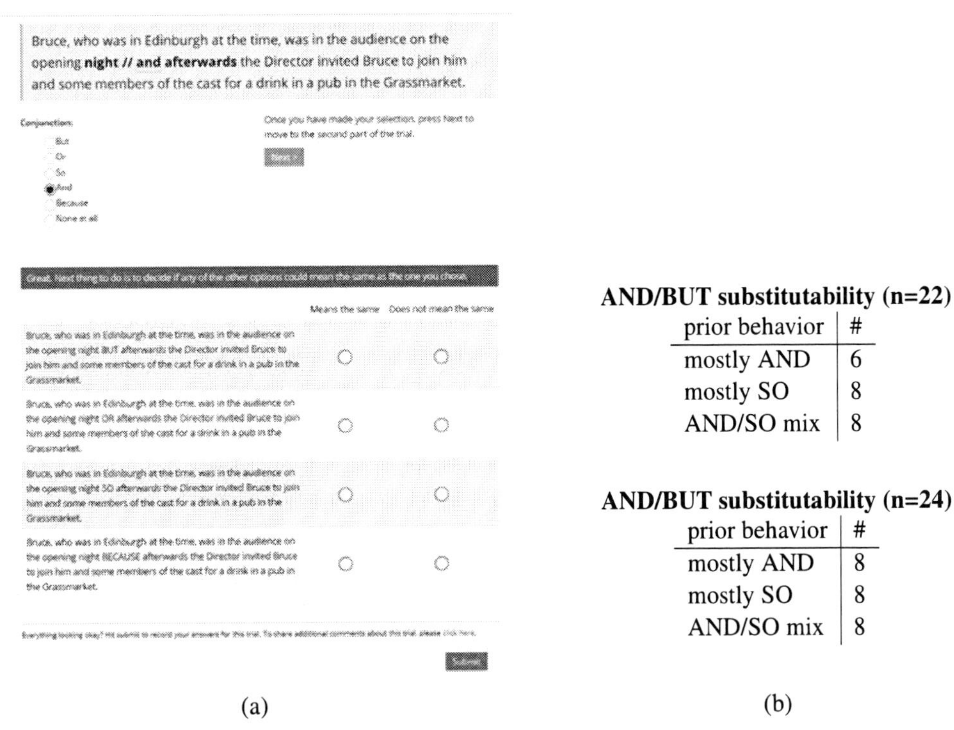

AND/BUT substitutability (n=22)

prior behavior	#
mostly AND	6
mostly SO	8
AND/SO mix	8

AND/BUT substitutability (n=24)

prior behavior	#
mostly AND	8
mostly SO	8
AND/SO mix	8

(a)   (b)

Figure 2: (a) Interface: first conjunction selection indicates participant's first choice; subsequent versions of the passage are then displayed with alternative conjunctions. (b) Materials: Distribution of passages according to their behavior in our prior studies.

4.1 Predictions of contingent substitutability

Recall that evidence for *contingent substitutability* between two connectives involves both (1) response profiles in which a participant licenses either one of the connectives but not the other and (2) profiles in which a participant licenses both. To examine whether participants' behavior reflects these two scenarios, we consider the relationship between AND/BUT and AND/SO.

For the analysis, we visualize the distribution of participant response profiles for the passages relevant to the substitutability of AND/BUT (n=24) and AND/SO (n=22). In Figures 3 and 4, each bar represents the response profiles for a single passage. Bar length indicates the number of participant response profiles (out of 16) which adhere to the contingent substitutability hypothesis. The colorful part of the bar (above the x-axis) shows response profiles satisfying the free-exchange aspect of contingent substitutability and the one-but-not-both aspect of contingent substitutability. The grey part of the bar (below the axis) shows response profiles in which the participant selected as their first choice one of the relevant connectives but then selected an unexpected connective as their second choice. Short bars correspond to passages whose response profiles are not relevant to the AND/BUT contingent substitutability hypothesis (i.e., where the first choice of many of the participants was neither AND nor BUT).

4.1.1 Substitutability between AND/BUT

Because the connectives AND and BUT are related in Knott's taxonomy via *contingent substitutability*, we check the response profiles of passages that previously had shown a mix of AND/BUT responses across participants. Figure 3 shows the distribution of response profiles. Some passages indeed favored BUT as the first or only choice (red bars on the left); others favored AND as the first or only choice (blue bars on the right). Crucially, as Knott predicts, most passages yielded response profiles fulfilling the two realizations of *contingent substitutability* (colorful tall bars). For a minority of passages, participants

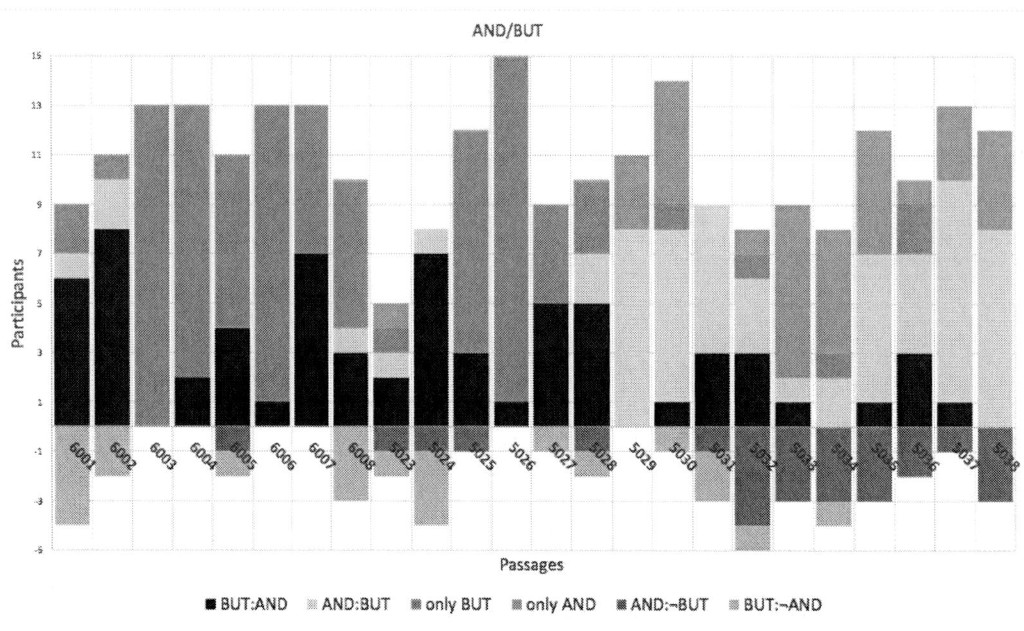

Figure 3: Distribution of response profiles for passages testing AND/BUT substitutability. Positive portion of bars (above the x-axis) corresponds to response profiles in keeping with contingent-substitutability predictions; negative portion (below the x-axis) corresponds to response profiles with unexpected substitutions.

diverge from the predicted patterns by selecting non-AND/BUT options like BECAUSE/SO/OR. We return in Section 4.2 to more systematic cases that violate this type of exclusivity.

4.1.2 Substitutability between AND/SO

Knott's taxonomy also relates AND/SO via *contingent substitutability*. We check the response profiles of passages that previously had shown a mix of AND/SO responses. Figure 4 shows the distribution of response profiles. Some passages favored SO as the first or only choice (dark blue/yellow bars on the left); others favored AND as the first or only choice (light blue/turquoise bars on the right). Crucially, as Knott predicts, most passages yielded response profiles fulfilling both realizations of contingent substitutability (colorful tall bars).

Figure 4 shows that there are some cases (e.g., the large gray negative bar for passage 5019) where the hypothesis that AND alternates with SO was not upheld. In that particular passage (Ex. 8), the adverbial *then* yielded an alternation between AND/BUT rather than AND/SO (akin to the pattern in Figure 3).

(8) *A bone-marrow transplant is a medical resurrection. First doctors all but kill a patient ____ then they bring him back to life.*

This finding is not that surprising since we selected passages to test the AND/SO hypothesis that contained adverbials that had previously permitted a mix of AND and SO, but (Ex. 8) had previously yielded a dominant AND bias and did not lend itself to a RESULT inference. This confirms the observation from (Rohde et al., 2017) that even though some adverbials introduce preferences regarding the implicit relation participants infer, the content of the passage is crucial as well.

4.2 Predictions of exclusivity for connectives

Knott also predicted that particular pairs of connectives are *exclusive*, meaning that they cannot substitute for one another in any context and convey the same sense (Section 2.1). Our current study provides

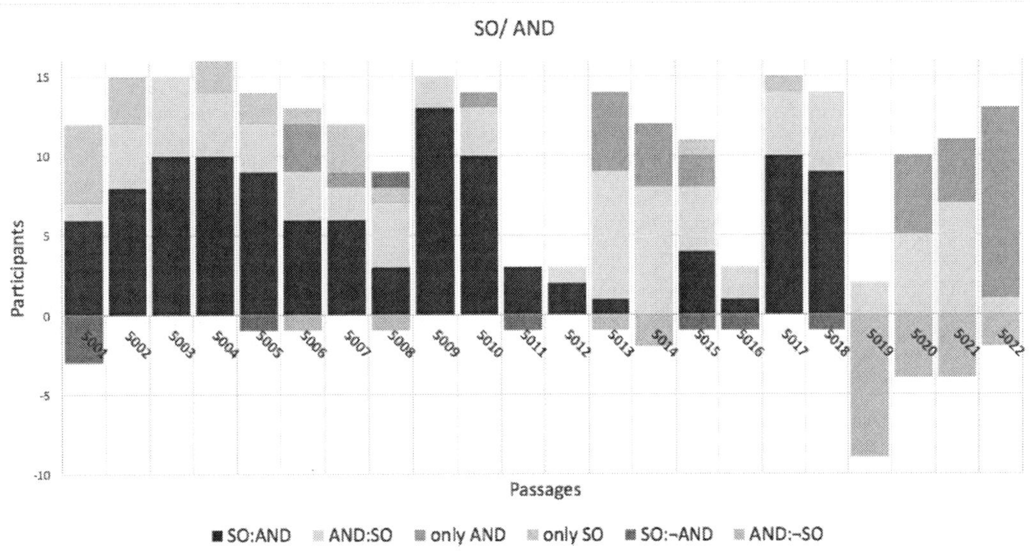

Figure 4: Distribution of response profiles for passages relevant to the hypothesis of AND/SO substitutability. Figure properties (above and below the x-axis) match those of Figure 3.

evidence against such exclusivity. While taken as a whole, the results of our study may not surprise the reader, they allow one to start pursuing a better explanation of what discourse connectives do and how they do it, and how one may need to alter one's predictions in the presence of a discourse adverbial.

Here we examine pairs of connectives that should be *exclusive*: In some cases, members of the pair belong to only one sense category, but the categories differ. In other cases, at least one member of the pair appears in multiple sense categories but nonetheless fails to share a category with the other. We discuss possible explanations for two of these in the Discussion in section 5.

because/but   BECAUSE only belongs to the category CAUSE, while BUT belongs to the sense category NEGATIVE POLARITY. As such, they should not be *substitutable*. Nevertheless, the response profiles for Ex. 9–10 (involving the adverbials *previously* and *after all*) showed that at least half of our participants endorsed both BECAUSE and BUT, with a slight preference for BECAUSE as first choice and BUT as the other connective expressing the same meaning. The remaining responses consisted of "only BECAUSE" and "only BUT" profiles (plus two "BUT:AND" profiles, a pairing already highlighted as contingently substitutable and confirmed in our results in Section 4.1.1). This pattern of response profiles suggests that BECAUSE/BUT are contingently substitutable in the context of *previously* and *after all*.

(9) *The demand for tickets continued so strong yesterday that several carriers, including United and Delta, extended until Sunday the period in which customers must pick up the tickets they had booked by telephone. ____ previously they were required to do so within 24 hours.*

(10) *Yes, I suppose there's a certain element of danger in it, that you can't get around ____ after all, there's a certain amount of danger in living, whatever you do.*

because/so   BECAUSE only belongs to the category CAUSE, while SO belongs to the sense category RESULT. As such, they should not be *substitutable*. Nevertheless, the response profiles for Ex. 11–12 involving the adverbial *then* showed that nearly all participants endorsed both BECAUSE and SO (with a strong preference for BECAUSE as first choice and SO as the other connective expressing the same meaning). This was the case for all 16 participants for Ex. 11 and 14 out of 16 for Ex. 12, with a 15th participant who selected AND as their first choice in an "AND:BECAUSE,SO" profile. This pattern of response profiles suggests that BECAUSE/SO are not always exclusive.

(11) *With a $50 credit in an on-line account, Jordan eagerly logged on. But as he tried to decide which video games to buy, he realized he had a new problem: shipping costs put him over budget. It took him a few weeks to figure out a solution: when he finally made his first purchase in July, he opted for less expensive items – videotapes – ____ then he could afford to pay the shipping costs.*

(12) *On a sunny day, upward of 2,000 hot dog vendors are at large in New York. Like many veteran frankfurter men, Mr. Stathopoulos is his own boss. There are a number of small companies who have a dozen or so carts and hire people to operate them, paying them a salary. All hot dog men, though, dream of owning a cart ____ then they can set their own hours and the harder they work the more money they make.*

but/or   BUT belongs to one category, NEGATIVE POLARITY, while OR belongs to multiple categories: SEQUENCE (where it is a synonym for 'or else'), RESTATEMENT (where it is a synonym for 'or rather'), and NEGATIVE POLARITY (no synonyms). As such, BUT/OR should only be *substitutable* in contexts in which a *negative polarity* relation is operative. However, in the context of the discourse adverbial *more specifically*, BUT/OR/AND are substitutable as examples of RESTATEMENT. The response profiles for Ex. 13–14 showed that BUT/OR is endorsed by 10 and 16 of the 16 participants, respectively. A number of participants also add AND, which is contingently substitutable for BUT.

(13) *Windows is a way of life to some degree ____ more specifically it's Microsoft's way of life, and you'd better like to live the way they tell you to live, or else.*

(14) *"The Wild Hawaiian" is a Hawaiian rock album ____ more specifically it's an album of songs in the Hawaiian language, against a whiplash of percussion and distorted guitars.*

or/because   As noted, BECAUSE belongs to only the sense category CAUSE, and does not overlap with any of the categories that OR belongs to. Passages Ex. 15–16 contain *otherwise*. The response profiles showed that 14 of 16 participants endorse OR/BECAUSE for Ex. 15 while 12 of 16 do so for Ex. 16.

(15) *"If people want to get rid of an animal, they'll do so," she said. "My thing is to get the animal here ____ otherwise they're going to end up wandering in the streets."*

(16) *Gouges are deep scratches that must be filled as well as colored ____ otherwise they will collect dirt and become permanently discolored.*

or/so   Like BUT and BECAUSE, SO belongs to only one sense category (RESULT), and does not overlap with any of the OR categories. Passages Ex. 17–18 contain *in other words*. The response profiles showed that 10 of 16 participants endorse OR/SO for Ex. 17, and 13 of 16 do so for Ex. 18.

(17) *In recognizing their special responsibilities and working sensitively in developing countries, multinationals can expect a smoother and more sustained market development in the long run ____ in other words good ethics is good business.*

(18) *Unfortunately, nearly 75,000 acres of tropical forest are converted or deforested every day ____ in other words an area the size of Central Park disappears every 16 minutes.*

We stress that the above results depend crucially on having sufficient participants to show more than one strong pattern of responses. With only a few participants, this might simply look like noise.

5   Discussion

The results we report here demonstrate a wider range of substitutability than previously assumed, but the experiments themselves do not answer why such a range is possible and what its limits are likely to be. In speculating about possible explanations of our observed patterns of substitutability, the picture is complicated – we have not found a uniform explanation that holds across the board to account for all passages for all adverbials. Rather, the substitutability patterns of families of different adverbials appear to invite different explanations, where those families of adverbials reflect shared patterns of substitutability that can cross-cut their semantics and function.

Below we review two patterns we see with regards to conjunction alternations, where the minimal explanation for the observed patterns of alternations appears to involve *both* the coherence relation signalled by the discourse adverbial *and* an additional coherence relation derived through pragmatic inference.

5.1 Disjunction and alternatives

Both the adverbials *otherwise* and *in other words* were found to license substitutability of the conjunction OR – specifically OR/BECAUSE in the presence of *otherwise* and OR/SO in the presence of *in other words*. We speculate that this substitutability arises due to the fact that both adverbials encode 'otherness' in their lexical semantics, as well as in their surface forms. Because these adverbials always convey an alternative, this aspect of their meaning can be made explicit with OR (albeit redundantly) whenever they appear. Then if an *otherwise* passage also supports inference of causality, OR can alternate with BECAUSE. The passage in Ex. 15 allows such a causal inference: The reason for the speaker's particular goal is BECAUSE the alternative is worse.

However, *otherwise* passages that do not support a causal inference do not permit this alternation. For example, the constructed *otherwise* passage in Ex. 19 lists a set of alternatives without describing a reason for a particular course of action; in that case, no OR/BECAUSE alternation is predicted to arise.

(19) For dinner, sometimes we go to a restaurant or to visit friends _____ otherwise we eat at home.

A related pattern emerges for *in other words*. The sense of an alternative is implicit in the adverbial itself since its meaning is about reformulation, thereby licensing OR in all cases. But OR can be seen to alternate with SO in the context of *in other words*, as shown in Ex. 20: The generalization about the rate of deforestation has the consequence that a more specific reformulation of that calculation must also be true.

(20) *Unfortunately, nearly 75,000 acres of tropical forest are converted or deforested every day _____ in other words an area the size of Central Park disappears every 16 minutes.*

We speculate that this OR/SO alternation for *in other words* arises because of the nature of reformulation: When one formulation holds, it follows that the alternative formulation must also hold. In this way, *otherwise* and *in other words* are similar in permitting the alternation between OR and a causal conjunction. They differ in that *otherwise* allows only conditional substitutability between OR/BECAUSE, whereas *in other words* may always license the alternation.

5.2 Apparent Symmetry in Causality

We normally assume that causality is asymmetric: If X BECAUSE Y (i.e., reason), then it can't also be the case that X SO Y (i.e., result). Nevertheless, as we noted in Section 4.2, the response profiles for Ex. 11–12 involving the adverbial *then* showed that nearly all participants endorsed both BECAUSE and SO for the same passage.

In this case, the explanation revolves around both an inference of purpose and a fact that we hadn't considered – that SO can be ambiguous between conveying result and conveying purpose. For example, in the constructed example Ex. 21a, SO can convey purpose, while in the minimally different Ex. 21b, it conveys only result.

(21) a. Nathan renewed his passport this year so (that) he could travel abroad.

b. Nathan lost his passport this year so (therefore) he could not travel abroad.

While we were aware that the purpose sense of SO can be expressed by the explicit phrase SO THAT, we had ignored the fact that this can (and is) often reduced to simply SO.

This sense of purpose can be inferred in both Ex. 11–12. However, it is not associated with the adverbial *then*, but rather the modal (*could* in Ex. 11, and *can* in Ex. 12). Thus we would predict that, whatever the discourse adverbial, if purpose can be inferred, then participants will identify BECAUSE and SO as substitutable.

There are other circumstances in which SO/BECAUSE can alternate – in particular, the epistemic uses of these conjunctions that capture reasoning about WHY a conclusion can be drawn or what conclusion can be drawn as a RESULT of certain evidence. The alternation depends on reasoning about the events that happened in the world versus reasoning about how a speaker's conclusion is drawn. Consider the well-known example Ex. 22 from Van Dijk (1977) (see also earlier work by Rutherford (1970)):

(22)   a.   John is home so/because the lights are burning.

b.   The lights are burning so/because John is home.

The conjunction SO primarily conveys consequence, whereas BECAUSE primarily conveys cause. So if the order is "Real-world-cause ____ Real-world-effect", as in Ex. 22a, then SO will express real-world causality, while BECAUSE will express epistemic inference (the opposite causal direction: reasoning backwards). Conversely, if the order is "Real-world-effect ____ Real-world-cause", as in Ex. 22b, then BECAUSE will express real-world causality, while SO expresses epistemic inference.

6   Conclusions and Future Plans

The experiment reported here collected multiple judgments from multiple participants on naturally-occurring passages containing discourse adverbials. The data provide evidence confirming two of Knott's *contingent substitutability* pairs and denying several *exclusivity* pairs. We have offered reasons for three of the surprising non-exclusivity judgments: for OR/SO, OR/BECAUSE, and BECAUSE/SO. But there is clearly more to explain and more evidence to gather in support for possible explanations. The question of how different discourse connectives are used to realize particular types of coherence relations remains unresolved. We plan to continue our pursuit of an answer via experimentation and classification of patterns of use in these contexts.

Acknowledgments

Our thanks to Alexander Johnson for enlightening in-person discussion, to Ali Knott for enlightening discussion over email, and to Larry Horn for pointing us to the work of Rutherford (1970). This project has been supported in part by a grant from the Nuance Foundation.

References

Knott, A. (1996). *A Data-driven Methodology for Motivating a Set of Coherence Relations*. Ph.D. dissertation, Department of Artificial Intelligence, University of Edinburgh.

Knott, A. and C. Mellish (1996). A feature-based account of the relations signalled by sentence and clause connectives. *Language and Speech 39(2-3)*, 143–183.

Rohde, H., A. Dickinson, C. Clark, A. Louis, and B. Webber (2015). Recovering discourse relations: Varying influence of discourse adverbials. In *Proceedings, First Workshop on Linking Computational Models of Lexical, Sentential and Discourse-level Semantics*, Lisbon, Portugal, pp. 22–31.

Rohde, H., A. Dickinson, N. Schneider, C. Clark, A. Louis, and B. Webber (2016). Filling in the blanks in understanding discourse adverbials: Consistency, conflict, and context-dependence in a crowdsourced elicitation task. In *Proceedings of the Tenth Linguistic Annotation Workshop (LAW-X)*, Berlin, pp. 49–58.

Rohde, H., A. Dickinson, N. Schneider, A. Louis, and B. Webber (2017). ConnText: Recognizing concurrent discourse relations. Second annual report to the Nuance Foundation.

Rutherford, W. E. (1970). Some observations concerning subordinate clauses in English. *Language 46*, 97–115.

Sandhaus, E. (2008). New York Times corpus: Corpus overview. LDC catalogue entry LDC2008T19.

Spooren, W. (1997). The processing of underspecified discourse relations. *Discourse Processes 24*, 149–168.

Van Dijk, T. A. (1977). *Text and Context*. London: Longmans.

Finite State Intensional Semantics

Mats Rooth
Cornell University
`mr249@cornell.edu`

1   Introduction

Suppose possible worlds are strings, rather than physically structured worlds like ours. Then the proposition corresponding to a sentence or a formula in logical language is a set of strings; an epistemic acquaintance relation is a relation between strings; and in a relational construction of partition semantics for questions, a question meaning is a relation between strings. If discourse referents, too, are encoded in the same strings, then dynamic information states are sets of strings, and distributive updates are relations between strings. Finally, in a construction of the temporal development of worlds in an action logic, actions are also relations between strings.

This paper makes the further assumption that the sets and relations mentioned above are regular sets and regular relations. These are the sets of strings and relations between strings that can be represented by finite state acceptors and transducers. In this framework an analysis of intensional complementation in *that*- and *wh*- clauses is developed. A version of dynamic semantics is used to formalize sub-clausal compositional semantics. The analysis is cast as a defined logical language in a finite state calculus that includes function definitions. Finally, an English fragment that maps to the logical language is formulated in an extended categorial grammar.

In a running example, a robot walks through a string of characters with a sequence of turns and steps, and picks up information by looking at the character in front of it. A world state is a string such as $>+b._-a_-t_-$, where the letter string is bat and the character $>$ represents the robot facing right at the start of the string. We conceive of this world as resulting from the robot starting in the configuration $<-b._-a_-t_-$, then turning and looking at the letter in front. In this world, the extensional sentence (1a) is true. The intensional sentence (1b) is false, because world $>+b._-a_-b_-$ is an epistemic alternative for the robot, and in that word the complement sentence (2c) is false.

(1) a. A B precedes an A that is adjacent to a T.
     b. He knows that there is a T in position three.
     c. There is a T in position three.

A semantics for English sentences will be obtained by parsing sentences with a categorial grammar, to assign the logical forms (2a,b) for (1a,b). Then in the finite state calculus, a set of strings as represented by a finite state machine is computed for each LF. This is a model-theoretic propositional content for the sentence or formula. Finally, truth values in particular worlds are found by checking membership in the propositions.

(2) a. *Indef(Let(t), Indef(Intersect(Let(a), Bind(Trace(Indef(Let(b), Pre)))), Adj))*
     b. *Kt(Indef(Let(a), Indef(Pos(3), In)))*

The paper is organized like this. Section 2 presents a statement of Hintikka semantics for intensional complements in the finite state framework. Section 3 looks at sub-clausal compositional semantics, using an encoding of discourse referents in strings. Section 4 presents the syntax-semantics interface, based on a categorial grammar. Section 5 extends the semantics to question complements, using partition semantics for questions. Section 6 describes the implementation. Section 7 comments on applications and related work.

2 Intensional complementation

A regular Kripke frame is a tuple $\langle \Sigma, W, R \rangle$, where Σ is a finite alphabet, W is a regular subset of Σ^*, and R is a regular relation on W. This is an ordinary Kripke frame, where the set of worlds W is a regular set of strings, and the accessibility relation R is a regular relation. Suppose we are given the semantic value of the complement clause ϕ in (3a) as a regular subset of W, and want to define the semantic value of the whole sentence as a set of strings. Or for the LF language, we are given the semantic value (3b) and want to define (3c).

(3) a. He knows that ϕ.
    b. $[\![\phi]\!]$, a regular subset of W
    c. $[\![K(\phi)]\!]$, a regular subset of W

Hintikka semantics for intensional complementation holds $K(\phi)$ to be true in w if and only if ϕ is true in every world v that is an alternative in w. This is stated using world quantification in (4). We want an equivalent semantics in the finite state calculus, which is an algebra of regular sets of strings and regular relations on strings, with operations including Boolean operations, composition of relations, Kleene closure, domain and co-domain of relations, and restriction of relations to domains and co-domains.[1] (5) defines $K(\phi)$ using set difference $(X - Y)$, domain of a relation $(Do(R))$, and restriction of a relation R to a codomain X $(R \circ X)$. It subtracts from W those worlds that are R-related to a world where ϕ is false. The latter is enforced by restricting R to the codomain $W - [\![\phi]\!]$.

(4) $[\![K(\phi)]\!] = \{w | \forall v. R(w, v) \to [\![\phi]\!](v)\}$

(5) $[\![K(\phi)]\!] = W - Do(R \circ (W - [\![\phi]\!]))$

In the running example, R is a knowledge modality, so it should be an equivalence relation. Beyond this, it should tie in a particular way to the development of world states. As the robot acts, it never loses information. Second, it picks up information by knowing how it acts, and by looking at the letter in front of it. This provides for a way of encoding the epistemic state of the robot in the world string. To capture the epistemic state of the robot, all that matters is where the robot is, how it is oriented, what letters the robot has looked at. In a world state like >+b._-a_-t_, plus characters + precede the letters that the robot has looked at, and minus characters – precede the characters that it has not looked at. We assume the initial state for any world-time line has only minus marks, indicating that the robot has no a-priori knowledge about the letter sequence in its world.

To develop the running example, define the set of worlds W by the sequence of definitions in (6). A world is a character sequence with CVC shape, where C is either t or b, and V is either a or e. Each letter is preceded by a sign + or –, indicating whether the robot has looked at that letter. Finally each plus/minus sign is preceded by a slot for the agent. This is a character position containing either < (robot facing left), > (robot facing right), or _ (no robot). A character position of this same shape also finishes the string. The conjunct $[\cdot * A_1 \cdot *]$ in the definition of W at the bottom in (6) ensures that a world string contains at least one robot. The center dot is a variable over all characters, and the star is asteration (Kleene star). The subtracted term $[\cdot * A_1 \cdot * A_1 \cdot *]$ ensures that a world string does not contain two robots. The syntax maps directly to the Fst language that is implemented in the Xfst and Foma interpreter-compilers (Beesley and Karttunen, 2003; Hulden, 2009). See the code and replication material Rooth (2017a,b).

---

[1] We assume the finite state calculus that is implemented in Xfst and Foma (Beesley and Karttunen, 2003; Hulden, 2009). Function definitions in Xfst are described in Karttunen (2010). For definition (5), an algebra is needed with Boolean set operations, domain for relations, and restriction of a relation to a co-domain. Later parts of the paper use relation composition.

$$(6) \quad \begin{aligned} C &:= & t \mid b \\ V &:= & a \mid e \\ S &:= & + \mid - \\ A_1 &:= & < \mid > \\ A_2 &:= & < \mid > \mid \_ \\ W &:= & [[A_2SC][A_2SV][A_2SC]A_2] \wedge [\cdot * A_1 \cdot *] - [\cdot * A_1 \cdot * A_1 \cdot *] \end{aligned}$$

R in the running example is defined by making substitutions for letters that are marked by a minus sign, i.e. letters in positions that the robot has not seen. Letters that the robot has seen remain constant when moving to an epistemic alternative. In (7), substitution is stated using the rewrite notation of the finite state calculus, which is a defined notation for relations that make substitutions in specified contexts (Kaplan and Kay, 1994; Kempe and Karttunen, 1996). Rewriting in the finite state calculus is inspired by the rewrite notation of classical generative phonology (Chomsky and Halle, 1968).

$$(7) \quad \begin{aligned} R_c &:= & C \to C \parallel -\underline{} \\ R_v &:= & V \to V \parallel -\underline{} \\ R &:= & W \circ R_c \circ R_v \circ W \end{aligned}$$

That R is an equivalence relation can be shown by reasoning about the definition, and can also be checked computationally for equal-length relations. (8) defines properties characterizing a relation as being reflexive, symmetric, and transitive, with equivalence relations satisfying all of these. Such properties in the finite state calculus are modeled as functions that map to truth values, where *False* is the empty set and *True* is the unit set of the empty string. The definitions use a conditional in the finite state calculus, which is defined in (9). R being an equivalence relation is checked by evaluating $Eqv(R)$.

$$(8) \quad \begin{aligned} \mathit{Rfl}(U) &:= & \mathit{If}(\mathit{Id}_W - (U \wedge \mathit{Id}_W), \mathit{False}, \mathit{True}) \\ \mathit{Sym}(U) &:= & \mathit{If}(U - \mathit{Conv}(U), \mathit{False}, \mathit{True}) \\ \mathit{Trs}(U) &:= & \mathit{If}((U \circ U) - U, \mathit{False}, \mathit{True}) \\ \mathit{Eqv}(U) &:= & \mathit{If}(\mathit{Rfl}(U) \wedge \mathit{Sym}(U) \wedge \mathit{Eqv}(U), \mathit{True}, \mathit{False}) \end{aligned}$$

$$(9) \quad \mathit{If}(X,Y,Z) \quad := \quad (Z - Co(X \circ (\cdot * \times \cdot *))) \mid (Y \wedge Co(X \circ (\cdot * \times \cdot *)))$$

The above definition of R leaves the robot in the same place and orientation, and keeps the length of the world constant. So in this example, the robot has a priori knowledge of its location and of the size of the world. Nothing about this is essential: the general account assumes nothing about W and R, beyond being a regular set and a regular relation on it. This is as usual in Kripke semantics. It is possible for W to be countably infinite—the replication supplement includes a version of the running example where the size of worlds in not bounded.

3   Compositional semantics

Type theoretic approaches to compositional semantics use functions to express lexical content and the semantics of complex phrases (Montague, 1973; Janssen, 1996). While function definitions are used in the finite state calculus in the way illustrated above, functions are not first class objects that themselves can be the arguments of functions or algebraic operators—really there are only one or two types in the finite state calculus. Further, the modal space of world-strings as presented above does not represent individuals. What then is the interpretation of the constants *Adj* (for adjacent) and *Pre* (for precede)? The approach taken here is to include in the model specification a set W_1, which we think of as a space of worlds with a distinguished individual. Similarly for a set W_2, a space of worlds with two distinguished individuals. In the running example, an element of W_1 is a string with an index 1 inserted after some letter, interpreted as a discourse referent for that token letter. So <+b._-a1_-b_ is the world <+b._-a_-b_ with a discourse referent for the middle letter. Using terminology from dynamic semantics, in the extended world <+b._-a1-b_, the token letter a is the center (e.g. Bittner 2003). <+b._-a1_-b2_ is the world <+b._-a_-b_ with a center for the second letter, and a secondary center for the third letter. In the running example, *Fol* is a subset of W_2 that is used as an interpretation for *follow*. The object is encoded as the center, and the subject as the secondary center (or pericenter). *Fol* includes the two-centered worlds listed in (10).

```
(10)  _+b1_-a2>-t._   _-t1<-e2_+b._   _-b._-a1_-b2>   _-t._-a1_+t2>
      _-t1_-e2>-t._   _-t1<-e2_+b._   _+t._+a1>+t2_   _-b1_-e2>-b._
      _-t1_-e2<+t._   _-b._-a1_-t2>   _-b._+e1_+b2<   _+b1>+a2_+b._
      _+b1<+a2_+b._   _+t._+e1<+t2_   _+t._-e1>+t2_   _-t1_-a2>-t._
```

The function *Indef*(X, Y) seen in (11) is used as a co-predicator on the center. It intersects its arguments, and then pops the center, with the input pericenter if present being the output center. (11a) is a subset of W that includes the worlds listed in (11b). *Indef* is used as a predicator both for the object and the subject.

(11) a. *Indef*(*Let*(*t*), *Indef*(*Let*(*a*), *Fol*))

```
    b. >+b._+a._+t._   _-t.<+a._+t._   <-t._-a._-t._
       >+t._-a._-t._   _+t._-a.<+t._   <+b._+a._-t._
       _+b.<-a._-t._   _+b._-a.<-t._   >+b._+a._+t._
```

Traces are treated along the same lines, using the marker 0 for traces. The operator *Trace* maps the center to the trace center, and maps the pericenter (if present) to the center. *Trace*(*Fol*) conceptually has a trace in the object position of *follow*, and *Trace*(*Indef*(*Let*(*a*), *Fol*)) conceptually has a trace in the subject position of *follow*. (12) and (13) show samples of these propositions.

(12) a. *Trace*(*Fol*)

```
    b. _-b0_+a1_+b.<   _+t._+e0_+t1>
       <+t0_-e1_-t._   _-b._+e0<-b1_
```

(13) a. *Trace*(*Indef*(*Let*(*a*), *Fol*))

```
    b. _+b._-a.<+t0_   _-t._+a.<-t0_
       <-b._-a._+b0_   _-t._-a._-t0>
```

The *Bind* operator seen in (2a) maps the trace center to the ordinary center, converting a phrase with a free trace to a property of individuals. The *Intersect* operator intersects two properties of individuals, and is used to combine a noun with a relative clause.

See the end of Section 6 for a complex LF that includes most of the operators.

4 Syntax-semantics interface

The material from Section 2 and Section 3 is concerned with a formal language with terms such as $K(\textit{Indef}(\textit{Let}(a), \textit{Indef}(\textit{Let}(t), \textit{Fol})))$. The terms get a model-theoretic interpretation as regular sets of strings. To tie this in with natural language, lexical items, phrases, and sentences of the natural language should be mapped to the formal language. Here this is accomplished with a categorial grammar. (15) lists some simple lexical entries, with word forms in in the first column, categorial types in the second column, and logical terms in the third. $e\backslash_N t$ is the categorial type for a noun. It is a multimodal slash type that is not active as a function in the grammar—it enters into a derivation only as an argument of a determiner. In type theoretic semantics, terms of syntactic category $e\backslash_N t$ have semantic type et, the type of functions from individuals to truth values. We keep the syntactic category, but interpret phrases of that category as subsets of W_1. $(e\backslash t)/e$ is the categorial type label for a transitive verb. In type theoretic semantics, this corresponds to type eet, while in the present system, it is semantically a subset of W_2.[2]

---

[2]The type labels *et* and *eet* are written in the notation from Link (1979), with right association and without commas or brackets.

(14) A $e\backslash_N t$ *Let(a)*
      B $e\backslash_N t$ *Let(b)*
      follow $(e\backslash t)/e$ *Fol*

The indefinite determiner is in the lexicon twice, once for use with an object, and once for use with a subject. In each case the semantics uses *Indef*, the co-predication operator on the center. See (15).

(15) a $(((e\backslash t)/e)\backslash(e\backslash t))/(e\backslash_N t)$ $\lambda X \lambda Y.Indef(X,Y)$ object determiner
      a $(t/(e\backslash t))/(e\backslash_N t)$ $\lambda X \lambda Y.Indef(X,Y)$ subject determiner

(16) is the first part of the analysis of traces and binding. The syntactic category of a clause with a bound trace is $e\backslash_T t$. This is again a nominally functional slash type that is not active as a function in the grammar. The relative morpheme *that* combines with $e\backslash_T t$ on the right, and a noun $e\backslash_N t$ on the left, to form a noun $e\backslash_N t$.

(16)   that $((e\backslash_N t)\backslash(e\backslash_N t))/(e\backslash_T t)$ $\lambda X \lambda Y.Intersect(X,Y)$

(17b) is the target LF for the relative clause (17a), with an object trace. The object trace should trigger the operator in the term *Trace(Fol)*, converting the center to a trace center. At the level of the relative clause, the *Bind* operator should convert the trace center back into an ordinary center. Thus the trace has both a local semantic effect, and an effect at its scope level. This is enforced in Barker and Shan's continuation scope calculus, using the categorial type $(e\backslash_T t)/\!\!/(((e\backslash t)/e)\backslash(e\backslash t)\backslash\!\backslash t)$. This indicates a local type $((e\backslash t)/e)\backslash(e\backslash t)$, which combines with a transitive verb (type $(e\backslash t)/e$) to form a predicate (type $e\backslash t$). Second there is a scope shell $(e\backslash_T t)/\!\!/(-\backslash\!\backslash t)$. This indicates that the trace takes scope at the clausal type t to form the bound-trace category $e\backslash_T t$. The first line in (18) is the lexical entry for the object trace. The semantics $\lambda k.Bind(k(Trace))$ has the effect of applying *Trace* to the verb meaning *Fol* downstairs, because the continuation variable k is applied to *Trace* in the term $k(Trace)$. The second line in (18) is the analogous lexical entry for a subject trace. The traces are in the lexicon with the spelling "e".

(17) a. a B follows e $(e\backslash_T t)$
     b. *Bind(Indef(Let(b), Trace(Fol)))*

(18) e $e\backslash_T t/\!\!/(((e\backslash t)/e)\backslash(e\backslash t)\backslash\!\backslash t)$ $\lambda k.Bind(k(Trace))$ object trace
      e $e\backslash_T t/\!\!/((t/(e\backslash t))\backslash\!\backslash t)$ $\lambda k.Bind(k(Trace))$ subject trace

(19) a. e follows a B, $(e\backslash_T t)$
     b. *Bind(Trace(Indef(Let(b), Fol)))*

Some observations are in order about the system of categories and the semantics. Familiar syntactic categorial symbols are used, such as $(e\backslash t)/e$ for a transitive verb. However, the corresponding semantics is not ultimately used as a function of type *eet*, contrary to what happens in type-theoretic interpretation using function application. The reason is that a term of the form $Fol(x)$ is not a term of the target logical language. The semantic terms in (15), (16), and (18) use lambda. These terms are meaningful in an extension using variables and binding by lambda of the logical language described in Section 2 and Section 3. However, since it is the basic logical language that is targeted, it is important that the lambdas are eliminated by beta reduction in complete derivations.

5 Question complements

In partition semantics for questions, a question complement contributes an equivalence relation on worlds (Groenendijk and Stokhof, 1984). Suppose ϕ is a question complement associated with the relation Q. Informally, w and w' are related by Q if and only if the complete answer to the question is the same in w and w'. Here we will use regular relations between worlds as question denotations.

In a whether-question such as the complement in (20a), there are two cells in the partition associated with the equivalence relation, one consisting of worlds where the clause (20b) is true, and the other consisting of worlds where the clause is false. The corresponding relation is defined in the finite state calculus using Cartesian product and union, see (21).

(20) a. He knows whether there is a B in three.

     b. There is a B in three.

(21) $Whether(X) := \quad (X \times X) \,|\, ((W - X) \times (W - X))$

The other half of the problem is to define a semantics for question-embedding *know* in terms of the epistemic accessibility relation R, and a relation between worlds contributed by a wh-complement. The robot knows whether Q if his knowledge as represented by R resolves the question encoded by Q. This is true in a given world w when the set of worlds that are R-related to w are all within a single cell of the partition corresponding to Q. Let $\bar{Q}$ be the complement of Q, which relates worlds that are in different cells of the partition. Let Id_W be the identity relation on worlds. The relation $R \circ \bar{Q} \circ R^{-1}$ relates pairs (w, w') such that one can start at w, jump to an epistemic alternative to w in some cell of the partition, jump using $\bar{Q}$ to a different cell of the partition, then jump back to w' using R^{-1}, the inverse of R. Intersecting with Id_w gives us the set of pairs (w, w) such that w is related by R to worlds in different cells of the question partition. This characterizes worlds w where the robot does not know whether Q. The set of worlds where the robot knows whether Q is the complement. This leads to the definition (23) for question-embedding *know*.[3]

(22) $Kw(Q) := \quad W - Do((R \circ (W \times W - Q) \circ R^{-1}) \wedge Id_W)$

Unfortunately, the relative complement $(Q' - Q)$ is not defined in the finite state calculus for arbitrary relations Q' and Q, only for equal-length relations. These are relations where any pair of related strings have the same length. The running example has worlds with fixed length, so all relations between worlds are length-preserving. But since we want to include the possibility of countably infinite sets of worlds, it is not desirable to rely on worlds having a fixed string length.[4] We are better off if the question complement contributes the complement relation to begin with. This is easy enough for whether-complements. See the revised definitions (23) and (24).

(23) $Whether_2(X) \quad := \quad (X \times (W - X)) \,|\, ((W - X) \times X)$

(24) $Kw_2(Q) \quad := \quad W - Do((R \circ Q \circ R^{-1}) \wedge Id_W)$

We would also like to interpret embedded constituent questions such as the ones in (25). This is not in the current system.

(25) a. He knows what letter is in position three.

     b. He knows what vowels follow what consonants.

---

[3] If R is assumed to be symmetric, R can be substituted for R^{-1}. In the finite state calculus as implemented in Xfst and Foma, the identity relation on a given set is not distinguished from the set, so W can be substituted for Id_W. For the same reason, the domain operator Do can be dropped.

[4] Possibly the problem can be partially finessed, by including for a world w of basic length n also a world of lenght $n + m$ that is obtained from w by adding m dummy characters.

6 Computational implementation

The proposal is implemented using a parser for categorial grammar, and a toolkit for the finite state calculus. The parser is Barker and Shan's parser for continuation categorial grammar (Barker and Shan, 2005). The grammar is a lexicon given in Scheme-Lisp format, consisting of a list of tuples of word forms, syntactic category symbols, and semantic terms. (26) is the lexical entry that corresponds to the first version of the indefinite article in (15). This lexical entry and the rest are isomorphic to what was seen in Section 4.

(26)   `(("a" (((e \ t) / e) \ (e \ t)) / (e \N t))) (^ P (^ f (Indef P f))))`

A sentence is presented to the parser with a Scheme parse command (see (27b). If the parser finds a derivation, an LF is printed in Lisp format, see (27c). This is converted to the logical language using a Lex program, by moving parentheses and inserting commas, to obtain (27d). Now this formula is read as a term denoting a regular set into an interpreter for the finite state calculus, in an environment where functions have been defined in the way characterized in Sections 2 and 3. Xfst or Foma is used as the interpreter for the finite state calculus. To illustrate the proposition that results, a random set of elements of the proposition are printed. Or one can test entailment or equivalence between propositions contributed by two sentences. (28) shows the procedure for printing a sample of the proposition in Xfst. (In the code the letter nouns are written "ay" and "bee", rather than "A" and "B".)

(27) a. a ay that a bee follow e follow a tee

     b. `(parse '(a ay that a bee follow e follow a tee))`

     c. `(Indef (Intersect (Bind (Indef (Let b) (Trace Fol))) (Let a))`
           `(Indef (Let t) Fol))`

     d. *Indef(Intersect(Bind(Indef(Let(b), Trace(Fol))), Let(a)), Indef(Let(t), Fol))*

(28)   `regex Pr(Indef(Intersect(Bind(Indef(Let(b),Trace(Fol))),Let(a)),`
                    `Indef(Let(t),Fol)));`
     `xfst[17]: print random-words`
     `_+t._-a._-b.<`
     `_-t._+a.>+b._`
     `_+t._-a.>-b._`
     `_-t._-a._-b.>`
     `_-t._+a.<+b._`
     `...`

These steps are tied together using file interfaces. With the input sentence in an input file `s1.snt`, parsing can be triggered from a make file, with the LF written into a file `s1.lf`, and the sample written into a file `s1.wld`. See the examples in the replication supplement.

In the implementation of the running example, a term is actually not interpreted directly as a set of strings like the ones seen at the end in (28), and elsewhere in the paper. Instead, a world is a 15-element bit vector that can be printed to a world string of the other kind, see (29.)[5] This explains the presence of the operator `Pr` in (28). The motivation for this is two-fold. First, it results in more structured definition of the modal space, based on the primitive propositions listed in (30).

(29)   `regex Pr({011110110000000});`
     `xfst[19]: print words`
     `>+t._+a._-b._`

---

[5]Curly brackets in {011110110000000} explode the contained string into the character sequence 0 1 1 1 1 0 1 1 0 0 0 0 0 0 0.

(30) A b vs. t is in letter position 1
      B a vs. e is in letter position 2
      C b vs. t is in letter position 3
      D letter position 1 has been seen
      E letter position 2 has been seen
      F letter position 3 has been seen
      G robot is in position 1 or 2 (and not 3 or 4)
      H robot is in position 1 or 3 (and not 2 or 4)
      I robot is facing left
      J dref2 in 2 or 3 (vs dref2 in 1 or no dref2)
      K dref2 in 1 or 3 (vs dref2 in 2 or no dref2)
      L dref1 in 2 or 3 (vs dref1 in 1 or no dref1)
      M dref1 in 1 or 3 (vs dref1 in 2 or no dref1)
      N trace dref in 2 or 3 (vs trace dref in 1 or no trace dref)
      O trace dref in 1 or 3 (vs trace dref in 2 or no trace dref)

A second motivation has to do with a goal of incorporating actions and the temporal development of worlds in the modal space. The idea is to assume four primitive actions Step (the robot stepping forward), Turn (the robot turning), Look (the robot picking up information from the position in front of it) and R. The latter is a pseudo-action of non-deterministically moving to an epistemic alternative. In a development of the action logic in Kleene algebra with tests (Kozen, 1997), the Kleene elements are *Step*, *Turn*, *Look*, and the propositions in (30) are generators for the Boolean algebra of tests. A world at a time is a sequence of Kleene elements (actions), with interleaved stative propositions. Models with this structure are generally comparable to the action and epistemic models that figure in research on situation calculus (Moore, 1984; Reiter, 2001; Scherl and Levesque, 2003; Levesque and Lakemeyer, 2008). They have the specific structure of trace models for Kleene algebra with tests. We have developed a partial axiomatization of the logic based on an implementation of KAT with hypotheses (Pous, 2015). This is strictly work in progress, but is relevant here as motivation for the definition of the finite state semantics using generating propositions.

Figure 1 and (31) give an abbreviated derivation for the complex sentence (31a). In the figure, only phrases that have an interpretation in the finite state calculus are listed. A sample is included of four words from the proposition that corresponds to the LF in the example model. The proposition corresponding to (31a) and (31b) is a set of eight worlds, which are listed in (31c). They differ just in the position and orientation of the robot, giving 4×2 worlds. Each of them has the letter sequence t a b, and in each of them the robot has seen each letter. Moreover, restricted to this set, R is the identity relation. In other words, in the example model, (31b) is true only when the robot has identified its world.

(31) a. He know that a tee adjacent a ay that follow a bee.

    b. $K(Indef(Let(t), Indef(Intersect(Bind(Trace(Indef(Let(b), Fol))), Let(a)), Adj)))$

    c.
```
<+t._+a._+b._
>+t._+a._+b._
_+t._+a.<+b._
_+t._+a.>+b._
_+t._+a._+b.<
_+t._+a._+b.>
_+t.>+a._+b._
_+t.<+a._+b._
```

he know that a tee adjacent a ay that follow a bee , t
$K(\mathit{Indef}(\mathit{Let}(t), \mathit{Indef}(\mathit{Intersect}(\mathit{Bind}(\mathit{Trace}(\mathit{Indef}(\mathit{Let}(b), \mathit{Fol})))), \mathit{Let}(a)), \mathit{Adj})))$

a tee adjacent a ay that follow a bee , t
$\mathit{Indef}(\mathit{Let}(t), \mathit{Indef}(\mathit{Intersect}(\mathit{Bind}(\mathit{Trace}(\mathit{Indef}(\mathit{Let}(b), \mathit{Fol})))), \mathit{Let}(a)), \mathit{Adj}))$

```
<+b._+a._-t._
_-b._-a._-t.>
_-b._-a.<-t._
_-b._+a.<+t._
```

tee, $e\backslash_N t$
$\mathit{Let}(t)$

```
>-t1_+a._-t._
_+t12_+e0<+b._
_-t._+a.<+t012_
_-b2_+a0>+t1_
```

adjacent a ay that e follow a bee,$(e\backslash t)$
$\mathit{Indef}(\mathit{Intersect}(\mathit{Bind}(\mathit{Trace}(\mathit{Indef}(\mathit{Let}(b), \mathit{Fol})))), \mathit{Let}(a)), \mathit{Adj})$

```
_-b1>-a._+t._
<-b._+a._+b1_
_-b1_-a._+t.>
<-b1_-a._-b._
```

adjacent,$(e\backslash t)/e$
Adj

```
_-b1>+a2_-b._
_-b.>-e2_-b1_
_-t._-e2>+t1_
_-t2>+a1_+b._
```

ay that e follow a bee, $e\backslash_N t$
$\mathit{Intersect}(\mathit{Bind}(\mathit{Trace}(\mathit{Indef}(\mathit{Let}(b), \mathit{Fol})))), \mathit{Let}(a))$

```
_+b.<-e1_-b._
_+b.<-e1_-t._
_+b.>+a1_+b._
<-b._-e1_+t._
```

ay, $e\backslash_N t$
$\mathit{Let}(a)$

```
_-b._+a1>+b._
_+b._+a1_+t.>
_-b._-e1_+b.>
_+b.>-a1_-b._
```

e follow a bee, $e\backslash_T t$
$\mathit{Bind}(\mathit{Trace}(\mathit{Indef}(\mathit{Let}(b), \mathit{Fol})))$

follow a bee,$e\backslash t$
$\mathit{Indef}(\mathit{Let}(b), \mathit{Fol})$

follow,$(e\backslash t)/e$
Fol

bee, $e\backslash_N t$
$\mathit{Let}(b)$

Figure 1: Abbreviated derivation for a complex sentence, including word sequence, syntactic category, LF, and a sample of four words from the proposition.

7 Discussion

The material presented here has been used in a second semester graduate course in linguistic semantics. The course adds computational topics and methodology to the curriculum on compositional semantics and possible worlds semantics. This is done in part by using parsers and derivation calculators, including a categorial-grammar parser (Barker and Shan, 2005), and a derivation calculator that interprets logical forms in a typed intensional logic (Champollion et al., 2013). Finite state intensional semantics adds the possibility of actually computing propositional denotations as sets of worlds, rather than just computing logical terms associated with phrases. In addition to the material on intensional complementation and questions, the course included computing with premise semantics for modality (Kratzer, 1981; Lewis, 1981), in a framework where the ordering propositions are a finite set of regular propositions.

Research and publications in linguistic semantics frequently refer to toy possible worlds models with a handful of worlds, in order to illustrate and test ideas. The methods introduced here allow this to be scaled up, even to countable sets of worlds, and to avoid error, by virtue of the formal methodology. And they start to bridge ideas about model structures and computation between possible worlds semantics as applied in natural language semantics, and the research program of cognitive robotics, where constructed possible worlds models are used to reason about action, planning, modality, and knowledge (Moore, 1984; Reiter, 2001; Scherl and Levesque, 2003; Levesque and Lakemeyer, 2008).

Tim Fernando and Lauri Carlson have developed approaches to natural language semantics using finite state methods (Fernando, 2007; Carlson, 2009). They mostly focus on tense, aspect, and the structure of events, rather than as here the syntax-semantics interface for intensional complementation. Fernando discusses intensions in his system of finite state semantics in Fernando (2017). Comparing and integrating the approaches is an important topic for future work.

The epistemic model in the running example is constructed to reflect certain intuitions, but this is done in an ad-hoc way. The topic of constructing epistemic action models in a systematic way was approached by Baltag et al. (1999) using action alternatives, and a large body of research has followed. See Van Ditmarsch et al. (2007) and Van Ditmarsch et al. (2015) for surveys. It is hoped that connecting with this literature and methodology will lead to richer examples, and an expansion in the set of embedding verbs that are can be covered.

Systems of quantified modal logic and intensional typed interpretation use models built from a set of worlds and a set of individuals (Lewis, 1968; Gallin, 2011). Where are the individuals in the current system? In Section 3, the strings in W_1 were described as worlds with a distinguished individual, or worlds with a discourse referent marking an individual. It is possible to directly view W_1 as the set of individuals. In model structures as defined by Lewis, individuals are not shared between possible worlds, and each individual can be mapped to its world. This suggests using model frames $\langle \Sigma_w, \Sigma_D, W, D, \pi, R, C \rangle$, where Σ_w and Σ_D are alphabets, W is a regular subset of Σ_W^*, D is a regular subset of Σ_D^*, π is a functional regular relation between D and W, and R is a regular relation on W, and C is a regular relation on Σ_D. π maps individuals to their worlds. C is the cross-world counterpart relation. It is hoped that the addition of C will make it possible to include de re LFs with *know* in the analysis. Another part of the analysis of *know* is presupposition. Collard (2016) introduced a version of the finite state system explained here that uses three-valued evaluations, in order to model presupposition.

Acknowledgments

Thanks to Jacob Collard, Todd Snider, Ede Zimmermann, and three IWCS 2017 reviewers for comments. Prior to the conference, this matierial was presented at the Goethe University/Frankfurt in July, 2017. Thanks to the audience for their comments and reactions.

References

Baltag, A., L. S. Moss, and S. Solecki (1999). The logic of public announcements, common knowledge, and private suspicions.

Barker, C. and C.-c. Shan (2005). Reference parser for explaining crossover and superiority as left-to-right evaluation. URL `semanticsarchive.net/Archive/TI1M2UxN`.

Beesley, K. R. and L. Karttunen (2003). *Finite State Forphology*. Center for the Study of Language and Inf.

Bittner, M. (2003). Word order and incremental update. In *Proceedings from the Annual Meeting of the Chicago Linguistic Society*, Volume 39, pp. 634–664. Chicago Linguistic Society.

Carlson, L. (2009). *Tense, Mood, Aspect, Diathesis*. Book ms., University of Helsinki.

Champollion, L., J. Tauberer, M. Romero, and D. Bumford (2013). The lambda calculator for students and teachers of natural language semantics. URL `github.com/nyusemantics/ LambdaCalculator`.

Chomsky, N. and M. Halle (1968). *The Sound Pattern of English*. ERIC.

Collard, J. (2016). A finite state model of semantics with presupposition. Manuscript, Cornell University.

Fernando, T. (2007). Observing events and situations in time. *Linguistics and Philosophy 30*(5), 527–550.

Fernando, T. (2017). Intensions, types and finite-state truthmaking. In *Modern Perspectives in Type-Theoretical Semantics*, pp. 223–243. Springer.

Gallin, D. (2011). *Intensional and Higher-order Modal logic: With applications to Montague semantics*, Volume 19. Elsevier.

Groenendijk, J. and M. Stokhof (1984). *On the Semantics of Questions and the Pragmatics of Answers*. Foris.

Hulden, M. (2009). Foma: a finite-state compiler and library. In *Proceedings of the 12th Conference of the European Chapter of the Association for Computational Linguistics: Demonstrations Session*, pp. 29–32. Association for Computational Linguistics.

Janssen, T. (1996). *Compositionality*. Institute for Logic, Language and Computation (ILLC), University of Amsterdam.

Kaplan, R. M. and M. Kay (1994). Regular models of phonological rule systems. *Computational linguistics 20*(3), 331–378.

Karttunen, L. (2010). Update on finite state morphology tools. *Ms., Palo Alto Research Center*.

Kempe, A. and L. Karttunen (1996). Parallel replacement in finite state calculus. In *Proceedings of the 16th conference on Computational linguistics-Volume 2*, pp. 622–627. Association for Computational Linguistics.

Kozen, D. (1997). Kleene algebra with tests. *ACM Transactions on Programming Languages and Systems (TOPLAS) 19*(3), 427–443.

Kratzer, A. (1981). The notional category of modality. *Words, worlds, and contexts*, 38–74.

Levesque, H. and G. Lakemeyer (2008). Cognitive robotics. *Foundations of artificial intelligence 3*, 869–886.

Lewis, D. (1981). Ordering semantics and premise semantics for counterfactuals. *Journal of philosophical logic 10*(2), 217–234.

Lewis, D. K. (1968). Counterpart theory and quantified modal logic. *the Journal of Philosophy 65*(5), 113–126.

Link, G. (1979). *Montague-Grammatik Die Logische Grundlagen.*

Montague, R. (1973). The proper treatment of quantification in ordinary english. In *Approaches to Natural Language*, pp. 221–242. Springer.

Moore, R. C. (1984). A formal theory of knowledge and action. Technical report, DTIC Document.

Pous, D. (2015). Symbolic algorithms for language equivalence and kleene algebra with tests. In *ACM SIGPLAN Notices*, Volume 50, pp. 357–368. ACM.

Reiter, R. (2001). *Knowledge in Action: Logical foundations for specifying and implementing dynamical systems.* MIT press.

Rooth, M. (2017a). Finite-state-intensionality. URL `github.com/MatsRooth/Finite-state-intensionality`.

Rooth, M. (2017b). Replication data for: Finite state intensional semantics. Harvard Dataverse Network. DOI `10.7910/DVN/EV6KLF` URL `http://dx.doi.org/10.7910/DVN/EV6KLF`.

Scherl, R. B. and H. J. Levesque (2003). Knowledge, action, and the frame problem. *Artificial Intelligence 144*(1-2), 1–39.

Van Ditmarsch, H., J. Y. Halpern, W. van der Hoek, and B. P. Kooi (2015). *Handbook of Epistemic Logic.* College Publications.

Van Ditmarsch, H., W. van Der Hoek, and B. Kooi (2007). *Dynamic Epistemic Logic*, Volume 337. Springer Science & Business Media.

When Conditional Logic met Connexive Logic

Mathieu Vidal

CHArt (PARIS), Université Paris 8, France
Univ. Grenoble Alpes, PPL, F-38000 Grenoble
vidal.math@yahoo.com

Abstract

Conditional logic and connexive logic are two theories whose goal is the correct formalization of the way conditionals (i.e. sentences of form *if A, C*) are used in natural language. However, both approaches are never combined in the literature. I present here the first formal system which allows modeling the ideas behind these two approaches in a unique framework. Furthermore, the resulting system allows explaining the different ways conditionals are negated in natural language.
Keywords: Conditional Logic, Connexive Logic, If, Negation

1 Introduction

It is generally agreed that the material conditional from classical logic does not correctly represent the conditional sentences from natural language. First, some critics argue that it validates too many schemas of reasoning that are intuitively incorrect. The first cases identified were called "paradoxes of material implication" and this list of defective inferences increased when classical logic was used to model natural language. In particular, counterexamples to the patterns of inference called *strengthening of the antecedent* "$A \to C \vDash (A \wedge B) \to C$", *contraposition* "$A \to C \vDash \neg C \to \neg A$" and *transitivity* "$A \to B, B \to C \vDash A \to C$" were found in English and the new systems that were devised to get rid of theses schemas were called *conditional logics* (Adams, 1965; Stalnaker, 1968; Lewis, 1973).

Second, other critics argue that some patterns of inference which are intuitively correct are not valid with the material conditional. New valid schemas should therefore be added. However, as classical logic is Post complete, it has no consistent proper extension. The new logics which are needed to solve this issue must therefore be non-classical. In particular, this argumentation is used by some logicians which consider that the notion of connection must be at the center of an analysis of conditionals and this trend is called *connexive logic*.

By taking into account these two criticisms, the conclusion is that the conditional theorems of classical logic constitute neither a superset nor a subset of the intuitively correct conditional inferences of natural language (Figure 1).

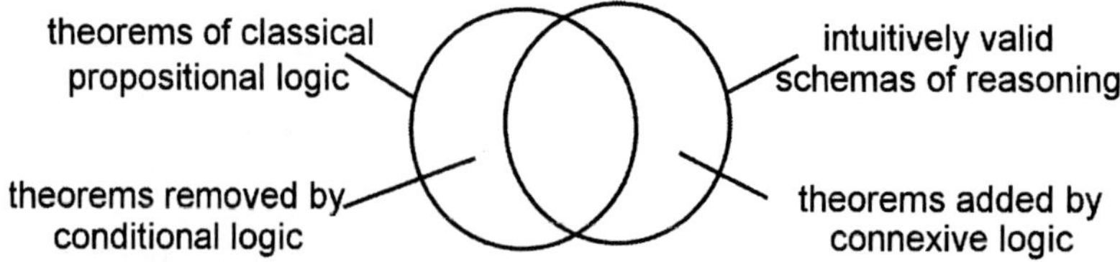

Figure 1: The partial overlapping of classical logic with intuitively correct reasoning schemas

This article is the first attempt to construct a logic which is both conditional and connexive, in order to model as closely as possible the use of conditional sentences in natural language. In section 2, a general solution validating the connexive schemas is presented. In section 3, this solution is applied to a particular conditional logic and it is formally shown that this new system validates the connexive

principles. In section 4, the utility of this approach is illustrated through an explanation of the two main
ways conditionals are negated in natural language. In section 5, a least drastic version of this approach
is presented.

2   A Solution to Connexive Principles

In connexive logic, some schemas repelled from classical logic are deemed valid. The exact list of
schemas can vary and I will here consider only the most usual. These six patterns are called AT and AT',
AB and AB', and BO and BO', in reference respectively to Aristotle, Abelard and Boethius.

$$\textbf{(AT)} \ \models \neg(\neg p \to p)$$

$$\textbf{(AT')} \ \models \neg(p \to \neg p)$$

$$\textbf{(AB)} \ \models \neg[(p \to q) \wedge (\neg p \to q)]$$

$$\textbf{(AB')} \ \models \neg[(p \to q) \wedge (p \to \neg q)]$$

$$\textbf{(BO)} \ p \to q \models \neg(p \to \neg q)$$

$$\textbf{(BO')} \ p \to \neg q \models \neg(p \to q)$$

They can be illustrated with the following examples:

(AT) It is false that if it does not rain, then it rains.

(AT') It is false that if it rains, then it does not rain.

(AB) It is false that both if I trigger the alarm, then it rings and if I do not
trigger the alarm, then it rings.

(AB') It is false that both if I trigger the alarm, then it rings and if I trigger the
alarm, then it does not ring.

(BO) If I trigger the alarm, then it rings. Thus, it is false that if I trigger the
alarm, then it does not ring.

(BO') If I trigger the alarm, then it does not ring. Thus, it is false that if I
trigger the alarm, then it rings.

These six patterns of inference share a common feature: they use only two connectives, the negation
and the conditional. This is why there exists three principal ways to solve this issue. Comparatively to
classical logic, either the conditional (Rahman and Rückert, 2001), the negation (Priest, 1999), (Francez,
2016) or both (MacColl, 1908),(McCall, 1967; Routley, 1978; Wansing, 2005; Pizzi and Williamson,
2005) are modified.

To devise a solution, let us come back to the reasons why some logicians consider these schemas of
reasoning as intuitively convincing. In a funny way, the AT sentences are directly supported not from
Aristotle but from Abelard's following quotation: [1]

> No one doubts that [a statement entailing its negation] is improper and embar-
> rassing (*inconveniens*) since the truth of one of two propositions which divide
> truth [i.e., contradictories] not only does not require the truth of the other but
> rather entirely expels and extinguishes it.

Conversely, the AB sentences seem a direct translation from the following principle expressed in Aristotle's *Prior Analytics* 57b3 (Smith, 1989):

---

[1]This translation is issued from Priest (1999) which also presents interesting historical observations.

> But it is impossible for the same thing to be of necessity both when a certain
> thing is and when that same thing is not (I mean, for example, for B to be large
> of necessity when A is white, and for B to be large of necessity when A is not
> white).

Finally, the BO principles are issued from Boethius' *De Syllogismo Hypothetico* where he defends that the negative of 'if A then B' is 'if A then not B' (Kneale and Kneale, 1962, p.191)

These three justifications turn around the reject of contradictions. In AT principles, a sentence cannot entails its negation. In AB principles, the same sentence cannot be the consequent of two contradictory sentences and the same antecedent cannot lead to two contradictory consequents. The justification for BO principles comes from the direct observation of the way conditionals are usually negated in natural language. Furthermore, if a consequent is obtained from an antecedent, its negation cannot be deduced, following the non-contradiction principle. Hence, the most direct way to interpret connexive principles through the oldest texts which justify their intuitive content is to say that their prime reason is the **rejection of contradictions**. Apart from the fact that it is the clear initial motivation for these three groups of principles, McCall (2012) notices also that it corresponds to the third variety of implication presented by Sextus Empiricus in *Outlines of Pyrrhonism*, in a passage which sums up the different positions hold during Greek Antiquity concerning the conditional:[2]

> And those who introduce connection or coherence say that a conditional holds
> whenever the denial of its consequent is incompatible with its antecedent.

Hence, the root principle behind the connexive conditional is the rejection of contradictions. How is it possible that such repelling which is relatively intuitive is not supported by most modern formal systems? The answer is quite simple. The advent of mathematization in modern logic gave place to sentences that are false in every interpretations. But in natural language, conditionals seldom if ever use contradictions as their components. Connexive principles, well adapted to represent conditional reasoning in our daily life, fell short as soon as contradictions are introduced by the mathematization. Notice also that because connexive principles systematically examine one sentence and its negation, they will also have difficulties to deal with tautologies which are negations of contradictions.

In support of this analysis, we can notice that tautologies and contradictions furnish counterexamples to connexive principles. Let us imagine a talk about the weather here and now. By allowing tautologies and contradictions, we could obtain the following sentences. The two first counterexamples assume the De Morgan's laws.

---

[2]This translation is from (Sanford, 2003).

(1) If it does not rain and it rains then it rains or it does not rain.

(Formal representation) $\neg p \wedge p \to p \vee \neg p$

(Counterexample to AT) $\neg(p \vee \neg p) \to p \vee \neg p$

(Counterexample to AT') $\neg p \wedge p \to \neg(p \wedge \neg p)$

(2) If it rains then it rains or it does not rain; and if it does not rain then it rains or it does not rain.

(Counterexample to AB) $(p \to (p \vee \neg p)) \wedge (\neg p \to (p \vee \neg p))$

(3) If it rains and it does not rain then it rains; and if it rains and it does not rain then it does not rain.

(Counterexample to AB') $((p \wedge \neg p) \to p) \wedge ((p \wedge \neg p) \to \neg p)$

(4) From "If it rains and it does not rain then it rains", we cannot conclude that it is false that "if it rains and it does not rain then it does not rain".

(Counterexample to BO) $(p \wedge \neg p) \to p \not\models \neg((p \wedge \neg p) \to \neg p)$

(5) From "if it rains and it does not rain then it does not rain", we cannot conclude that it is false that "If it rains and it does not rain then it rains".

(Counterexample to BO') $(p \wedge \neg p) \to \neg p \not\models \neg((p \wedge \neg p) \to p)$

One objection to this list of counterexamples could be that the ones which use contradictions are not convincing. Indeed, these sentences are not easy to understand in natural language because we have no firm intuitions about whether they can receive a truth-value and which one to attribute if they have any. On the contrary, I think that this difficulty is just another reason to forbid contradictions in the construction of conditionals, in order to judge whether connexive principles are respected in natural language. Usually, this forbidding is done at the pragmatic level. However, an investigation of the results obtained for a repelling at the semantic level is worth doing, in order to see whether a semantic validation of the principles would be possible.

The general strategy that I adopt in order to cope with the connexive schemas is therefore the following one. The semantics of the conditional will be adapted in order to forbid contradictions and tautologies in its construction. Antecedents and consequents cannot be anymore contradictory or tautological sentences. This choice is motivated by two main reasons. It falls within the spirit of the principles argued by Aristotle, Boethius and Abelard which repel contradictions and which are at the origin of connexive principles. Furthermore, the use of contradictions in natural language conditionals does not allow to obtain clear judgments about their meaning and consequences. It is therefore preferable to dismiss them and their negations (i.e. tautologies) as soon as possible, namely at the semantic level.

3   A Conditional Logic Adapted to Connexive Principles

The goal of this section is to test whether the repelling of contradictions and tautologies as constituents of hypothetical sentences in conditional logic allows validating the connexive principles.[3] Defenders of conditional logics argue that their theories offer a better representation of the way we use conditional sentences in natural language. We just saw that connexive principles are based on the rejection of contradictions in the constructions of such sentences also for natural language. Therefore, if these two hypotheses are correct, the combination of both approaches would lead to a validation of connexive schemas in conditional logic.

---

[3]The original exposition of this idea can be found in (Vidal, 2012).

Let us notice first that connexive principles are not valid in the most well-known conditional logics which are Stalnaker's **C2** system (Stalnaker, 1968) and Lewis's **VC** system (Lewis, 1973).[4] In these systems, a conditional is true if the 'closest' or 'most similar' possible worlds where the antecedent is true are also worlds where the consequent is true.[5] In particular, this set of the 'closest' or 'most similar' possible worlds where the antecedent holds can be the empty set, when such worlds cannot be found. In that case, the conditional is systematically true. As a consequence, a contradictory antecedent which is true nowhere will be systematically mapped to this empty set, and the resulting hypothetical sentence will automatically be true.

This aspect of their theories could be considered as a borderline case whose treatment could be modified. However, both Stalnaker and Lewis justify this choice. The first reason advanced in (Lewis, 1973, p.21) is that the 'might' counterfactual can be defined in terms of the 'would' counterfactual. In the same way that the existential quantifier can be defined through the universal quantifier in classical logic, with the consequence that the formula '$\exists x F x$' needs a non-empty domain to be true contrary to the formula '$\forall x F x$' which is true in empty domains, the 'might' counterfactual needs at least one world where the antecedent is true to be able to be true contrary to the 'would' counterfactual. (Stalnaker, 1984, p.120-121) reuses another argument already offered in (Lewis, 1973, section 1.6) to defend his choice. Any sentence is the semantic consequence of a contradiction. Therefore, the same relation must hold for the conditional connective. However, as noticed by Lewis, these "reasons are less than decisive." Finally, Unterhuber (2013) shows that the validity of (AB') is impossible in these two systems without leading to inconsistency.

We will therefore explore the consequences of the dismissal of contradictions and tautologies in hypothetical constructions for another conditional logic which is the one exposed in Vidal (2016) and Vidal (2017). We make this choice because this theory offers a basic semantics for the *if* construction which can be combined with the meaning of additional particles like *even*, *then* and *only*. This approach offers therefore a more diverse and fine-grained representation of conditionals in natural language than concurrent theories because the meaning of the forms "if A, C", "even if A, C", "if A, then C" and "only if A, C" are compositionally constructed and distinguished. Moreover and as I will explain soon, the repelling of contradictions and tautologies naturally extends the intuitive ideas behind this system. In this semantics, the evaluation of a conditional is processed along two phases. I will present here the version of the semantics for the *if then* conditional because connexive principles are generally considered to hold for this form. During the first phase of evaluation, both the antecedent and the consequent are inhibited. This means that they are no more believed true or false. This allows obtaining a neutral position concerning their truth-value. This is why this stage is called the *inhibition* or *neutralization* phase. During the second phase of the process, the antecedent is reconstructed. If in all these reconstructions, the consequent is obtained, the conditional is deemed true. This second phase is the *expansion* stage.

The first advantage of positioning such a process is that before the evaluation, three attitudes are possible concerning a sentence. It is believed either true or false or indeterminate. The inhibition allows removing all the circumstances too particular to be interesting for the evaluation and that were attached to the sentences under scrutiny. Hence, the resulting situations obtained after the reconstruction can slightly differ from the initial situation. If the antecedent was initially true, by passing through the phases of inhibition and reconstruction, we can now examine other ways it could have been true. In particular, if both the antecedent and the consequent were initially true, by inhibiting both of them and by constructing various new situations where the antecedent is true, the consequent is no more certain to be obtained if there was no connection between the two. Hence, *unconnected conditionals*, which are compounded from two independent sentences that are true, like "if Mickey has four fingers, Pacific is an ocean" are not declared true in this semantics, contrary to what is obtained in **C2**, **VC** and in most conditional logics.[6] If the antecedent was initially false, we can now consider different situations where

---

[4]The most well-known actual development of this trend represented by the work of Kratzer (2012) does not change this treatment.

[5]In this paper, we expose Chellas (1975)'s version of Stalnaker's semantics, where a set of possible worlds and not a single world is the result of the search of the closest worlds.

[6]Notice that several psychological experiments (Matalon, 1962; Skovgaard-Olsen et al., 2016; Vidal and Baratgin, 2017)

it would be true and avoid contradictions with the initial situation. Finally, if the antecedent was initially considered indeterminate, the neutralization phase does not change anything and we can safely consider situations where it is obtained.

This intuitive process of judgment can be turned into a formal semantics in terms of possible worlds. Starting from the initial world of evaluation which is bivalent, the antecedent and the consequent are first inhibited through what is called a *neutralization function*. Notice that the set of possible worlds resulting from this neutralization are all worlds where these two sentences are neither true nor false. They are indeterminate and the possible worlds used must therefore be trivalent (a sentence evaluated in one world receive one truth-value among three possibilities: true, false or indeterminate). To be deemed successful, this phase must conduct to a non-empty set of possible worlds. During the second phase, the antecedent is added again to these possible worlds, through what is called an *expansion function*. After that, we check whether the consequent is true in all these situations where the antecedent was reconstructed. If this is the case, the conditional is true. Different variations concerning the truth or falsity of the antecedent are considered during this second phase. However, not all possibilities are explored because some of them are too absurd or not sufficiently relevant for the case at hand. They are therefore limited to what is called a *universe of projection* which is the set of the envisaged alternatives. Notice that in the present semantics, we enforce that all the possible worlds in this universe of projection are bivalent concerning the antecedent and the consequent of the conditional judged.

This semantics is detailed in (Vidal, 2017, Appendix A) and completed in Vidal (2016) for the *if then* conditional. In Fig. 2, we depict the meaning of "if A, then C", in which w stands for the starting world of evaluation and the square for the universe of projection.

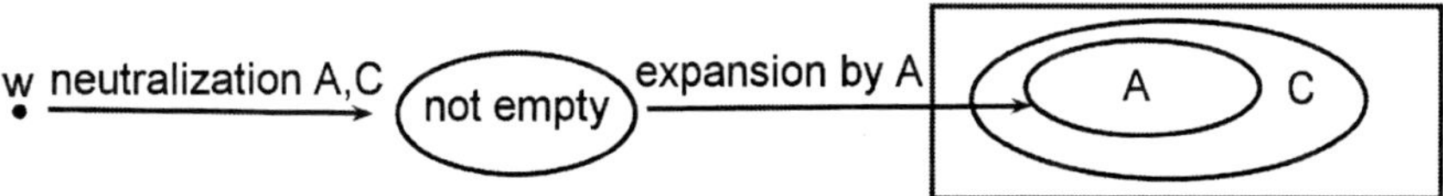

Figure 2: Semantics of the *if then* conditional

More formally, we obtain the following truth-conditions for the sentence *if A, then C*, with $[C]^U$ the set of possible worlds in the universe of projection U where C is true.

Definition 3.1 (Truth-Conditions for If A Then C).
$\vDash_w A \to C$ iff in the associated universe of projection U, with n the neutralization function and e the expansion function

i) $n_w(A, C) \neq \varnothing$

ii) $e_{n_w(A,C)}(A) \subseteq [C]^U$

In this system, connexive schemas are not valid. In order to obtain this validity, let us see how to improve this semantics by removing contradictions and tautologies. We can first notice that such improvement is a natural extension of the intuitive ideas behind this approach. Indeed, during the first phase of judgment, the sentences are inhibited, which means that they are no more believed true or false. To obtain such an evaluation for contradictory and tautological sentences seems impossible and this is a good reason to repel them in the construction of conditionals. Furthermore, during the second phase, several alternatives are envisaged, some in which the antecedent is true and some in which it is false, in order to constitute the universe of projection. Again, contradictions and tautologies are not well suited for respecting the intuitions behind this constraint.[7] In order to extend this semantics, we will add now

---

confirmed that subjects do not validate the reasoning $A, C \vDash A \to C$.

[7]Based on different intuitions than the present proposal, classical variably strict account of conditional ((Stalnaker, 1968), (Lewis, 1973)) and strict accounts of conditionals ((Lewis, 1918), (Warmbröd, 1981), (von Fintel, 2001)) have no real reasons to repel contradictions and tautologies from hypothetical constructions. They would have therefore more difficulties to justify such an extension of the system.

the following requirement. In the universe of projection, the set of possible worlds representing the antecedent and the consequent cannot be the empty set nor the totality of possible worlds. In that way, the two sentences whose relation is examined cannot respectively be true or false in all the alternatives envisaged. With this additional constraint, we not only repel the logical tautologies and contradictions but also the sentences that would be tautological or contradictory only relatively to the universe of projection considered. Formally, this extension of the semantics is expressed by the following truth-conditions where the items iii) and iv) are added comparatively to the previous definition:

Definition 3.2 (Connexive Truth-Conditions for If A Then C).
$\vDash_w A \to C$ iff in the associated universe of projection U, with n the neutralization function and e the expansion function

i) $n_w(A, C) \neq \varnothing$

ii) $e_{n_w(A,C)}(A) \subseteq [C]^U$

iii) $[A]^U \neq \varnothing$ and $[A]^U \neq U$

iv) $[C]^U \neq \varnothing$ and $[C]^U \neq U$

Let us prove now that the connexive principles are valid with this new formal semantics for the conditional. Let us remark first that $e_{n_w(A,C)}(A) = [A]^U$, that is the set of possible worlds where the antecedent is rebuilt is the same as the set of the possible worlds where the antecedent is true in the universe of projection.

Proof of AT.

For any world w, $\neg(\neg p \to p)$ is true in w iff $\neg p \to p$ is false in w.

We prove by contradiction that $\neg p \to p$ cannot be true in w. Indeed, to be true, we would need:

i) $n_w(p, p) \neq \varnothing$ and

ii) $[\neg p]^U \subseteq [p]^U$ and $[\neg p]^U \neq \varnothing$ and $[\neg p]^U \neq U$ and $[p]^U \neq \varnothing$ and $[p]^U \neq U$

But this last relation is a set-theoretic contradiction equivalent to:

iii) $(U \smallsetminus P) \subseteq P$ and $(U \smallsetminus P) \neq \varnothing$ and $(U \smallsetminus P) \neq U$ and $P \neq \varnothing$ and $P \neq U$ (contradiction)

Hence, by bivalence, $\neg p \to p$ is false in any world w. $\square$

The validity of the other schemas is demonstrated in the same way. The negation of the semantic consequence leads to a set-theoretic contradiction. We show below these contradictions for AB and BO, the proofs for AT', AB' and BO' being totally equivalent.

Proof of AB.

iii) $P \subseteq Q$ and $(U \smallsetminus P) \subseteq Q$ and $P \neq \varnothing$ and $P \neq U$ and $(U \smallsetminus P) \neq \varnothing$ and $(U \smallsetminus P) \neq U$ and $Q \neq \varnothing$ and $Q \neq U$ (set-theoretic contradiction) $\square$

Proof of BO.

iii) $P \subseteq Q$ and $P \subseteq (U \smallsetminus Q)$ and $P \neq \varnothing$ and $P \neq U$ and $Q \neq \varnothing$ and $Q \neq U$ and $(U \smallsetminus Q) \neq \varnothing$ and $(U \smallsetminus Q) \neq U$ (set-theoretic contradiction) $\square$

Hence, by enforcing the repelling of contradictions and tautologies in our conditional logic, we managed to validate the connexive principles.

The following objection could be addressed to the present proposal. The identity principle (ID) would be lost: $\nvDash p \to p$. Indeed, we do not accept anymore tautologies and contradictions in the construction of conditional sentences. This objection can be answered in the following way. First, an antecedent of a conditional is hypothetical. By saying "if A", we consider that A could have been true. But this truth is not necessary and so A could also have been false. Obviously, this cannot be the case for tautologies and contradictions. So, their repelling in antecedent is natural and the consequence is that (ID) cannot be universally valid but only applies to contingent propositions. Second, the loss of this principle does not cause damage. Indeed, this conditional does not carry any interesting information. By learning that p holds, from $p \rightarrow p$, we can only deduce that p. Hence, we learn nothing from this conditional. This means that the identity principle has no informative utility and can be safely removed from our logical system. Finally, notice that the rejection of the identity principle is a respectable position which is as old as the philosophical discussions on conditionals. Indeed, according to Sextus Empiricus and following Sanford (2003)'s translation, "those who judge by 'suggestion' declare that a conditional is true if its consequent is in effect included in its antecedent. According to these, 'If it is day, then it is day,' and every repeated conditional will probably be false, for it is impossible for a thing itself to be included in itself."

4   How to negate a conditional

If a person says the sentence "If A, then C" in which I do not believe, I will often express my disagreement with the locution "If A, then not C." Hence, this is not the whole conditional which is negated but its sole consequent. The following sentences illustrates this point:

> **(6)** If it's sunny, then Mary will go to the beach.

> **(7)** It is false that if it's sunny, then Mary will go to the beach.

> **(8)** If it's sunny, then Mary won't go to the beach.

To negate sentence (6), sentence (7) is rarely used because it is too pedantic. Sentence (8) will be preferred because it is shorter. The connexive principles and in particular the schema (BO') allows explaining why the negation of the consequent is a way to negate the whole conditional.

> **(BO')** $p \rightarrow \neg q \vDash \neg(p \rightarrow q)$

With the schema (BO'), we can directly deduce sentence (7) from sentence (8). Hence, this principle allows explaining why negating the consequent of a conditional is a way to negate the whole conditional.

However, as noticed by Dummett (1996) and Woods (1997), there exists another way to negate a conditional, which is more nuanced. For instance, we could negate sentence (6) in the following way:

> **(9)** If it's sunny, then it is possible that Mary won't go to the beach.

In sentence (9), the speaker lets a possibility for Mary to go or to not go to the beach, while in sentence (8), it is certain that she will not go there. Let us call these two ways to negate a conditional respectively the *weak negation* and the *strong negation*. The *strong negation* is expressed by the (BO') principle. The *weak negation* means that there exists another way to negate a conditional. As a consequence, the converse of (BO') cannot be valid in a system because it would make the *weak negation* impossible:

> **(ConvBO')** $\neg(p \rightarrow q) \nvDash p \rightarrow \neg q$

The logical system that we described in this paper validates (BO') but invalidates (ConvBO'). It gives therefore place for both the *strong* and the *weak* negations. This can be illustrated by two pictures. In Figure 3, we see that as soon as all possible worlds where the antecedent is true are also worlds where the negation of the consequent is true, none of them can be worlds where the consequent is true, simply by bivalence.

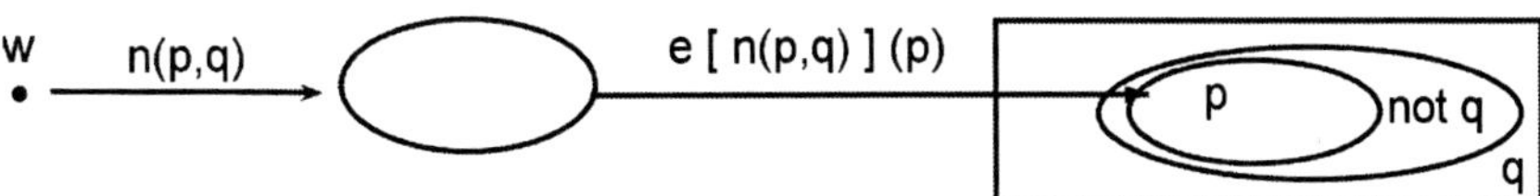

Figure 3: Strong negation of a conditional

To illustrate the *weak* negation, we just need to have a part of the possible worlds where the antecedent is true being also worlds where the consequent is true. By bivalence, the other part will be worlds where the negation of the consequent is true. This way to negate a conditional is illustrated in Figure 4.

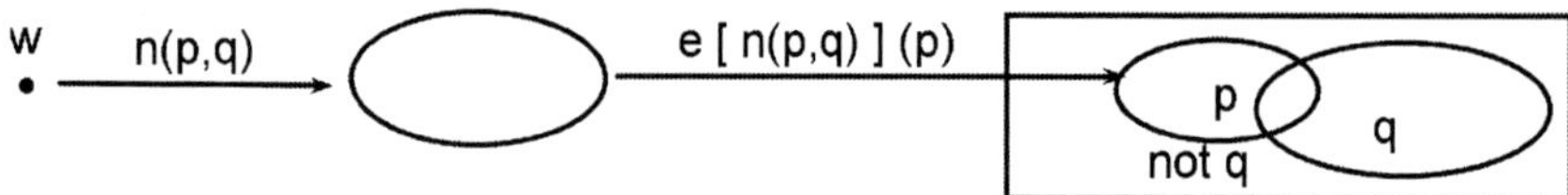

Figure 4: Weak negation of a conditional

The validation of the schema (BO') and the invalidation of its converse are therefore crucial features for a logic aiming to model the way we negate conditionals in natural language. It is therefore important for a conditional logic to be extendable both technically and intuitively in order to incorporate these two principles. We already saw that conditional logics do not validate in general connexive principles and in particular the schema (BO'). This is the case in particular for the systems of Lewis (1973) and Adams (1975). Stalnaker (1968)'s system **C2** could be seen as a notable exception because it does not validate (BO') but it contains the axiom (a4) which is very close: $\Diamond A \supset [(A \to C) \supset \neg(A \to \neg C)]$. This axiom stipulates that if the antecedent is possible, the truth of a conditional implies the negation of the same conditional with a negated consequent. Stalnaker notices rightfully that to negate the consequent is a usual way to negate the conditional. Because this feature is represented by his axiom (a4), it is an advantage of his approach. However, the default of Stalnaker's system is that it validates the schema (ConvBO') and as we saw, this schema forbids the *weak negation*. Hence, Stalnaker's solution is incomplete concerning the problem of negating conditionals in natural language.

5 A least drastic solution

The solution proposed so far repels contradictions and tautologies from conditional constructions in order to validate connexive principles, because we determined that they were only applicable to contingent propositions. But there exists another option that we will now examine. Its basic idea is that the initial truth-conditions for conditionals should be kept (Definition 3.1) and that we should check whether the connexive principles simply hold when its constituents are contingent.

The first step to devise this solution is to define what is a contingent proposition for a conditional construction. In the present system, two properties are required. First, the constituent of the conditional can be inhibited, in conjunction with the other constituents. Second, in the universe of projection obtained, the truth-set of the contingent proposition is neither the empty set nor the totality of possible worlds.

More formally, we obtain the following definition for the notion of contingency that we note ◆.

Definition 5.1 (Contingent proposition).
◆A iff for every conditional containing A as a component, w being the starting world of evaluation of this conditional and U its associated universe of projection:

i) $n_w(A, ...) \neq \varnothing$

ii) $[A]^U \neq \varnothing$ and $[A]^U \neq U$

With this definition, tautologies and contradictions cannot be contingent. Furthermore, we obtain the following valid schemas of reasoning which are the connexive principles limited to contingent propositions.

(AT♦) $\blacklozenge p \vDash \neg(\neg p \to p)$

(AT'♦) $\blacklozenge p \vDash \neg(p \to \neg p)$

(AB♦) $\blacklozenge p, \blacklozenge q \vDash \neg[(p \to q) \wedge (\neg p \to q)]$

(AB'♦) $\blacklozenge p, \blacklozenge q \vDash \neg[(p \to q) \wedge (p \to \neg q)]$

(BO♦) $\blacklozenge p, \blacklozenge q, p \to q \vDash \neg(p \to \neg q)$

(BO'♦) $\blacklozenge p, \blacklozenge q, p \to \neg q \vDash \neg(p \to q)$

The additional advantage of such a definition of contingency is that we can express that the identity schema is valid for contingent propositions in conditionals, whether we adopt the first version of its semantics (Definition 3.1) or its strengthened form (Definition 3.2).

(ID♦) $\blacklozenge p \vDash p \to p$

With this second version of our solution, we have a theory that makes sensible predictions for both contingent and non-contingent clauses. Linguistically, this seems to be the better option. But strictly speaking, we have no more a connexive logic.

6 Conclusion

Let us sum up the results obtained. The first version of the solution presented in this paper manages to validate connexive principles in the frame of a conditional logic. An important advantage of such an extension is the capacity to explain the way conditionals are negated in natural language. The price to pay is the repelling of contradictions and tautologies in conditional constructions, in line with the initial motivations given by the Greek philosophers arguing for connexive principles. If this price is too high to pay, our second version of the solution where the notion of contingency is defined must be preferred. With this new notion, it is possible to express that connexive principles are only valid for contingent propositions, which seems to be linguistically more satisfying.

References

Adams, E. W. (1965). The logic of conditionals. *Inquiry 8*, 166–197.

Adams, E. W. (1975). *The Logic of Conditionals*. Dordrecht: D. Reidel Publishing Co.

Chellas, B. (1975). Basic conditional logic. *Journal of Philosophical Logic 4*(2), 133–154.

Dummett, M. (1996). *The Seas of Language*. USA: Oxford University Press.

von Fintel, K. (2001). Counterfactuals in a dynamic context. In M. Kenstowicz (Ed.), *Ken Hale: a Life in Language*, pp. 123–152. Cambridge, Massachusetts: The MIT Press.

Francez, N. (2016). Natural deduction for two connexive logics. *IfCoLog Journal of Logics and their Applications 3*, 479–504.

Kneale, W. and M. Kneale (1962). *The Development of Logic*. Oxford: Clarendon Press.

Kratzer, A. (2012). *Modals and Conditionals: New and Revised Perspectives*. Oxford Studies in Theoretical Linguistics. Oxford University Press.

Lewis, C. I. (1918). *Survey of Symbolic Logic*. Berkeley, California: Univeristy of California Press.

Lewis, D. K. (1973). *Counterfactuals*. Cambridge, Massachusetts: Harvard University Press.

MacColl, H. (1908). "If" and "Imply". *Mind 17*, 151–152.

Matalon, B. (1962). Etude génétique de l'implication. In J. Piaget (Ed.), *Etudes d'Epistémologie Génétique XVI*. Paris: PUF.

McCall, S. (1967). Connexive implication and the syllogism. *Mind 76*, 346–356.

McCall, S. (2012). A history of connexivity. In D. Gabbay, F. J. Pelletier, and J. Woods (Eds.), *Logic: A History of its Central Concepts*, Handbook of the History of Logic Vol.11, pp. 415–449. Elsevier.

Pizzi, C. and T. Williamson (2005). Conditional excluded middle in systems of consequential implication. *Journal of Philosophical Logic 34*(4), 333–362.

Priest, G. (1999). Negation as cancellation, and connexive logic. *Topoi 18*, 141–148.

Rahman, S. and H. Rückert (2001). Dialogical connexive logic. *Synthese 127*, 105–139.

Routley, R. (1978). Semantics for connexive logics. i. *Studia Logica 37*, 393–412.

Sanford, D. H. (2003). *If P, then Q: Conditionals and the foundations of reasoning*. New York: Routledge.

Skovgaard-Olsen, N., H. Singmann, and K. C. Klauer (2016). The relevance effect and conditionals. *Cognition 150*, 26–36.

Smith, R. (1989). *Aristotle's Prior Analytics*. Hackett Publishing Company.

Stalnaker, R. C. (1968). A theory of conditionals. In N. Rescher (Ed.), *Studies in Logical Theory*, pp. 98–112. Oxford: Basil Blackwell Publishers.

Stalnaker, R. C. (1984). *Inquiry*. Cambridge, Massachusetts: The MIT Press.

Unterhuber, M. (2013). *Possible Worlds Semantics for Indicative and Counterfactual Conditionals. A Formal Philosophical Inquiry into Chellas-Segerberg Semantics*. Heusenstamm: Ontos Verlag.

Vidal, M. (2012). *Conditionnels et Connexions [Conditionals and Connections]*. Ph.D. dissertation, Institut Jean Nicod, E.H.E.S.S., Paris.

Vidal, M. (2016). A compositional semantics for 'if then' conditionals. In M. Amblard, P. de Groote, S. Pogodalla, and C. Retoré (Eds.), *LACL 2016, LNCS 10054*, pp. 291–307. Springer.

Vidal, M. (2017). A compositional semantics for 'even if' conditionals. *Logic and Logical Philosophy 26*, 237–276.

Vidal, M. and J. Baratgin (2017). A psychological study of unconnected conditionals. *Journal of Cognitive Psychology 29*(6), 769–781.

Wansing, H. (2005). Connexive modal logic. In R. Schmidt, I. Pratt-Hartmann, M. Reynolds, and H. Wansing (Eds.), *Advances in Modal Logic. Volume 5*. London: King's College Publications.

Warmbrōd, K. (1981). Counterfactuals and substitution of equivalent antecedents. *Journal of Philosophical Logic 10*(2), 267–289.

Woods, M. (1997). *Conditionals*. Oxford: Oxford University Press. Published posthumously. Edited by David Wiggins, with a commentary by Dorothy Edgington.

Comprehensive annotation of cross-linguistic variation in the category of tense

Zymla, Mark-Matthias
University of Konstanz
Mark-Matthias.Zymla@uni-konstanz.de

Abstract

In this paper, we present part of a new, cross-linguistically valid annotation scheme for annotating tense and aspect information on a syntactic and semantic level, focussing on the category of tense. Primarily, the annotation maps morphosyntactic information to representations of eventualities. We specify mapping conventions which are represented as inference rules expressing language specific variations of the syntax/semantics interface. Eventualities are expressed in terms of a cluster of features whose values can each be mapped to a formal description based on insights from the tense and aspect semantics literature. The annotation is integrated into a broader effort of achieving cross-linguistically viable temporal annotation and combines recent efforts of bringing together computational and formal approaches to temporal semantics. This allows for an overall comprehensive representation of syntax, semantics and the syntax/semantics interface regarding tense and aspect. The annotation scheme is especially well suited for computational research seeking to understand and extract tense/aspect information across languages.

1 Introduction

Annotation of temporal information as a whole has made steady progress in recent years following the TimeML ISO standard (Derczynski et al., 2013; Pustejovsky et al., 2003, 2002) and going beyond it (Bethard and Parker, 2016; Gast et al., 2016, 2015). However, there are only limited possibilities readily available to use this information to gain a better understanding of the relation between explicitly stated temporal information such as temporal expressions and and the category of tense. This has two implications: First, the fine nuances in meaning encoded in the interplay between verbal form and meaning cannot be captured, and second, existing efforts cannot provide a cross-linguistically adequate representation of tense and aspect categories. In this paper we address these issues by providing a tripartite annotation of tense. Thereby, we bring together deep linguistic parsing and a novel semantic annotation of eventualities. The system may be supplemented by elements from existing temporal annotation schemes ultimately providing a comprehensive description for temporal information and its relation with tense syntax and semantics.

Current temporal annotation schemes are well equipped with expressive power to describe the overall temporal situation within a text or sentence. However, the current state of the art focuses more on the annotation of explicit temporal expressions rather than on the meaning that remains implicit in the morphosyntactic form of verbal predicates. Thus, a great deal of the information with regard to the mapping from syntax to semantics is difficult to access. For example, Chinese timeML annotations in the 2010 TempEval shared tasks (UzZaman et al., 2012) are not marked up for tense and aspect at all, although, several morphosyntactic as well as semantic and pragmatic factors for analyzing tenses have been identified in the formal literature. This is shown for example in Bittner (2014); Smith (2006), among many others.

This makes it difficult to use existing efforts to get a better understanding of the interactions between temporal structure as a whole and different instantiations of tense and aspect categories cross-linguistically. Following approaches such as Gast et al. (2015) or Bethard and Parker (2016), we propose an annotation scheme that is faithful to the interaction between syntax and semantics in this paper.

The paper is structured as follows: We begin with identifying the main issues we want to address wrt. the annotation of tense. Section 3 illustrates the syntactic and semantic annotation of tense features and their realization in terms of the semantics we propose for eventualities. We illustrate the annotation in terms of the concrete annotation of the category of tense. In 4 we apply the entire annotation scheme to data stemming from the formal semantic literature illustrating how the scheme deals with cross-linguistic variation. Section 5 wraps up the paper with some remarks on implementability of the proposed annotation scheme.

2   Research questions

In this paper we focus on answering two questions: First, how to map morphosyntax to meaning in an implementable way, and second, which properties of eventualities are required (and of interest) for a linguistically rich representation of tense and aspect features. To address the first question, we propose separate levels for syntactic vs. semantic annotation, complemented by an alignment system that links syntactic features to semantic features by applying a set of inference rules. Such a system allows us to maintain parallelism in terms of syntactic and semantic features of languages while still explicitly capturing cross-linguistic variation. In terms of the abstract semantic foundations, the annotation is independent of a syntactic system. Nevertheless, our approach entails that the richer the syntactic representation, the more detailed the interactions between syntax and semantics can be modeled.

The alignment system is based on two different linking operations between syntactic and semantic features: a compatibility relation and an implication relation, such that for example the following simple rules are possible:

(1)   a. The people killed   the king.
      the people kill.**Past** the king

   b. logoN=ne   baadshaah=ko maar daalaa.
      people=Erg king=Acc   hit   **put.Perf**

   c. Das Volk   hat   den König getötet.
      the people have.Pres.3.Sg the king **kill.Perf**

   d. Orang membunuh raja
      people **AV.kill**   king

(2)   a. *indicative mood* ∧ *syntactic past*
         → *semantic past*

   b. *indicative mood* ∧ *syntactic perfect*
      ∘ *semantic past*

   c. *indicative mood* ∧ *syntactic present* ∧
      syntactic perfect → *semantic past*

   d. *indicative mood* ∘ *semantic past*

Example (1) and (2) illustrate how tense might be annotated in four different languages. The semantic interpretation might be a obligatory inference of a syntactic tense marker as in (2a) (English), a non-obligatory byproduct of a syntactic marker that does not necessarily express semantic past tense as in (2b) (Urdu), an obligatory inference of a combination of a syntactic tense with a syntactic perfect marker as in (2c) (German), or simply not inferable from the syntactic structure but merely a feature that overlaps with it as in (2d) (Indonesian). [1] Overall, the semantics in (2) are parallel; mapping the syntax to the semantics, however, captures cross-linguistic variation, even in tense systems that are more on par with one another than the ones described above.

The second aim of this paper is to define different types of variation in the syntax/semantics interface across languages and to illustrate how this variation is encoded in our annotation scheme. We introduce a crucial distinction of different form-to-meaning mappings that allows us to identify primary and secondary meaning features of certain syntactic constructions. Primary meaning features are those that follow directly from morphosyntactic grammaticalization (and are thus readily available from the syntactic analysis), while secondary meaning features describe semantic properties that are based on complex semantic and pragmatic processes, such as implications or alternative, semantically-constructed meanings of morphosyntactic material. Thus, the system presented here allows us to explicitly capture variations of the form-to-meaning mapping within a language, such as for example the so-called Sequence-of-tense phenomenon. Sequence-of-tense (hence: SOT) describes an unexpected pattern in the interpretation of

---

[1]In cases such as the latter, the semantic interpretation is usually contextual, a problem that is discussed in depth in Zymla (to appear)

past tense morphology in embedded contexts. This is illustrated in (3). SOT sentences result in two different possible paraphrases, undermining the assumption that syntactic past tense is always synonymous with a temporal back-shift of the respective eventuality (denoted in (3) by the two predicates E1 and E2).[2]

(3) Tom said$_{E1}$ that Karen was sick$_{E2}$.
     a. Tom said: Karen is sick.
     b. Tom said: Karen was sick.

Furthermore the annotation presented here allows us to capture cross-linguistic variation of tense categories. In the upcoming sections, we discuss syntactic variation of tense categories across languages such as the ones already introduced in (2). Moreover, we present a case of cross-linguistic semantic variation based on the SOT-phenomenon sketched above. Concretely, we illustrate the explicit annotation of syntax/semantics interface processes that vary between languages that express the SOT phenomenon on the one hand and languages that do not express the SOT phenomenon on the other hand. By explicitly annotating syntax, semantics and the interface, we can capture formal linguistic insights that at best remain implicit in existing annotation schemes.

3 Syntactic and semantic annotation of tense and aspect

The main innovation of our annotation system are the semantic features representing various properties of (verbally expressed) eventualities. The term eventuality thereby covers both events as well as states, following the classical ontology of Bach (1986). We treat eventualities as semantic objects similar to event variables in event semantics with certain semantic features. Relating these features to a sufficiently rich syntactic representation is the important first step for a comprehensive annotation of tense (and aspect). For this purpose we make use of the computational grammars developed within the ParGram project (Butt et al., 2002; Sulger et al., 2013) as syntactic input. This is done for two reasons: first, parsers are already available for a wide number of languages (for a full list and more description, see Sulger et al. (2013)) and second, the syntactic annotation of tense and aspect features is sufficiently exhaustive and more importantly parallel across languages. This allows us to clearly define parameters of syntactic variation.

The ParGram grammars are all developed using the XLE parser (Crouch et al., 2017) and are couched within the syntactic theory of Lexical Functional Grammar (LFG, Dalrymple (2001); Bresnan (2001)) which describes syntax in terms of two distinct representations: the c(onstituent)-structure and the f(unctional)-structure. The c-structure in LFG is a tree representation of the surface structure of a given sentence loosely based on X'-theory (Bresnan, 2001); since it is entirely language-specific and does not serve for encoding tense and aspect categories, our approach does not make use of it. The f-structure is a flat, quasi-logical (Crouch and King, 2006) representation of syntactic relations in terms of attribute-value matrices (Butt et al., 1999). F-structures contain information about syntactic dependencies (predicate-argument structures) as well as further morphosyntactic information such as number, gender, person or tense and aspect. At f-structure, ParGram grammars encode a language-universal level of syntactic analysis, allowing for crosslinguistic parallelism at this level of abstraction.

---

[2]It is well known that past tense markers do not always express a temporal backshift in non-indicative constructions (e.g., conditionals). However, the variation we are concerned with here is situated within constructions that fall under indicative mood.

(4) Er   schrieb Brief-e
     pron.3sg.m write.past letter-pl
     'He wrote letters.'

$$
\begin{bmatrix}
\text{PRED} & \text{'schreiben} < [\boxed{1}\text{:Er}], [\boxed{2}\text{:Brief}]>\text{'} \\
\text{SUBJ} & \boxed{1}\begin{bmatrix}\text{PRED} & \text{'pro'} \\ \text{NUM} & \text{sg} \\ \text{CASE} & \text{nom}\end{bmatrix} \\
\text{OBJ} & \boxed{2}\begin{bmatrix}\text{PRED} & \text{'Brief'} \\ \text{NUM} & \text{pl} \\ \text{CASE} & \text{acc}\end{bmatrix} \\
\text{TNS-ASP} & \begin{bmatrix}\text{TENSE} & \text{past} \\ \text{MOOD} & \text{indicative}\end{bmatrix} \\
\text{VTYPE} & \text{main} \\
\text{VFORM} & \text{fin} \\
\text{CLAUSE-TYPE} & \text{decl}
\end{bmatrix}
$$

Figure 1: f-structure: *Er schrieb Briefe*

As (3) illustrates, the syntactic features are categorized in terms of grammatical functions (the LFG term for syntactic arguments such as SUBJ and OBJ), as well as tense and aspect (TNS-ASP) features of the main verb *schreiben* and other relevant morphosyntactic features. The f-structure is a projection alongside the c-structure that makes accessible morphosyntactic information that is semantically relevant. The information is rendered in terms of feature-value pairs (e.g. [*TENSE past*]). The f-structure can thus readily serve as input to a syntax-semantics interface. The syntactic features for tense and aspect used in the ParGram grammars specifically are the same cross-linguistically. Thus a wide variety of features is available and distinctly describable. They are carefully carved out with the consideration of several different languages and language families in mind (Butt et al., 2002; Sulger et al., 2013). If a language does not express a feature, then the feature is not expressed at f-structure level. Thus, only overtly realized morphosyntactic properties can be read off the f-structure. This allows for a clear-cut differentiation between structural, morphosyntactic and semantic as well as pragmatic features.

3.1 Annotation of eventualities at the interface

As stated before, semantic and pragmatic information is encoded in terms of properties of eventualities. On the one hand, there are properties that are concerned with the internal structure of an eventuality, such as telicity or verbal number. In this paper we omit an analysis of these properties, since they are not crucial to the argument defended in this paper. On the other hand, there are properties that relate eventualities to temporal intervals, i.e. tense and grammatical aspect. In what follows we focus on the category of tense which is traditionally understood as an operator relating two time intervals putting them in sequence on a time line (Goranko and Galton, 2015). This notion will be refined in the forthcoming pages. In general, the annotation of a semantic feature always requires the formalization of an inference rule that leads to the annotation. The resulting meaning features are of the form in (5).

(5) ⟨attribute ::= [...],tier ::= [t1 | t2]⟩

Effectively, the annotation is flat, i.e. a set that consists of tuples of the form presented above. Thereby each attribute has a designated feature space as illustrated in figure 2. For the sake of visualization we group certain features under a governing *main feature* presented in angular brackets. The main feature is such that it generalizes the semantic features it subsumes onto a cross-linguistically valid feature space. The main feature should be a cross-linguistically parallel, sufficiently general annotation of the respective *semantic category* it classifies making it an important point of meta data for the comparison of semantic categories. In other words, the main feature is a meta label for a semantic category, while the semantic properties it governs represent the instantiation of the category in a specific language. Consider as a concrete example the category of tense: the logical possibilities of temporal reference are universal to all languages by the nature of its definition, however, some languages further restrict temporal reference as is shown in (6). In this example a temporal remoteness morpheme glossed with *IMM* marks that the sentence is about a time in the immediate past rather than about a time far back in the past which would be marked with a different temporal remoteness morpheme. This restriction is encoded in the *restr* feature and is a non-necessary modification of a tense category. As such *ref 'past' ∧ restr 'immediate'* or *ref 'past' ∧ restr 'unspec'* are different realizations of the semantic, cross linguistic category (or main feature) *past*.

(6) **Temporal remoteness in Gĩkũyũ (Cable, 2013):**

    a. Nĩ-ma-**∅**-gũr-ire   TV njeru

        ASRT-3pl-**IMM**-buy-<u>PST.PRV</u> TV new

        'They bought a new TV (**today**)'

$$
\text{b.}\quad \left[\text{TEMP-REF} <\text{'past'} > \quad \begin{bmatrix} \textbf{ref} ::= \text{'past'} \\ \textbf{restr} ::= \text{'imm'} \end{bmatrix} \right]
$$

Overall, the mapping from form to meaning is straight forward. We can map tense markers on values for the feature *ref* (short for (temporal) reference) and temporal remoteness markers to further restrict certain values of *ref*. The full spectrum of semantic tense categories and their specific configurations is shown in Figure 2 below. In comparison to the existing state of the art, we provide a more fine-grained set of features that is necessary to annotate cross-linguistic variations of the category of tense.

$$
\left[\text{TEMP-REF} <\text{'past' | 'present' | 'future' | ... } > \quad \begin{bmatrix} \textbf{ref} ::= \text{'past' | 'present' | 'future' |} \\ \text{'non-past' | 'non-present' | 'non-future' | 'unspec'} \\ \textbf{restr} ::= \text{'immediate' | 'non-recent' | 'remote' | 'unspec'} \end{bmatrix} \right]
$$

Figure 2: Possible annotations for temporal reference

The mapping from morphosyntax to semantics is not always as straight forward as in the example above. Recall example (2) where we claimed that at least two different types of relations between syntax and semantics obtain. We model these relations in so-called inference rules consisting of a source and a target. The source, represented by the premises of the inference rules, may either be a syntactic or a semantic feature or a set of features. The target is a semantic feature. The most simple inference rules represent a mapping between a meaning feature and its syntactic exponent. However, more complex rules are possible. The basic syntax of inference rules is illustrated below.

(7) ϕ, ψ are semantic feature/value pairs; α, β, γ are morpho-syntactic features, such that the following types of rules are possible:

    a. $\alpha \to \phi, \psi \to \phi$

    b. $\alpha \wedge \beta \wedge ... \wedge \gamma \to \phi$

    c. $\alpha \circ \phi, \psi \circ \phi$

In (7) $\to$ describes the implication relation and $\circ$ describes the compatibility relation. A feature or set of features implies a semantic feature, iff there are no two equally strong rules that generate the respective feature. The compatibility relation holds if there are two or more equally strong rules that generate a value for the same feature or if the feature is optional, i.e. an implicature. This means, for each syntactic feature or feature complex, there might be multiple rules that target it, such that we need to formalize certain principles — principles of strength — according to which these rules operate:

Firstly, the implication is stronger than the compatibility relation. This means if we have two rules $\beta \to \alpha$ and $\gamma \circ \alpha'$, where β and γ are semantic or syntactic features and α and α' are two different annotations of the same feature, then the attribute/value pair α is generated. Secondly, a rule is stronger if it requires more premises. This means, if there are two rules $\beta \to \alpha'$ and $\beta \wedge \gamma \to \alpha$, where β and γ are semantic or syntactic features and α and α' are two different annotations of the same feature, then, again, the attribute/value pair α is generated.

Based on these rules we now can define primary and secondary meanings. The primary meaning of any syntactic element is the meaning that is generated by the weakest implication rule that exists for this element. The corresponding meaning is labeled the *tier-1* meaning (t1 above) of its syntactic exponent. All other meanings are labeled t2 (*tier-2*), although the range of possible t2 meanings is less coherent than the range of t1 meanings. Tier 2 covers both semantic and pragmatic processes that generate semantic features, while tier 1 only covers the direct mapping from syntax to semantics. For illustrative purposes assume that α, β, γ are syntactic features, ϕ, ψ are attribute-value pairs(avps) describing semantic features. ϕ, ϕ'... are alternative annotations of the respective semantic attribute.

(8) **Inference rules for syntactic feature α:**

$\alpha, \beta, \gamma \rightarrow \phi \rightarrow$ **tier 2**
$\alpha, \psi \rightarrow \phi' \quad \rightarrow$ **tier 2**
$\alpha \rightarrow \phi'' \quad\quad \rightarrow$ **tier 1:** ϕ'' **is the primary meaning of** α

The alignment system introduced above is complemented by cross-linguistically universal assumptions about hierarchical relations between features. We illustrate this in terms of the semantic feature of temporal reference that is formalized such, that we can sort the domain of time intervals D_i so that each time interval in D_i belongs to a set representing a possible value for tense. This is done using the temporal precedence relation $\prec$ and the temporal overlap relation $\otimes$ wrt. a given evaluation time t_0. The resulting sets can be realized as set that is partially ordered in terms of the inclusion relation (omitting the empty set). In formal semantics a prevalent assumption is that the tense feature is determined by the relation of the so called topic time to the evaluation time Klein (1994). This theory has also been incorporated within the existing TimeML standard by Gast et al. (2016). Keeping future compatibility in mind we also presuppose topic times although we will not explicitly illustrate the system in this paper. This means we will not concern ourselves with complex tense constructions such as the perfect at this point. Depending on the membership of the topic time wrt. the sets introduced in figure 3 the tense feature is then determined. For example if a verbal predicate is restricted to topic times that are included within yesterday, then the verbal predicate is automatically past tense (see section 3.2 and following).

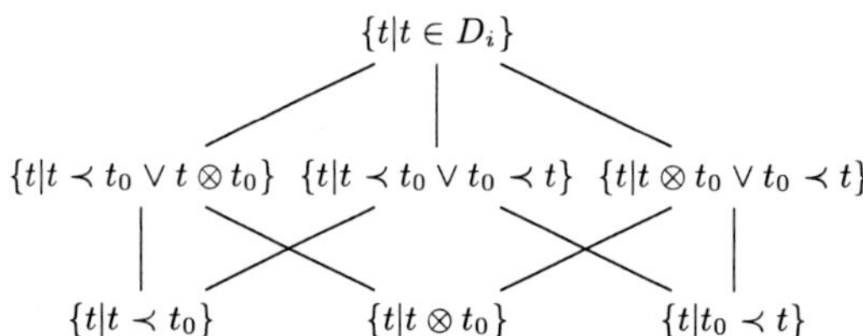

Figure 3: Formalization of tense features

The order by inclusion visualizes the hierarchical structure of the different values for tense. For example, the value past $\{t|t \prec t_0\}$ provides a stronger restriction than non-future $\{t|t \prec t_0 \vee t \otimes t_0\}$, thus, if two rules of equal strength compete such that one rule attributes the value 'past' to the feature tense and one rule attributes the value 'non-future' to the feature tense, then the former is applied since it makes a stronger claim.

The formal system introduced above covers a wide array of syntactic and semantic variations in the category of tense and a similar point can be made about aspect. It should be made clear again, that the rules introduced above are language specific. In parallel corpora we assume that the semantics are fairly comparable between languages, however, the inference rules that describe the processes that occur during the mapping from syntax to semantics and within the semantics express the actual variation between different languages.

3.2 Advanced annotations – The sequence-of-tense phenomenon

We initially illustrated the annotation in terms of the category of tense. It is not surprising that the form to meaning mapping varies between languages, however, even within languages the mapping from form to meaning is not always completely clear. A famous example that has been widely discussed in the formal semantic literature is the Sequence-of-tense (SOT) phenomenon. A case where syntactic tense is not distinctly mappable to a specific meaning. It is illustrated in (9) below.

(9) Tom said that Karen was sick.

a. Tom said: Karen is sick.

b. Tom said: Karen was sick.

As shown above the SOT-phenomenon allows for two different interpretations of the sentence *Tom said that Karen was sick*. Following the guiding principles introduced in the last section we can provide the following basic tense rule for English. However, it does not allow us to capture the two readings that arise in the SOT sentence.

(10) a. *TENSE past* $\wedge$ *MOOD indicative* $\rightarrow$ *ref ::= past*

The rule above basically says that the syntactic past tense marker and indicative mood produce a semantic past tense. If the topic times of both eventualities are linked to the speech time of the sentence via a past operator, the resulting semantics are not quite right. Assume that t^m is the topic time of the propositional attitude verb and t^c is the topic time of the verb embedded in the complement, then the the the rules above would give us the following three logical possibilities: $(t^m \prec t^c) \prec t^0, (t^c \prec t^m) \prec t^0$ and $(t^c \otimes t^c) \prec t^0$. However, only two of these logical possibilities fit the SOT data, namely the latter two. Either, the eventualities overlap at some point in the past, or the embedded eventuality precedes the matrix eventuality. This also means that we cannot infer the appropriate temporal sequence of eventualities directly from the syntax without assuming some intermediate semantic processes. The virtue of the annotation scheme presented here is that we can explicitly formalize these processes.

We have seen above that the feature past relates the topic time of an eventuality such that it is prior to some evaluation time. Above, we hooked both topic times to the speech time of the sentence. However, tenses may be relative, rather than absolute. In formal semantics absolute tenses are always interpreted with respect to the speech time while relative tenses are (possibly) relative to topic times provided by other tense markers. Usually these tense markers govern the tense in question syntactically (Kusumoto, 2005). However, simply assuming relative tenses does not suffice to reach the proper semantics, because if we interpret the embedded tense as past wrt. the matrix tense, then we only get the so-called past under past reading: $(t^c \prec t^m) \prec t^0$. We have to provide a more elaborate semantic system to account for SOT readings.

Following the formal semantic literature we treat SOT as an ambiguity (Grønn and von Stechow, 2010; Kusumoto, 2005). Seemingly, this ambiguity arises only in specific syntactic contexts as shown in the f-structure in Figure 4. The crucial point in the f-structure template for prototypical SOT sentences above is that two verbal PREDs (the *matrix* verb and the embedded *comp* verb) marked for past tense stand in a syntactic complement relation (COMP), i.e. a past-under-past structure. Thereby, the matrix verb has to be a propositional attitude verb, e.g. *say, believe, think*. Since this information is not part of the annotation of temporal properties of verbal predicates we follow the annotation guidelines of the TimeML standard differentiating between eventualities and instances of eventualities. For the feature *class* we use the dummy feature *propositional attitude*.[3]

---

[3]This information is annotated in the EVENT tag in the TimeML architecture as the attribute `class` Pustejovsky et al. (2003). At this point we do not roll out the discussion of this feature. For this paper we assume that propositional attitude verbs are certain I_STATE (e.g. believe, think) or REPORTING (e.g. say, report) that occur in (counter-)factive or (negative) evidential subordination links (SLINKS). Concretely, *CLASS(E1) propositional attitude* $\wedge$ *COMP(E1,E2)* equates such an SLINK. Without going into detail, these SLINKS can be derived from syntactic information and the annotation of the event attribute `class` in terms of inference rules that are coherent with the formal system introduced above. In terms of implementability Crouch and King (2006) provide a semantic system that centers around these types of verbs and the links they invoke. Thus, their system readily provides the means to infer such links inside our implementation.

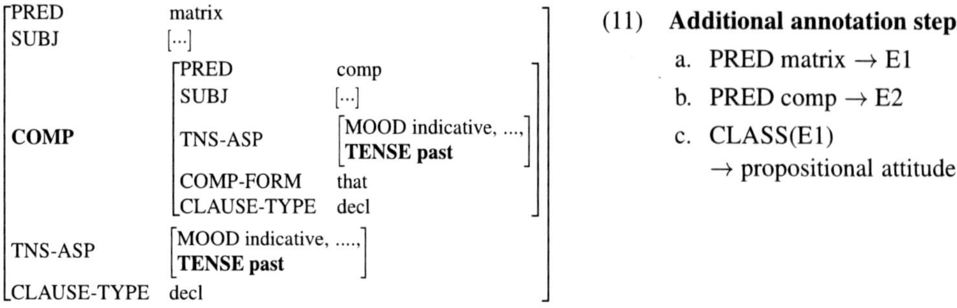

Figure 4: f-structure skeleton for SOT

With this information in place we can provide an additional rule that fulfills the SOT requirements in English. As (12b) shows the rule is incomparably more complex than the basic tense rule we presupposed before. It results in non-future temporal reference. Due to the definition of tense given above the non-future value for the embedded tense subsumes both cases: simultaneous readings and back-shifted readings. At the core of this rule are *propositional attitude* feature of the matrix predicate and the syntactic complement construction. In short, if an event is subordinated under an event via this rule and both of these events are annotated as past tense, then the embedded tense receives the value *non-future* or *non-successive* for temporal reference. This feature is interpreted with respect to the topic time of the matrix tense rather than the speech time. In this respect English is relative in this annotation scheme. The respective rules are illustrated below in a simplified manner:

(12) **Inference rules for (past) tense in English:**

    a. *tier 1:*
        TENSE past $\wedge$ MOOD indicative $\rightarrow$ temp-ref 'past'

    b. *tier 2:*
        CLASS(E1) propositional attitude $\wedge$ COMP(E1,E2) $\wedge$ MOOD indicative $\wedge$
        TENSE(E1) past $\wedge$ TENSE(E2) past $\rightarrow$ temp-ref(E2) 'non-future'

In TimeML the annotation of a SOT sentence may be obtained, as is illustrated below (omitting optional/unnecessary tags):

```
(13)   a. EVENT : eid ::= e1, class ::= reporting
          EVENT : eid ::= e2, class ::= state
       b. MAKEINSTANCE : eiid ::= ei1, eventID ::= e1
                         pos ::= 'VERB'
                         tense ::= 'PAST'
                         aspect ::= 'NONE'

          MAKEINSTANCE : eiid ::= ei2, eventID ::= e2
                         pos ::= 'VERB'
                         tense ::= 'PAST'
                         aspect ::= 'NONE'
       c. SLINK : lid ::= 1, eventInstanceID ::= ei1
                  subordinatedEventInstance ::= ei2
                  relType ::= 'Evidential'
       d. i. TLINK : lid ::= 2, eventInstanceID ::= ei1
                     relatedToEventInstance ::= ei2
                     relType ::= 'BEFORE'
          ii. TLINK : lid ::= 2, eventInstanceID ::= ei1
                      relatedToEventInstance ::= ei2
                      relType ::= { 'SIMULTANEOUS' | 'IS_INCLUDED' }
```

As example (13d) shows, it is difficult to find a unique annotation for the SOT sentence wrt. the relation between the matrix event and the embedded event (TLINKs to the speech time have been omitted for reasons of space). In the annotation presented in this paper we obtain a semantic restriction at sentence level for the embedded event, namely, that is has to be non-successive (or non-future) wrt. the matrix event. This seems like a small gain, however, it captures that, cross-linguistically, languages behave differently wrt. the SOT-parameter: They build a different semantic frame for interpreting temporal relations. The importance of such a frame becomes more apparent when the SOT phenomenon is explored cross-linguistically, as shown in, for example, Bochnak (2016); Mucha (2015), where the role of a purely morphosyntactic frame is challenged. Furthermore, the next section will show, that an annotation along the lines of timeML sketched above is not sufficient to describe cross-linguistic variation of tense categories.

4 Cross-linguistic variation in the category tense

In this section we apply the overall annotation scheme to different linguistic expressions. We define two types of variations which mark cornerstones in the spectrum of variation within syntax/semantics interface: Syntactic variation and semantic variation. Syntactic variation occurs when two eventualities that have the same semantic features are realized differently on a morphosyntactic level. Semantic variation occurs when syntactically similar constructions result in different annotations of the corresponding eventualities. We illustrate the two types of similarity in terms of minimal pairs so as to keep variation within a reasonable degree.

4.1 Syntactic variation

Syntactic variation is arguably the simpler of the two types of variation. We define it in terms of similarity on f-structure level, that is, two sentences are syntactically similar if they express alignable f-structures, i.e. they are non-contradicting (Sulger et al., 2013). We focus on variation in terms of the TNS-ASP grammatical functions in this paper (However, not all syntactic variation relevant for annotation of eventualities is necessarily confined within the TNS-ASP node). Thus, the two f-structures below are syntactically identical except for the lexical instantiation of the PRED.

(14) $\begin{bmatrix} \text{PRED 'schreiben} < ... >' \\ ... \\ \text{TNS-ASP} \quad [\text{TENSE past, MOOD indicative}] \end{bmatrix}$ (15) $\begin{bmatrix} \text{PRED 'write} < ... >' \\ ... \\ \text{TNS-ASP} \quad [\text{TENSE past, MOOD indicative}] \end{bmatrix}$

Assume now a language that does not express tense overtly such as for example Indonesian (Arka et al., 2013). A corresponding TNS-ASP matrix is shown in (16).

(16) $\begin{bmatrix} \text{TNS-ASP} \quad [\text{MOOD indicative}] \end{bmatrix}$

The minimal difference between the TNS-ASP matrix in (16) and the matrices in (14) and (15) is that there is no syntactic tense. Consider the sentences in (17), where this would be the minimal difference (in terms of tense) between the two sentences. Out of the blue the two sentences would be different in their compatibility with semantic features. However, they occur in a specific context such that both of the sentences are about an event in the past. Thus, in a context-driven annotation both sentences are semantically past. However, the explicit past should be annotated as conveying past time reference while the contextual past in Indonesian is only compatible with past time reference.

(17)   Q: What did the farmer do (yesterday)?

     a. The farmer groaned.

     b. Petani itu   mengaduh
        Farmer that groan

Since the past time reference in Indonesian has no overt syntactic exponent as reflected in the partial f-structure in (16), we have to provide inference rules that exhibit the difference between English and Indonesian. The first step is to annotate syntax and semantics. The second step is to annotate the corresponding inference rules for English and Indonesian as shown in (18). The resulting representations of the two different instantiations of the category past tense are illustrated in (19).

(18)   a. English:
          TENSE past $\wedge$ *MOOD indicative* $\rightarrow$ *ref ::= past*

      b. Indonesian:
          MOOD indicative $\circ$ *ref ::= past*

(19)   a. I met Peter (at the market).

F-Structure:

$$\left[\text{TNS-ASP}\quad \left[\text{TENSE } \textbf{past}, \text{MOOD indicative}\right]\right]$$

ParTMA Temporal reference:

$$\boxed{101}\left[\text{TEMP-REF} <'\text{past}'> \quad \begin{bmatrix}\text{ref} ::= \textbf{'past,t1'} \\ \text{restr} ::= \text{'unspec'}\end{bmatrix}\right]$$

      b. Saya bertemu Peter (di pasar (itu)).

F-Structure:

$$\left[\text{TNS-ASP}\quad \left[\text{MOOD indicative}\right]\right]$$

ParTMA Temporal reference:

$$\boxed{101}\left[\text{TEMP-REF} <'\text{past}'> \quad \begin{bmatrix}\text{ref} ::= \textbf{'past,t2'} \\ \text{restr} ::= \text{'unspec'}\end{bmatrix}\right]$$

These rules capture the relationship between syntax and semantics in these two languages. In English there is a very direct mapping from syntax to semantics. In Indonesian the connection is only apparent. The compatibility relation between indicative mood and past time reference does not entail that every sentence that is marked in indicative mood has past time reference. Where does the past time reference come from? Intuitively, the answer is that the past time reference is a result of contextual inference based on an available, salient time interval. In the context above this time interval is denoted by *yesterday*. We claimed before that tense sorts the available temporal intervals respective to the evaluation time. However, this does not mean that a past tense annotation denotes every interval that qualifies as that tense. Rather a tense annotation is appropriate if the temporal interval that a sentence is about, the Kleinian topic time (Klein, 1994), is included in the set described by the respective feature. With Gast et al. (2015) and following Klein (1994) we claim that finite verbs introduce topic times. In formal semantics topic times are treated as pronominal elements that point to a specific time interval (Partee, 1973). This leads to the following annotation process for English:

(20) **Annotation of:**
      Q: What did the farmer do yesterday?
      A: The farmer groaned.

      a. Syntactic parsing

      b. did $\rightarrow$ E1, groaned $\rightarrow$ E2

      c. temporal expressions:
          $\rightarrow$ [*yesterday, evaluation time*]

      d. Relate events to temporal intervals
          $\rightarrow$ [*E1, E2* $\subseteq$ *yesterday*]

      e. time reference:
          E2 $\subseteq$ *yesterday* $\wedge$ <u>*TENSE(E2) past*</u> $\rightarrow$ *ref ::= 'past',t1*

In Indonesian the process would be similar for the most part. The only difference would be the underlined part, which would be void. Thus, the inference of past time reference would be purely semantic(/pragmatic). This would also mean that the Indonesian annotation would receive the label *tier 2* since we can't relate the semantics to any syntactic exponent via an implication relation as illustrated in (18).

The example above illustrates the interaction between the module of syntax, semantics and a contextual component currently carried out through manual disambiguation which regulates the interactions between topic times and (salient) temporal variables (step d. above). For current annotations we employ the dummy label ctx for elements outside of the syntactic and the eventuality module, such that *ctx(past)* $\wedge$ *MOOD indicative* $\circ$ *ref ::= 'past',t2* describes a rule that, given some context that requires a past interpretation combined with a sentence in indicative mood determines semantic past tense such as in the Indonesian example in (17). We, thus, slightly revise the rule given in (18).

4.2 Semantic variation

In section 3.2 we introduced the Sequence-of-tense phenomenon and illustrated how our annotation scheme captures shifts in meaning within a language. However, this anomaly is not cross-linguistically robust. There seems to be a parameter that distinguishes two groups of languages. Those that express the phenomenon such as English and those that do not express it, such as for example, Japanese.

(21) Tom said that Karen was sick.
    a. Tom said: Karen is sick.
    b. Tom said: Karen was sick.

(22) Jon wa Karen ga byōkida   to   itta
    John top Karen subj be-sick.past comp say.past
    'Tom said: Karen <u>was</u> sick.

Table 1: SOT vs NON-SOT language

Readings	SOT	NON-SOT
$(t^c \prec t^m) \prec t^0$	+	+
$(t^c \otimes t^c) \prec t^0$	+	-
$t^m \prec t^c) \prec t^0$	-	-

The annotation system provided here provides a simple solution to capture the difference in the semantics – namely a variation in terms of the syntax/semantics interface. If we treat SOT as a parameter that allows for specific rules, there is simply no SOT rule in Japanese. Concretely, applying the simple past tense rule we provided initially, we will get the required result for Japanese. Thereby, both English and Japanese tenses are treated as relative tenses rather than distinguishing between absolute and relative tense systems.

Overall, we have shown that the annotation scheme presented here can handle different cases of variations in terms of tense categories easily. Thus, the annotation scheme provides a valuable tool for qualitative analysis of tense categories while pertaining integratability in the broader picture of temporal annotation. A similar point can be made about various aspectual features as well, but we leave this endeavor for elsewhere (see e.g. Zymla (to appear)).

5 Summary

In this paper we presented a novel annotation for tense using as example different variations related to the category of tense. The research presented here is situated within a broader effort to provide a linguistically and formally sound annotation for tense and aspect for NLP applications. We focused on small data examples from the formal semantic literature to illustrate the overall architecture. We bring together syntactic resources as well as existing resources in the realm of temporal tagging to provide annotations that encode the intrinsic meaning variations that arise from the morphosyntactic marking of tense or the absence thereof.

We did not go into detail with regards to the implementability of the system presented here with regards to the language specific inference rules. Complemented with a suitable database for lexical semantics the presented annotation could be automated to a large degree relying on human supervision for disambiguation and resolving contextual inferences the system cannot make due to the lack of a formalized pragmatic module. The biggest semantic resource specifically for XLE grammars is the semantic system employed in the ParcBridge Q & A system. Crouch (2005); Crouch and King (2006). We work on an extension of this system to incorporate the annotation presented in this paper. Languages without the respective semantic resources have to be annotated manually or at least require substantially more manual labor.

To summarize, we provide an annotation scheme for primarily qualitative research on the syntax/semantics interface cross-linguistically. Thereby we use the parallel grammars of the ParGram project as a foundation. We integrated the annotation scheme into the broader effort of temporal annotation and thus provide means to bring temporal annotation and deep linguistic parsing closer together. This promises to allow us to better test formal linguistic insights concerning the mapping from syntax to semantics. Furthermore, we have shown, how the separation of syntax, semantics and the syntax/semantics interface provides a more clear representation of various tense categories in general.

Acknowledgments

We thank the anonymous reviewers for their helpful feedback. Furthermore, we thank the participants of the ParGram project and the INESS infrastructure for their collaboration. The research presented here is part of the project *Tense and Aspect in Multi-Lingual Semantic Construction* founded by the Nuance foundation.

References

I Wayan Arka et al. 2013. On the typology and syntax of tam in indonesian. *Tense, aspect, mood and evidentiality in languages of Indonesia* pages 23–40.

Emmon Bach. 1986. The Algebra of Events. *Linguistics and Philosophy* 9(1):5–16.

Steven Bethard and Jonathan L Parker. 2016. A semantically compositional annotation scheme for time normalization. In *Proceedings of the Tenth International Conference on Language Resources and Evaluation (LREC 2016)*.

Maria Bittner. 2014. *Temporality: Universals and variation*. John Wiley & Sons.

M Ryan Bochnak. 2016. Past time reference in a language with optional tense. *Linguistics and Philosophy* 39(4):247–294.

Joan Bresnan. 2001. *Lexical-functional Syntax*, volume 16 of *Blackwell textbooks in linguistics*. Blackwell Publishing.

Miriam Butt, Helge Dyvik, Tracy Holloway King, Hiroshi Masuichi, and Christian Rohrer. 2002. The parallel grammar project. In *Proceedings of the 2002 workshop on Grammar engineering and evaluation*. Association for Computational Linguistics, volume 15, pages 1–7.

Miriam Butt, Tracy Holloway King, María-Eugenia Niño, and Frédérique Segond. 1999. *A Grammar Writer's Cookbook*. CSLI Publications.

Seth Cable. 2013. Beyond the past, present, and future: towards the semantics of 'graded tense'in Gĩkũyũ. *Natural Language Semantics* 21(3):219–276.

Dick Crouch, Mary Dalrymple, Ronald M. Kaplan, Tracy Holloway King, John T. Maxwell III, and Paula Newman. 2017. *XLE Documentation*. Palo Alto Research Center.

Richard Crouch. 2005. Packed rewriting for mapping semantics to KR. In *Proceedings of the Sixth International Workshop on Computational Semantics (IWCS-6)*. Tilburg, pages 103–114.

Richard Crouch and Tracy Holloway King. 2006. Semantics via F-Structure Rewriting. In Miriam Butt and Tracy Holloway King, editors, *Proceedings of the LFG06 Conference*. CSLI Publications, Stanford, CA, pages 145–165.

Mary Dalrymple. 2001. *Lexical Functional Grammar*, volume 34 of *Syntax and Semantics*. Academic Press, New York.

Leon Derczynski, Hector Llorens, and Naushad UzZaman. 2013. Timeml-strict: clarifying temporal annotation. *arXiv preprint arXiv:1304.7289* .

Volker Gast, Lennart Bierkandt, Stephan Druskat, and Christoph Rzymski. 2016. Enriching timebank: Towards a more precise annotation of temporal relations in a text. In Nicoletta Calzolari (Conference Chair), Khalid Choukri, Thierry Declerck, Sara Goggi, Marko Grobelnik, Bente Maegaard, Joseph Mariani, Helene Mazo, Asuncion Moreno, Jan Odijk, and Stelios Piperidis, editors, *Proceedings of the Tenth International Conference on Language Resources and Evaluation (LREC 2016)*. European Language Resources Association (ELRA), Paris, France.

Volker Gast, Lennart Bierkandt, and Christoph Rzymski. 2015. Creating and retrieving tense and aspect annotations with graphanno, a lightweight tool for multi-level annotation. In *Proceedings 11th Joint ACL-ISO Workshop on Interoperable Semantic Annotation*. page 23.

Valentin Goranko and Antony Galton. 2015. Temporal logic. In Edward N. Zalta, editor, *The Stanford Encyclopedia of Philosophy*, Metaphysics Research Lab, Stanford University. Winter 2015 edition.

Atle Grønn and Arnim von Stechow. 2010. Complement tense in contrast: the sot parameter in russian and english. *Oslo Studies in Language* 2(1).

Wolfgang Klein. 1994. *Time in language*. Psychology Press.

Kiyomi Kusumoto. 2005. On the quantification over times in natural language. *Natural language semantics* 13(4):317–357.

Anne Mucha. 2015. *Temporal interpretation and cross-linguistic variation*. Ph.D. thesis, PhD thesis, University of Potsdam, Potsdam, Germany.

Barbara Hall Partee. 1973. Some structural analogies between tenses and pronouns in english. *The Journal of Philosophy* 70(18):601–609.

James Pustejovsky, José M Castano, Robert Ingria, Roser Sauri, Robert J Gaizauskas, Andrea Setzer, Graham Katz, and Dragomir R Radev. 2003. Timeml: Robust specification of event and temporal expressions in text. *New directions in question answering* 3:28–34.

James Pustejovsky, Roser Saurí, Andrea Setzer, Rob Gaizauskas, and Bob Ingria. 2002. Timeml annotation guidelines. *TERQAS Annotation Working Group* 23.

Carlota Smith. 2006. The pragmatics and semantics of temporal meaning. In *Proceedings, Texas Linguistics Forum*.

Sebastian Sulger, Miriam Butt, Tracy Holloway King, Paul Meurer, Tibor Laczkó, György Rákosi, Cheikh M Bamba Dione, Helge Dyvik, Victoria Rosén, Koenraad De Smedt, Agnieszka Patejuk, Özlem Çetinŏglu, I Wayan Arka, and Meladel Mistica. 2013. ParGramBank: The ParGram Parallel Treebank. In *ACL*. pages 550–560.

Naushad UzZaman, Hector Llorens, James Allen, Leon Derczynski, Marc Verhagen, and James Pustejovsky. 2012. Tempeval-3: Evaluating events, time expressions, and temporal relations. *arXiv preprint arXiv:1206.5333* .

Mark-Matthias Zymla. to appear. Cross-Linguistically Viable Treatment of Tense and Aspect in Parallel Grammar Development. In *Proceedings of the LFG17 Conference*. CSLI Publications.

Association for Computational Linguistics
209 N. Eighth Street
Stroudsburg, Pennsylvania 18360

ISBN 978-1-5108-5282-2